A HISTORY OF
Australian Tra
and Tourism

A HISTORY OF

Australian Travel and Tourism

John I Richardson

HOSPITALITY
P R E S S
MELBOURNE

Hospitality Press Pty Ltd
38 Riddell Parade
P.O. Box 426
Elsternwick Victoria 3185
Australia
Telephone (03) 9528 5021   Fax (03) 9528 2645

A History of Australian Travel and Tourism

First published 1999

National Library of Australia
Cataloguing-in-publication data:

Richardson, John I. (John Ivor), 1931– .
   A history of Australian travel and tourism / John I. Richardson.
   Bibliography.
   Includes index.
   ISBN 1 86250 483 0.
   ISBN 1 86250 496 2 (pbk).

   1. Tourism—Australia. 2. Tourism—History. 3. Tourism.
   4. Tourism—Economic aspects—Australia. 5. Australia—
   Description and travel. I. Title.
338.479194

Designed by Lauren Statham (Alice Graphics)
Edited by Frances Wade (Wade's Distractions)
Typeset by Melbourne Media Services
Production by Publishing Solutions, Richmond, Victoria
Published by Hospitality Press Pty Ltd (ACN 006 473 454)

For Janet, who loves books

History is the essence of innumerable Biographies.
Thomas Carlyle (1795–1881) *Essays: On History*

Contents

Preface

THERE ARE DIFFERENT ways of approaching a history of travel and tourism in Australia, just as there are different definitions of what constitutes tourism. It depends on the point of view. For instance, tourism history may be approached from the viewpoint of an economist, a sociologist, an archaeologist—or a fair number of others. J. Towner has pointed out that tourism is an interdisciplinary field of interest and that the social sciences and history share a wide range of approaches.[1]

This book deals primarily with the history of the *business* of Australian travel and tourism. The original idea was that it would form part of an introductory text for students seeking a career in one of the many different types of businesses that make up the industry. An industry builds on what has gone before, and its history is important to an understanding of the way it works today.

As time went on, it became clear that to make sense of the subject the work would be longer than originally anticipated. It was then decided to make it a separate book. The original intention had been to confine the work to the main sectors of the industry in accordance with the plan for the larger book, of which the history was to be a part. However, a separate book required a broader approach.

What does it encompass? The term 'travel and tourism' has been used in the sense that tourism is a subset of travel. 'Travel' is not difficult to define—we all know that it means to go from one place to another. 'Tourism' is another matter. It involves travel and a temporary stay away from home, and its prime purpose is something other than earning money in the place or places visited. Beyond stating these simple facts, there is no single definition that satisfies all interests.

Definitions can be put into two categories. The first is the 'technical' group, which defines tourists to distinguish them from other travellers so that statistics can be collected uniformly and different collections can be aggregated and compared. Technical definitions usually include three elements: distance travelled, duration and purpose. The second category contains the 'conceptual' group of definitions, which seek to determine the nature of tourism or some aspect of it. This is a large and ever-expanding group, because what is perceived as the nature of tourism depends on the interest and viewpoint of the person seeking to define it.

Some of these are important to people in tourism businesses. For instance, there is a school of thought that prefers to define tourism in behavioural terms; the behaviour of tourists is important to tourism marketers, among others. However, the definitions most relevant to an introductory book for students of tourism businesses are the technical ones, because they tell us who is counted as a tourist. In this way, we can understand the numbers that are issued around the world.

The World Tourism Organization's 'technical' definition of tourism is:

> the activities of persons travelling to and staying in places outside their usual environment for not more than one consecutive year for leisure, business and other purposes.

The WTO regards all types of travellers engaged in tourism as 'visitors'. Its definitions for statistical purposes are:

- International visitor:
  any person who travels to a country other than that in which he/she has his/her usual residence but outside his/her usual environment for a period not exceeding 12 months and whose main purpose of visit is other than the exercise of an activity remunerated from within the country visited.

- Domestic visitor:
  any person residing in a country, who travels to a place within the country, outside his/her usual environment for a period not exceeding 12 months and whose main purpose of visit is other

than the exercise of an activity remunerated from within the place visited.[2]

There are difficulties. For example, no single definition of 'usual environment' has been found that can be applied all over the world. Nevertheless, the statistics collections work for tourism organisations and the definitions listed above need to be kept in mind when reading parts of this book. In particular, it should be noted that the definition of a tourist is a broad one; the term is applied not just to the leisure traveller, as it was in the past (and some would argue should be the case today). It should also be noted that day-trippers, or excursionists, are included in the compass of the book.

In appreciating the scope of the book, it is also necessary to define the travel and tourism 'industry'. The travel and tourism industry cannot be defined in terms of the goods and services it produces, as are other industries (for instance, the automotive industry produces cars; the coal industry digs up coal). There is no product called 'tourism'; in theory a tourist can consume or use just about anything produced. So the industry is defined in terms of the many disparate organisations that provide goods and services for tourists: it is tourism demand that brings them together as an 'industry'.

In these circumstances a workable definition of the travel and tourism industry is: 'a composite of organizations, both public and private, involved in the development, production, distribution and marketing of products and services to serve the needs of travelers, especially tourists'.[3] Note that this definition includes some government organisations that are engaged in tourism activities.

The history of Australian travel and tourism begins with the first settlement of this continent more than 40 000 years ago. However, this book is mainly concerned with modern tourism; that is, from the time technology began to make travel possible for ordinary people.

In the period after the first white colonists arrived in 1788 travel was extraordinarily difficult, though necessary to link settlements and develop trade routes. Meanwhile, in other parts of the world changes were beginning to take place. By the time of the gold rushes in Australia, technology had changed travel for ever in Europe and North America. For the first time in those parts of the world ordinary wage-earners—not just the rich and elite—could leave home for pleasure or simply to satisfy curiosity. Visionaries like Thomas Cook had begun to fashion the industry, serving travellers and extending tourism into its modern form.

Australians were not far behind. To understand how they behaved in respect to travel and tourism and developed an industry to serve their needs, it is necessary to understand what was happening elsewhere. This book is divided into three parts, separated by the two world wars. Each part is opened by a chapter that examines important developments in the wider world.

One of the purposes of this is to allow the reader to see how Australians responded to inventions, innovations and trends in other countries. Have Australians simply followed, or have they developed a recognisable Australian tourism product? It is a question worth keeping in mind as the reader progresses through the book. If the past is a guide to the future, there are other questions that may present themselves from the start. Is there evidence of a growing professional approach to tourism, particularly in regard to service? As there seems to be no end to its growth, what clues are there as to how we may manage tourism in the future? To what extend can tourism be managed?

Some of these questions would not have occurred to our predecessors in travel and tourism. Travel was always important, but tourism as an organised and, to some extent, manageable item among those that affect the competitiveness of nations is a new concept.

Technology has been a principal factor in bringing about the change. Australia's first discoverer probably arrived by accident in a bark canoe or on a flimsy raft made of roped logs, perhaps even clinging to a single log that had been swept out to sea from an Indonesian river by the tide. The distance would have been measured in tens of kilometres at the most, but it was a notable voyage. Even at the time of white settlement in 1788 there were many unknowns about the earth. Australia was to remain isolated, beset by the tyranny of distance, for most of the time between then and the present day.

This book shows how technology has conquered distance and ended Australia's isolation. However, being part of a globalised world has its price. The final chapter takes a brief look at the future, the likely effect of new technology, and some of the current and future issues that concern Australian tourism.

Each section of the book follows a similar pattern, although the chapter organisation has been adapted to varying needs. The idea was to examine the world scene in each period, give an overview of Australian travel and tourism in that period and then examine progress in various kinds of travel, the hospitality sector, the activities that have attracted tourists and the ways in which tourism has been organised, measured and promoted. The comparatively recent interest in the research and development of tourism education has been covered in the last section.

Much of the research for this book was desk work and I owe a debt of gratitude to a number of libraries: RMIT University's Central, Victoria University of Technology, the State Library of Victoria, the Toorak-South Yarra branch of the City of Stonnington Library and, in particular, the Prahran Mechanics' Institute Library, where I found the answers to many of the harder questions I was asking.

But much of the material, particularly material about the period after the Second World War, came directly from people who were involved at the time. After 30 years in Australian tourism, it was not much of an effort to locate the right people, especially as my own involvement first encompassed the Australian Tourist Commission and then—directly or as a consultant—State and Territory organisations, coach companies, airlines, hotels, motels and tour operators.

When I still needed help, I had guides who, apart from being informative themselves, were able to pass me on to others who could help with cloudy areas. For this service I thank, in particular, Alan Greenway, Don Beresford, Kim Dunstan, David Raven, Pierre Chaperon, John Evans, Peter Watson, John McKirnan, Jack Woods and Stewart Moffat. Foolishly, perhaps, I did not keep count of everybody I spoke to on one relevant subject or another during the course of writing the book; it ran into scores and I thank all of them. There were some splendid occasions: examples are two memorable afternoons at the home of Stewart Moffat talking about half a century of business adventures; a fine lunch with Sammy Heifitz in a Carlton restaurant near the office where four decades before he decided to add student travel to an already burgeoning retail business; and a Melbourne Skal Club lunch where Frank Christie, with some argument, put the history of international hotel management in Australia to rights. Correspondence with Nancy Richardson, whose husband Don opened Australia's first motel, was another highlight of many months searching the past. Sadly, Stewart Moffat, who took such an interest in my progress, will not see this book. He died in early 1999.

I must also thank Associate Professor Neil Leiper, of Southern Cross University, for his help during the writing of the book, and Professor Brian King, of Victoria University of Technology, for his interest in the project, for his suggestions as to sources and for taking the trouble to read the draft and give valuable advice on how to improve it. For some reason, the book was much more of an editing challenge than my earlier works and I thank Frances Wade for handling the task—and me—with her customary skill. Above all, I thank my wife Janet for her

xviii support day after day over many months and her invaluable, expert and persistent help with research.

A short history moves quickly and omits detail, but I hope the sense of the spirit of enterprise and persistence characteristic of those who built Australian travel and tourism has not been lost. In apologising for omissions, I can only say that choices had to be made. The responsibility is mine alone.

John I. Richardson

ENDNOTES

[1] Towner, J. (1988), 'Approaches to tourism history', *Annals of Tourism Research*, vol. 15, pp. 47–62.

[2] WTO (1994), *Recommendations on Tourism Statistics*, Madrid, p. 3.

[3] Adapted from Gee, C. Y., Makens, J. C. & Troy, D. J. L. (1989) *The Travel Industry*, Van Nostrand Reinhold, NY, p. 4.

The foundation: Australian travel and tourism up to 1914

I N SPITE OF ALL we read about famous journeys, throughout history most people did not move more than a day's walk from their homes unless they had to. Technology—particularly steam-power—made the difference. The impact of the steam engine on travel was being felt in Europe and North America during the first half of the nineteenth century, just as the settlements in Australia were finding their feet. Overseas, people began to move in their hundreds of thousands on cheap, fast and commodious railways where only hundreds had gone before; ships driven by steam were bringing a new reliability to travel on water.

Australians were quick to adapt to new ways and they were self-reliant. The white population of the colonies was smaller than 100 000 in 1831 when the first steam vessel arrived in Sydney from Britain under sail, its engine dismantled for the journey. Yet a home-built steamer was already nearing completion in a Sydney Harbour bay and actually raised steam first. Twenty-three years later, when it became likely that the steam locomotive intended for Australia's first railway in Melbourne would be late arriving from Britain for the opening, the colonists built their own. Within a few years of the appearance of the first car in Germany and the first heavier-than-air flight in the United States, Australians were making cars and planes.

2   There were problems with roads and costly mistakes with railway gauges, but by the Centennial in 1888 Australia, with a population of about three million,[1] had developed a stable and expanding travel industry. The events of the Centennial, especially the celebrations in Sydney and the Great Exhibition in Melbourne, proved that the colonists could organise tourism on a considerable scale. The travel infrastructure rapidly expanded from 1888 until the start of the First World War and so did tourism organisations; most of the States by that time had tourism bureaus that packaged and sold travel and tourism products. The foundations of today's industry had been laid.

ENDNOTE

[1] The population figures are from J. C. Caldwell (1987), 'Population' in *Australians: Historical Statistics*, ed. W. Vamplew, Australians: A Historical Library series, Fairfax, Syme & Weldon Associates, Sydney, p. 26. While figures for each year are not available, returns for the colonies in other years close to 1831 make it clear the total population was under 100 000. There is no figure for 1888, but the population in 1891 is given as 3 174 392.

The world: how travel and tourism developed

The start of it all

Mass tourism is a relatively new phenomenon, though people have travelled since the beginnings of civilisation.[1] There have always been compelling reasons for some people to leave their homes: for example, to search for food, to wage war, to make religious pilgrimages and above all to carry on trade; the merchant has always had to move about to find merchandise or customers. The growth of cities, the building of sea-going ships and the use of money as a means of exchange all helped in the development of commerce around the Mediterranean and in other seas and oceans as well. Muscat and Omani traders sailed to India and China and their adventures are still recalled in the tales of Sindbad the Sailor. Indian merchants were travelling to South-East Asia 2000 years ago.

In other parts of the world, too, there were voyages of discovery. Some 1500 years ago Polynesians were sailing the Pacific in boats with two hulls, exploring among its 25 000 islands and navigating partly by the 'feel of the sea'.[2] The Vikings made notable voyages from their Scandinavian homes in little 15-metre boats across wild seas, to Greenland in the tenth century and to Newfoundland in the eleventh century. A Norwegian book of 1240 gives us an early explanation as to why people travelled: 'One motive is fame, another curiosity and the third is lust for gain.'[3]

4   The Silk Road, which began as a collection of caravan routes and eventually linked China with the Mediterranean countries, dates back thousands of years.[4] The Chinese Emperor Mu is said to have ventured along it into Central Asia around 1000 BC. However, it was usual in ancient China to say that emperors had achieved great things when it was really someone else, so it may have been Chinese merchants who actually made the journey.[5]

The Ancient Greeks travelled to Olympia, the most sacred site of Zeus, ruler of the gods, at intervals from 776 BC to AD 394 for the original Olympic Games. But Olympia was only one kind of specialised destination developed by the Greeks. There was also Delphi, a religious shrine for worshipping and for consulting oracles, and the island of Cos, the archetypal health resort and the residence of Hippocrates and his disciples.[6] The Romans had holiday resorts at spas, at beaches and in the mountains and their excellent road system made long-distance travel possible. Some people in China and Japan were attracted to nature tourism and journeyed hundreds of miles to stand before a waterfall or a cherry tree.

In the Middle Ages a number of Arab tourists went east into Asia, taking their harems with them. This was not a notable period for travel in Europe, but 'the scholar was unhampered and free to move, he visited important schools and enjoyed his travels as a way of life.'[7] Religious travel was imperative for many: to Rome and Jerusalem for Christians, to Mecca and Medina for Muslims and to the Ganges for Hindus.

In the fifteenth century the Incas built an impressive road network in South America. The main route, the Royal Road, ran from Santiago in Chile north to the capital, Cuzco, in Peru and on to Quito in Ecuador at altitudes of up to 3600 metres. It was probably the longest operating road in the world until well into the nineteenth century. Roadside lodges were built a day's walk apart. This was typically 20 kilometres, but sometimes the distance was as short as 10 kilometres because of the difficult terrain.[8]

The English ruling classes made their Grand Tours of Europe in the seventeenth and eighteenth centuries for the cultural experience, particularly in the early years—and not always with propriety in the latter. Tobias Smollett, a well-known novelist and humorist who died in 1771, wrote that Britain sent young men abroad 'on purpose to bring her national character into contempt.'[9] The word 'tourist' dates from the days of the Grand Tour, though it and 'tourism' did not come into common use until the early nineteenth century.[10]

Provision was also made for leisure closer to home. Pleasure gardens, the ancestors of today's theme parks, made their appearance in the eighteenth century, first in France and then in other parts of Europe. Among them were royal parks, like Versailles near Paris and the Prater in Vienna. In England the best-known were the Vauxhall and Ranelagh Gardens. The Tivoli Gardens came later—they opened in 1843—and remain as a major attraction in Copenhagen today. The gardens were for passive recreation at first, with elaborate horticultural displays, but later on entertainment was offered: musical performances, balloon ascensions, circus acts and games.[11]

Famous travellers

There are travellers famous in history, largely because they have left readable accounts of their adventures. The first was the Greek historian and geographer Herodotus, who became known as 'the father of history' and is sometimes credited with having been the first tourist. During the years 464 to 447 BC he visited many islands in the Greek Archipelago, the capital of the Persian Empire, Susa, the shores of the Black Sea as far as the mouth of the Dnieper River, and Egypt.

> From these expeditions, Herodotus brought back eye-witness reports full of picturesque details, extravagances and marvels, wit and humour, pathos, tragedy and heroism. (G. Sigaux, *History of Tourism*, 1966)[12]

The Venetian Marco Polo (1234–1324) wrote of his experiences in China in one of the most influential travel books ever published. Before it became available, few Europeans had heard of China. It also gave them their first information about Tibet, India, Sri Lanka, Burma, Japan, Indo-China and Java. Sigaux describes *The Book of Marco Polo* as 'a vivid descriptive narrative by one who was a natural tourist as well as an accomplished businessman and diplomat'.[13] Accomplished he was: he became a diplomat and city governor in the service of the Mongol emperor Kublai Khan. With his uncles he stayed in China for 17 years.

Herodotus and Marco Polo were rare travellers, but travel of one's own free will was in itself rare in their times and for most of history. Although there were spectacular explorations, pilgrimages, migrations and wars in distant places, to travel for adventure or pleasure or merely to experience other peoples' cultures was uncommon before the mid-nineteenth century.

6 How steam-power changed the world

Before steam-power, travel was slow and uncomfortable, often danger-ous—and expensive. 'Travel' has the same origins as 'travail', meaning 'painful or laborious effort', which helps to explain why few people travelled unless they had to. Those who did were usually the rich and members of the elite with time to travel, curiosity nurtured by learning and the means to make the best of a difficult undertaking. Many Britons became rich in the Industrial Revolution and went to the Continent in unprecedented numbers after the defeat of Napoleon in 1815; by 1840 there may have been 100 000 a year.

Impressive as this was at the time for a nation of 27 million people, it was hardly tourism on anything like the scale we know it at the end of the twentieth century. Most people, particularly the poor, rarely left their home districts. A Cornish vicar wrote that a visit to a distant market town was 'an achievement to render a man an authority or an oracle among his brethren' and Dr Matthew Arnold, the famous head-master of Rugby School, said in 1829 that 'more than half my boys never saw the sea, and never were in London.'[14]

The eighteenth and nineteenth centuries saw great developments in the means of travel used in Europe and North America—improvements in roads and stage coaches[15] and in the reliability of sailing ships. However, it was steam-power that brought the greatest change to the way the world travelled, although it took time and imagination to see its potential. There was the occasional steamboat in Napoleon's day and the first locomotive ran at a mine in England in 1804, the year when Napoleon crowned himself Emperor of the French. But there was little awareness that soon the speed of human travel would no longer be governed by horse-power[16] and wind-power.

So Napoleon's armies moved no faster than did Caesar's, and many people thought that that was the way land travel should stay. Ten years after the Battle of Waterloo, however, progress was being made with steamships. The *Savannah*, an American ship with an engine as well as sails, had crossed the Atlantic in 1819, some of the time under steam.[17] But there was much doubt about the wisdom of people travelling on railways. This is what the English journal *Quarterly Review* said in March 1825:

> What can be more palpably absurd and ridiculous than the prospect held out of locomotives travelling twice as fast as stage coaches! We should as soon expect the people of Woolwich to suffer themselves to be fired off upon one of Congreve's ricochet

rockets as trust themselves to the mercy of such a machine going at such a rate ... We trust that Parliament will, in all railways it may sanction, limit the speed to eight or nine miles an hour, which we entirely agree with Mr. Sylvester is as great as can be ventured on with safety.[18]

Nevertheless, in 1829 George Stephenson built his Rocket,[19] the first locomotive suitable for a regular passenger railway operation, and its speed was much more than eight or nine miles an hour. In fact, it reached 29 miles an hour (46 kilometres per hour) at its trials. The railway era began on 15 September the next year with the opening of the London-to-Manchester Railway.

There were still critics. Pope Gregory XVI forbade the construction of railways in the Papal States on the ground that they could harm religion and the English writer and art critic John Ruskin dismissed them as a means by which 'every fool in Buxton can be at Bakewell in half an hour and every fool in Bakewell at Buxton.'[20]

The elite might sniff, but technology triumphed and it was also a triumph for ordinary people. Railways provided not only capacity and speed; they cut the cost of travel from about threepence-halfpenny a mile to a penny. By the 1830s passengers of all social classes in Britain were using the railways. Life would never be the same again. 'Feudality is gone for ever,' said Dr Arnold when the Birmingham railway reached Rugby.[21]

The inventive mind of Thomas Cook

Steam-power's potential for tourism was not realised fully until after 1841, when Thomas Cook organised a group of 570 to go from Leicester to Loughborough in England for a temperance meeting. Cook, a 32-year-old printer, saw the new railways as an instrument of social education and reform. He thought most social problems were related to alcohol and that, if travel were available to ordinary men and women, it would give them something better to do than drink. In putting together this first excursion he became immersed in the mechanisms of tourism: he was the tour operator and also the meeting organiser. The railway company soon asked him to be its agent.

Many have followed him as tour operators, meeting organisers and travel agents. This is not to say that Thomas Cook was the first travel agent—the Romans had travel agents. Nor was he the first tour operator —Venetians could buy a package tour to the Holy Land in the fifteenth century which included transport there and back with guides and two

8   hot meals a day, all for the one price of 60 gold ducats. Closer to home, a Mr Emery of Charing Cross was organising 14-day coach tours to Switzerland for 20 guineas in 1818.

Cook claimed to have organised the first public excursion train in England. In fact, he did not originate railway excursions. However, his temperance excursion caught the public imagination like none before. In the words of Piers Brendon, it was 'the first hesitant step on an immensely long and arduous journey'.[22]

He not only took advantage of the new steam trains and steamships; his great achievement was in simplifying, popularising and cheapening travel to places as far away from England as Australia. He developed close contacts with hotels, shipping companies and railways throughout the world and obtained the best service and the lowest prices for his clients. His innovation took many forms: he bought tickets from the railway companies for resale; he published guidebooks. In 1868 he invented the hotel voucher, in 1872 he took 11 people on the first Cook's round-the-world tour[23] and in 1874 he launched the 'circular note', the forerunner of the traveller's cheque. Through his knowledge and attention to detail he took the worry out of travel for many thousands of people.[24]

Other innovators:
Murray, Baedeker and American Express

Thomas Cook was not the only, or indeed the best-known, publisher of guidebooks. Guidebooks had already been produced for European travellers in the 1830s by two publishers who were to have considerable influence as tourism reached a new impetus in later decades. They began by producing guidebooks for the same countries—John Murray of London brought out his *Handbook for Holland, Belgium, and North Germany* in 1836 and Karl Baedeker of Coblenz produced his guide in 1839.

As time went on there were many guidebook publishers and the destinations they covered multiplied, but Murray and Baedeker were the chief rivals in the nineteenth century. Baedeker sold more copies than Murray, but then his books were cheaper. Their books guided travellers not only to all parts of Europe but to other parts of the world as well. Baedeker offered guidance as far as Beijing or across Canada and the United States, while Murray even published guidebooks on Japan and New Zealand.[25]

In the United States in 1850, as the result of a merger between Wells   **9**
Fargo and two other freight companies, the American Express company
came into existence. It was to be no ordinary freight company. Its enterprise took a number of forms, but from its early years it devised innovative financial services for travellers. It first underwrote a money order in
1880; it also pledged to pay money on telegraphic orders between
places thousands of kilometres apart. In 1891 it introduced the first
traveller's cheque, representing dollars that could be converted into a
variety of currencies. In 1900 it opened its most famous office at 11 Rue
Scribe in Paris, which became a focal point for Americans in Europe,
particularly when they were in trouble after the outbreak of war.[26]

The passenger ships get bigger and faster

When two paddle-steamers—the *Sirius* and the *Great Western*—created
public excitement by both exceeding an average speed of eight knots
crossing the Atlantic in April 1838, a group of shipping magnates
decided that the passenger ship logging the fastest transatlantic crossing
should be honoured with the privilege of flying a blue ribbon from its
mast. Thus began the tradition of the Blue Riband.

The *Great Western*, which had arrived in New York a day after the
Sirius but had achieved the higher average speed of 8.66 knots, had
been designed by the famous engineer Isambard Kingdom Brunel, who
was also chief engineer of Britain's Great Western Railway. He designed
the *Great Britain*, the first ocean screw steamer, in 1848 and then in
1858 the *Great Eastern*, an enormous passenger ship for the times. At
18 915 tons,[27] the *Great Eastern* was the first vessel to exceed 10 000 tons
and it was almost five times bigger than anything then afloat. It was not
until 1899 that a longer ship was built, and its overall size was not
exceeded until 1901. It had six masts to carry sails and screw propellers
as well as paddle wheels. Its owners, the Great Ship Company, put it
into service between Southampton and New York in 1860, but the ship
was not a success because it made its passengers sick if the sea got up. It
wallowed so heavily in a seaway that its paddle wheels were often damaged; on one occasion one was destroyed entirely. The *Great Eastern* was
withdrawn from passenger service in 1864 and became a cable layer.

While it had its problems, the *Great Eastern* was the portent of things
to come. The 30 years before the First World War were an era of impressive development for passenger ships. During the 1880s steel became
the favoured building material because it was as strong as iron and
lighter in weight. Twin screws became normal, driven by quadruple

10 engines which increased speed and economy. Then came the steam turbine.[28] The new, bigger, faster ships went all around the world, including to Australia, but the Atlantic was the glamour ocean, the route between European ports and New York the arena for national rivalry, the prize the Blue Riband for the fastest crossing.

The 'German decade' began in 1897 when the North German Lloyd liner, the 14 749-ton *Kaiser Wilhelm der Grosse*, averaged 22.35 knots to take the Blue Riband.[29] The Hamburg-America line's *Deutschland* exceeded that speed in 1900 and again in 1901 (23.51 knots) and held the 'fastest' title for six years.

The 31 550-ton *Lusitania*, built for the Cunard Line with financial help from the British government, was the next 'biggest ship in the world' when it was launched in 1907. It captured the Blue Riband for Britain later that year, only to lose it the next year to its sister ship the *Mauretania*. The *Lusitania* made its fastest voyage in 1909 to retake the Riband with an average of 25.85 knots, but lost it permanently to the *Mauretania* in September 1909.[30]

The most famous incident of this era at sea was the sinking of the 46 329-ton White Star liner *Titanic* in the early hours of 15 April 1912. The *Titanic* and its sister ship the *Olympic* were the largest vessels in the world and supposedly unsinkable. But the *Titanic* hit an iceberg in the Atlantic on its maiden voyage and went down with the loss of some 1500 lives, a maritime disaster that writers, underwater explorers and film-makers have kept famous for successive generations. The *Olympic*, which was partly rebuilt after the *Titanic* disaster to increase its safety measures and provide for additional life-boats, was in service until 1935.[31]

For all the drama, the *Titanic* tragedy did not set back the progress of travel at sea, though the fortunes of its owner, the White Star Line, began to decline from that time. In terms of consistent high-quality passenger service, it is the *Mauretania* that stands out among ships built before the First World War. This ship was to hold the Blue Riband unchallenged for 20 years and, in the opinion of a respected German maritime historian, was 'the most famous express steamer of all time'.[32]

The spread of railways

Railways had put stage coaches out of business. In Britain, the coach industry had reached its peak in 1836 with some 150 000 horses, 30 000 people and 3000 coaches providing 700 regular postal runs. But in 1841 the railways began to carry mail and the death knell for the long-distance coach business had been sounded.[33] The effect of the railways on the number of people who travelled was remarkable. Coaches had taken 50 000 people from London to Brighton in the year 1837 and people in England thought that was a record that might never be exceeded. In 1862, however, 132 000 went there from London by rail on a single day—Easter Monday.

It was not only in Britain that engineers were busy in the mid-nineteenth century. Railways soon spread in Europe and the United States. In the 1850s, tourists could get to Rome from London in four-and-a-half days—a journey that once took weeks—by taking the train as far as Marseilles and a boat to Civitta Vecchia, where the novelist Stendhal, who popularised the word 'tourist', had been the French consul in the 1830s. By 1872 the railway to Rome went via Paris, Munich, Innsbruck and the Brenner Pass, taking three days.

In 1848 about half the continental width of the United States was permanently settled by white people. Nearly a hundred little railways, with lines from 8 to 250 kilometres long, were scattered over the eastern states and about another twenty of the same dimensions were operating inland. Twenty-one years later a railway had been built across the continent from the Atlantic coast to the Pacific, and there were 85 000 kilometres of railway lines laid throughout the country.

Sleeping and dining cars

Railway travel in the United States had become more comfortable. In 1863 George Mortimer Pullman patented his invention of the first modern railway sleeping car, which had folding upper berths and seats that could extend into lower berths. In 1867 he organised the Pullman Palace Car Company to manufacture sleeping cars, parlour cars and dining cars.

By the turn of the century the train was the only practical form of land transport for medium- and long-distance journeys. Most people travelled in some comfort. This was certainly a long way from the 'tubs': the open, seatless carriages that early British railways provided for their third-class passengers.

For those who could afford to pay a premium price there was luxury on wheels. Perhaps the best example of the time was the New York Central's *Twentieth Century Limited*, a train capable of covering the 1577 kilometres between New York and Chicago in 20 hours. When it was introduced in 1902, the express carried a mere 42 passengers in its five cars.[34] These passengers had a choice of accommodation extending to palatial staterooms (two of which could be joined to become a bridal chamber); a gentlemen's club car with wine bar, barber's shop and

12   white-tiled bathroom; an observation car to which ladies could retire; and a dining car which, apart from the sumptuous meals it offered, was notable for its moulded mahogany décor, wall-hung pot plants, linen-covered tables and real silverware.[35]

In Europe there were no Pullman cars. Instead sleeping, dining and saloon cars were operated by the International Sleeping Car Company, which was formed in 1876 by Georges Nagelmackers, a Belgian mining engineer. Nagelmackers was only 22 when he first conceived of his plan after travelling on Pullman cars during a visit to the United States in 1867. He returned to Belgium believing he could improve on the American achievements. For one thing, he considered that the Pullman sleeping cars did not give women sufficient privacy; his solution was to have sleeping compartments with doors instead of the Pullman's coach-dormitory, which had only a curtain to separate the sleepers in their niches.[36]

The Franco-German war of 1870–71 delayed his project and so did the problems of dealing with a large number of European railways with different gauges, different braking, lighting, heating and signalling systems and different regulations. But eventually his company—its full title was the Compagnie Internationale des Wagons-Lits et des Grands Express Européens—began operations and by the First World War had a fleet of 550 specialised cars. Most of these were concentrated in de luxe trains, though sometimes individual cars were included in the make-up of ordinary trains.

In 1883, the best-known of the great Wagons-Lits trains, the *Orient Express*, made its first run from Paris—though not all the way to Constantinople (now Istanbul) on this first trip, because the Balkan railway systems were not good enough. So the *Orient Express* went only as far as Giurgewo (now Giurgiu), a little Romanian port on the banks of the Danube. It took a couple of boat trips and a short journey on another train to complete the journey to the Turkish capital.

However, from 1889 the *Orient Express* went all the way from Paris to Constantinople after the line from Belgrade to Nis was linked. The 3200-kilometre journey was made in less than three days and the train linked a great range of peoples—French, Bavarian, Austrian, Hungarian, Serbian, Bulgarian, Romanian and Turkish—at a time of intrigue, tension and diverse national ambitions.

> ... the *Orient Express* has always enjoyed a rather special reputa-
> tion. Spies and shady characters rubbed shoulders with fallen
> Princes and Diplomats bearing State secrets. Oriental merchants
> rich in leather and furs were so wealthy ... that they put their

diamonds in their luggage. (J. Des Cars & J. P. Caracalla, *The*   **13**
Orient Express: A Century of Railway Adventures, 1984)[37]

The first modern hotels

Nagelmackers' Wagons-Lits company also went into the hotel business, because its trains pulled into terminals where the accommodation was not adequate for its passengers. The reasoning was similar to that of the airlines in a later era. In 1890 it founded the Compagnie Internationale des Grands Hôtels, the first international hotel chain. The first hotels were in Brindisi, Ostend, Monte Carlo, Nice, Constantinople, Lisbon and Cairo. In 1904 the Grand Hôtel des Wagons-Lits opened in Beijing.

There was an increased demand for accommodation in many parts of the world, with so many people travelling. Hotels as such were relatively new. Their predecessors had been inns—and these had existed from the earliest times to serve merchants and other travellers. The Romans called them *mansionis* and placed them along the road system to accommodate travellers. In later periods many inns were operated by monastic brotherhoods. The number of inns increased with the growth of stage coach travel in the eighteenth century, but many of these left much to be desired. They were often just part of a dwelling, dirty and run by a disreputable landlord.

There was a great improvement during the Industrial Revolution—especially in Britain, where new standards of comfort and cleanliness were set and there was some service to guests rather than the practice of leaving them to look after themselves, as had been the earlier custom. In this period, from 1750 to 1820, English inns were generally considered to be the finest in the world.[38]

The development of large city hotels began in the early nineteenth century in North America and in Europe. These embodied a different set of ideas from anything that had gone before. Rather than being merely places to sleep and eat on a journey, they became important centres for a number of activities, offering restaurants, bars and places for meetings and receptions as well as accommodation.

The Americans build bigger

The word 'hotel' was adopted by early American proprietors from the French word, which referred to a substantial city residence or large public building.[39] The Americans had always built larger inns than the Europeans. When the City Hotel was opened in New York in 1794 it was considered immense because it had 73 rooms, although it was no

14   more than an overgrown inn. Before that, inns in America had usually been converted dwellings.

Later the Americans developed the larger hotel with its own architecture, innovative construction and a greater ratio of bathrooms to bedrooms than in previous eras. According to Montgomery-Massingberd and Watkin:

> This was partly due to the greater fluidity of American society, the longer distances which the traveller there had to cover, and the relative scarcity of the kind of hostelries or family hotels to be found in Europe.[40]

The first modern hotel was the Tremont House in Boston. When it was built in 1829 it was the largest and costliest building in the United States. Whereas the typical inn of the day consisted of one or two large rooms containing from three to ten beds, the Tremont House was the first to have private single and double rooms. Each room was supplied with a bowl and pitcher and free soap—considered an extreme luxury—and the door could be locked. French cuisine was introduced in the dining-room and the first bellboys were employed.

Luxury hotels were built in many cities of the United States after that, among them the old Waldorf-Astoria hotel in New York,[41] the Brown Palace in Denver and the Palace in San Francisco. The latter was the most ornate and expensive hotel of the day. Much less impressive hotels were built near railway stations, some of them little better than rooming-houses. By the end of the century there was a demand for something better for travellers who could not afford the luxury hotels; this led to the modern commercial hotel. The first of these was the Statler Hotel in Buffalo, opened in 1908. Each room had its own bathroom, circulating iced water, and a light switch located just inside the door so that it could be easily found. A free newspaper was delivered to each guest in the morning. The hotel's owner, Ellsworth Milton Statler, later started the first great American hotel-keeping chain.

The luxury hotel appears in Europe

In Britain, unimaginative hotels had been built for railway travellers near stations in the 1850s and 1860s. The more impressive Westminster Palace, opened in 1859, was the first London hotel to have lifts, although it had only 14 bathrooms to its 286 bedrooms. On the Continent, luxury resort hotels were built on the French and Italian Riviera, but it was in Switzerland that the concepts of hotel luxury, management and service were most advanced. In the 1880s the Grand Hôtel Nationale in Lucerne was considered the most elegant in Europe.

The first hotel school started in the same city in the next decade. This **15** reinforced the perception that Swiss hotels and training were the best in the world. For decades to come, the top management of the world's best hotels was to be dominated largely by Swiss hotelkeepers and their style of operation.[42]

The influences of Ritz and Escoffier

In the latter years of the 1880s London and Paris were catching up, using American techniques to build hotels and absorbing the influences of outstanding figures such as the former Grand Hôtel Nationale's manager César Ritz and the great chef Auguste Escoffier. The leading hotels in the European capitals became centres of style and were able to influence social changes. Ritz had such a passion for cleanliness that he was considered to have helped alter public attitudes towards hygiene and sanitation. He insisted on having a bathroom to every bedroom in the Paris Ritz, which opened in 1898. The London Ritz came later, in 1906: it had 150 bedrooms and 75 bathrooms, arranged in two-bedroom suites with a sitting-room and separate lavatory.[43]

Savoy Hotel dining-room, London (Source: The Savoy Group)

The original restaurant of the Savoy Hotel, where César Ritz changed the social life of London in the 1890s. One of his innovations was to hire Johann Strauss and his orchestra to play waltzes for the diners, but his success was also due to changes in the licensing laws.

16   Earlier, in 1889, Ritz had become manager of the new Savoy hotel in London. Assisted by the actress Lillie Langtry and others, he campaigned to have the licensing laws changed so that the Savoy restaurant could stay open until after midnight and on Sundays. He then hired Johann Strauss and his orchestra to play waltzes for diners and brought a baker from Vienna so that on Sundays crusty fresh bread could be served. With such innovations he succeeded in changing the pattern of London social life by persuading people it was smarter to dine in the Savoy restaurant than in their own dining-rooms. Sir Hugh Wontner, chairman of the Savoy group in the 1980s has said that, before Ritz began at the Savoy, 'it was not the thing to eat in a public restaurant, and certainly never to be seen there with your wife.'[44]

Coney Island shows the way

Although attractions on piers at seaside resorts were being built in Britain in the nineteenth century, the first amusement parks on the outskirts of cities came into being in the United States. The best known were at Coney Island, which was in reality a series of pier amusement parks stretching along New York City's most popular bathing beaches. Sea Lion Park, which opened in 1895, was the first to group rides and attractions into a single, enclosed amusement park with an admission fee charged at the gate. Within nine years, the three most famous Coney Island amusement parks, Steeplechase Park, Luna Park and Dreamland, were opened.[45]

The car and the plane make their entry

In a period of 17 years straddling the turn of the century, two new vehicles made their appearance. In future eras they would change travel and tourism more profoundly than anything that had gone before.

In 1886 two Germans made the first successful motor cars powered by internal combustion engines. Karl Benz produced a three-wheeled car powered by a petrol engine and Gottlieb Daimler, working independently of Benz at about the same time, built a four-cycle single-cylinder petrol engine that was in advance of anything previously built. He attached this to an American horse carriage, though he also built a vehicle to a new design that could achieve a speed of 16 kilometres per hour. Both men established automobile companies that were to be merged as Daimler-Benz in 1926. They never met.[46]

Queen Victoria thought the car a 'very shaky and disagreeable conveyance' and Rudyard Kipling described it as a 'petrol-piddling monster',[47] but by the turn of the century there were 11 000 cars in the world and by 1906 50 000 were being made a year, 60 per cent of them in Europe. Large-scale manufacturing had begun in Detroit, however. Henry Ford introduced the moving assembly line in 1913 and 300 000 cars were sold in the United States the next year.[48]

The first limited access road—precursor of the freeway—was the Long Island Motor Parkway in the United States. It was opened in 1908 as a toll road for cars only and was the first public road to use overpasses to eliminate intersections and to employ banking on curves.[49]

In December 1903, the American brothers Orville and Wilbur Wright made the first flights in a power-driven heavier-than-air machine—an aeroplane. Orville was at the controls when their biplane, powered by a four-cylinder engine of their own construction, made the first 12-second flight at Kitty Hawk, North Carolina. In the subsequent three flights that day, the brothers alternated as pilots.

The internal combustion engine that drove aeroplanes and cars was to change the way we travelled as profoundly as had the steam engine that powered railway trains and steamships. But World War I intervened before the next phase of development began. The war brought about an end to a political and social era. It also marked the end of the beginning of the modern age of travel and tourism.

ENDNOTES

[1] The term 'mass tourism' is used to denote not only numbers, but also the era when the ordinary person earning a weekly wage has the time and money to travel for leisure purposes. This has required a reduction in the cost of travel, the concept of paid holidays and an increase in prosperity spread throughout communities.

[2] Gould, D. (1995), *How Was It Done? The Story of Human Ingenuity Through the Ages*, Readers Digest Association Limited, London, p. 12.

[3] ibid., p. 13.

[4] In 1997, the WTO produced a brochure to promote tourism to 16 Silk Road countries, with financing from the Japanese government. Other projects to promote Silk Road tourism included a 26-part television series by a New Zealand media group and a congress of Silk Road tour operators (*WTO News*, November 1997, p. 12).

[5] 'The Travels of Emperor Mu' was included in a collection called *The Bamboo Annals*, edited in the third century BC. Emperor Mu is supposed to have been a ruler of the Chou Dynasty, around 1000 BC. He is said to have travelled into the 'Wild West' until 'they arrived at the domain of the Royal Mother of the West'. Some scholars have thought this to be the Queen of Sheba, who is said to have ruled in south-western Arabia, controlling trade on the Incense Road to Syria and Mesopotamia. (I. M. Franck

18

& D. M. Brownstone, 1986, *The Silk Road: A History*, Facts on File Publications, pp. 33–5). According to M. G. Lay (1993, *Ways of the World: A History of the World's Roads and of the Vehicles that Used Them*, Primavera Press, Sydney, p. 46), the Silk Road was extended to meet the Middle Eastern system in about 200 BC and by about 100 BC it had become an active trade route between China and the Mediterranean.

[6] Mumford, L. (1961), cited by N. Leiper (1980), An interdisciplinary study of Australian tourism: its scope, characteristics and consequences, with particular reference to governmental policies since 1965, Master of General Studies thesis, University of New South Wales, p. 123.

[7] Wagner, F. E. (1970), cited in Schmidhauser, H. (1989), 'Tourist needs and motivations' in *Tourism Marketing and Management Handbook*, ed. S. F. Witt & L. Moutinho, Prentice Hall International, Hemel Hempstead, p. 570.

[8] Lay (1993), op.cit., p. 90.

[9] Brendon, Piers (1991), *Thomas Cook: 150 Years of Popular Tourism*, Secker & Warburg, London, p. 9.

[10] The Oxford English Dictionary gives examples of the use of 'tourist' in 1780 and of 'tourism' in 1811. The French novelist Stendhal (Henri Marie Boyle, 1783–1842) is sometimes credited with inventing 'tourist' (cf. Feifer, Maxine, 1985, *The Ways of the Tourist from Imperial Rome to the Present Day*, Macmillan, London, p. 2, 'The word 'tourist' itself was coined by Stendhal in the early nineteenth century'), but it is clear from the Oxford English Dictionary examples that the word was in use before he was born. Stendhal wrote *Les Mémoires d'un Touriste* in Paris when on prolonged sick leave from consular duties at Civita Vecchia between 1836 and 1839.

[11] Corzé, J. C. (1989), 'Theme and leisure parks', in *Tourism Marketing and Management Handbook*, ed. S. F. Witt & L. Moutinho, Prentice Hall International, Hemel Hempstead, p. 459; Leisure and Recreation Concepts, Inc. (1978), *Economic Profile of Dreamworld: A Proposed Family Entertainment Center in Cooma, Queensland, Australia*, Dallas, Texas, p. 7.

[12] Sigaux, G. (1966), *History of Tourism*, Edito-Service Ltd, Geneva; English translation, Leisure Arts Ltd, London, p. 8. No doubt there were tourists before Herodotus, but they did not leave accounts of their wanderings as he did in his famous *Histories*. According to Sigaux, the title of his work really meant 'researches' and applied as much to the study of countries and customs as to historical events.

[13] ibid., p. 21.

[14] Brendon, op.cit., p. 12.

[15] Stage coaches provided regular service between cities and towns. They made their journeys in stages, changing their horses at post houses. By the end of the seventeenth century coaches were operated over stages of about 25 kilometres and a traveller could usually manage two or three stages in a day. The word 'coach' was first used to describe a vehicle with a passenger compartment suspended by straps or chains. It comes either from the name of the fifteenth-century Hungarian vehicle builder Kotze, who invented the technology, or the small town of Kocs where he lived. It progressed through Germany (*Kutsche*), Italy (*cocchio*) and France (*coche*) to become the English word 'coach' (Lay, 1993, op.cit., pp. 123, 124).

[16] Horses were not the only domesticated animals used for motive power, of course, though they are the most familiar. Lay (1993, op.cit., p. 19) also lists cattle, onagers, donkeys, dogs, goats, mules, camels, elephants, buffaloes, llamas, reindeer, yaks and humans as some of the better-known species that have been used for transport.

[17] The *Savannah* took a month on the crossing, mostly under sail, using engines intermittently. The British vessel *Great Western* was the first ocean-going steamship and it did not sail until 1838.

[18] *A History of Travel in America*, The Bobbs-Merrill Co., NY; new edition Tudor Publishing Co., NY, 1937, p. 906. The victor of Waterloo, the Duke of Wellington, did not like railways. 'In my opinion people never acted so foolishly as we did in allowing of the Destruction of our excellent and commodious [post roads] in order to expend Millions Sterling on these Rail Roads! [he wrote to Miss Angela Burdett-Coutts, who was investing heavily in them in September 1848]. It appears to me to be the Vulgarest, most indelicate, most inconvenient, most injurious to Health of any mode of conveyance that I have seen in any part of the World!' (C. Hibbert, 1997, *Wellington: A Personal History*, HarperCollins Publishers, London, pp. 385–6).

[19] Stephenson's parents were too poor to send him to school. Born in the north of England in 1781, he learned to read at night classes when he was 18.

[20] Brendon, op.cit., p. 15.

[21] ibid., pp. 12–16.

[22] ibid., p. 17.

[23] Griggs, T. (1997) (ed.), *Superbrands: An Insight into 65 Australian Superbrands*, Superbrands Pty Ltd, Sydney, p. 130.

[24] Brendon (op.cit.) provides a detailed and readable account of Cook and his times.

[25] Sillitoe, A. (1995), *Leading the Blind: A century of Guide Book Travel, 1815–1914*, Macmillan, London, p. 5.

[26] Griggs, op.cit., p. 12.

[27] 'Tons' is used throughout to indicate the relative sizes of ships. The term as used here means 'gross tons', which is a measurement of volume: 100 cubic feet (2.83 cubic metres) equals one gross ton. It cannot be converted to today's Australian usage of the metric 'tonne', which is a unit of weight (1000 kilograms) and close to being the equivalent of a long ton (2240 pounds or 1016 kilograms). Gross tonnage is the measurement of the internal capacity of a ship, not its weight.

[28] Dean, I. (1991), *Great Ocean Liners: The Heyday of Luxury Travel*, B. T. Batsford Ltd, London, p. 18.

[29] Because transatlantic routes vary in length, the 'fastest passage' is based on average speed rather than elapsed time for the voyage.

[30] The *Lusitania* was torpedoed by the German submarine *U20* off the Irish coast in May 1915. Of the 1959 people on board, 1198 died.

[31] It had its share of drama. In 1918 it was attacked by the German submarine *U103*, which ran under its bows and was sunk. In 1934 it rammed and sank the Nantucket lightship in heavy fog. A third vessel in the class, the 48 158-ton *Britannic*, was completed as a hospital ship in 1915 and sank the next year after hitting a mine.

[32] Kludos, A. (1975), *Great Passenger Ships of the World*, vol. 1, 1858–1912, tr. Charles Hodges, Patrick Stephens Ltd, Cambridge, p. 137.

[33] Lay (1993), op.cit., pp. 126, 127.

[34] 'Express' has nothing to do with speed. The word means 'explicit' or 'expressly stated'. It was first applied to trains in 1845 and signified a special train, which operated for an express purpose (C. Taylor, 1986, *Great Train Non-journeys of Australia*, University of Qld Press, St Lucia, Qld, p. 45).

[35] Allen, G. F. (1983), *Railways of the Twentieth Century*, Sidgwick & Jackson Ltd, London, p. 8.

[36] Des Cars, J. & Caracalla, J. P. (1984), *The Orient Express: A Century of Railway Adventures*, tr. George Behrend, Great Express Books, London, pp. 12–17.

[37] ibid., p. 40.

[38] Lattin, G. W. (1990a), 'Hotels', in *Collier's Encyclopedia*, vol. 12, Macmillan Education Co., NY, p. 294.

[39] Inskeep, E. (1991), *Town Planning: An Integrated and Sustainable Development Approach*, Van Nostrand Reinhold, NY, p. 8.

[40] Montgomery-Massingberd, H. & Watkin, D. (1989), *The London Ritz*, new ed., Aurum Press, London, p. 18.

[41] The first Waldorf-Astoria was at 34th Street and Fifth Avenue. The present hotel of the same name is on Park Avenue.

[42] Lattin (1990a), op.cit., p. 298.

[43] None of the Ritzes was big by today's standards. As configured in the 1990s, the Paris Ritz had 187 rooms, including 46 suites and the Madrid Ritz 161 rooms, including six suites. Another famous Paris hotel, the George V, has 292 rooms including 59 suites.

[44] Sir Hugh Wontner, Chairman of the Savoy Group in the 1980s, quoted by Montgomery-Massingberd & Watkin, op.cit., p. 20.

[45] Leisure and Recreation Concepts, Inc., op.cit., pp. 7–8.

[46] It has been said that Daimler built the first petrol-powered engine and Benz built the first petrol-powered vehicle. This statement reflects the difference in their approaches. Benz focused on the whole vehicle, designing it from scratch to suit the engine and Daimler concentrated on the engine and then looked around for a chassis to carry it (Lay, 1993, op.cit., p. 155). Daimler died in 1900 and Benz in 1929. The first modern car in all essentials is said to have been the 1901 Mercedes, designed by Wilhelm Maybach and produced by the Daimler company. The Mercedes was named after the daughter of an Austrian-born Parisian banker and car dealer Emile Jellinek, who had urged the construction of the new vehicle and ordered the first 36. The new name was chosen because Jellinek did not think a car with a German name would sell well in France (ibid., pp. 158–9).

[47] Lay (1993), op.cit., p. 174.

[48] ibid., p. 168.

[49] ibid., p. 314.

Travel in Australia to 1914

Before 1788

The same kinds of technological advances that brought such dramatic changes to Europe and North America would in time also change Australia. But it had to await the efforts of struggling colonists. Australia's original inhabitants, the Aboriginal people, were remarkable travellers but they had little technology of their own and the country did not provide them with animals they could ride or harness to a wheeled vehicle. They had few possessions to carry and, in the normal course of their lives, no need for land vehicles.[1] They walked. They explored and settled a huge continent and developed a network of communication throughout it for trade and social contacts, all on foot.

Australia was settled by sea travellers more than 40 000 years ago, long before people recorded their achievements. Scientists have pieced together what we know from skeletons and tools—even charcoal from ancient fires and bones of animals eaten tens of thousands of years ago. These can be compared with relics found elsewhere in the world and, in some instances, with characteristics of various people today to give us some scanty knowledge of the first settlers.

Scientists also know that at the time of the first settlement the waters of the oceans were colder than they are now and that the sea levels were much lower. This meant that New Guinea and Tasmania were joined to Australia, which was about 20 per cent larger than it is today. Geoffrey Blainey has speculated that the discoverer of Australia waded ashore somewhere on the north-west coast, perhaps on the western coast of the land link between the present New Guinea and the present Australia. In Blainey's words, this ancient voyager was the first of 'a host

21

22   of people taking part in a long, long relay race that perhaps extended over thousands of years'.[2]

These people came from South-East Asia, island-hopping on frail rafts or in simple canoes, and the distances they travelled across the narrow straits that existed then were probably less than 100 kilometres.[3] Short though their voyages were, they were worthy of a place in history:

> They were the only people in the world's history to sail across the seas and discover an inhabitable continent. (G. Blainey, *Triumph of the Nomads*, 1975)[4]

The Aboriginal settlement of the whole continent may have taken as long as 10 000 years. The Aboriginal people were always nomads; they did not herd animals, grow crops or cultivate gardens. Instead, they roamed over a wide terrain in search of food, but usually within clan boundaries. For travel on water they used a variety of canoes and rafts: mostly flimsy craft that were quickly built from bark or stakes tied together with vines. In the north, Aboriginal groups learned from Indonesian fishermen how to build stronger dug-out canoes and some copied the outrigger dug-outs of the Torres Strait Islanders and the Papuans.

For all their lack of contrivances, they were living well by most standards of the time when white settlement began in 1788. Blainey, taking the main ingredients of a good standard of living to be food, health, shelter and warmth, says:

> Aboriginals of course could not match the comfort and security of the upper classes of Europe, of the wealthiest one-tenth of the population, but they were probably much better off than the poorest one-tenth.[5]

When food became scarce they simply moved camp to find it.

> [The Aboriginal people] often ate foods which would have been rare luxuries to European peasants or town labourers, and at the same time they had plenty of the starchy foods which were the main or only course at European tables.[6]

Their travel to find food was not haphazard. They understood the land and what it could supply them with and they understood the changes of the seasons. They also travelled for trade, barter and the ceremonial exchanging of gifts with other tribes or groups, and to see their friends and relatives. Their paths usually ran from waterhole to waterhole and distance was measured by the time it took to walk between them.[7]

The longest recorded individual journeys involved the Dieri people east of Lake Eyre, who periodically walked several hundred kilometres to the Flinders Ranges for red ochre and also visited the Simpson Desert to obtain the narcotic plant pituri. If the same people undertook both journeys, then they visited places more than 800 kilometres apart.[8]

The white settlers could not match the Aboriginal people's endurance on land nor their ability to live from it. But Australia's second settlement came at a time when science and technology were beginning to transform Europe and North America and would also change the way people travelled in Australia.

> Transport, in the conventional sense of a permanent and mapped road system, established seaways and regular shipping, navigable river routes and eventually modern rail and air transport, only began in Australia with the arrival of the technology and engineering capability of the Old World. (B. Inglis, in *Technology in Australia 1788–1988*, 1989)[9]

Technology conquers distance

By the mid-nineteenth century Australia was developing fast and confidently under the impetus of the gold rushes. The travel revolution had begun. Steamships had been on coastal runs for 20 years. The first train hauled by a locomotive ran from Flinders Street in Melbourne to what is now suburban Port Melbourne in September 1854, carrying passengers and freight over a distance of some four kilometres. The other colonies soon followed Victoria's lead. New South Wales had a railway in 1855, South Australia followed in 1856, Queensland in 1863, Tasmania in 1871 and Western Australia in 1879. The Northern Territory's first railway, between Darwin and Pine Creek, opened in 1889.

Communication by water was of paramount importance in the early years. Ships, of course, were the only means of reaching Britain or any other part of the world; coastal vessels connected the colonies and local transport was also dependent on water. Thus Rose Hill (now Parramatta) and Windsor were settled with the help of river craft before roads were built. The *Rose Hill Packet*, known as 'the Lump', was built by the colonists in 1789, the year after their arrival in Sydney. Propelled by oars and sail, this boat carried stores and passengers along the Parramatta River to Rose Hill.

24 Slow progress on land

Progress in land communications was slow at first. Few roads were built in the first decades after settlement in New South Wales. Even when they were built, they were a long way from what we are accustomed to today. They could be dangerous. In 1847 Lady FitzRoy, the wife of the Governor of New South Wales, Sir Charles FitzRoy, was thrown from a carriage at Parramatta and killed.

As for public conveyances, riding in a bucking, swaying coach over corrugated roads was uncomfortable and frequently frightening. Some intrepid passengers rode on the roof where they were likely to suffer from wind, rain, flying dust or mud, and also had to watch out for low-hanging branches. In the early days there was the possibility of coming upon hostile Aboriginal people and later there were bushrangers: travellers were vulnerable to assault, robbery and even murder on the roads. Bushranging increased after the gold rushes of the 1850s and the years between 1860 and 1880 were especially dangerous.

When railways were extended throughout much of the country, travelling by land may have become less hazardous but it could still be tiresome. Going from one capital to another frequently meant combining rail and coach travel, which usually required an early start. It was often necessary to make an overnight journey by coach in order to catch a train. For instance, to go from Melbourne to Adelaide in 1882 meant taking a train from Melbourne to Hamilton, then a coach from Hamilton to Naracoorte, then another train from Naracoorte to Kingston, and then a coach from Kingston to Meningie. This connected with a ship, which steamed across Lake Alexandrina to Milang. From there, a coach took the passenger into Adelaide.[10]

The sea: a ring road

Eventually railways would bring about the decline of the shipping companies, but the process was slow and for most of the nineteenth century ships were the principal means of travel between the main settlements.

> If we are to understand transport in the nineteenth century, we must think of the sea not as a border but as a ring road. (G. Davison, J. W. McCarty & A. McLeary, eds, *Australians: 1888*, 1987)[11]

Travelling that 'road' was not always comfortable or without hazard, as a report in the *Gippsland Mercury* in 1879 illustrates. This article tells of a relatively short journey along the Victorian coast by the steamer

Bairnsdale. The *Bairnsdale* left Melbourne on Friday, 11 April bound for **25** Sale in Gippsland. But the vessel could not even clear Port Phillip Heads into Bass Strait for four days because of a gale. It reached Wilson's Promontory, no great distance from the Heads, on Wednesday, 16 April and Lakes Entrance the next day. It failed to cross the bar at its first attempt, grounding hard, and had to be hauled off with the help of the anchor. It was not until Friday night that the *Bairnsdale* made its next attempt to cross the bar, this time successfully, and finally reached Sale at mid-afternoon the next day. That was Saturday, 19 April. The trip had taken eight days. Today it is a pleasant drive of a few hours.[12]

A changing world

The problems—of dangerous roads, of disconnected train journeys, of perils at sea—were real enough, but on the other hand the development of transport between 1850 and 1870 was extraordinary for a collection of colonies with small populations. And progress accelerated. In 1870, Australian railways carried nine million passengers, in 1890 they carried 70 million and in 1915 270 million.[13]

Though isolated from the rest of the world—or perhaps because they were, and were therefore reliant on their own resources—the colonists participated in the early development of the new vehicles. Even the first locomotive that ran in Victoria was home-made because the English steam engines ordered for the railway had not arrived in time for the opening (see page 1).

Despite this ingenuity, it took a long time for Australians to master one of the most fundamental necessities of travel—the road. It was not so much a matter of engineering capability, though that was in short supply in the early years. The real problems were money and labour resources.[14]

The period before the First World War ended with Australian travel and tourism firmly established. This was based on a transportation system which was remarkably efficient for the day, considering the distances it had to contend with and the relatively sparse population.

The world was changing. A few thousand Australians were already driving motor cars and motor coaches were being used to take tourists around the sights. Despite the awful roads, some people were beginning to go on overnight trips. This was a new kind of tourism. And there was a new sound in the air.

26   The first flight controversy

There is controversy about who made the first powered flight in Australia. Colin Defries, an Englishman who had learned to fly in France, made the first attempt in a Wright Flyer at Victoria Park racecourse, Sydney, on 9 December 1909. However, while the *Sydney Morning Herald* reported that he had successfully completed a short flight, the *Daily Telegraph* and the Aerial League claimed that he did not leave the ground.[15]

There is little doubt that Harry Houdini, the famous escapologist, took to the air in a Voisin box-kite biplane at Digger's Rest, Victoria, on 18 March 1910. Nine witnesses testified in a signed statement that Houdini, whose real name was Ehrich Weiss, made three controlled flights. The Aerial League reviewed all flight attempts at the end of the year and presented Houdini with a trophy for 'the First Aerial Flight in Australia'.

The first flight in an Australian designed and built aircraft also occurred in 1910. On 16 July, John R. Duigan flew his pusher-engined biplane at Mia Mia, 40 kilometres from Kyneton in Victoria. The distance was only about seven metres, not even as far as the Wrights had flown seven years before, but Duigan continued to improve the performance of his plane and by October 1911 was able to fly 1000 metres on a semicircular course.[16]

There was a long way to go before Australians would board a Qantas 747 or an Ansett aeroplane, but the first steps had been taken towards the global era of travel and tourism and Australia was going to be part of it. The First World War ended the long period in history when it had taken days or weeks to travel the same distance we can now cover in an hour. In Australia's history this was a period in which a firm foundation was laid for the next stage of development.

Travel by sea

Shipping development until the First World War may be looked at in three periods:

1   The pioneering period. From settlement to the beginning of the gold rushes in 1851 small sailing ships and paddle-steamers explored routes, first linking settlements within their own colonies and from 1825 beginning regular inter-colonial services.
2   The expansion period, 1851–1879. Services were extended around the coasts, encompassing a large number of ports from the north-west of Western Australia to the far north of Queensland. Regular

service with modern ships was maintained between Tasmanian and mainland ports. New companies were formed. However, most packet ships running regular routes were paddle-steamers, which made little concession to passenger comfort.

3 The consolidation period, 1880–1914. Competition was strong on the popular routes between capitals and new screw-steamers, much larger than their predecessors, were introduced. These became more comfortable as time went on and offered passengers properly constructed cabins as well as luxurious public areas.

The pioneering period

In the early days of settlement, few British-built craft were available. It was mostly with the ships they built themselves that the colonists developed the inland waters and coastal trades. The shipbuilders usually had plenty of timber to build first-class ships—jarrah, blue gum, cedar and Huon pine—and sheltered shores nearby to accommodate their shipyards.

By 1804 there were at least 20 vessels under construction in Sydney and in other coastal settlements of New South Wales. The first vessel launched in Tasmania—then called Van Diemen's Land—was the schooner *Henrietta* in 1812. The *Lady Stirling* was built in Western Australia in 1836 and Victoria's first shipyard was established on the banks of the Yarra River at Melbourne in 1839. As time went on, top British craftsmen came out to work at the yards.

In Tasmania alone, government records show that 445 vessels were built between 1825 and 1872: 313 on the Derwent shoreline and the rest in northern yards.[17] Australia's first screw-steamer, the 139-ton *City of Melbourne*, was launched on the Yarra in 1851. It was very slow, averaging about three knots in its trials on the river, but was put on the run to Launceston. In smooth water it had less power than contemporary paddle-steamers, but when the weather was bad it had a decided advantage over them because its screw was always under water.[18]

The sailing ships in each colony established services from the main settlements, around the harbours and bays, along rivers like the Derwent, Tamar, Swan, Hunter and Hawkesbury, and around the coasts.

Regular sailing by packet ships between Sydney and Newcastle had begun by the 1820s. A 'packet' ship was one that had been commissioned by the government to carry mails and dispatches between designated ports. For passengers, the packets offered an all-inclusive passenger fare. Thus the cutter packet *Lord Liverpool* made weekly sailings between Sydney and Newcastle, a voyage of 12 hours, for a cabin fare

28   which included wine and spirits.[19] Regular packet services between Hobart Town and Sydney were organised in 1825. The fare charged was ten pounds cabin and five pounds steerage.[20]

South Australia built up a large fleet of small sailing vessels in later decades to provide the essential link with outlying agricultural settlements, including such places as Wallaroo, Port Augusta, Port Lincoln, Onkaparinga, Willunga, Port Wakefield and Robe. Over the years the fleet grew to more than 100 vessels serving more than 40 ports.

The coming of steam

From the 1830s the trading routes of the steamers developed on those already established and the new vessels quickly became more important for passenger traffic than sailing ships. However, there were still hundreds of ships under sail in the rivers, estuaries and around the coasts and would be for many more years.

The first ship driven by steam on the Australian coastal trade was a 256-ton paddle-wheeler, the *Sophia Jane*, which arrived in Sydney Harbour from Britain on 13 May 1831. Then five years old, it was 38.4 metres long and had three cabins—the women's cabin with eleven beds, the men's with sixteen, and steerage with ten. The *Sophia Jane* was rigged as a schooner and had sailed from Britain with its paddle-wheels removed and stowed on board. On its arrival they had to be refitted and the 50-horsepower engine reassembled.

This took some time, and allowed a home-built vessel to claim the honour of being the first to operate under steam in Australian waters. A little steam ferry, the 18-ton *Surprise*, was nearing completion in Neutral Bay when the *Sophia Jane* arrived. Time was needed to convert the *Sophia Jane* to a steamer. This was in progress on 25 May when the *Surprise*'s builder, Robert Millard, and its owners, brothers Henry and Thomas Smith, raised steam for the first time and took their boat on trials in Sydney Cove and around Pinchgut Island. On 1 June the *Surprise* made the 25-kilometre voyage to Parramatta, going aground at Red Point on the way, and returned the next day. The *Sophia Jane* did not make its first trip under steam until ten days later, when it carried the Governor and other guests on a morning cruise. It left Sydney on its first commercial voyage only two days after this, under steam, bound for the Hunter River.[21]

Of the two pioneer steamships, the career of the *Sophia Jane* was by far the more significant. For nearly 13 years it helped establish trade routes both north and south of Sydney, going as far north as Moreton Bay. In April 1845 it strained its hull when it went aground on a reef off

Wollongong, was not considered worth repairing and was broken up the next year.

The little *Surprise* was not a success for the venture it had been built for—the ferry service to Parramatta—partly because it rolled uncomfortably in the wider reaches of Sydney Harbour. The next year, with its paddle-wheels stowed, it was sailed to Hobart to work as a ferry on the Derwent. Under steam it could do four-and-a-half knots, which enabled it to maintain an hourly service across the river between Kangaroo Point (Bellerive) and New Wharf. In 1842 its boiler blew up after the safety valve jammed, and that ended its days as a steamer. It was cut down and became a schooner named the *Anna Jane*, almost as though its new owner 'disliked new-fangled ships and names'.[22]

In the 1830s other steamers were built in Sydney, Newcastle and Hobart. While usually the engines were made in England, components for the engine of a paddle-wheeler built in Hobart were made or modified in a local foundry. More of the steam-powered craft came from Britain. By 1838 ten steamers operated out of Sydney. Four of these worked Port Jackson and the river to Parramatta; the rest were on coastal routes, the main route being between Sydney and the Hunter River. The small ships called at Newcastle and travelled upriver to Morpeth and Maitland.

The early steamers plying Australian coastal waters had sails, but their engines made them independent of fickle winds and so they were faster and more reliable. Sailing ships usually remained at the docks until they were fully laden, making it a matter of conjecture whether they would depart on the day advertised. Once under way, they were dependent on wind and tides, which made the dates of their arrival at their next ports even less predictable. Paddle-steamers might be, in the words of Atkinson and Aveling, 'noisy, greasy and heavily vibrating vessels', but they could maintain a regular sailing pattern and advertise their schedules in advance.[23]

Although some metal-hulled paddle and screw steamers were built in Australia—most of them in New South Wales—the majority of orders for new craft built of iron or steel went to yards in Britain because Australia did not have iron and steel works until the early twentieth century.

At the time steamers were beginning to make an impact along Australian coasts, there were three colonies: New South Wales, Western Australia and Van Diemen's Land. But soon there were four: South Australia became a separate colony in 1836. Victoria was separated from New South Wales in 1851, followed by Queensland in 1859.

30   Not surprisingly, since it is an island and given its history in building ships and providing whaling and sealing ports, Tasmania had a strong influence on early Australian shipping history. Its own coasts were explored by daring captains like James Kelly in the early years of the nineteenth century. As mining, logging and agriculture were developed and settlements formed, shipping services to a lengthy list of little ports on all coasts and to the Bass Strait islands followed.

Services across Bass Strait to the mainland have always been of great importance to Tasmania; they still are today. The first inter-colonial voyages by a steamer were made by the 33.8-metre wooden-hulled paddleboat *James Watt,* which had been built in Britain. It arrived in Hobart Town from Sydney on 31 March 1837 and then visited Melbourne, being the first steam vessel to enter Port Phillip Bay. Later in the same year, it went north from Sydney to become the first steamer to visit Brisbane, though it did not actually enter the river, but anchored in Moreton Bay. It was some years before these pioneering voyages led to regular services.

The expansion period

The gold rushes starting in mid-century stimulated shipping services, as they did all other economic activity. As fortune-hunters from overseas and from the other colonies wanted to get to the richest diggings—those in Victoria—hundreds of sailing ships anchored in Port Phillip and Hobsons Bays. Coastal ship-owners competed vigorously to cash in on the huge demand for passages. By 1853, 15 steamers and numerous sailing craft were employed on the route between Melbourne and Sydney.

The style of company organisation for the new transport system had been established by the Hunter's River Steam Navigation Co., formed in 1839. It was reorganised as the Australasian Steam Navigation Company (A.S.N.) in 1851 and became a leader in the Australian coastal trade in the 1860s and 1870s. In 1887 its ships and heritage passed to the Australasian United Steam Navigation Company, owned by the British India Steam Navigation Company.

Captain Howard Smith, who had arrived in Victoria at the time of the gold rush, formed a company which bore his name in 1854; it was to be a strong competitor of the A.S.N. Other companies were established in the 1870s or later, among them the Adelaide Steamship Company, Melbourne Steamship Company and Huddart Parker & Company. Captain Peter Huddart was another seaman who had arrived at Port Phillip during the Victorian gold rush. The Union Steamship

Company of New Zealand became an Australian operator late in the century when it bought the ships and business of the Tasmanian Steam Navigation Company. Thus the pattern was set for the development of the sea trade and, through it, a principal means of travel till past the middle of the next century.

While there was so much bustle in the east after the gold rushes—the establishment of companies and ordering new ships, followed by periods of cut-throat competition—in the west sea traffic was at a much more primitive stage. Overall, development in Western Australia was behind that in the east. Albany in the south was settled in 1826 and Perth in 1829, but the port of Bunbury did not develop until after 1841, and Geraldton and Esperance not until 1851.

There was no ready source of local coal, so steamships did not come into coastal service until the 1870s, 40 years after they had been introduced in the eastern colonies. The port of Fremantle was not opened until 1900 and the town did not even have a jetty until 1877. Before that, cargo and passengers had to be taken by lighters from vessels standing offshore to wharves in the Swan River. From 1852, the mail steamers from Britain called at the southern port of Albany.

The story of the little 337-ton steamer *Georgette*, one of the first on the Western Australian coast, illustrates what the sea trade was like in those waters in the 1870s. The *Georgette* arrived from Britain in September 1873 to provide a regular service between Geraldton in the north and Albany in the south, calling at Fremantle, Busselton and Bunbury with passengers, mail and cargo. The arrival of the mail steamers at Albany was the key to its scheduling so that it could fulfil its owners' mail contracts with the Western Australian government. Business people were pleased and so was the general community at having at last a reliable steamer service on the coast.

In 1876, when the *Georgette* was in Bunbury taking on 350 tons of cargo and 70 passengers for Albany, one of the heavy logs it was loading crashed into its hold. Nobody noticed the damage at the time, but when the ship was out at sea it sprang a leak, and although it drifted to shore near the Margaret River it was a total loss. There was no other steamer to carry on the *Georgette*'s regular trade and so there could be no collection of the overseas mails from Albany. The colonial government had to get a replacement vessel from the east.

Tasmania, on the other hand, was always in the forefront of the sea trade. Its most influential company of the times, the Tasmanian Steam Navigation Company (T.S.N.), was established in 1852. The company's first steamship was the *Tasmania*, an iron vessel of 600 tons, which

32

The last word in luxury at sea (Source: SA Maritime Museum)

The 1711-ton Adelaide was considered palatial when it entered the Adelaide Steamship Company's inter-colonial service in 1883. Not only did it have polished timber panels in its public rooms, but it also had a steam machine for making coffee and tea and the latest thing in baths and lavatories.

began running between Hobart Town, Launceston, Port Phillip and Sydney in 1853. It was a powerful vessel made of iron with a propeller measuring 2.4 metres in diameter. By 1868 the T.S.N. had eight ships serving not only Sydney, Melbourne and Hobart but also Launceston, Twofold Bay and the Snowy River goldfields.[24]

The consolidation period

By the end of the 1870s, a network of steamer routes extended from Albany in the west to North Queensland on an inter-colonial basis and from Wyndham to Cooktown via the south coast and Tasmania, if colonial services and trans-shipment are included. What followed was a development of a three-part service: from north-west ports south to Fremantle, from Fremantle to east coast capital ports, and from southern Australian ports to Cairns, the Gulf of Carpentaria and Thursday Island.[25]

The ships in which Australians travelled round their coasts grew bigger and more comfortable as the century went on. As an example, the 'palatial' vessel *Adelaide* of 1711 tons entered the Adelaide Steamship Company's inter-colonial passenger service in 1883.[26] However, many sea journeys in the second half of the century were on much smaller, smelly coastal steamers that were certainly not luxurious and anything but comfortable in rough weather.

The steam packets that had operated in the 1860s and 1870s were mostly paddle-steamers, small with spartan accommodation. The next group of vessels to come on the scene were composite design screw-steamers, built to carry a mixed payload of both cargo and passengers and with accommodation that improved as time went on from saloons with convertible bunk beds to properly constructed cabins. The vessels representing the final stage of design were the full passenger ships, luxuriously appointed steamers of much larger size and power than anything that had gone before; these could compete with the railways. Twenty-one were commissioned for the Australian coastal services before the First World War started in 1914.[27]

Ship-owners had expanded aggressively where they could. In Western Australia, the slow start with steamer operations on the coast had left the colony's ship-owners with neither the experience nor the resources to compete with the Adelaide Steamship Company when it moved west in 1883 and took over most of the routes along the Western Australian coast. The company had been formed in 1876 to trade between Port Adelaide and Port Phillip, but a few years later it extended its Western Australian routes as far north as Derby and ten years after that entered the Queensland trade. Thus it could offer a service between ports in the north of both colonies: a service no other ship-owner could match.

There was also competition in the south, which led to the Tasmanian Steam Navigation Company's being bought out by the Union Steamship Co. of New Zealand in 1891. The Union company had started operations out of Dunedin in 1875 and expanded rapidly, partly by the acquisition of other companies. Within two years it had entered the trans-Tasman trade with services to Sydney and Newcastle. It then developed what became known as the 'horse shoe' route: the long way round from Sydney to Melbourne via Wellington, Lyttleton, Bluff and Hobart. Six vessels were employed on this route as early as 1880, with an additional steamer on stand-by.

When the Union Steamship Co. took over the T.S.N. it entered the direct run between the mainland colonies and Tasmania with these five services: Melbourne–Launceston twice weekly, Melbourne–Hobart every ten days, Melbourne–Northwest Coast twice weekly, Sydney–Launceston fortnightly and Sydney–Hobart weekly. The company had many fine, large ships. One that became particularly well known because it crossed the Strait to Melbourne for 32 years was the 2448-ton *Loongana*, the first turbine ship in the fleet and the first full passenger liner solely on the Strait when it entered service in 1904. On one trip it was timed at more than 22-and-a-half knots.

Huddart Parker competed on the Bass Strait routes, having entered service in 1889 at the request of Tasmanian graziers and fruit-growers who were discontented with the T.S.N.[28] To compete with the *Loongana*, the company ordered the *Nairana* from the same British shipyard that had built the Union Steamship Company vessel, but delivery was held up by the First World War. They were to become partner ships in a later era.

Other companies put notable ships into service in the years before the war, among them Howard Smith with the *Bombala* and the *Cooma*, destined for the Queensland tourist trade, and McIlwraith McEacharn with the *Karoola* and the *Katoomba*. The *Katoomba*, a ship of 9424 tons, was built in 1913. It carried 800 passengers and its public rooms were of world standard, which made it particularly suitable for the cruising programs it would undertake in a later era.

The neglect of road transport

Road transport was the Cinderella of Australia's transportation system until the Second World War. From the start of white settlement, making roads was a formidable task. The settlers had little to work with in terms of people, animals or money. The bush could be thick and tough and the land dry and hard, except when rain came and turned it to mud. In the cities and towns streets were so badly drained that holes were worn in them by the rain. These sometimes grew so big that when they filled with water people and animals drowned in them. Getting to the diggings during the gold rushes was a painful process and other journeys were not only slow—they were often dangerous. It did not pay to drop off to sleep while riding on the outside of a coach travelling over rough ground.

For the first 35 years of white settlement, a journey of more than 25 kilometres was hard going. In the Sydney area there were 14 main roads by the early 1820s, but in total they covered a distance of only 444 kilometres. There was promise of better things in Van Diemen's Land. This became a separate colony in 1825, at which time there were some 14 500 people living there as against 36 300 in New South Wales.[29] The following year, a road was completed between Hobart and Launceston. It was of a good enough quality for stage coaches drawn by six horses to cover the 190 kilometres in 12 hours, at a speed equal to that achieved by only the best mail coaches in England.

In the next decade there were improvements in New South Wales. A network of roads was built by convicts, most notably the Great North Road to the Hunter Valley, the Great Western Road to Bathurst and the Great South Road to Yass. The busiest road on the continent was between Bathurst and Sydney. However, despite the grand names some of the main roads were given, they were incredibly rough by today's standards. This is how one traveller described the road from Sydney to Goulburn:

> It is ridiculous to denominate as a road a winding track along an alternate succession of mounds and ditches and across the beds of rivers, perpetually obstructed by stumps of trees and other vegetation, destitute of either drainage or macadamisation, impassable for weeks in the wet season. (J. Gunn, *Along Parallel Lines*, 1989)[30]

In the towns the streets were so poorly constructed they could be impassable in wet weather and ruts and holes would fill with water. In Adelaide in 1848 a drunk was fined for attempting to swim the liquid mud of Hindley Street from one end to the other and a bullock drowned in the quagmire of Wakefield Street near the site of the Town Hall.[31] In 1858 a man and his horse drowned in Elizabeth Street in Melbourne and another pair in Swanston Street were swept into the Yarra River. Even in the late 1870s cabmen were charging pedestrians to ferry them across Elizabeth Street.[32]

Country roads in the 1850s were described by a Select Committee of the Victorian Legislative Council as being 'in a state of nature'.[33] The gold rushes were not 'rushes' in terms of transportation; progress to the gold fields could be agonisingly slow.

> ... the roads were in a horrible state and the cart got bogged several times but we managed to shove him out till towards night when we got stuck so badly that it took 4 bullocks to do it and the bullock driver charged 2 pounds for pulling us out ... (Edward Snell, prospector, 1852)[34]

36   Nevertheless, there was movement by land. Sydney and Melbourne were linked in 1838 by a regular mail service on a route via the Sydney road to Berrima and on to Melbourne by a track. The mail was transferred from a coach to horseback at Yass. The first road in South Australia, from Adelaide to Port Adelaide, was built in 1839 and 1840. Brisbane's first road was made in 1826 and by 1847 a road linked Brisbane with the Darling Downs, which had been settled originally from what is now northern New South Wales. Major road construction started in Western Australia in 1836, to connect Perth with Fremantle and Perth with Albany. In 1841 the first four-horse light van carried the mail from Albany to Perth, taking 72 hours.[35]

Coaches could operate only on the better roads. Stage coach services from Sydney to Bathurst began in 1824, the 220-kilometre trip taking four days. A network of private mail coaches serving Bathurst, Kelso, Yass, Singleton and Maitland in New South Wales was built up in the 1830s, but only a few thousand passengers a year travelled with coaches anywhere. The numbers were certainly few on the twice-weekly mail service Mary Ann Cox ran between Hobart Town and Launceston under contract to the Van Diemen's Land government. Her light chaise had room for only one passenger.

Travellers could find 'rent-a-gig' operators in the larger towns. One was George Jones, who transferred his livery stables to George Street, Parramatta, in August 1838 and advertised that his horses and gigs were 'always on hire at a moment's notice'.[36] Hiring vehicles was expensive and people who could afford them had their own. Apart from the convenience, a carriage was a sign of social status.

English carriages were fashionable in the cities and towns, but outside them rugged American vehicles were found to be more suitable. The buckboard and the buggy were popular for private use. The buckboard was a simple vehicle—two wheels, no springs, and a platform of tough, stringy boards complete with seat. Light and almost indestructible, it was much more suitable than an English gig to negotiate rough Australian roads and to ford rivers. The buggy was a light American vehicle also suited to Australian conditions and not expensive.

The first coaches used on the early New South Wales and Tasmanian services had been imported from England or built in the colonies to English patterns. They were too heavy for rough Australian roads and their steel springs made the ride uncomfortable and, worse still, often broke with the strain.

American vehicles like the Concord coach were imported after the middle of the century. They had been developed to transport pioneers to the American West over rough, roadless land—conditions similar to those found in Australia. The body of the vehicle was not attached to the undercarriage by steel springs as in other coaches, but was suspended by long oxhide straps called 'thoroughbraces'. When the coach jolted over rough ground, the body swayed backwards and forwards on its leather braces but did not bounce violently up and down like coaches mounted on steel springs. There was much less strain on the horses as well as the passengers and driver.

The first Concords were imported by Freeman Cobb, an American who had been in the coaching business during the Californian gold rush. With other Americans, he started a service from Sandridge (Port Melbourne) to Melbourne in 1853 and the next year began running to the diggings at Ballarat, Bendigo and Castlemaine.

In the years that followed, Cobb & Co. was by no means the only company operating coaches, but it became the biggest. More gold rushes in New South Wales and Queensland in the 1860s created a huge demand for the company's services. At one time it was harnessing 6000 horses a day and its coaches were covering 45 000 kilometres a week. Its service between Melbourne and Sydney took five days. Cobb & Co. was to remain in business until 1924, when its last service from Surat to Yeulba in southern Queensland was closed down.

That service had lingered on long after coaches had been put out of business elsewhere by other forms of transport. Where there were railways they could not compete. They could, perhaps, travel at an average of eight kilometres an hour, including stops for meals and changes of horses. But that was much slower than the trains and they were far more expensive. In the 1880s travellers from Sydney could reach Bourke by train in 22 hours. For 800 kilometres of travel they paid a little over two pounds. If they then went to Wilcannia by coach another 370 kilometres, they paid six pounds and were in the coach for another two full days.[37]

But as much as Australians took to trains, they retained their affection for the horse. By the end of the nineteenth century there was one horse for every two people in Australia, as against one for every four in the United States and one for every ten in Britain. There was good and bad in this. As much as the horse was useful, it also caused problems. A horse was said to eat as much as eight men and required two hectares to sustain it. The surfaces of city streets were composed partly of dried manure, which caused health hazards.[38] And of course it stank. Horses contributed a great deal to Melbourne's reputation as 'Smelbourne'.

38 The first railways and mixed gauges

It was intended that the first steam-operated public railway in Australia would run between Sydney and Goulburn. Construction of the line was supposed to begin after 3 July 1850 when Mrs Keith Stewart, the New South Wales Governor's daughter, symbolically dug up a piece of turf with an engraved spade in a paddock at Redfern before a large crowd.

The railway had been first discussed at a public meeting in 1846. The discussion was followed by years of talk and not much action; Mrs Stewart's flourish with the spade in 1850 made little difference. The Legislative Assembly set up a select committee; lengthy correspondence passed between the colonial administration and the government in Britain (which encouraged the project); and there were seemingly endless arguments about financing the venture, land acquisition, the source of labour to build the railway, the believability of cost estimates, the company manager's salary, the location of the Sydney terminus and so on.

The first name of the company—the Australian, Southern and Western Railway—lasted only two months before it was changed to the less ambitious-sounding Sydney Tramroad and Railway Company. It was later replaced by a new company called simply the Sydney Railway Company.

Of all the changes of mind that happened over the years, none was to have such consequences as the one over what gauge was to be adopted. In England at the time two gauges were in use: 1435 millimetres (4 feet 8½ inches) and 2134 millimetres (7 feet). The narrower gauge was considered more suitable for general traffic, although it had some drawbacks including wear and tear on the line. Therefore, attention was focused on a third gauge, 1600 millimetres (5 feet 3 inches), which had been chosen for the railways in Ireland because it had been found to increase the effective power of locomotives. Consequently, the 1600-millimetre gauge was adopted by the company.

The New South Wales Executive Council agreed that the superiority of the 1600-millimetre gauge had been 'admitted by the highest authorities [in England] ... and should be approved',[39] the Legislative Council included the specification of the gauge in legislation, the British government gave its approval and the governments of South Australia and Victoria were told of the decision.

No track had been laid in July 1852 when James Wallace arrived from England as the company's new engineer-in-chief. He gave the Sydney Railway Company a different account about the 1435-millimetre gauge.

The narrow gauge has been found to combine in a higher degree than any other the great commercial requisites for a railway, namely speed, safety, convenience and economy. For these reasons it has been adopted, with little exception, throughout Europe and America and in India and Egypt, where the highest engineering talent has been employed.[40]

As a result of Wallace's persuasion, the New South Wales authorities changed their minds, repealing legislation on the 1600-millimetre gauge in favour of the narrower gauge. South Australia and Victoria were not interested. They had already ordered rolling stock overseas for the 1600-millimetre gauge and were put off by what seemed to them 'capricious and offhand behaviour' in New South Wales.[41]

Nevertheless, the Lieutenant-Governor of South Australia, Sir Henry Young, wrote to the British government in 1854 suggesting a 'grand trunk route' connecting Adelaide, Sydney and Melbourne, with the terminal station in each city to be alongside a dock capable of handling the largest ships afloat. He thought this could be constructed in seven years, which seemed ambitious considering the progress being made in New South Wales.

Along the way, there had been another change to the original plan. The destination from Sydney was no longer to be Goulburn, 206 kilometres away, but Parramatta, only 22.5 kilometres away. As there were still problems with finance, the government took over the assets of the Sydney Railway Company and the 1435-millimetre line to Parramatta was completed at last. On 26 September 1855, the first train ran. But New South Wales had missed having the first steam railway in the colonies.

That had become Victoria's achievement. A year earlier—in September 1854—service had begun on a four-kilometre track between Port Melbourne and Melbourne with a 1600-millimetre gauge. The line had been developed privately by the Melbourne and Hobson's Bay Railway Company.[42]

Ideas of a 'grand trunk route' connecting the colonies' capitals were forgotten. Victoria and South Australia were committed to a different gauge from that of New South Wales, and that was that. By 1861 there were 390 kilometres of railways in the three colonies. Ten years later, Queensland and Tasmania also had track laid and there were 1627 kilometres in total. There was also a new narrow gauge in vogue—1067 millimetres (3 feet 6 inches). Track of that gauge was cheaper to lay than the others and it had been adopted by Tasmania and Queensland—and also Western Australia when it began to create

40   railways about that time. Some South Australian lines also used the narrow gauge.

The river steamboats

Another era had started at the time of the railways' debut—that of the river steamboats. William Randell, a grazier, built the first of them, the 16-metre *Mary Ann*, on the banks of the Murray at Noa-No, launching it in February 1853. It had an unusual feature: its boiler had been made in Adelaide with flat sides, which began to swell under pressure when steam was first raised. As steam was raised for the first time the boiler took on the shape of a football and the engineer, convinced it was about to explode, headed for the bush. The boiler did not blow up. As this appeared to be due more to good luck than good design, strengthening struts were placed along each side and chains wrapped around the entire structure.

Despite this nerve-wracking beginning, Randell turned the *Mary Ann*'s second voyage into a race, putting maximum pressure on the vessel's boiler as it surged upriver with full steam up in competition with a larger paddle-steamer, which he had not even known was on the river.

The South Australian government had offered a prize of 4000 pounds for the first iron steamer of not less than 40 horsepower, and not exceeding 61 centimetres draft of water when loaded, to navigate the Murray from Goolwa to the junction of the Darling, a distance of 887 kilometres. This was of no interest to Randell because the *Mary Ann* did not qualify; she had a wooden hull and was too small.

However, Captain Francis Cadell, the son of a Scottish shipbuilder, had built the *Lady Augusta*, a 32-metre paddle-wheeler, in Sydney and sailed it to Goolwa to seek the prize. The *Lady Augusta* was an impressive-looking vessel with two decks and two funnels; it had accommodation for 16 first-class and 8 second-class passengers. It headed upriver from Goolwa on 25 August 1853.

Randell was already on his way to Swan Hill from Mannum, unaware that the *Lady Augusta* existed. Within a few days of his destination he moored the *Mary Ann* by the bank of the river while he and his crew had a rest. They were awakened 'by an unusual noise upon the water' and saw that the 'cause of the commotion' was a paddle-steamer twice the size of the *Mary Ann* heading up the river at the rate of three or four knots.[43]

They cast off, not worrying about the *Mary Ann*'s swelling boiler as the
furnace was stoked, and began to race the *Lady Augusta*. The lead
changed several times over the next two days; when one boat stopped so
that wood could be cut for fuel, the other would surge ahead. But on
17 September the *Lady Augusta* established a permanent lead and
arrived in Swan Hill three hours ahead of the *Mary Ann*. Swan Hill was
declared the finishing line but Randell went on as far as Maidens Punt,
today known as Moama, opposite Echuca, while Cadell returned to
Goolwa to claim his prize. Randell, although not eligible for the prize,
was awarded 300 pounds by the South Australian government and a
public subscription raised another 700.

Randell and Cadell had proved that steamers could navigate the
Murray. They continued their pioneering work by exploring the major
tributaries, the Darling and the Murrumbidgee. Cadell formed a company and put a number of other paddle-steamers on the Murray, while
Randell converted the *Mary Ann* into a catamaran, with the paddle-
wheel inserted between the two hulls. Renamed the *Gemini*, it was difficult to handle and sank after hitting a snag. Nevertheless, once raised,
this boat was to continue to go where others had not gone before on the
Murray and its tributaries.

Sir Thomas Elder, a prominent Adelaide businessman and pas-
toralist, was a passenger on one of Cadell's steamboats, the *Gundagai*, on
its first voyage from Goolwa to Albury in 1855. He wrote of the
experience:

> The saloon is raised above deck with windows on both sides, a
> large airy space, used as a dining room and a sitting room during
> the day, and as a sleeping apartment for gentlemen at night, cur-
> tains extending from the roof ensuring the requisite privacy.
> Several state cabins at the stern are reserved for the ladies and
> children. One of the first things passengers do on coming aboard
> is to select the place they propose to sit at table, which is kept
> during the voyage. Considering the small sum charged for passage
> money from Goolwa to Albury, a distance of 2,000 miles [3200
> kilometres], namely £15, including provisions, we had good
> reason to be satisfied with our fare and steward's attendance.[44]

Sir Thomas described a mode of travel which at the time could not have
been equalled for comfort by any other in Australia. Most steamboats,
however, were built to carry cargo, especially bulk goods like wool
bales, and often towed one or more barges. They were cheaper and
faster than their competition, bullock teams and wagons. Other ship-

42 owners joined Cadell and Randell and 27 steamboats were chugging and tooting their way along the Murray and its tributaries by 1865. The value of properties along the river banks doubled. Eventually 6640 kilometres of waterways, more than double the length of the navigable Mississippi, were opened to river traffic. The vessels called at dozens of sheep stations as well as established ports, notably Echuca, which became Victoria's second largest port. Up to 16 steamboats and their barges could be tied up at its wharves at any one time.

The largest steamers on the river were the passenger boats. An example was the *Gem*, rebuilt in 1882 to carry 100 passengers in 'commodious cabins' on three decks. There were also saloons and smoking-rooms and a dining-room seating 60. Another passenger boat was the *Ellen*, which had a tendency to roll very badly when going round bends in the river—so much so that its captain was said to have been able to lean out with a cup and scoop up a drink of water. For passengers in the dining-room the *Ellen*'s roll was not so convenient; their meals would shoot off the tables as it rounded a bend at speed.

Despite such mishaps, the river boats brought touches of civilisation to pastoralists and their families.

Glass replaced hessian squares in windows, household necessities ceased to be such unobtainable luxuries and mail arrived more frequently. Orders for clothes could be given to ship-board seamstresses who fashioned clothes and delivered them the next time they moored. Bush missionaries leaned on the rails, shearers lounged on the decks, theatrical companies practised their entertainment on the other passengers ... whenever the steamers moored they brought a taste of excitement from the outside world. (A. Howard, *Coaches, Riberboats and Railways*, 1982)[45]

The railways take over

As the river trade flourished, the railway lines were creeping up to the river on both sides. By 1862 lines from Melbourne had reached Ballarat and Bendigo and in 1864 the Melbourne–Bendigo line was extended to Echuca. This helped establish Echuca's importance as a port, but as the lines spread they began to strangle the river boat business. Trains were cheaper, faster and more reliable. The upper Murray trade was adversely affected by rail links to Albury, Yarrawonga, Cobram and Coroway, established between 1881 and 1892, and in 1890 the Melbourne–Swan Hill line cut off Echuca from the lower river. The decline of the Darling River steamboat trade began with the completion of the Sydney–Bourke line in 1885. After a series of droughts made the Murray unnavigable during the First World War, the bulk of the remaining trade was taken by the railways.[46]

The Victorian portion of the Melbourne–Sydney railway reached Wodonga in 1873, but it was another ten years before the line from Sydney reached Albury and a railway bridge was put across the Murray. Passengers had to change trains because of the different gauges, but it was possible to go from Sydney to Melbourne in about 19 hours. The Melbourne–Adelaide line was completed in 1887 and the Sydney–Brisbane line in 1889. By 1891 more than 16 000 kilometres of track had been laid in Australia, compared with 2560 in 1875.

The railways also hurt the other main forms of transport: the coastal steamers and coaches. In the 1880s the sea route between Sydney and Newcastle became the busiest on the Australian coast, with two companies running ships each way six nights a week. But in 1888 the different rail systems in New South Wales that terminated in Sydney and in Newcastle were connected and the new line formed part of a system which went as far as Brisbane via Newcastle.

> The steamers changed their timetable to fit in with the new train service north and lowered their fares, but could not compete with the through passenger trade. Since it cost the same to go north from Newcastle as it did from Sydney, the steamers would have had to charge nothing to entice people to take the first part of the journey by sea as they had done previously. (G. Davison, J. W. McCarty & A. McLeary, eds, *Australians: 1888*, 1987)[47]

The railways also poached passengers from the steamers by setting a cheap fare for the Newcastle–Sydney sector. The steamers were still cheaper, but rail was quicker and less likely to make its passengers sick. Share prices of steamship companies fell.

Although generally train travel was not cheap—and more expensive than steamship travel when they were in competition—it was becoming more comfortable. The New South Wales railways were the first to introduce sleeping cars, on the services to Bourke and Hay. These were Pullman cars, similar to the American design—that is, they were open carriages without compartments. At night the seats were converted to a row of beds and upper bunks were lowered from the ceiling. Curtains shielded the sleepers from the central aisle.

Sleepers of this kind were introduced on trains running between Melbourne and Brisbane, but for the Melbourne–Adelaide express the first sleeping cars were imported from the United States and were of a dif-

44   ferent style. These had separate compartments, which gave more privacy than the Pullmans, and became the standard Australian sleeper.[48]

In the inland, railways had become the symbol of progress—the means to end isolation. 'Railway leagues' were formed and set out to persuade parliaments that a line to their particular town would pay. The Wilcannia (New South Wales) correspondent of the *Town and Country Journal* complained that, because there was no railway, most of the townspeople were more or less strangers to Sydney.[49]

By Federation, each of the six States had its own railway system run by its government. A network stretched from capitals and key ports and by 1901, the year of Federation, 20 241 kilometres of track had been laid.[50]

All States except Western Australia were linked by rail, but of course there was the issue of the different gauges. Unification was a subject of discussion at the Federation Convention that preceded the adoption of a Commonwealth Constitution. Delegates from the colonies were asked to consider if the new Commonwealth Government might take control and unify the country's railways. But the issue was evaded. In the words of J. Gunn:

> Political self-interest in the separate States was to perpetuate the railway mess of broken gauges. (*Along Parallel Lines*, 1989)[51]

One of the promises made to Western Australia, which was unsure about joining the Federation, was that there would be a transcontinental rail link, which meant constructing 1682 kilometres of track between Port Augusta and Kalgoorlie. However, after Federation became a fact, a number of States were less than enthusiastic about paying for it.

> Queensland heard nothing about the assurances [for building the east–west railway] during the Federation campaign and is under no obligation to Western Australia. (D. Burke, *Road Through the Wilderness*, 1991)[52]

Western Australia, with a population of only 184 000 out of a national total of 3 780 000 at the time of the 1901 census, was not a powerful force in the Federation. Its champion in the Federal Parliament, however, was the formidable Sir John Forrest, former explorer, State Premier and later Federal Treasurer and Baron Forrest of Bunbury, the first native-born Australian to be made a peer. In his first speech to the House of Representatives in May 1901, Forrest said he would use every constitutional means in his power to undo the Federation if the east–west line were not built.[53]

But it was another six years before survey work began on the route. Two survey teams set out, one from the east and one from the west, using camels to carry their stores and equipment. The obstacles they found were not physical features that would require bridges or tunnels, but 'an arid remote terrain for most of it, and not a drop of surface water'.[54]

Despite the inhospitability of the area the surveyors completed their work in 13 months, but the parochial wrangling persisted and Western Australia continued to question the value of remaining in the Commonwealth. There was powerful support for the line from Lord Kitchener, Chief of the Imperial General Staff, who on a visit from Britain in 1911 inspected military establishments and met with defence force chiefs. In his report to the Commonwealth Government, he referred specifically to the east–west rail connection, saying:

> Unless this line is built Australia will lie helpless before any aggressor who is able to mount an attack in which intelligence and outflank are the order of the day. The country could be seized in twenty different places without one Australian defender appearing on the scene.[55]

That did not end the arguments, though it did quieten some of the critics. At the end of that year, the Commonwealth Parliament agreed to go ahead with the building of the railway and the Governor-General signed the Act on 12 December 1911, authorising the expenditure of four million pounds to build the railway. The new line was to be of 1435-millimetre gauge and the railways it was to connect—South Australian at Port Augusta and Western Australian at Kalgoorlie—were both narrow gauge (1067 millimetres).

The transcontinental line was built—a saga in itself[56]—and the first train left Port Augusta 32 minutes behind schedule at 9.32 p.m. on Monday, 22 October 1917, arriving at Kalgoorlie on Wednesday, 24 October at 2.50 p.m.—a journey of 42 hours and 48 minutes.[57] From then on Australians were able to go from Brisbane to Perth by rail, but it required travel on six different trains because of the various rail gauges. It was not until 70 years after Federation that there was regular passenger service on a single-gauge line across the continent between Sydney and Perth.

46   The coming of the motor car

Australians in a number of States experimented with steam cars in the last years of the twentieth century and one built in Melbourne in 1896–97 even had pneumatic tyres—a rare thing in those days. The first vehicle powered by an internal combustion engine in Australia may have been a three-wheeler built by Charles Highland of Sydney in 1894. Driven by a Daimler engine, it had the habit of catching fire when the engine backfired. Of greater engineering interest was the car built in Melbourne in 1897 by Harry A. Tarrant.

> Colonel Tarrant was a remarkable entrepreneur whose inventive ability in producing early petrol driven cars places him among the pioneers in international automobile production. (B. Inglis in *Technology in Australia 1788–1988*, 1989)[58]

Tarrant, later joined by a bicycle maker named Harold Lewis, produced another car in 1901 powered by a six-horsepower Benz engine mounted in the rear. This was called the Tarrant. Cars that followed included the first fully-enclosed body made in Australia and locally designed and made engines, gear boxes and rear axles. Tarrant won Australia's first motor car race at Sandown Park, Melbourne, in 1904 at an average speed of 44 kilometres per hour over 5 kilometres in a car he had built a year earlier, with his own engine.[59]

In the 1890s cars were being made by a number of companies in Europe and the United States, but in 1902 a customs duty was placed on vehicles imported into Australia to encourage local manufacture. In 1913, about 2000 cars were made in Australia and about 5000 imported, mainly from the US.[60] By 1915 the motor vehicle population was about 38 000.

Motoring organisations were formed in New South Wales (the Sydney Automobile Club), South Australia and Victoria in 1903 and in other States a little later. This was partly defensive because their members were unpopular with other road users.

> Pedestrians and those who used horses and horse-drawn vehicles were united in their opposition to these automobiles that seemed to be taking over the roads, and there were many stories of stones being thrown at people travelling in cars and of drivers being struck by whips as they passed wagons or drays.[61]

The new motoring organisations started lobbying for better roads, with little or no effect. But in spite of the terrible roads, the hostility of others and the uncertain endurance of their vehicles, early motorists

Catering for motorists in 1908 (Source: RACV Heritage Collection)

By 1908 motorists were being offered services that included fuel and garaging, as this advertisement for the Prince of Wales Hotel in Geelong demonstrates. The choice of meal plans is an interesting marketing feature.

48   began travelling so much to new places that among the early concerns of the motoring organisations was to help them find out where they were going. The provision of directional signs and maps was high on the list of issues tackled.

For a start, the organisations lobbied State and local governments about signs. In South Australia, councils got the message as early as 1913 and then asked the Royal Automobile Association to supply the signs. It did and was a major supplier of directional signage in South Australia until the 1960s. The Royal Automobile Club of Western Australia also decided to do the job itself and in 1913 the Postmaster-General gave it permission to attach mileage signs to telegraph poles.

The Western Australian RAC was an early provider of maps. It appointed a subcommittee to prepare a south-west road map at a scale of 10 miles to the inch in November 1910. By 1912 the club had its first strip maps. In December 1914 it resolved to put two maps of the State on the market at a cost of not more than five pounds. The RACV compiled a list of approved hotels in Victoria in 1908—places where they could not only stay, but could also receive attention for their vehicles.

The 'keep left' rule had been instituted by Governor Lachlan Macquarie in 1820. Now there was a need for more rules of the road. New South Wales introduced a Metropolitan Traffic Act as early as 1900 and all the States had enacted similar legislation by 1919. There were motor convictions before those Acts were passed. The first was in Sydney in 1897, when a man was booked for speeding at 13 kilometres per hour in a motorised Dion tricycle. In 1903 a Victorian motorist, Dunlop's local general manager, was convicted under the 1865 Steam Roller and Traction Engine Act of exceeding five kilometres per hour without being preceded by a man carrying a red flag. The 1904 South Australian Act set a general speed limit of 25 kilometres per hour. However, councils could raise the limit to 30 kilometres per hour, which led to instances where different speed limits applied on different sides of the same road.[62]

As motor vehicles became increasingly reliable, they were adapted as buses to replace stage coaches, originally on solid rubber tyres. The first buses[63] made in Australia are thought to have been those constructed in 1903 by Humble and Son, a Geelong engineering works,[64] and the 16-passenger model built by the Albion Magnet Company of Melbourne for a Tasmanian bus operator in the same year.[65]

Apart from providing feeder services to railway stations and their popularity on country routes, the suitability of buses for tourism purposes was immediately apparent. The South Australian Government

Tourist Bureau was running motor tours in an Albion charabanc in   **49**
1910.[66] A photograph in the State Library of Victoria shows a group of
more than 20 formally dressed tourists sitting in an open-topped white
charabanc in Melbourne in 1917.

These developments again showed the ability of Australians to keep
up with the rest of the world in modern travel equipment and tourism
practice. Much of their huge country was still inaccessible, but to service
the coastal areas where almost all of them lived, they had developed an
efficient travel network which enabled them to move from one place to
another by ship, train and coach—and now by bus and car.

ENDNOTES

[1] Blainey gives an instance where vehicles would have helped. The burden of moving heavy slabs of stone for use as millstones at least 200 miles in north-west Queensland was shared by a slow relay of carriers. (Blainey, G., 1975, *Triumph of the Nomads: A History of Ancient Australia*, Macmillan, Melbourne, p. 206)

[2] ibid., p. 24.

[3] White, J. P. & Lampert, R. (1987), 'Creation and discovery' in *Australians to 1788*, ed. D. J. Mulvaney & J. P. White, Australians: A Historical Library series, Fairfax, Syme & Weldon Associates, Sydney, p. 8.

[4] Blainey, op.cit., p. v.

[5] ibid., p. 225.

[6] ibid., p. 226.

[7] Mulvaney, D. J. (1987), 'The end of the beginning: 6000 years ago to 1788' in *Australians to 1788*, ed. D. J. Mulvaney & J. P. White, Australians: A Historical Library series, Fairfax, Syme & Weldon Associates, Sydney, p. 92; Ferguson, W. C. (1987), 'Mokaré's domain', ibid., p. 134.

[8] Mulvaney, op.cit., p. 94. The most abundant groves of the pituri bush grew along the Mulligan River on the northern fringes of the Simpson Desert. The dried leaves were chewed, producing a sense of well-being that included hallucinatory effects. The drug was probably one of the most precious items exchanged along the trade routes of central Australia. (McBryde, I., 1987, 'Goods from another country: Exchange networks and the people of the Lake Eyre basin' in *Australians to 1788*, ed. D. J. Mulvaney & J. P. White, Australians: A Historical Library series, Fairfax, Syme & Weldon Associates, Sydney, pp. 265–6).

[9] Inglis, B. (1989), 'Transport' in *Technology in Australia 1788–1988*, Australian Academy of Technological Sciences & Engineering, Melbourne, p. 446.

[10] Gilltrap, Terry & Gilltrap, Maree (1981), *Romance of Australian Transport*, Rigby Publishers Ltd, Adelaide. However, in 1887 train travel between Melbourne and Adelaide began, inaugurating the first inter-capital service that did not require a change of trains.

[11] Davison, G., McCarty, J. W. & McLeary, A. (eds) (1987), *Australians: 1888*, Australians: A Historical Library series, Fairfax, Syme & Weldon Associates, Sydney, p. 94.

[12] *Gippsland Mercury*, 2 April 1879, cited in Pemberton (1979), *Australian Coastal Shipping*, MUP, pp. 106–7.

[13] Vamplew, W. & McLean, I. (1987), 'Transport and communications', in *Australians: Historical Statistics*, ed. W. Vamplew, Australians: A Historical Library series, Fairfax, Syme & Weldon Associates, Sydney, p. 166.

[14] No Royal Engineer officers accompanied the early regiments. There were no purely 'civil' engineers among the early settlers. Most of the military engineers had only a crude knowledge of surveying, roadmaking and bridge building (Lay, 1984, p. 6). Macquarie was denied funds for roadbuilding by the Colonial Secretary and introduced tolls as early as 1811. Victoria had some 123 toll gates in operation in 1870. They were unpopular and were abolished in 1877 (ibid., p. 11).

[15] Isaacs, K. (1988), 'Aviation', in *The Australian Encyclopaedia*, v. 1, The Australian Geographic Society, Sydney, p. 322.

[16] ibid. See also Parnell, N. & Broughton, T. (1988), *Flypast: A Record of Aviation in Australia*, AGPS, Canberra, pp. 8 & 10.

[17] Lawson, W. (1949), *Blue Gum Clippers and Whale Ships of Tasmania*, facsimile copy 1986, D. & L. Book Distributors, Launceston, pp. 110 & 144.

[18] Cox, G. W. (1986), *Bass Strait Crossing*, Melanie Publications, Hobart, pp. 86–7.

[19] Pemberton, op.cit., p. 77.

[20] Lawson, op.cit., pp. 27–8.

[21] Plowman, P. (1992), *The Wheels Still Turn: A History of Australian Paddlewheelers*, Kangaroo Press, Sydney, pp. 18–22, Koskie, J. (1987), *Ships that Shaped Australia*, Angus & Robertson, Sydney, pp. 44–6 and Andrews, G. (1994), *Ferries of Sydney*, 3rd edn, Sydney Univ. Press in association with OUP Australia, Sydney, pp. 4–5.

[22] Lawson, op.cit., p. 207.

[23] Atkinson, A. & Aveling, M. (1987), *Australians: 1838*, ed. A. Atkinson & M. Aveling, Australians: A Historical Library series, Fairfax, Syme & Weldon Associates, Sydney, p. 187.

[24] Advertisements in the *Hobart Town Advertiser*, cited by Pemberton, op.cit., p.115.

[25] Pemberton, op.cit., p. 135.

[26] ibid., p. 136.

[27] ibid., p. 115.

[28] The Tasmanian Steam Navigation Company made a great contribution to travel and trade over 40 years, but in its last years it became very unpopular. According to Cox (op.cit., p. 101), complaints were made of exorbitant charges, disgraceful accommodation, arrogance from officers and careless handling of passengers' baggage.

[29] Caldwell, op.cit., p. 25. These are official 1825 figures. Those for New South Wales excluded military personnel and families.

[30] Gunn, J. (1989), *Along Parallel Lines: A History of the Railways of New South Wales, 1850–1986*, MUP, p. 2.

[31] Whitelock, D. (1977), *Adelaide 1836–1976*, UQP, St Lucia, Qld, p. 74.

[32] Lay (1984), op.cit., p. 10.

[33] Anderson, W. K. (1994), *Roads for the People: A History of Victoria's Roads*, Hyland House, Melbourne, p. 14.

[34] ibid., p. 13. Edward Snell noted these words in his diary on his way to the diggings in Bendigo in 1852 where he prospected for gold. He was a trained and experienced engineer who later built the Melbourne–Geelong railway line.

[35] Lay (1984), op.cit., pp. 8–12.

[36] Atkinson & Aveling, op.cit., p. 190.

[37] Davison, McCarty & McLeary, op.cit., p. 101.

[38] In London in the 1860s, a Dr Letherby analysed London road mud and found 60 per cent was organic matter and manure. Another doctor, writing about the same time, said the amount of irritation to noses, throats and eyes from dried manure was 'something awful' (Lay, 1993, op.cit., p. 132).

[39] Votes and Proceedings of the Legislative Council of New South Wales, Deas Thomson to Cowper, 2 July 1850, cited by Gunn, op.cit., p. 23.

[40] Wallace to the Sydney Railway Company, 8 September 1852, cited by Gunn, op.cit., p. 28.

[41] Gunn, op.cit., p. 29.

[42] The line was converted to an electric light rail link, serviced by trams, in 1987.

[43] Randell's own account quoted in Koskie, op.cit., p. 72.

[44] Plowman, op.cit., p. 117.

[45] Howard, A. (1982), *Coaches, Riverboats and Railways*, Bay Books, Kensington, NSW, p. 16.

[46] A few boats continued trading until the end of the 1960s. Passenger service was not consistent, but did not cease entirely until 1952.

[47] Davison, McCarty & McCleary, op.cit., p. 95.

[48] ibid., p. 96.

[49] ibid., p. 102.

[50] Spearritt, P. (1987b), 'Railways' in *Australians: A Historical Dictionary*, ed. G. Alpin, S. G. Foster, M. McKernan & I. Howie-Willis, Australians: A Historical Library series, Fairfax, Syme & Weldon Associates, Sydney, p. 345.

[51] Gunn, op.cit., p. 240.

[52] Burke, D. (1991), *Road Through the Wilderness*, NSW Univ. Press, p. 62. The speaker was Senator R. S. Sayers of Queensland.

[53] ibid., p. 53.

[54] ibid., p. 69.

[55] ibid., p. 71.

[56] One of the by-products was that the Broken Hill Proprietary Company (BHP) went into steel-making to take advantage of the huge requirement for rails. The company established coking ovens, furnaces and rolling mills on the waterfront at Newcastle. The first order for the transcontinental railway was for 10 000 tonnes of 36 kg steel rail in 12.2 metre lengths. It put the BHP plant in business. In building the railway there were many problems to overcome—not only to do with the heat, dust and flies, lack of cool water and distance from amenities of civilisation, but also with the supply of sleepers, a shortage of locomotives, late delivery of rails, arguments over wages . . . the crises were continuous. Nevertheless the work was completed. The line was built from both east and west with the two teams meeting near Ooldea, 676 km west of Port Augusta on 12 October 1917. At its peak in 1916, the construction force numbered 3395 men. (ibid., pp. 80–247 for the building of the railway. See pp. 87–8 for the BHP contribution).

[57] Times are local and different time zones account for the apparent discrepancy in the elapsed time. Forrest was an honoured guest on the inaugural trip. He became Lord Forrest the next year, but died at sea on 3 September 1918 on his way to London to seek treatment for cancer and to take his place in the House of Lords.

[58] Inglis, op.cit., p. 486.

[59] Lay (1984), op.cit., p. 26.

[60] Spearritt, P. (1987a), 'Motor Vehicles', in *Australians: A Historical Dictionary*, ed. G. Alpin, S. G. Foster, M. McKernan & I. Howie-Willis, Australians: A Historical Library series, Fairfax, Syme & Weldon Associates, Sydney, p. 277.

[61] Gilltrap & Gilltrap, op.cit., p. 73.

52

requiring one horse for every eight passengers. The term 'bus' came from a similar service in another French city, Nantes, in 1826. It passed by a hat-maker's shop where the owner, M. Omnès, had a punning sign 'Omnès Omnibus' (Omnès for all). This appealed to the bus operator, Stanislaus Baudry, who adopted 'omnibus' for his own operation (Lay, 1993, op.cit., p. 129).

[64] Inglis, op.cit., p. 500.

[65] Gilltrap & Gilltrap, op.cit., p. 77.

[66] An early name for a motor coach. It is from the French words meaning 'seated carriage'.

Where they stayed: the development of the hospitality industry

The first inns and hotels

The Australian inns in the early days of white settlement were primitive affairs which outwardly did not look any different from the rough dwellings of the time. They were nowhere near as well appointed as the inns in England—which were considered the finest in the world—and the lack of furniture in most of them led to the uniquely Australian habit of 'perpendicular drinking'. In England people sat down to drink; in the early Australian inns, more often than not, they stood because they had nothing to sit on.[1]

The early inns were centres for a variety of activities, not all of them desirable. Some of them were brothels, others conducted cock-fights and a few had boxing rings. They often served as labour exchanges. For several decades from the 1830s, the custom was for pastoral workers to sign up with squatters for three months and then be paid at the end of the contract with the equivalent of a cheque. Usually the men cashed this at the nearest inn and, having been starved of companionship, stayed there until the money ran out. The process was known as 'work and burst'. Having 'burst', the men were ready for work again. When squatters needed workers for their runs, they were usually sure of finding a pool of men at the local inn.

The typical roadside inn was set back from the roadway. This allowed coaches and other vehicles to be driven off the main road so that passengers could alight without obstructing other traffic. The arrival of the coach brought welcome noise and bustle to an otherwise monotonous life and helped make the inn a gathering place for the district. As the coach drew up and the passengers got down, men came forward to take the horses, which had to be watered and possibly changed. The landlord bustled around his guests and the locals gathered to see who the travellers were and what news they brought of the outside world.

In the inn itself sleeping was usually a communal affair, as in other countries—often on the earthen floor, unless the guest was lucky enough to find a sofa. We have a description of what it was like in 1841 at the Bush Inn, some 56 kilometres from Melbourne near present-day Heathcote. Edward Micklethwaite Curr, a young squatter, was on his way to his station with two companions when he stopped at the inn at about nine o'clock on a hot night.[2]

> The sitting room, into which we have found our way, was about fifteen feet long. In the middle of it was a deal table, one end of which was laid with washing utensils for the morning. In the centre of the table was a large brass bell, such as is used by criers, and a single tallow candle in a disreputable candlestick, which guttered complacently on to the oilcloth covering ...
>
> There were also in the room four sofas, of the poorest sort, on two of which beds had been made, the one having an occupant who was already asleep. He was probably a squatter, travelling between his station and town. His boots, hat, and clothes had been thrown on the floor beside him; a tobacco-pouch hung suspended by a leather belt from the head rail of the sofa or bedstead (the one by day, and the other by night), and from under his pillow protruded the end of a valise and the butt of a horse pistol. (*Recollections of Squatting in Victoria*, 1883)[3]

Another man was awake sitting on the edge of a second sofa, his shirt unbuttoned, his hair dishevelled, 'his eye being wild, haggard and restless'. He ignored the new arrivals, now and then getting up, wringing his hands 'with the air of a maniac' and muttering 'a string of bitter imprecations on some, to us, unknown individual'. Curr learned later that the man's brother had been mortally wounded in an encounter with Aborigines and his widow, after consenting to marry the man in the inn, had jilted him.

Sleep was all but impossible, not only because of the antics of the discarded lover but also because, among other things, the mutton-bird feather pillows had an unsavoury smell and half a dozen drunken men in the bar continued singing and swearing until almost daylight. In the morning Curr and his men washed in a nearby creek before paying their bill and moving on. He considered this establishment a 'fair specimen' of the bush inns around Melbourne at the time.[4]

Victoria was a raw new colony; by the 1840s some of the inns around Sydney were sophisticated by comparison. The Black Horse Hotel at Richmond catered for honeymooners with a bridal chamber described by F. Walker as 'a large and roomy apartment, with low ceiling, and two quaint windows facing the east'. The happy couples arrived from Sydney in carriages, 'with four or five horses, postillions and out-riders accompanied by all the ceremony which our forefathers loved'.[5]

The Black Horse had had time to gather a few comforts and attract a specialised market. It was first licensed in 1819. In those days glasses were filled behind a screen and then passed to the guest through a little square opening in the wall. This did not prevent Paul Randall, the plump and presumably merry first licensee, from mingling with the guests. But when the bar counter was introduced in the 1840s it separated staff from the guests psychologically as well as physically and changed the character of the inns.[6]

The first Melbourne inn hardly deserved the name. Soon after his arrival in Melbourne from Launceston in 1835, John Pascoe Fawkner opened a rickety grog shop for which he had no licence on land to which he had no title, but then the first police magistrate did not arrive until the next year. It was well patronised because it was without competition.

> Here he established a queer sort of *table d'hôte* (or, as he translated it, 'table hotty'), over which he invariably presided himself, and in distributing the viands he was not only capricious but peremptory. One had to take whatever the host gave him, fat or lean, under or over done; the whimsical taste of the carver was alone consulted, and if any eater dared to have a choice or opinion or taste of his own, the knife and fork were twirled in his face, and he was snarlingly told that if he did not like what he got (though too good for him) he had better clear out and go elsewhere, the irascible little Boniface being well aware that his 'elsewhere' meant 'nowhere'. (E. Finn ('Garryowan'), *The Chronicles of Early Melbourne 1855–1832*, 1988, p. 541)[7]

56   Fawkner's Hotel was 'little more than a clumsy and comfortless booth'[8] and the land on which it was built was soon taken by the government for a custom-house. Fawkner, one of Melbourne's founders, then put up a more substantial two-storey hotel on the south-east corner of Market and Collins Streets.

This time he had competition. In 1838 there were seven licensed victuallers in Melbourne. The popular Lamb Inn, nearby in Collins Street, was a sizeable property with 39 rooms and stabling for 16 horses. It took business away from Fawkner, who gave up his hotel licence in 1839, and his property became the club house of the newly-formed Melbourne Club.[9]

Without competition, customer service was often lacking. There was a time when Brisbane had but one inn. A traveller from the Darling Downs writing years later avoided naming it, though he did place it in Queen Street. Arriving with half a dozen others, he asked a waiter if they could get beds. 'Can't tell,' he was told, 'there's some coves in them there bunks: they can make room for you, rouse 'em out.' What about dinner then? 'You'll have to take what ye can get then, so I tell-ee.' What they could get were chops or steaks 'shot out of a frying pan in company with potent onions and floods of boiling grease' served from a 'filthy kitchen'.[10]

Involvement in sport, drama and music was a feature of Adelaide inns from the early days of the colony of South Australia. Cricket was a passion. The London Tavern in Currie Street put together one of the first cricket clubs in 1838 while John Bristow, landlord of the Great Tom of Lincoln in Thebarton, organised what may have been the first recorded match in Adelaide in 1839. John Crocket, who ran the Kentish Arms after arriving in 1846, had played for Kent against All England. He formed the Kent and Sussex Club, which had a ground on parklands near the end of Stanley Street.[11]

The Royal Hotel, which opened in Sydney's George Street in 1829, was to nurture an early theatre. The hotel was established in the front part of a building which had been intended to be a mill and ware-house—an enterprise that had failed. It was here, probably in a temporary building attached to the hotel, that the first performances of legitimate drama in Australia took place in the 'Theatre Royal' on 26 December 1832. About 500 people turned up to see two plays, *Mr. Meredith* and *Monsieur Tonson*. Later an old store at the back of the hotel was fitted out as a more permanent theatre. However, it closed in 1838 and both it and the hotel were destroyed by fire in 1840.

A new Royal Hotel was soon opened, but the building was not com- **57** pleted before 1848. It was to become one of the two leading hotels in Sydney, the other being Petty's, which had nearly one hundred apartments as well as a large saloon and dancing room where concerts, meetings and fairs were held.[12]

The second Royal Hotel was of the new kind of public house that had begun to take shape in Australian cities and towns about mid-century. Although not all were as large as the Royal, one of the factors that distinguished them from the old inns was that they no longer resembled dwellings. They looked like places of commerce both inside and out. They offered accommodation, food and drink, and sometimes entertainment and facilities for people to hold meetings, dances and concerts. There was an attempt to separate social classes with public and saloon bars and parlours. The gold rushes also brought different types of customers, including Americans who wanted mixed drinks with ice in them.[13]

Petty's Hotel, on Church Hill, had been first licensed in 1833 as Cumming's Hotel in what had been a Presbyterian minister's manse. It was virtually rebuilt in 1850 and became established, in the words of J. M. Freeland, as 'the prima donna of Australian metropolitan hotels until the Menzies in Melbourne appeared, and which even well into the present century was the grand old lady of Sydney's hotels'.[14] Petty's offered good food served on silver plate in a gold and white dining room. Its interior constantly changed, but the decorations always reflected a love of horses and horse-racing. It became more fashionable as time went on and in 1904 its popularity required further extensions, including the addition of a third storey in the 1850s style.

In Melbourne Americans met at the Criterion Hotel in Collins Street. Samuel Moss, its licensee after its renovation in 1853, had come from the United States himself. The Criterion had much to offer: a billiard saloon, a hair-cutting shop, a bath-house that could provide hot, cold, vapour or shower baths on demand, and a bowling saloon. There was also a vaudeville theatre, capable of holding an audience of 500, which later became a concert room and was for a time the headquarters of 'Rainer's Celebrated Troop of Ethiopian Serenaders'.[15] The Criterion became the Melbourne base of the goldfields entertainer Lola Montez.

Melbourne was a boom town. People flooded in not only from Britain and the United States but from all over the world. In July 1852 it was reported that 'gold has ceased to come into Melbourne in ounces; pounds are nearly obsolete and hundredweights are all but replaced by tons. The last weekly escorts brought six tons of the

58   precious metal from the diggings!'[16] The hotels reflected the affluence the gold brought with it.

The first coach with passengers for the Victorian diggings left John Cowen Passmore's hotel on the north-west corner of Elizabeth and Lonsdale Streets in Melbourne on 6 October 1851. Known later as Hockin's Hotel and from the time of Federation as the Commonwealth Hotel, it had 41 rooms, two cellars and kitchen pantries. The hotel had a ballroom 20 metres long by 10 metres wide and for a time was the centre of Melbourne's social life.

Grand hotels

As the century moved on from its mid-point, the cities began to build larger hotels, which could compare with most of those overseas. The first of the 'true grand hotels' was the five-storey Menzies Hotel built by Archibald Menzies on the corner of Bourke and William Streets, Melbourne, in 1867. Menzies had opened a private hotel soon after his arrival from England in 1852; as a result of the experience he gained in that establishment, he saw an opportunity for a grand hotel in the European style, with a palatial building and service to match.

A rambling white building with three steepled towers, the hotel was supposedly built on the lines of a French château, but was not considered an architectural success in its original form.[17] However, inside all was luxury; there was even a bathroom on every floor. Furnishings were superior to anything seen before in an Australian hotel and guests could gaze at rich panelling, carved stairways, gas chandeliers and fine curtains. Food was prepared under the direction of A. H. Bennett, who previously had controlled the kitchens at Buckingham Palace.

Fittingly, one of Menzies' first guests was Prince Alfred, Duke of Edinburgh, Queen Victoria's fifth child and a naval officer who commanded the 3500-ton Royal Navy warship *HMS Galatea*. In 1867 he received orders to visit Australia and made an extensive tour which included Adelaide, Melbourne, Hobart, Sydney and Brisbane.[18]

In Hobart he stayed at Webb's Hotel, which had begun trading in Murray Street in 1849. Known at first as the Marquis of Waterford, it was built from sandstone by convict labour on a site previously occupied by the Golden Anchor Inn, which had been opened in 1834. The Duke of Edinburgh was its second royal guest: the Duc de Penrieve, of the House of Orleans, had also stayed at the hotel in the 1860s.

Its name had been changed to Webb's Hotel after its then owner, who had been sent to Van Diemen's Land for housebreaking and when

pardoned had become caterer to Government House. John Webb died   **59**
in 1881 and the hotel was bought by John and Mary Hadley, who
renamed it Hadley's Orient Hotel. In 1912 Roald Amundsen proclaimed to the world from Hadley's that he had beaten Britain's
Captain Robert Scott to the South Pole. He also noted in his diary that
when he checked into the hotel he was treated as a tramp and given a
'miserable little room'.[19]

Melbourne had other up-market hotels besides Menzies. Edward
Scott had built a new hotel on the site of the Lamb Inn in Collins Street
in 1861. It had opened as the Port Phillip Club Hotel, but in 1862
became Scott's Hotel.[20] For more than a century Scott's was a favourite
for country people and racehorse owners. It was rebuilt in 1914, just
before the war, in two sections, one of four storeys and the other of six.

Melbourne had a spate of hotel-building during the 1880s and early
1890s, largely due to the determination of temperance interests led by
businessman and politician James Munro, to provide the city with
alcohol-free accommodation.[21] Melbourne's Grand Hotel opened in
Spring Street in 1883 with 94 rooms on six levels. In 1886 it was
bought by a company of which Munro was a director. Under its new
ownership the hotel became the Grand Coffee Palace, the term 'coffee
palace' then being used for a temperance hotel. By 1895 there were 23
coffee palaces in and around Melbourne, including the Victoria in Little
Collins Street (opened in 1880), the Melbourne (1882) and the Federal
(1888).

The Grand's new owners decided on a very large extension of the
hotel and within two years another 275 rooms, new kitchens, a grand
main corridor and a dining-room 31.2 metres long by 10 metres wide
were added. The hotel then had some 400 rooms, of which 300 were
bedrooms. It was usual for nineteenth-century hotels to have many
more rooms than bedrooms. Most bedrooms at the time, even in hotels
as splendid as the Grand, were for sleeping in only and were not much
bigger than a bed and wardrobe.

> In those days before television there was little reason to actually sit
> around in a room; if you wanted to read you went to the library or
> reading-room, if you wanted to write there would be a writing
> room, parlours were for socialising, lounges were for tea and
> sandwiches in between main meal times when you went to the
> dining room, and the smoking room was for ... well ... smoking.
> Bathrooms were still down the hall; in the Grand the male bath-
> room was in the north corner and the ladies' bathroom was in the
> south corner at the rear of the hotel on each floor ... gender

division was typical . . . and led to duplication of rooms in turn, so that there would be one writing room for the men and another for the ladies, a smoking room for the men and a drawing room for the ladies, and so on. (C. J. Spicer, *Duchess: The Story of the Windsor Hotel*, 1993)[22]

In the financial troubles of the 1890s, Munro's Federal Building Society and Real Estate Bank closed their doors and it took liquidators several years to sort out the financial affairs of those and other companies with which he was associated. Munro was not there to help. While still Premier, he was appointed Victorian Agent-General in London, resigning from the board of the Grand Coffee Palace Company before he left. Within a few years shareholders and directors were considering serving alcoholic beverages again. These were hard times and the hotel was not making any money out of liquor, although large quantities were being drunk by its patrons surreptitiously. It made more sense to sell it openly and make a profit. So in 1897 the Grand was re-licensed and became once more the Grand Hotel.

At about the same time the Federal Coffee Palace in Collins Street was also licensed and became the Federal Hotel. It was very large for the times, with 500 rooms, and it remained the biggest hotel in Australia until well into the twentieth century. The hotel was eye-catching. It had seven floors topped by an iron-framed domed tower and the grand lobby had a 3.8-metre-wide white and red marble staircase that split into two, rising to meet arched arcades that surrounded an early version of an atrium, which rose through four floors to a stained-glass ceiling.[23]

The Federal Coffee Palace Company had been formed in 1885 to build the hotel and the Federal Hotel Group, which in the next century would introduce hotel-casinos to Australia, dated its origins as a company from this time. This made it the second oldest hotel company in the world. At the time it was built, the Federal was considered to be ideally situated. At the corner of Collins and King Streets, it was only minutes from Spencer Street railway station, which was the central station for passengers at the time, and the main Yarra wharves. The wholesale business centre of Melbourne was just at hand and cable trams passing the door on Collins Street made it convenient to get to other parts of the city.[24]

Brisbane's two grandest hotels were built in the 1880s. Lennon's Hotel, in George Street, was completed in 1884 and the handsome Bellevue Hotel opened on the corner of George and Alice Streets two years later. Lennon's was originally a wooden structure but was substantially rebuilt and added to over the years.

The Australia Hotel is now open for business with ample accommodation" for man and beast." It will be seen from the above "picter" that the bedrooms are large, airy and commodious, and everything else is on a corresponding scale.

lephope.

Luxury at Sydney's Australia Hotel (Source: La Trobe Collection, State Library of Victoria)

The opening of the Australia Hotel in 1891 had Sydney journalists searching for superlatives. The Bulletin's cartoonist was impressed with the 'ample accommodation'. However, hotel bathrooms were small by today's standards.

Sydney's finest hotel of the period, the Australia Hotel, opened its doors on to Castlereagh Street on 11 July 1891 with its first guest, the celebrated actress Sarah Bernhardt, already in residence. The social writer of the *Bulletin* reported at the time:

> ... unless one 'inventorises' like an auctioneer, one couldn't give a general idea of the artistic sumptuousness of this splendid hotel. The Australia certainly has 'success' written all over its gilded brow. Fancy, oh women! the rapture of camping in a palace where the management sets apart a private room for ladies who are too lazy (the courteous, violet-eyed manager said, 'Indisposed') to rise and dress for the general breakfast.'[25]

In an editorial, the *Sydney Morning Herald* noted that the hotel had been designed and fitted out without regard to cost as the result of careful inspection of the greatest hotels of Europe and America; and 'if there is anything in any other institution of the kind which is perfect for its purpose, and which has not been adopted, it is only because it has not been found.'[26]

The first manager was an American, Hugh Edwin Moore, who made sure his guests had service by keeping a small army of porters, bellboys and waiters on hand at all times. He also had a selection of side dishes offered in the dining-room.

> ... this novelty, like many of the others for which the establishment was to become noted, was a great success with the local inhabitants quite unaccustomed to such niceties in their hotel fare. (C. Rühen, *Pub Splendid: A History of the Australia Hotel, 1891–1971*)[27]

The section of Castlereagh Street between Moore Street—later called Martin Place—and King Street was to become known as Hotel Row. On the other side of the street from the Australia were the Carlton Hotel and on the corner of King Street, Usher's.[28] Another big, sumptuous hotel favoured by many country people was the Metropole, which had opened in Bent Street in 1890.

In Adelaide, the first part of the elegant South Australian Hotel in North Terrace was built in 1894. In about 1900 the adjoining buildings were rebuilt and the magnificent three-storeyed veranda was added. Adelaide had another fine hotel a few years later, when the Grand Central Hotel was opened on the south-east corner of Rundle Street and Pulteney Street in 1910. In contrast to the relatively simple lines of the South Australian, the facades of the Grand Central were elaborately

decorated with a complex pattern of string courses, pilasters and   **63**
mouldings. The bay windows rose to almost the full height of the
building and the corner bow window was capped with an open turret.

Perth acquired its top hotels in the 1890s under the impetus of new
wealth from the goldfields. The Palace, in St George's Terrace at the
corner of William Street, was built in 1895 by John de Baun, an
American who had made money on the goldfields and Stock Exchange.
J. M. Freeland writes that it was 'undoubtedly without peer in Australia
when it opened in 1895, a model of good taste and quality when osten-
tation was the order of the day.'[29] The Esplanade at 20 The Esplanade,
which opened three years later, was owned by Nat Harper, who had
also been on the goldfields during the roaring days.

Guest houses

Outside the cities, at mountain and seaside resorts, the wealthy built
substantial homes. Guest houses were opened for those who did not
have their own accommodation. Unlicensed guest houses were the
only alternative to hotels—and were sought after by more genteel
travellers. They were standard accommodation at holiday places
frequented by families and often included recreational facilities such as
croquet and tennis courts.

Women in inns and hotels

The temperance movement was one of the factors, although not the
only one, that made it difficult for women to work in the hotel business
in the latter years of the nineteenth century and the first decades of the
twentieth century.

In the early days of the Australian hospitality industry many publicans
were women. Sarah Bird was the first. She established the Three Jolly
Settlers in Sydney in 1797. Sarah Baxter, an enterprising servant girl,
opened the Royal Admiral in 1798 when she was 19. In the 1830s
women held a quarter of the licences in New South Wales and for a
time the proportion of women running hotels was 40 per cent.

It was a different story in the early years of the twentieth century,
when there was active discrimination against women in hotels, both
as licensees and as barmaids. When Carlton and United Breweries set
out on a program to buy hotels in the early twentieth century, it specified that only men were to run them. Other landlords had the same
attitude. Legislation designed to restrict women holding liquor licences

64   appeared in Tasmania in 1902 and in South Australia in 1908. Control of women licensees involved questions of age, marital status and prior industry experience. The Licensed Victuallers' Association in South Australia claimed in an annual report that its association experienced 'a weakness through the presence of so many women licensees' and suggested that licensing authorities exercise more discretion than they had done in granting licences to young single women.[30]

Attempts to control barmaids began in the 1880s, although it was years later before legislation was passed—1908 in South Australia, 1910 in Western Australia and 1917 in Victoria. Many women preferred working in hotels because the pay was much better than they could get elsewhere. For example, a barmaid in Melbourne in the 1890s could expect to earn 65 pounds a year, while if she were a domestic servant she would earn only about 35 pounds a year. Barmaids worked longer hours but they still had a freer life than women in domestic service, who were on call outside regular working hours. Many barmaids were given considerable independence, managing their bars as they saw fit so long as they attracted a certain level of trade.

However, moral crusaders like the members of the Women's Christian Temperance Union thought that barwork was unbecoming to women. Moral temptation was another of the issues in the parliamentary debates, as well as a concern that women were leaving domestic service and forsaking their 'nobler purpose'. Victorian politicians considered ways to allow plain girls to work in bars but not attractive ones, because they thought good-looking young women were being employed as a lure to encourage men to drink. Indeed, an earlier Royal Commission had come to this conclusion. But the issue was dropped because it was impossible to define 'plain looking barmaids'.[31]

South Australian legislation required the registration of all barmaids and made no provision for new entrants. Thus the time would come when there would be no barmaids at all—or so it was thought. While it did not happen quite like that, there were very few barmaids in South Australia by the late 1930s and those who remained were not the youthful women of the past. The number also declined in Victoria, but not to the same extent.

It would be many years, and two world wars, before discrimination against women in the hotel business would be swept away by social change. The structure of the accommodation industry—a few grand hotels plus a relatively large number of public houses and guest houses—was to remain unchanged for about the same period.

ENDNOTES   **65**

[1] Bronwyn Hicks (Department of Hospitality, Tourism and Marketing, Victoria University of Technology, interview May, 1998).

[2] A squatter was a farmer who paid the Government a fee to 'squat' on land not already occupied by a white settler. Curr says that in 1841 the annual fee was ten pounds. His father had bought a sheep station situated on the 'Major's line' about 112 kilometres from Melbourne and about eight kilometres south-west of Heathcote. The 'Major's line' signified the track, line or road formed by the drays of Major Thomas Mitchell on his explorations. As there was plenty of country available in 1841, the selling value of a run or station was little more than the cost of improvements—huts, fences, woolsheds etc. (Curr, E. M., 1883, *Recollections of Squatting in Victoria*, Facsimile Editions No. 130, reproduced by the Libraries Board of South Australia from a copy held in the State Library of South Australia, 1968, Adelaide)

[3] ibid., p. 25.

[4] ibid, pp. 26–7.

[5] Walker, F. (1921), 'Australian roadside inns', *The Royal Australian Historical Society Journal and Proceedings*, v. VII (III), p. 122.

[6] Bronwyn Hicks, interview.

[7] Finn, E. ('Garryowen') (1888), *The Chronicles of Early Melbourne 1835–1852*, vol. 2, Fergusson & Mitchell, Melbourne, p. 541.

[8] ibid., p. 542.

[9] This was later moved, eventually to its present site at 36 Collins Street. The Lamb Inn had several owners and was closed more than once. Eventually it was bought and rebuilt by Edward Scott and in 1862 it became Scott's Hotel, regarded as one of the finest Melbourne hotels until well into the twentieth century. (Cole, R. K., 1950, 'Early Melbourne hotels', *The Victorian Historical Magazine*, v. XXIII(2), June, Royal Historical Society of Victoria, Melbourne, pp. 50–1).

[10] Russell, H. S. (1888), *The Genesis of Queensland*, Turner & Henderson, Sydney, in Ward & Robertson (1964), *Select Documents in Australian History*, v. 1, Ure Smith, Sydney, pp. 285–6.

[11] Whitelock, op.cit., p. 231.

[12] Bertie, C. H. (1927), *The Story of the Royal Hotel and the Theatre Royal, Sydney*, Simmons Ltd, Sydney, pp. 21–31. The Royal was a club for soldiers during the First World War and was demolished in 1926. The Dymocks book company erected a building on the site.

[13] Bronwyn Hicks, interview.

[14] Freeland, J. M. (1977), *The Australian Pub*, Sun Books, Melbourne, p. 64.

[15] Cole, op.cit., p. 59.

[16] Cox, op.cit., p. 88.

[17] Freeland, op.cit., p. 103: 'Achitecturally however, Menzies was one of the less successful of [architect Joseph] Reed's works. Square towers topped by inelegant pyramids marked the corners of the five-storey pile. A heavy arcaded balcony, supported on thick stone pillars, linked them. The north wall with its unprotected windows had a scattering of classic details but, while these were happy enough in themselves, they were were overwhelmed by the ill-conceived form of the building itself.'

[18] On 12 March 1868, the Duke was shot in the side by an Irishman, James O'Farrell. The Duke quickly recovered after the bullet was removed. The crowd tried to lynch O'Farrell at the time. He was later tried for attempted murder, found guilty and hanged.

66

[19] Notes by Simon and Georgina Miller, June 1998. Mr Miller was general manager of Country Comfort Hadley's Hotel. In the 1990s one of the hotel's suites was named after Amundsen.

[20] Cole, op.cit., p. 51.

[21] Munro was a member of the Victorian Legislative Assembly and became Premier in 1890. He held positions of particular influence within four major temperance organisations and was president of the international temperance conferences held in Melbourne in 1880 and 1888. 'He was ... accurately summed up by fellow Victorian politician and later Prime Minister Alfred Deakin as a sound financier and cunning political chief, but untrustworthy and unscrupulous.' (Spicer, C. J., 1993, *Duchess: The Story of the Windsor Hotel*, Loch Haven Books, Main Ridge, Vic., p. 9).

[22] ibid., p. 13.

[23] ibid., p. 77.

[24] History of the Hotel Federal (formerly the Federal Coffee Palace), unnumbered pages, copied and held in the Federal Hotel's archives.

[25] Rühen, C. (1995), *Pub Splendid: The Australia Hotel 1891–1971*, John Burrell in association with Murray Child and Co., Cullaroy, NSW, pp. 18–19.

[26] ibid., p. 21.

[27] ibid., p. 20.

[28] ibid., p. 25.

[29] Freeland, op.cit., p. 133.

[30] Hicks, B. (1991), *But I Wouldn't Want my Wife to Work There! A History of Discrimination against Women in the Hotel Industry*, Australian Feminist Studies, No. 14, Summer, p. 76.

[31] ibid., p. 74.

Early tourism and government involvement

For the pleasure of it all

Australians began travelling for pleasure early in the life of the nation. Although organised tourism did not start until the 1880s, people in earlier days were prepared to go even long distances for a change of scene.

They had summer leisure. The combination of English and Scottish traditional holidays and hot weather meant that the concept of an extended holiday over the Christmas–New Year period was established early in Australia's history.[1]

It was the affluent who spent holidays outside Australia. Throughout the century there was a strong sentiment favouring travel to the British Isles. For a great many people, going 'home' had the force of a religious pilgrimage. As wealth increased, so did the numbers setting out for Britain. Some went to show off their wealth to relatives; politicians looked to Britain for guidance and endorsement of their policies; businessmen visited Britain for technical assistance and capital; others sought the inspiration of social movements; many went there to find British examples of what they felt to be the social graces. There were republicans in Australia,[2] but generally the feeling was overwhelmingly in favour of the Crown, the Empire and things British.

But while many, perhaps most, would have liked to visit Britain, only a small percentage could because most had neither the time nor the money. In fact, most people were working an eight-hour day, or

68 48-hour week, by the end of the nineteenth century. Annual leave was unpaid in all but the most exceptional circumstances. For city people, a break from routine was usually a one-day or half-day trip close to home—to the seaside, on a train or on an excursion boat. Country people moved around more; they visited the cities on business and for pleasure, their numbers reaching a peak at Show time.[3]

A half-century earlier, when there was money to be made at the Victorian diggings, gold miners took a break to go south to Tasmania for a holiday. Crossing the often stormy seas of Bass Strait in a little steamer was not everyone's idea of relaxation, but that did not stop the tough miners with money in their pockets. The first director of the Tasmanian Government Tourist Bureau, E. T. Emmett, who began his working life as a railway clerk in 1888, wrote a brief history of the State's tourism after he retired. He said:

> It is of course impossible to pinpoint any year as the starting date of the tourist traffic, for the very first person who voyaged across Bass Straits for no particular reason except to have a look at the place was the first tourist. Perhaps a more or less regular traffic began in the fifties of last century, for it is recorded that when the gold diggings of Victoria were in full swing, many of the luckiest miners treated themselves to a holiday in Tasmania, helping the island's economy by 'knocking down' a considerable portion of their newly acquired wealth, and returning to the field in hope of further lucky strikes.
>
> It is certain, however, that the traffic had assumed some dimensions prior to 1870, for Anthony Trollope [the well-known English novelist] who paid a visit to Tasmania then, in referring to the many grumblers he met wrote in his travel book: 'Hobart town, they say, is kept alive by visitors who flock to it for the summer months from the other colonies.' (E. T. Emmett, History of Tasmania's Tourist Bureau, 1958–59)[4]

Mountains and beaches

The earliest resorts on the mainland were in the mountains, because people valued air that was purer and cooler than in the city. For this reason many in the nineteenth century showed a preference for the mountains over the seaside. The Blue Mountains, the Jenolan Caves, the Dandenong Ranges, Tamborine Mountain and the Mount Lofty Ranges were particularly popular with honeymooners.[5] In the 1870s Sydney holidaymakers took Cobb & Co. coaches to Katoomba; in the

1880s the opening of the railway increased the resort's popularity. Sir Thomas Elder built a Scottish baronial castle on Mount Lofty and other Adelaide business leaders also had mansions there. In 1891 Marble Hill, a two-storey Gothic building with 40 rooms and a 30-metre tower, was built near Norton Summit as a summer residence for South Australia's governors.[6]

Some of those who headed for the heights had more athletic pursuits in mind than taking the mountain air. A hotel was built at Mount Kosciusko (New South Wales) in 1909 and a chalet at Mount Buffalo (Victoria) in 1910 mainly for summer recreation, but hardy adventurers explored the mountains on skis during the winter. Scandinavian miners in the New South Wales gold rush town of Kiandra made the first skis in this country in the winter of 1860 and called them snow shoes. The next year, the *Monaro Mercury*, published in Cooma, reported:

> Kiandra is a rather dreary place in the winter, but yet the people are not without their amusements. The heaven-pointing snow-clad mountains afford them some pleasure. Scores of young people are frequently engaged climbing the lofty summits with snow shoes and then sliding down with a volancy that would do credit to some of our railway trains. (J. M. Lloyd, 1986)[7]

One of the oldest ski clubs in the world, the Kiandra Snow Shoe Club, was formed in the 1860s—the exact year is uncertain. Later Charles Kerry, a photographer, created interest in Sydney with his pictures of the mountains in winter and formed the New South Wales Alpine Club. A 'snow shoe carnival' was a feature of Kiandra's winter season, but with the opening of the Kosciusko Hotel interest was transferred to the other side of the mountains near the hotel, where there was better access.[8] In Victoria, members of the Bright Alpine Club made trips to the snow in the 1880s and there was skiing on Mount St Bernard around the turn of the century. Later, most of Victoria's skiing activity was near the Mount Buffalo Chalet. Only a few short slides were available and ski touring was the most popular activity.

Although the general trend to beach holidays did not start until the first decades of the next century, seaside places were certainly not ignored. Indeed, some took on the attributes of resorts, examples being Queenscliff and Sorrento on Port Phillip Bay, which were accessible by bay steamer.

The planning of holiday resorts was becoming sophisticated by the 1880s. The announcement in the *Bairnsdale Advertiser and Bruthen News*

70 in April 1886 of a new guest house to be built at Lake Tyers in Gippsland, Victoria, stated:

> ... a line of coaches is to be laid on the run from Lakes Entrance to Lake Tyers, also a first class steam yacht and a fleet of pleasure boats are to furnish means of enjoyment to visitors in the new house.[9]

In Queensland Southport and Coolangatta, which had been established as timber settlements in the 1870s, had become resorts a decade later. With the extension of the railway to Beenleigh in 1886, Southport became fashionable—so much so that the Governor, Sir Anthony Musgrave, and other dignitaries holidayed there. Beach resorts further south in the early years of the twentieth century were busy. An early tourist bureau reported in 1917:

> ... the bathers may be numbered in thousands [at holiday times], and at no time of the year will the Tweed Heads and Coolangatta hotels and boarding houses be without their companies of strangers.[10]

By 1911 the Queensland government was promoting its South Coast beaches in Melbourne and Sydney, and a small number of wealthy southern visitors were journeying north. When they went home again they took word of the wonderful winter climate they had experienced.[11]

City attractions

People from the country went to the capitals on holiday. Here there was activity after the quiet and loneliness of the country—and things to see and experience: shops, theatres, restaurants, impressive buildings and the energy of places on the move. 'Marvellous Melbourne' in the 1880s was described by a young traveller as 'a human ant-hill where everyone was making money ... and where everyone was in a hurry.'[12]

With the building of railway lines country people could travel more readily, but train travel was expensive. Colonial governments were under constant pressure to provide cheap fares or free passes and they did provide special excursion rates for trips to agricultural shows, races or sports meetings. The first Royal Easter Show was held in Sydney in 1889. The first Melbourne Cup was run in 1861. In 1889 Huddart Parker, which had just entered the Bass Strait service, chartered the fast paddle-steamer *Newcastle* 'in order to convey excursionists to the Melbourne Cup Carnival' from Tasmania.[13]

The first inter-colonial cricket match was played in 1851,[14] the first visit by a team from England was in 1862 and the first Test match was played in 1877. Sailing and rowing regattas were common. The first annual regatta held on the Derwent was in 1838 and the attendance was thought to be 10 000 out of a possible 12 000 population in Hobart and the surrounding district.[15]

There were man-made attractions for visitors to wonder at. A copy of London's Cremorne Gardens was built on Sydney's Robertson's Point in the 1850s offering an Italian Walk, an Avenue, a Serpentine Maze, supper rooms and park furniture. There were dances and fireworks. But by the 1870s the gardens were attracting the wrong clientele—they became notorious for bad behaviour and families went elsewhere.[16]

Melbourne had its own Cremorne Gardens on the banks of the Yarra at Richmond, but they lasted only ten years. They were opened in 1853 with facilities for music and dancing. Fireworks and attractions were added over the years, culminating in a 75-metre painted panorama of Sebastopol behind which live rockets and fireworks exploded.[17] The gardens closed in 1863. Luna Park, a Coney Island-style fun park, was opened at St Kilda, another suburb of Melbourne, in December 1912 and attracted huge crowds.

The popularity of theatre

Theatre was popular from early times. Lieutenant-Colonel G. C. Mundy, ADC to New South Wales Governor FitzRoy, thought the dramatic talent in the 1840s compared with that at most provincial theatres in England and the behaviour of the audience of the Sydney Theatre Royal[18] much better than in theatres in English seaport towns.

But there were dangers for visitors outside the Theatre Royal. Lurking nearby was a set of loafers known as the 'cabbage-tree mob'—so called because they wore low-crowned cabbage palm hats. Their usual sport was to knock the black hats of 'respectable persons' over their eyes as they passed or entered the theatre. Colonel Mundy told the story of what happened after he had given his servant a ticket to go to the theatre. First the man was 'furiously assailed' by the 'Cabbagites' and his hat was driven down over his eyes. Then, in a rage and unable to see, he struck out and punched a policeman. He spent the night in the watch-house and the next morning had to prove that the 'glaring case of assaulting a constable in the execution of his duty' was not intentional nor of malice aforethought.[19]

Melbourne had four theatres in 1882, Sydney and Adelaide two each. Hobart had had the Theatre Royal from 1837[20] and Adelaide's

72   theatrical history went back to 1841 when the short-lived Queen's Theatre opened. Perth did not have a permanent theatre until the 1890s, when the gold rush provided the money for it and stimulated the audiences.

Each city had its special places where the citizens gathered and the out-of-towners visited. Adelaide's were its surrounding parks and the beaches at Glenelg and Brighton. Perth had its huge King's Park with its bush and wildflowers and Honour Avenue, a stylish promenade. In Melbourne people took a short train ride to the beach at St Kilda to take the sea air and to swim. By 1888 there were five 'baths' there, enclosed establishments which allowed bathing in the sea without fear of sharks and with some privacy. The sexes were segregated.

Harbourside baths became popular in Sydney, too, but laws which had been in force since the 1830s had to be rescinded first: these had prohibited bathing in the harbour or the ocean between 6 a.m. and 8 p.m. Manly Council was the first to rid itself of the old laws in 1903 and the other councils followed. In 1906 Australia's first surf club was founded at Bondi.[21]

Given the reliance on water transport in the early days, it is not surprising that day-tripping in sheltered waters was a common form of recreation. Features of the Sydney scene from the 1870s on were picnic launch companies and individual boatmen who could take people to any number of picnic spots along Middle Harbour and the Lane Cove and Parramatta Rivers.

In Perth, river steamers were converted to excursion work when the river trade fell away in the early twentieth century because of railway competition. Excursions by boat from Brisbane to the South Passage and the Ocean Beach were popular.

Melbourne day-trippers took to a variety of 'bay steamers' for excursions on Port Phillip Bay. A regular service to Mornington had begun in the 1870s. Later the standard run was from Station Pier to Sorrento, Mornington and Queenscliff. Three big paddle-steamers, delivered successively from the late 1880s—the *Ozone*, *Hygeia* and *Weroona*—were particularly well known. The *Ozone* was nearly 80 metres long and it was the smallest. The *Weroona*, delivered in 1910, could carry 2000 passengers at a time.

Cruising in the Pacific

In the 1850s miners had gone south for relaxation and adventure. Thirty years later, others were going north in rather more comfort.

Burns, Philp & Co. Ltd advertised in the *Sydney Morning Herald* in **73**
February and September 1884 for passengers for a five-week cruise to
New Guinea aboard the 'comfortable clipper yacht' *Elsea*. The advertisement stated that the cruises offered 'capital shooting and fishing and
intending passengers should take rifles and fishing tackle.'[22]

Burns, Philp & Co. began as a merchant and agency partnership in
Townsville, entering shipping mainly to supply its own stores and businesses in New Guinea and the Pacific islands. It was to become the
biggest company in Australia but its initials, 'BP', were used by some to
mean 'Bloody Pirates' because of the company's allegedly tough island
trading practices.

Burns, Philp & Co. published a guidebook titled *British New Guinea*
in 1886 and continued to promote cruises. By 1913 it had a tourist
office at its headquarters in Sydney and travel experts in its other main
offices. Its cruising itinerary by that time included remote outstations as
well as Port Moresby in Papua New Guinea (then separately governed)
and, in addition, various ports in the New Hebrides (now Vanuatu), the
Solomon Islands, Lord Howe Island and Norfolk Island. Despite the
promotional language, the 'cruises' were basically cargo runs.

The company targeted teachers in their promotion because they had
the time and the money to make voyages of four to six weeks. Often
most of the passengers were female.

> This delighted the many resident bachelors [in the small
> European settlements visited] who were able to obtain dancing
> partners for the social gatherings which occurred whenever the
> ships were in a port of any size. Indeed, full evening dress was
> considered absolutely essential in the wardrobe of both residents
> and excursionists, regardless of heat, humidity and health risks.
> (N. Douglas & N. Douglas, 'P & O's Pacific', *Journal of Tourism
> Studies*, 1996)[23]

The event of the century

The hundredth anniversary of the landing in Sydney Cove of Captain
Arthur Phillip and the convicts, officials, marines and their families
who had arrived with him in the First Fleet was commemorated on
26 January 1888. There were celebrations throughout the colonies and
governors, church dignitaries, politicians, mayors, trade union officials
and civil servants from all over the colonies came to Sydney for the

74   principal ceremonies. There were then some three million people living in six colonies, of whom about a third lived in the capital cities, as is shown in the table below.

Melbourne	419 000
Sydney	358 000
Adelaide	115 000
Brisbane	86 000
Hobart	34 000
Perth	9 000

Source: Davison, McCarty & McLeary, eds, *Australians: 1888*, 1987, p. 189.[24]

People were able to travel from every colony and from many parts of New South Wales with an efficiency undreamt of only 50 years before, let alone 100. In fact, so many people went to Sydney for the week-long celebrations—including all manner of dignitaries and officials—that the *Adelaide Register* commented, 'It is appalling to think how far-reaching the consequences would have been if Sydney had been swallowed up by an earthquake within the last two or three days.'[25]

The visitors were able to travel in style because of the network of railways—albeit inconvenienced by the changes of gauge—and the coastal shipping system. Making a journey on a ship like the *Adelaide*, with its polished timber panels, gentlemen's smoking room and ladies' boudoir, a steam machine for making coffee and tea and the latest thing in baths and lavatories, was not roughing it as in the old days. The railways had improved in speed, reliability and comfort and some had sleeping cars on long journeys.

The New South Wales government offered cheap fares on its railways so that people would come to Sydney for the celebrations. This was so successful that there were complaints that the government had undermined local celebrations. At Narrabri, a centennial banquet was cancelled because so many of the guests set off for Sydney. The editor of the local newspaper said it was a plot to enrich Sydney's shopkeepers at the expense of country people.

The week's celebrations included the unveiling of a statue of Queen Victoria in Hyde Park, the dedication of Centennial Park, the laying of a foundation stone for a new Trades Hall and numerous social and sporting events. The New South Wales towns mostly celebrated with sports and picnics. Yass had a Centennial pigeon shoot, and Parramatta a procession of friendly societies that ended with the laying of the foundation stone of a Centennial memorial drinking fountain.

Outside New South Wales Hobart and Fremantle held regattas; the one in the Western Australian port attracted many railway excursionists from Perth. Queensland newspapers were enthusiastic about the Centennial, one including a poem congratulating New South Wales on its rise from serfdom.

South Australians were less impressed. Their colony had not had convicts and they were reluctant to spend money celebrating the founding of a penal colony; most tradespeople did not observe the holiday. The only notable events in Melbourne on Centennial Day were the Caledonian Society's sports and a bay excursion organised by the Australian Natives' Association. But Melbourne's time was to come later in the year. On 1 August, the Centennial Exhibition was opened in the Melbourne Exhibition Building. Eight nations sent official delegations to the Exhibition and twenty others were represented unofficially.

> Besides a full display of its traditional industries, the British court included a collection of painting and sculpture selected by the president of the British Academy. Even casual visitors, however, could see that Britain, so long the pacemaker in industrial progress, was lagging in the competition with its younger rivals. The German court, dominated by a great silver statue of Germania congratulating Australia, was generally reckoned to be the most impressive overseas exhibit. But for sheer ingenuity the Americans beat all comers. They gave Australians the first glimpse of the Edison phonograph, the petrol engine and a curious substance known as chewing gum. (G. Davison, J. W. McCarty & A. McLeary, eds, *Australians: 1888*, 1987)[26]

As an attraction the Centennial Exhibition surpassed anything else known in Australia up to that time. More than two million visitors saw it in the nine months it was open. Special trains brought people from throughout country Victoria to Melbourne at reduced fares.

> It brought Australians their first view of the art treasures of Europe and their first full season of symphony concerts. It showed them the world's latest technology. But most of all, it held a mirror to the achievements of Australia itself. (G. Davison, J. W. McCarty & A. McLeary, op.cit.)[27]

76   Organising tourism

The States establish bureaus

Government involvement in tourism in Australia began at the Centennial Exhibition in Melbourne in 1888. The Exhibition attracted so many thousands of interstate and overseas visitors that the Victorian Railway Department opened an 'Inquiry Office' at Spencer Street Station for those who wanted to see more of the State. This was so successful it was retained and became the forerunner of the Victorian Government Tourist Bureau.

Some other States followed Victoria's lead by also establishing official bureaus and as a result the organisation of tourism, including the selling of packaged tours, was well developed by 1914. In their early years, the bureaus usually sold rail and steamship tickets and sometimes booked accommodation. They also organised excursions by coach. At first, in the case of early bureaus like the ones in Tasmania and South Australia, these coaches were horse-drawn.

Australia was part of the tourism world. The Thomas Cook company opened an office in Melbourne in 1910. The shipping companies and the State and Commonwealth railways were among the most significant commercial organisations in the country and Australians had shown they could organise world-class events and market them. The Centennial Exhibition had attracted many visitors from outside Victoria and 'a larger share of its surrounding population than any of its European and American counterparts.'[28]

In New South Wales, official tourism promotion started with the establishment in 1905 of the curiously-named 'Intelligence Department'. This body played a general promotional and informational role for the government and provided a government tourist bureau.[29]

South Australia established a State Tourist Bureau in 1908 as a separate government department. Two years later it absorbed the State's 'Intelligence Department', which previously had been responsible to the Commissioner for Lands for general State publicity. The functions of the Bureau, as stated by its director-elect in 1911, included:

- sending framed enlargements of South Australian views to other States and various parts of the world, to be hung in places frequented by the public

- keeping a representative stock of lantern slides and delivering illustrated lectures throughout the country. 'Lantern slides are also loaned to persons competent to lecture who are travelling to old-world countries and who are willing to thus advertise the State'[30]

- the formation of local tourist associations in the important centres of the State, with the object of 'creating a live interest among the residents of the particular locality in the potentialities of their district as a field for tourists.'[31]

Tourism in Tasmania became organised following the laying out of the island's railway system between 1870 and 1890. Trains would meet the passenger steamers as they docked at Hobart's wharves and carry visitors and their baggage into the hinterland. The Tasmanian Tourist Association was formed in 1893 at a public meeting in Hobart Town Hall. The Association, which was subsidised by the government and by private donations, first informed visitors of the State's variety of natural attractions, but as tourism flourished it opened an information centre which became known as the Tourist Bureau and began issuing rail tickets and booking local trips.

This became too big an undertaking for a private organisation and in 1914 the Railway Department took over, forming a new branch called the Tasmanian Government Tourist Department and putting E. T. Emmett in charge as the first director. One of Emmett's qualifications was that he knew the State well; he was in his own words an 'ardent cyclist' who had seen much of Tasmania's beauty from the saddle of a 'safety' bicycle, which had replaced the penny farthing.[32]

As a result of this knowledge he had been instructed to produce an illustrated guidebook, which he wrote under gaslight. It was issued in 1913, the year Hobart first had electric light. The book ends—appropriately, considering its author's passion—with an itinerary for a fortnight's cycling tour and the statement that 'the roads are, as a rule, excellent.' And that, Emmett wrote in 1959, 'in spite of no bitumen at all. However, they can't have been too bad, for about the year 1900 I rode the 143 miles from Stanley to Launceston in a day.'[33]

The novel as a promotional tool

Melbourne's tourism was boosted in the last years of the century by the publication of a novel by Fergus Hume entitled *The Mystery of a Hansom Cab*, at one time said to be the most widely-read crime novel in the English language. More than half a million copies of the book were sold in Australia and overseas. Set in 1886, it was a murder mystery which included descriptions of Melbourne's streets and back alleys through which Hume's detective searched for a killer.

Within a few years tourists were arriving in Melbourne with Hume's book in hand, wanting to see the locations he'd used for

78   his story. It took such a hold on people's imagination the English writer G. K. Chesterton once quipped that the typical Australian was likely to be less interested in the mystery of the outback than the mystery of the hansom cab. (C. J. Spicer, *Duchess: The Story of the Windsor Hotel*, 1993)[34]

Collecting statistics

Without statistics it is not possible to measure tourism. In Australia, official statistics had been kept since the first days of white settlement because it was essential to keep a record of prisoners. Other statistics were kept by the colonial administrations so that the costs and progress of the colonies could be measured in Britain.

In later times all the States had official statisticians who had at their disposal the reports of the Registrars of Births, Marriages and Deaths, the population censuses and the reports of government departments on subjects such as lands, mines, education and railways.

It was difficult, however, to produce uniform statistics in some areas because the British administrators treated each colony as a separate entity. Difficulties with uniformly-accepted definitions continued after Federation. Tourism was not significant enough at the time for the statisticians to worry about trying to define a 'tourist'. They had enough trouble with the words they thought important; it took the States until 1902 to agree on a common definition for 'factory'.[35]

In 1905 the Commonwealth Government founded the Commonwealth Bureau of Census and Statistics and created the position of Commonwealth Statistician. Professor G. H. Knibbs was appointed to the post and the next year he presided over a meeting to standardise the States' statistical returns.

While tourism was not specifically addressed by the statisticians at the time, some collections of figures were of interest to the new breed of tourism officials. The most obvious were those related to shipping and railways, including the numbers of passengers arriving and departing.

The First World War disrupted normal patterns of travel and tourism, of course, and for some types of businesses—coastal shipping was the main example—the world would never be as good again. However, the basis for organising tourism in Australia had been put in place before the war started. That foundation was to be built upon when the conflict ended, leading to the country's being promoted as a tourism destination overseas.

ENDNOTES

[1] Leiper (1980), op.cit., p. 56.

[2] A Victorian journalist under the pen-name of 'Vagabond' wrote, 'I find a strong republican feeling among the masses in Sydney.' (Davison, McCarty & McLeary, op.cit., p 15).

[3] Van den Hoorn, R. (1991), *Dreams, Destinations, Directions: The Changing Face of Tourism in South Australia 1900–1992*, Tourism South Australia, Adelaide, p. 2.

[4] Emmett, E. T. (1958–59), History of Tasmania's Tourist Bureau, unpublished manuscript.

[5] White, R. & Frow, L. (1987), 'Tourism' in *Australians: A Historical Dictionary*, ed. G. Alpin, S. G. Foster, M. McKernan & I. Howie-Willis, Australians: A Historical Library series, Fairfax, Syme & Weldon Associates, Sydney, p. 402.

[6] Whitelock, op.cit., p. 258.

[7] *Skiing into History, 1924–1984*, Ski Club of Victoria, Melbourne, p. 39. The *Monaro Mercury*'s report was in the issue dated 2 August 1861. Ten days later the *Sydney Morning Herald* quoted a description of the skis from the *Braidwood Observer*. The 'skates' were said to have been 'constructed of two palings turned up at the front and about four feet long, with straps to put the feet in, and the traveller carries a long stick to balance himself and to assist him up hill.'

[8] Lloyd, op.cit., pp. 39–42. Neville Locker of Happy Valley, Adaminaby, whose family had lived in the mountains for more than a century, interview, August 1998.

[9] *This Bold Venture: The Story of Lake Tyers House, Place and People*, Alison Goding, Melbourne, p. 25.

[10] Fitzgerald, R. (1984), *A History of Queensland: From 1915 to the 1980s*, Qld Univ. Press, St Lucia, Qld, p. 547. It is not clear which tourist bureau was the source of the report. The Queensland State Tourism Authority was not set up until 1926, but Queensland tourism was being promoted long before this.

[11] McRobbie, A. (1984), *The Fabulous Gold Coast*, Pan News Pty Ltd, Surfers Paradise, Qld, p. 29.

[12] Davison, McCarty & McLeary, op.cit., p. 229.

[13] Cox, op.cit., p. 107.

[14] The match was between Victoria and Tasmania at the Launceston Racecourse. The first ball bowled in Australian first class cricket was an underarm delivery by William Henty of Tasmania sent down to Duncan Cooper of Victoria at 11 a.m. on 11 February 1851. 'The ground was of the roughest description and only with difficulty were the umpires Lyon and Weedon able to select a place to play.' (Hutchinson, G. & Ross, J., 1997, eds, *200 Seasons of Australian Cricket*, Pan Macmillan Australia in association with the Australian Cricket Board, Sydney, p. 16). Tasmania won the match by three wickets.

[15] Anderson, K. (1987), ed., *Australia 200 Years & Beyond*, John Fairfax & Sons, Sydney, p. 54.

[16] Andrews (1994), op.cit., p. 29.

[17] Cannon, M. (1993), *Melbourne After the Gold Rush*, Loch Haven Books, Melbourne, p. 281.

[18] Presumably the later and longer-lasting Theatre Royal rather than the theatre at the back of the Royal Hotel, burnt down in 1840 as already described.

[19] Mundy, G. C. (1855), *Our Antipodes: Or Residence and Rambles in the Australasian Colonies etc.*, 3rd edn, Richard Bentley, London, pp. 16–18, in Ward & Robertson, eds, 1964, *Select Documents in Australian History*, v. 1, Ure Smith, Sydney, pp. 273–4.

20 It was first called the Victoria Theatre. In its early years it was used as place for lectures, public meetings and sporting events as well as theatrical performances (The Wapping History Group, 1988, *'Down Wapping': Hobart's Vanished Wapping and Old Wharf Districts*, Blubber Head Press, Hobart, p. 42).

21 Spearritt, P. (1978), *Sydney Since the Twenties*, Hale & Iremonger, Sydney, p. 236.

22 Douglas, N. & Douglas, N. (1996), 'P & O's Pacific', *The Journal of Tourism Studies*, v. 7(2), December, p. 3.

23 ibid., p. 8.

24 Davison, McCarty & McLeary, op.cit., p. 189.

25 ibid., p. 18.

26 ibid., p. 24.

27 ibid., pp. 26–7.

28 ibid., p. 26.

29 Tourism New South Wales (1996), History of Tourism New South Wales, paper issued by Tourism New South Wales, Sydney.

30 Correll, Ted (1986), *The History of South Australia's Department of Tourism*, South Australian Department of Tourism, Adelaide, p. 2.

31 ibid.

32 The penny farthing had a very big front wheel and consequently the rider's seat was high off the ground. Sudden stops could be perilous. The safety bicycle's wheels were of equal size with the pedal chain drive supplying power to the rear wheel. The rider was relatively low to the ground. This was considered safer, hence the naming of the new bicycle as the 'safety'. Cycling was very popular in the last decades of the nineteenth century. The penny farthing was invented in 1874. The safety bicycle was introduced in 1877 by Henry Lawson in London but did not become popular until after 1885 when John Starley of Coventry produced the 'first recognisable modern bicycle' (Lay, 1993, op.cit., p. 143). There were a number of design variations, including three-wheeled 'sociables' in which two riders sat side by side, and the tandem where one rider sat behind the other.

33 Emmett, op.cit. Emmett died in Hobart in December 1970 at the age of 99. In 'Brief historical notes on tourism in Tasmania' (unpublished, dated June 1995), E. Patterson wrote: 'His death seemed to mark the passing of an era. He had been born when tourism was first recognised as a major social and economic phenomenon in Tasmania, had witnessed the formation of the early tourist associations, presided over the infancy of the Department of Tourism, nurtured it through its most difficult years, and had most ably fostered and guided the development of the State's tourist industry during his 52 years of Public Service.'

34 C. J. Spicer, op.cit., p. 25.

35 Vamplew (1987), Introduction, *Australians: Historical Statistics*, ed. W. Vamplew, Australians: A Historical Library series, Fairfax, Syme & Weldon Associates, Sydney, p. xv.

The years between: 1918–1939

S O MUCH HAPPENED in the 1920s and 1930s that the travel and tourism scene was changed for ever in those relatively few years. The development of aviation, in Australia as well as elsewhere, was exciting and dramatic. By the end of the period there were reliable passenger services. To travel first class by ship was to experience the ultimate luxury available. Railways became faster and more comfortable, although in Europe and North America motor vehicles were pouring on to the roads and taking away their business. In Australia cars were still too expensive and the roads too bad to trouble the railways seriously, but signs were appearing of things to come: coach companies were beginning to take people on tours to remote places and camping grounds and caravan parks were being built for the first time.

At the end of the 1930s the latest DC-3 airliners were in Australian skies, all-steel air-conditioned trains were on our railway lines and luxury motor ships were sailing between our ports. People had more time to travel, too—in 1936 one week's annual leave had been introduced for those in full employment.[1]

82   The Depression puts a brake on progress

All this was achieved in spite of the Great Depression. The Depression put a sharp brake on most progress in travel and tourism. In 1930 Australian airlines carried 91 415 paying passengers; in 1935 the figure was only 45 450.[2] Even grand hotels for the rich barely held on. Business at Menzies Hotel in Melbourne was so bad that those staff members who still had a job were willing to accept months off at a time.[3] Melbourne's population declined by 40 000 between 1930 and 1933.[4] The Depression hit all sectors of the economy and the effect on many people's ability to earn was devastating. The recovery, which began in 1934, was agonisingly slow. Many remained jobless for years.

Yet the impact was uneven. Some people were less affected than others; some were not directly affected at all. Some parts of the travel and tourism industry flourished in the gloom. When P&O announced a five-day cruise from Sydney to Norfolk Island by the liner *Strathaird* towards the end of 1932, it was sold out within three days. On Christmas Eve, the day after the *Strathaird* sailed, the Orient Line's *Oronsay* left Sydney on a round voyage to Noumea.[5]

The romance of travel

Looking back 60 years and more, travel away from our shores in the decade before the Second World War seems romantic and leisurely.

While the 1932 cruises were the first from Australian ports to be conducted by the giants of the Australia-to-England run—P&O and the Orient Line—cruising was not new to Australians. A cruise to Queensland waters from the south in winter was the equivalent of a visit by car or plane to a northern resort now. To give an example, the McIlwraith McEacharn liner *Katoomba*'s monthly Christmas cruise was initially to the Whitsunday group, but after 1933 that became the winter cruise itinerary and the ship sailed to Noumea, the New Hebrides (now Vanuatu), Norfolk Island, Suva and Lord Howe Island in January.[6]

Burns, Philp & Co. ran leisurely South Pacific cruises from Sydney to its trading ports in the vessels *Macdhui, Malaita* and *Bulolo*. The latter, at 6267 tons, was the biggest New Guinea passenger ship registered in Australia and was equipped with a dining-room, smoking-room, music-room, writing-room, library, veranda, cafe and pool.[7]

Luxurious ships like P&O's five 'White Sisters'—the Strath liners— were on the Australia-to-England run. A fast trip to Europe and back took ten weeks, so travellers needed time as well as money. Flying to other countries was for the very privileged few. But in the last years of the 1930s anybody in Sydney could see the great Qantas flying boats arriving from or leaving for faraway places.

In 1938 a Sydney newspaper asked a range of people where they would go if time and money were no object.

> ... wealthy people set out clear itineraries in which England, Italy, Germany and the United States were most popular, whereas those who had no chance of travelling spoke of a fantasy world made up of Hollywood, romantic fiction, and vague memories of school geography and stamp albums. Evelyn Davis, 'soda fountain dispenser', wanted to 'go to Hollywood to see if Clark Gable really is as handsome as he is on the films', and Norma Murphy, a salesgirl, 'grew dreamy-eyed at the thought of travelling. I want to see a Rajah riding a jewelled elephant', she said.[8]

It was not yet the time when ordinary working Australians like the two Sydney girls could think of travelling overseas. More technological advances would have to be made before the age of mass tourism could arrive.

But it seemed as if the travel and tourism industry was getting ready for it. There was a powerful entrepreneurial spirit making itself felt in the industry. And, as a symbol of the nation's vision of the future, Australia had already opened its first promotional offices overseas.

ENDNOTES

[1] Leiper (1980), op.cit., p. 59. Introduction of paid mandatory leave followed a decision of the International Labour Organisation Convention. The term was increased to a minimum of two weeks in 1944.

[2] Vamplew & McLean, op.cit., p. 172.

[3] Archer, F. (1984), *Tell Me More: More of the Story of Menzies Hotel*, Fred Archer, Melbourne, p. 37.

[4] Spicer, op.cit., p. 48.

[5] *Travelweek*, June 18 1997, p. 4.

[6] Pemberton, op.cit., pp. 143–4.

[7] ibid., p. 223. The *Malaita*, which traded in the South Pacific until 1965, was the second ship of that name operated by Burns Philp. The first, a former West Indies fruit ship bought by Burns Philp in 1905, had its moments of fame as a hulk in 1926, when it was dragged from its moorings in Victoria's Port Phillip Bay during a storm and

demolished the South Melbourne Sea Baths. The only way to clear the mess was to dismantle the ship and scuttle what was left outside the Heads.

[8] White, R. (1987), 'Overseas', in *Australians 1938*, ed. B. Gammage, P. Spearritt & L. Douglas, Australians: A Historical Library series, Fairfax, Syme & Weldon Associates, Sydney, p. 439.

Two *decades* of *rapid change*

The Great Depression

This was an era of contradictions. For many millions in the early 1930s life was anything but glamorous as the Great Depression swept the world. Banks failed, factories and mills closed and millions lost their jobs. The travel and tourism industry did not escape: as the Depression wore on, 85 per cent of hotels in the United States, for example, went into receivership or some form of liquidation.[1] The effects of the Depression were felt for years in all industrialised countries.

Ships and trains, cars and planes

The 21 years between the First and Second World Wars, however, were highly significant in the development of travel and tourism. They saw the birth and development of the airliner, from small beginnings in Europe immediately after the war with rickety wartime aircraft to large flying boats that flew over the oceans, joining continent to continent. The advances in air transportation during this period went far beyond the aircraft themselves and included weather forecasting, the development of navigation equipment and innovative management.

Ships became bigger and faster, and the fashionable liners became household names. American Express, a freight company which first had turned to financial services, expanded into travel. In 1922 it arranged the first round-the-world cruise.

This was also an era of great steam trains. However, the period also encompassed the end of that era—long before it ended, diesel-electric

86 locomotives were taking over. Another development that seriously affected the railways was the availability of the motor car. Assembly lines turned out cars by the millions. Cars and motor coaches changed the way people travelled on land and ended the dominance the railways had held in long journeys.

Travel had become part of popular culture. Intentionally or not, it was glamorised merely through the names of popular musical pieces like Gershwin's *An American in Paris* and movies like *Flying Down to Rio*.[2]

Luxury afloat

New technology made ocean liners faster, quieter and more luxurious than ever before. In the 1920s P&O, which had merged with British India, the largest shipping company east of Suez in 1914, made up its wartime losses and continued to expand, buying several other shipping lines and a controlling interest in the Orient Line. It had more than 500 ships in the 1920s and in the 1930s it put into service five liners whose names all started with 'Strath'—the *Strathaird*, the *Strathnaver*, the *Strathmore*, the *Stratheden* and the *Strathallan*. These became well known in Australian ports.

On the Atlantic, the *Mauretania* finally lost the Blue Riband, its times beaten in July 1929 by the 51 656-ton German ship *Bremen* of the North German Lloyd line. This was to be a period not only of fast ships, but of great luxury liners which were like floating hotels with magnificent dining-rooms, ballrooms, swimming-pools and sports courts. The first large transatlantic liner to be built after the war was the French Line's *Ile de France*, launched in 1926. The 43 500-ton ship was not particularly fast; it was built for elegance and good living and was an immediate success.[3] The French Line followed with the 80 000-ton *Normandie*, which carried only 1972 passengers in a variety of classes and accommodation including 28 de grand luxe suites, each consisting of five or six rooms. The *Normandie* easily gained the Blue Riband on its maiden voyage in May 1935.

Soon afterwards came Cunard's 81 235-ton *Queen Mary*, its construction delayed by the Depression. It made its maiden voyage in March 1936 and, after a couple of transatlantic crossings to work up to full speed, steamed from New York to Southampton in just four days at an average speed of 30.6 knots (57 kilometres per hour) to take the Blue Riband. It was as lavishly furnished as the *Normandie*. The difference, as one observer put it, was that 'the French built a beautiful hotel and

put a ship around it; the British built a beautiful ship and put a hotel
inside it.'[4]

The development of airliners

The aeroplane was developed rapidly as a passenger carrier, though it
was only the relatively few who flew in airliners until after the Second
World War. The foundations of British, French, German and Swiss air
transport were laid as early as 1919 with the use of war surplus aircraft.[5]
Daily international scheduled services began in August of that year
between London and Paris.

Flying as a passenger in the first few years was anything but comfortable. In some aircraft the passenger space was enclosed by a simple
cabin, but the windows had to be kept open for ventilation and the
noise of the engines was so deafening that passengers had to plug up
their ears and pass notes if they wanted to communicate.

Emergency landing grounds were spaced out along the routes
because planes frequently had engine trouble or were low on fuel due to
strong headwinds, or because the pilots couldn't see clearly on account
of the weather. One aircraft flying from London to Paris made 14 intermediate stops.[6] But as time went on, specialised transport aircraft with
comfortable passenger cabins came into service. British planes carried the
first airborne toilets in the early 1920s and a few years later Imperial
Airways (British) and the French Air Union introduced stewards and
meal services.

European countries with overseas connections began to fly across
oceans. The Dutch company KLM began a service from Amsterdam to
Batavia (now Jakarta) in 1929 with Fokker F-VIII aircraft stopping more
than two dozen times in twelve days. Also in 1929, Britain began a
commercial air route to India and by 1935 Britain's Imperial Airways
was circling the globe, with Qantas flying the Brisbane-to-Singapore leg
as part of the Australia–England route.

In the United States, development took a different course. Routes
were pioneered with air mail services, which by 1920 crossed the continent. Six years later, eleven routes were being serviced and on some of
them passengers were being carried. It was with air mail subsidies that
some of the best-known US airlines such as United Airlines, American
Airlines and Delta developed. United Airlines introduced the first stew-
ardesses in 1930, requiring that they be registered nurses and wear
nurses' uniforms during the flight.

88   The early mail runs gave the Boeing company valuable experience which later helped it develop successful passenger planes, leading up to today's family of jet airliners. In the 1930s Boeing changed the way airliners were built with its 247, which first flew in 1933. The Boeing 247D, an improved version, is usually considered the first successful modern passenger plane. It was an all-metal low-wing monoplane with two engines, a single tail fin and rudder and a retractable main undercarriage. Carrying ten passengers, it was a complete break with the past and earlier types could not compete.

But it was not without competition for long. Douglas followed the next year with the even more advanced DC-2, which could accommodate 14 passengers. A DC-2, operated by the Dutch airline KLM, won the handicap section of a race from England to Australia in 1934 to celebrate Melbourne's centenary, proving an American commercial aircraft could cover 18 000 kilometres in four days.[7]

The DC-2 was followed by the DC-3 which was bigger, with seats for more than 20 passengers. According to J. W. R. Taylor and A. Munson, it 'did more than any other type of aircraft to develop and establish a reliable system of worldwide airlines and create the traffic which led to the production of modern four-engined airliners.'[8]

Flying boats pioneer long-range routes

Flying boats played a major role in pioneering the world's long-distance routes. They were preferred on long routes because they did not require landing fields; they only needed a buoy to tie up to.

The British Short company had in mind the long distances Imperial Airways had to cover to reach the countries of the British Empire. It built a series of flying boats, starting with the Singapores in 1926. Its flying boat production culminated in the Empire class, of which the airline ordered 28 in 1935. By 1938 seven services a week were being flown to Egypt, four to India, three to East Africa and two each to South Africa, Malaya and Australia. American companies had also built a number of successful flying boats and in 1938 the Boeing 314 Clipper went into service with Pan American World Airways, enabling it to pioneer Pacific and Asian routes and maintain a transatlantic service during the Second World War.

Juan Trippe, the founder of Pan Am, also pioneered the concept of airlines that provided accommodation at their stopovers. In 1936 he sent crews to Midway Island, Wake Island and Guam to build exotic South Pacific hotels for passengers flying on Pan Am Clippers from San Francisco to Manila.[9]

The transformation of the railways

Railways underwent a transformation both in North America and Europe. On both continents they had to contend with competition from motor vehicles on a scale they could hardly have imagined before the war. At first, they simply offered better service for those who could afford to pay for it. In Europe Pullmans were introduced on some of the continental services, though it was the de luxe Wagons-Lits trains leaving from Paris Gare de Lyon for the Riviera, the Alps and Italy which captured imaginations and the patronage of the social elite in the 1920s.

In 1929 the *Orient Express* was held up for five days when the track was blocked by snow in appalling weather 80 kilometres from Istanbul. This event created a sensation and gave Agatha Christie the starting-point for her book *Murder on the Orient Express*, which was published in 1934 and later turned into a film. Graham Greene's simply-titled novel *Stamboul Train* had been published two years earlier. It was filmed three times.[10] In the 1930s the *Orient Express* was to become a family of trains with different routes and with Athens as well as Istanbul for a final destination. The Wagons-Lits company bought Thos. Cook and Son.[11]

But behind the glitter railways were losing money because of the competition from road traffic. To accommodate the increases in motor vehicles the Americans built more parkways, the Germans the auto-bahnen and the Italians the autostrada—all contenders for the title of first freeway.[12] Between 1925 and 1929 the number of private cars and motor coaches operating in Germany rose more than 125 per cent and the number of people taking a bus by more than 250 per cent. By the end of the inter-war period it was calculated that coach services had taken away from British railways more than 200 million passenger journeys a year.[13] Air travel was also emerging as a threat. The Germans were the first to show that it was effective for domestic inter-city operations.

When they realised what was happening, the railways fought back by offering better services to a larger market, targeting leisure travellers with cheap excursion fares. Thus seats on Italian excursion trains to popular resorts were priced at only 20 per cent of the normal return fare. Speed and frequency became part of the railways' competitive weaponry, helped by the introduction of high-speed diesel-electric locomotives. Diesel traction was first used on the 286.6-kilometre Berlin-to-Hamburg service in the early 1930s in a streamlined two-car train called the *Fliegende Hamburger*—a title 'quite innocent of the burlesque its English "Flying Hamburger" translation conjures up nowadays'.[14]

90   In the United States diesels were also used in the fight against road competition. Henry Ford had introduced his Model T in 1908. In 1914 he developed assembly-line production that caused prices to fall to the point where millions could afford his cars. In any year in the 1920s American companies never made less than 90 per cent of the world's cars.[15] As a result of pressure from motoring interests to improve roads, Congress approved a federal highway program in 1917. The new highways led to inter-city coach services in the 1920s and in that decade passenger-mileage and passenger-revenue on the railways fell more than 40 per cent.

The Burlington Railroad, which had seen its passenger volume drop from 18 million to 7 million a year between 1923 and 1933, was the first to adopt diesel power and the result was spectacular. Its streamlined *Pioneer Zephyr* ran non-stop between Denver and Chicago in May 1934 at an average speed of 124.9 kilometres per hour for the 1633 kilometres. Two-and-a-half years later a ten-passenger train called the *Denver Zephyr* began regular service on the Chicago–Denver route on a 16-hour overnight schedule that was almost 10 hours shorter than the previous best with a steam train. The following year the Sante Fe company introduced the first all-Pullman streamliner, the Chicago–Los Angeles *Super-Chief*.

The new trains were followed by others—some, like the *Super-Chief*, offering the latest in luxury, others all-economy configuration. They generated much more revenue than the steam trains that had preceded them and they were much cheaper to run. But they were working only on the main transcontinental routes and the chief inter-city corridors; they could not stop the losses on the American train system overall. Cars, coaches and, increasingly, aeroplanes were taking their toll on the railways.

The hotels get bigger

In the 1920s hotels in the United States got bigger and bigger. The biggest of them all was the Stevens Hotel (now the Conrad Hilton) in Chicago, which opened its 3000 rooms in 1929. Two other hotels dating from this period were New York's Waldorf-Astoria on Park Avenue and the Pierre on Fifth Avenue.

Traditionally, most of the hotel staff positions in the United States had been filled by Europeans. However, this supply of trained hotel people was cut off in the 1920s by new immigration laws.[16] Cornell University started teaching hotel management in 1922, and Michigan

State University followed in 1926. The Swiss had long been the leaders in food service training. The Americans now added a management emphasis to preparing people for careers in hospitality.

The motel also dates from the 1920s. The first was probably a set of tourist cabins built at Lincoln Park, Los Angeles, in 1922.[17] The first establishment to use the name was the Motel Inn on Highway 101 in San Luis Obispo, California, in 1925. One version of the creation of the name was that the architect abbreviated the words 'motor hotel' on his plans to 'Mo-Tel', another that the sign painter could not fit 'motor hotel' on the existing signboard and so saved the money for a new one by using 'motel'.[18] The idea of accommodation designed specifically for motorists did not sweep America immediately; it was not until the 1950s that motels would rapidly increase in number and size.

Holidays with pay

A resolution at an International Labour Organization convention in 1936 made vacations with pay mandatory in some countries, including Britain and France. The world was still emerging from the Depression, but the ILO decision made an immediate impact on tourism in Europe.[19]

> ... the summer Riviera was more popular than ever with middle-class vacationers. Beverly Nichols wrote of them, 'Ye Gods, the people! Drunken, debauched, heartless, of an incredible vulgarity —swooping, screaming, racketing.' Of the picturesque locals, Cyril Connolly remarked that 'elderly peasants ... seemed to have acquired an air of licentiousness from their customers'. At the same time, the idealistic strain of tourism as exemplified by Thomas Cook's paragon continued to flourish. With cars, trains, and ships at his disposal, the earnest student of culture and ethnography could visit more places than ever, thinking to spread international understanding and goodwill; it was a particularly popular mode amongst German tourists. (M. Feifer, *Going Places*, 1985)[20]

This, it seems, was the beginning of a new type of tourism. The day-trippers had been unleashed in great numbers by the steam train in the previous century and now increased leisure time was allowing ordinary people with jobs to seek the sun where only the rich had gone before. They aroused the displeasure of effete British writers, but not only these. As time went on some people did not want to be thought of as 'tourists', and preferred to be called 'travellers'.

92   The first definitions of the word 'tourist'

A different view had been taken in 1933 by an English economist, F. W. Ogilvie, who had noted that the words 'tourist' and 'tourism' were starting to receive wide recognition 'shorn of their more frivolous associations'.[21] Tourism had become important enough for people to start wondering what it really was, for it to be defined more precisely, starting a process which was to prove never-ending. Ogilvie himself attempted what Morley considers the earliest formal definition of 'tourists' in the English language:

> ... all persons who satisfy two conditions, that they are away from home for any period of less than a year and, second, that while they are away they spend money in the place they visit without earning it there.[22]

Ogilvie's view that tourism was being taken seriously was valid. A number of nations were already promoting it for its economic benefits and in 1924 the International Union of Official Travel Organizations (IUOTO) had been formed, with its head office first in London and later in Geneva. All its members at that time were European.

Another international organisation began in the 1930s. The first Skal Club was founded in Paris in 1932 by travel trade managers who had been on an educational tour of Scandinavia. In 1934 the Association Internationale des Skal Clubs was founded and Skal was on the way to becoming the great fraternal organisation of the international travel and tourism industry that it is today.[23]

In 1937 the League of Nations Statistical Committee took the first step towards the development of international definitions by recommending that an 'international tourist' for statistical purposes be regarded as one who 'visits a country other than that in which he habitually lives for a period of at least twenty-four hours'.[24]

The interest in tourism extended to European universities, where it was offered as a subject for the first time in the 1930s.

Another terrible war was to come and change much that was familiar, including the perceptions of ordinary people in industrialised countries with regard to travel. A great deal of preparatory work was done in the 1920s and 1930s to make possible the explosion in tourism that followed the Second World War. This not only affected advances in transport technology and new styles of accommodation, but also influenced the increase of leisure time and paid holidays. With all this came a recognition that there was such a thing as tourism, which would become very important to national economies.

ENDNOTES

[1] Lattin (1990a), op.cit., p. 295.

[2] *Flying Down to Rio*, made in 1933, was a musical starring Dolores Del Rio and Gene Raymond, but it was a relatively unknown dancer called Fred Astaire and his new dancing partner Ginger Rogers who dazzled the audiences. It was not a 'tourist movie'—one shot showed a dozen girls dancing on the wings of aeroplanes thousands of feet above Rio de Janeiro, something tourists were not likely to see in real life, let alone emulate— but the title was evocative of a romantic view of travel, and still is (Hirschhorn, 1981, *The Hollywood Musical*, Octopus Books Limited, London, p. 80).

[3] Dean, op.cit., p. 23.

[4] ibid., p. 24.

[5] Taylor, J. W. R. & Munson, K. (1972), *History of Aviation*, Crown Publishers, NY, p. 136.

[6] ibid., p. 163.

[7] There is a memorial incorporating the DC-2 at Albury airport. Encountering a storm over northern Victoria, the pilots were forced to land at Albury racecourse where the plane became bogged. Local residents helped move it to solid ground, passengers were off-loaded, and the DC-2 took off and completed its flight to Melbourne. On elapsed time, a De Havilland DH88 Comet came first in the race, the DC-2 second and a Boeing 247D third. The latter aircraft was not used by Australian airlines.

[8] Taylor & Munson, op.cit., p. 231. According to R. Bond (ed., 1997, *The Story of Aviation: A Concise History of Flight*, Greenhill Books, London, p. 55), the DC-3 resulted from American Airlines' approaching Douglas for an enlarged version of the DC-2 to accommodate sleeping berths and the DC-3 was first known as the Douglas Sleeper Transport. It was first flown on 17 December 1935 and the day version, the DC-3, became the world's most popular airliner. By the outbreak of the Second World War it was estimated that nearly 90 per cent of the world's airliner passengers flew in the DC-3.

[9] *Air Tranport World*, September, 1993, p. 60.

[10] Des Cars & Caracalla, op.cit., pp. 7 & 140.

[11] During the Second World War the Wagons-Lits headquarters in Brussels and Paris were occupied by the Germans. Thos. Cook and Son Ltd. was eventually made part of the nationalised British Railways. It was separated in 1972 and in 1977 became part of the Midland Bank group. It is now owned by Westdeutsche Landesbank, one of Germany's largest banks. (Griggs, op.cit., p. 131).

[12] Lay (1993), op.cit., p. 315. Edward Bassett, chairman of the American National Conference on City Planning, coined the word 'freeway' in 1930 to distinguish it from a toll road, which was not free. Later the word came to mean freedom from intersections and uncontrolled access (ibid., p. 316).

[13] Allen, op.cit., p. 84.

[14] ibid., p. 87.

[15] Lay (1993), op.cit., p. 161.

[16] According to Lattin (1990a, op.cit., p. 298), at one time 80 per cent of the employees and many department heads and executives in American hotels would have been European born and trained. Now most were American-born.

[17] Lay (1993), op.cit., p. 309.

[18] Dunstan, K. (1991), *Flag: The First 30 Years*, Flag International Ltd, Melbourne, p. 13; Lay (1993), op.cit., p. 309.

[19] Feifer, M. (1985), *Going Places: The Ways of the Tourist from Imperial Rome to the Present Day*, Macmillan London Ltd, p. 220.

[20] ibid.

[21] Morley, C. L. (1990), 'What is tourism? Definitions, concepts and characteristics', *Journal of Tourism Studies*, v. 1(1), May, p. 3.

[22] ibid.

[23] In the 1990s, Skal had more than 25 000 members in more than 500 clubs in 80 countries. In early 1999 there were 20 clubs in Australia.

[24] OECD, 1974, p.7 cited by Leiper (1980), op.cit., p. 14.

How they travelled and where they stayed

Faster and more comfortable trains

As the Australian railway system continued to expand after the war, travel by train became faster and more comfortable and the steam engine became one of the most potent symbols of technological advance. No train made a greater impact than Victoria's all-steel, streamlined *Spirit of Progress*, which went into service in 1937 between Melbourne and Albury. It was seen as an assertion of optimism in a country that was still emerging from the Depression.

Because most main lines had been completed before the war, not a great deal of track-laying was necessary. However, what was done was significant for reasons other than just the length of the track. The New South Wales Railways built standard gauge lines to link Sydney with Broken Hill in 1919 and Brisbane in 1930, but most activity was in the middle section of the country.

Commonwealth Railways, which ran the transcontinental link between Port Augusta and Kalgoorlie and the Darwin-to-Pine Creek narrow gauge in the Northern Territory, built the Central Australian Railway, which reached Alice Springs, 1339 kilometres north of Port of Augusta, in 1929. The train was the famous *Ghan*. The name was an abbreviation of 'Afghan', and was a reference to the camel drivers who had pioneered the north-south route. The *Ghan* ran in two sections, the first being on the standard gauge from Port Pirie to Marree. Here

96   passengers changed to another train with the same name, which ran on the 1067-millimetre gauge line to Alice Springs.

> They used to say 'if you want to see the land, ride the Ghan' and in fact a song was written about it. You had plenty of time. Without allowing for delays, which were many, caused by such trivialities as floods washing away miles of track or intense heat bending the rails, the old Ghan was allowed a generous thirty-one hours to cover its 870 kilometres of shaky narrow gauge track, laid slap on the desert floor without any proper foundation. At 28 km/h overall, it may well have merited the title of the slowest named train in the world. (C. Taylor, *Great Rail Non-journeys of Australia*, 1986)[1]

In 1931 there were 42 867 kilometres of track laid in Australia, with Queensland and New South Wales each having more than 10 000 kilometres.[2] This was close to the maximum, which was reached in 1941— 43 829 kilometres.

Standardisation of gauges became a political issue again in the 1920s and a Royal Commission in 1921 advocated a program to convert all lines in the country to the standard 1435-millimetre gauge at a cost of nearly 60 million pounds. This was a vast figure at the time, and the scale of the task combined with State rivalries ensured that the recommendation was shelved.

Gauge changes in South Australia

There was some rationalisation of gauges used in South Australia— though it was not to the standard gauge. Lines that had been built in isolation to take agricultural produce to ports were linked, which meant that some 1067-millimetre lines had to be widened to conform with the State's mainline 1600-millimetre gauge. The line from Adelaide to Red Hill to Port Pirie was converted to the 1600-millimetre gauge in 1937. In the same year, the standard gauge transcontinental line was extended from Port Augusta to Port Pirie. The town was also the terminal for a 1067-millimetre line from Broken Hill, built in 1887. Port Pirie then became the only major rail terminal in the world accommodating three different gauges.[3]

Almost all Australian railways were steam-powered until 1919, when Melbourne began to electrify its suburban system. Sydney followed in 1926. All other interstate and intrastate railways continued to use steam until the introduction of the diesel in the 1950s.

The period between the wars was the era of powerful locomotives in Australia—the smoke-belching, hissing, grunting monsters so beloved of

railway enthusiasts and remembered through those that have been pre-   **97**
served to run on a few historical lines and through the models found in
hobby shops. However, the people who travelled on trains drawn by
steam engines were not always so fond of them as today's railway
enthusiasts. They were only too conscious that the smoke and soot
these engines produced not only dirtied the stations but found its way
into the carriages.

The *Spirit of Progress*

There was improvement in this respect in the 1930s, instigated by the
Victorian Railways under Sir Harold Clapp.[4] In 1937 the *Spirit of
Progress* was introduced—the first air-conditioned, all-steel express train
in Australia—running between Melbourne and Albury. Clapp had
chosen a type of train operated by the Baltimore and Ohio Railroad in
the United States as his model. The *Spirit of Progress* consisted of eight
sitting cars, a parlour car and a dining car plus a brake van and a mail
van. The carriages were elegantly furnished and air-conditioned at a
time when this was a novelty in Australia.

Designed to haul it were four dark blue, streamlined, S-type locomotives, which in the words of S. Brooke 'bespoke power, everything about

The Spirit *beats a plane (Source: Department of Infrastructure, Victoria)*

The Spirit of Progress *was the fastest thing on rails in Australia when it
was introduced on the Melbourne–Albury run in 1937. In this picture the
Victorian Railways' sleek train is shown outspeeding a de Havilland Tiger
Moth.*

98 them screamed speed and strength.'[5] In a demonstration run between Melbourne and Albury the *Spirit of Progress* reached 127 kilometres per hour, a record for Australian trains at the time. As part of the publicity, it raced against a de Havilland Tiger Moth aircraft—and won. This was a stunt, but there was a serious side to it. The standard of railway services in Victoria and New South Wales was so good that commercial aviation had developed slowest in those States.[6]

There were other fine expresses—the *Overland* between Melbourne and Adelaide; the *Brisbane Limited* between Sydney and Brisbane—but nothing else had quite the glamour or performance of the *Spirit*.

The new ships

The coastal passenger trade was never the same after the war. In the decade before the conflict the ship-owners had been full of confidence, commissioning 17 new steamers. With the composites there were 27 ships providing more than 350 interstate departures a year on the mainland passenger services.

Some ships were lost during the war—the *Warilda* was torpedoed while acting as a hospital ship—and when it was over it was soon apparent that the best days of the coastal shipping trade were over too. Improved rail links west and north were part of the reason, but in the rest of Australia as well the railways were sapping the strength of the shipping lines. By 1921 the fleet of passenger ships on the coasts had been depleted to a dozen vessels serving ten mainland ports with fewer than half the number of sailings that there had been before the war.[7]

The ship-owners countered the land competition with a new breed of ships. The vessels, which went into service between 1929 and 1936, varied in size from just over 8000 tons to nearly 11 000 tons, carried between 300 and 400 passengers and offered them an array of public rooms: lounge, dining-room, library, smoking-room, writing-room and so on. Motor ships, not steamers, these were the *Manunda* and *Manoora* (Adelaide Steamship Company), *Westralia* (Huddart Parker), *Duntroon* (Melbourne Steamship Company) and *Kanimbla* (McIwaith McEacharn). Except for the *Westralia*, which had a false tall steamer funnel, they looked different from earlier vessels because of their single, squat motor ship funnels. They were efficient and with their quality accommodation and public rooms 'coastal passenger transport came of age.'[8]

It was not an era that would last. The last three ships delivered, the *Manunda*, *Duntroon* and *Kanimbla*, had hardly settled into their schedules before they were requisitioned for service in the Second World War.

The Bass Strait route

New ships came on the Bass Strait run after the war. The *Nairana*, at 3042 tons, arrived for Huddart Parker in 1920. This ship had been laid down in Britain before the war and on completion had been taken over by the Admiralty for service as a seaplane tender. At the end of the war, it was refurbished for its original purpose and sailed for Tasmania to begin its Bass Strait career, competing against the Union Company's *Loongana*, which had been in service for 16 years. Like the *Loongana* it was regarded as an 'express steamer', built along the same lines as the larger ships on the mainland interstate routes.

Huddart Parker and the Union Company merged their interests into a joint venture called Tasmanian Steamers Pty Ltd in 1922 and that company took over the *Nairana*, *Loongana* and *Oonah*. For the next 13 years, the *Loongana* and *Nairana* sailed between Melbourne and Launceston while the *Oonah* went from Melbourne to the Tasmanian ports of Burnie and Devonport.

In 1935, the 1753-ton *Oonah* was sent to the breaker's yard and the new 4300-ton *Taroona* took its place in the Bass Strait ferry trade. The *Taroona* had berths for 483 passengers and was equipped with a formal dining-room and lounge in true passenger ship style. All first class public rooms were wood panelled and there was a bar adjoining the oak-lined smoking-room.

The Bass Strait ships had their trials. Most of the *Taroona*'s fine pan-elling had to be replaced after it caught fire at its Melbourne berth in May 1936. The month before, the *Nairana* had been hit by a freak wave as it was about to enter Port Phillip Heads; three passengers had been washed overboard and another crushed to death. The ship went com-pletely about during the confusion and sailed two miles to sea again before turning back to Port Phillip Bay.[9]

Despite these mishaps the cross-strait service was considered very successful. Tasmanian Steamers provided sailings by the *Nairana* and *Taroona* from Melbourne to Beauty Point (Launceston), Devonport and Burnie. The *Nairana* carried on alone during the Second Word War when the *Taroona* was turned into a troop ship.

On the roads

Even before the war ended, Australians were importing cars in consider-able numbers—15 000 in 1917 alone, of which 10 000 were Model T Fords. The preponderance of American cars was not only due to the pop-ularity of the cheap and durable Ford but also because British and other

100 European industries had been fully occupied with the war. By 1920 there were 62 000 cars and 3500 trucks on the roads. The total was close to 200 000 vehicles by the end of 1924, and by 1936 there were 524 256 cars and 192 995 trucks registered throughout the Commonwealth.[10]

The road system was not ready for vehicles in the hundreds of thousands. From 1919 to 1921 branches of the National Roads Association of Australia were formed in most States, with the aim of seeing that more money—particularly Commonwealth money—was spent on roads. The Association also successfully campaigned for Australia's coastal highway to be named 'Prince's Highway' after the Prince of Wales, who visited Australia in 1920. In 1923 the Commonwealth Government began to make funds available to the States for roads and three years later the governments signed an agreement on Commonwealth aid for roads, which stayed in force with modification until 1947.

Road conditions did improve as a result. Bulldozers had been introduced during the 1920s and they and other new earthmoving equipment moved large quantities of rock and earth at a speed not known before. Bridges were built over waterways to make roads passable in wet weather.

But the task was enormous, considering past neglect, the vast distances that roads in Australia had to cover and the fact that there was a small population to supply the necessary resources. Outside city limits most roads were still made of dirt or gravel, and dust and mud were a problem. Nevertheless, as cars became more reliable motor touring was increasingly popular. Kerbside petrol pumps appeared in the early 1920s and later in the decade there were drive-in service stations.

The road authorities recognised the needs of motoring tourists and set out to satisfy them, even with limited resources. In 1923 the Victorian Government set up a tourism committee to administer funds allocated for making places of tourism interest more accessible. As a result the Victorian Country Roads Board was able to build tourist roads: the Hall's Gap–Wartook Road between Stawell and Horsham in the Grampians, the Warburton–Narbethong Road and the Lorne–Wye River section of the Great Ocean Road.[11]

However, when the Depression came, governments found it difficult to supply funds for basic road maintenance services, let alone extend the road network. Unemployed men were given jobs road-building, but overall there was not a lot of progress made.

> Governments, both Commonwealth and State, allowed the road network to stagnate or even regress during the 1930s and 1940s ...
> (W. K. Anderson, *Roads for the People*, 1994)[12]

Cars **101**

Although Australian car-builders such as Holden's in Adelaide had adopted Henry Ford's production line, a large number of cars were still custom-built. The customer selected the chassis (usually made overseas), then went to a bespoke coach-builder who offered a section of stock designs from which one was chosen and altered to suit the individuality of the buyer.

> It was a terribly expensive way of indulging in the pleasures of motoring, but it made for some interesting car designs.
> (M. Williams, *Australia: We Remember the Twenties and Thirties*, 1988)[13]

Most motoring organisations formally established touring departments in the 1920s, but a number of services besides the supply of maps were already in place; for instance, providing advice on accommodation. In 1917 the Royal Automobile Association of South Australia and the Commercial Travellers' Association had agreed on a method to identify 'the best hotels to accommodate members in country towns'. In the 1920s the RACV's list of 'approved hotels' became known as the Hotel and Guest House Guide.

The Royal Automobile Club of Queensland put its first patrols on the road in 1924:

> They are mounted on motorcycles and wear distinctive uniforms. Each one carries in his side car a good kit of tools and some of the more essential spares, also a fire extinguisher and medical first aid material. The service is one of mechanical first aid for emergency conditions and not for major repairs, which should be done in a workshop. The service is absolutely free, except that motorists are expected to pay for any spare parts which the patrols may supply.[14]

Guidance was still a concern in 1920 when the National Roads Association was formed in New South Wales.[15] One of its first services was to provide guides to help motorists visiting Sydney find their way about the city.

In November 1921 the Royal Automobile Club of Victoria organised its first 1000-mile Alpine Reliability Contest, which took six days and crossed alpine country from Omeo to Tallangatta. It became an annual event and in 1926 Mount Kosciusko was included on the route. By that time hundreds of motorists were passing over the alpine highway each summer.[16]

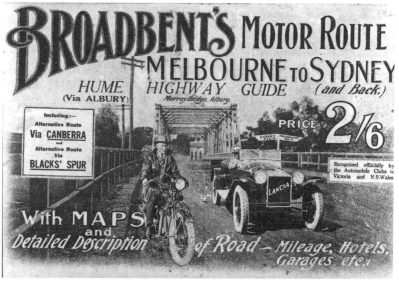

Car travel in the 1920s (Source: RACV Heritage Collection)

Top: the excitement of motor sport: the dust flies as a car takes a turn on a Mount Buffalo hill climb about 1923. Bottom: the cover of the 1920 Broadbent's guide for motorists travelling between Melbourne and Sydney conveys much about road travel at this time.

The Whippet that became a Greyhound (Source: Russell Penfold)

This photograph was taken in Russell Penfold's Brisbane garden in 1998. It was with a similar Whippet that Penfold's father, A. R. Penfold, started a passenger service between Toowoomba and Brisbane in 1928, a business that grew after the war into one of Australia's best-known coach companies. In 1951 the elder Penfold was deciding on a company name. He had heard of the Greyhound company in America. A greyhound could be thought of as a large whippet, and so Greyhound Coaches was born. The name lives on in Australia's biggest express company, Greyhound Pioneer Australia. Three Whippets were used in the Penfold passenger business but this is not one of them. Remembered in the family as 'Mother's car', it was restored in the early 1980s and used to promote Greyhound. After the picture was taken, the car was bought by Greyhound Pioneer Australia. The chassis for Whippet cars came from the United States and the vehicles were put together by the Holden Assembly Company in Adelaide.

However, despite all this motoring activity and the obvious increase in the number of cars between the wars, they were still too expensive for most people; by 1939 only one family in four had a car.[17]

Motor coaches go touring

By the end of the war there were coach excursions between Melbourne and Sydney. Despite the surfaces motor vehicles travelled on, the spirit

104 of road adventure was all over Australia. The State Library of South Australia has a photograph of a Studebaker articulated bus of the 1930s which carried passengers not only between Adelaide and Sydney but also between Adelaide and Central Australia.

Among the pioneers of coach touring whose legacies endure were A. A. Withers, a farmer, A. R. Penfold, a ticket-writer and window-dresser, and R. M. Ansett, at one time a sewing-machine mechanic. In 1905 Withers used a solid-tyred charabanc to start a one-vehicle passenger service that later became Pioneer Tourist Coaches. Penfold began a car passenger service in Queensland in 1928 which was to become Greyhound Coaches. Ansett, who started a passenger-carrying business in Victoria in 1931, began his operations between Ballarat and Maryborough with a seven-passenger used Studebaker car he had bought for 70 pounds.

The name 'Pioneer' has a special place in the history of coach touring in Australia. Albert Arthur Withers had first entered the road passenger business with horse-drawn vehicles at about the turn of the century. His business progressed in fits and starts. His first motor coach service did not last long because the vehicle he used did not belong to him and its owners wanted it for some other purpose. But within a year or two he had acquired four Milnes Daimlers and then, in 1913, several new 30-passenger vehicles which were painted white and known as Withers White Charabancs. With one of them, a Saurer, he ran the first Melbourne–Sydney–Melbourne tour in 1916. After his sons had returned from the war and three of them had rejoined the company, he bought new vehicles and renamed it the Pioneer Motor Company.

The company lived up to its name of 'Pioneer', especially after it introduced vehicles with pneumatic tyres in 1919. Among its first tour offerings was an eight-day tour from Melbourne to Mount Kosciusko. In 1922 Percy Withers, Albert's son, conducted a tour with 12 people over the Australian Alps as an extension of a tour from Melbourne to the Gippsland Lakes, then to Mount Hotham via Omeo, returning by way of Bright. In that year the company was renamed Pioneer Tourist Coaches Pty Ltd. A. A. Withers died in 1929.

In 1935 Bill Caffey, who had been working for the company for two years, took 12 tourists on a 14-week tour around Australia, clockwise from Melbourne, in a Reo coach accompanied by a Reo truck. The party camped out for some 80 days and had to rely on compass navigation where there were no roads and on government bores for water. Their vehicles wore out two sets of tyres.

By 1938 Pioneer Tourist Coaches was a major tour operator, with a **105** range of itineraries throughout Victoria, South Australia, New South Wales and Queensland.[18]

Penfold's Queensland services

Penfold, who lived in Toowoomba, saw his opportunity to get into the road passenger business during a rail strike in 1928. He owned a 1927 Whippet car and he advertised for passengers who wanted to go to Brisbane. When the strike was over he had done well enough out of the passenger service to give up window-dressing for good. He acquired service cars to increase his capacity on the Toowoomba–Brisbane run, later increased his route structure from Brisbane and even acquired a de Havilland DH-84 Dragon to start South Queensland Airways.[19]

Ansett, a pilot, was also to divide his interests between air and road passenger services. His first operations on the Maryborough–Ballarat route with his Studebaker car lost him money, so in December 1931 he moved to Hamilton and began running the car on the 180-kilometre route to Ballarat. In 1936 the Victorian government put him out of business because he was seen as a threat to the government-owned railway system. Ansett took to the air, carrying passengers between Hamilton and Melbourne in a single-engine plane. But he did not turn his back on road passenger travel. He took over Pioneer in 1944.[20]

In the air

Aviation was very exciting in Australia during this period, but it took some time after the war before planes provided a passenger service of importance. There were other things to do with war-surplus aircraft in the meantime. Some of the eager young pilots who had been trained in the war set out to prove that aeroplanes could conquer one of Australia's greatest handicaps—distance. The first were brothers Ross and Keith Smith, who flew a Vickers Vimy bomber from England to Australia in 1919 to win a race sponsored by the Australian government.

Perhaps the greatest Australian aviation pioneer of the time was Charles Kingsford-Smith, who with C. T. P. Ulm, another pilot, flew around Australia in 1926 in 10 days 5 hours: half the previous record. Kingsford-Smith, who was later knighted, and Ulm are best remembered for their flight across the Pacific from Oakland, California to Brisbane in 1928 in a Fokker Tri-Motor plane called the *Southern Cross*.

106   Kingsford-Smith was one of the first pilots for Western Australian Airways, which was founded by Norman Brearley (later Sir Norman), a highly-decorated veteran of the Australian Flying Corps, in 1921. Australian airline development followed the American pattern: the first services were paid for by mail contracts, not passengers, and the idea was to complement the State-owned railway systems, not to compete with them. The route first operated by Western Australian Airlines was between Geraldton and Derby.

Kingsford-Smith and Ulm founded their own airline, Australian National Airways, in 1928 but the company failed three years later during the Depression. The dismal financial environment was one of the reasons for the failure, but a contributing factor was the loss of one of the company's Avro Ten three-engine airliners, the *Southern Cloud*, with two pilots and six passengers aboard. It disappeared on its way from Sydney to Melbourne in March 1931. The aircraft wreckage was not found until October 1958 in the Toolong Range in the Snowy Mountains near Cabramurra, New South Wales.[21]

The founding of Qantas

Western Australian Airways was one of the first two Australian airlines to be given a mail contract. The other, which began operations in Queensland in November 1922 from a base at Longreach, had been formally established two years earlier by two former Air Force pilots, W. Hudson Fysh and Paul McGinness, with a wealthy grazier, Fergus McMaster, as chairman. It was called Queensland and Northern Territory Aerial Services Limited, but quickly became known by its acronym Q.A.N.T.A.S. The airline's first route was from Charleville to Cloncurry via Longreach and a number of other intermediate stops.

In those days, passengers were taken aloft frequently on joy flights and sometimes on charters. Scheduled flights were for carrying mail. Passengers were carried only if there was room for them and then they sat in an open cockpit wearing a helmet and goggles. For some the excitement must have outweighed the discomfort; in any case it could not have been too bad, because the first passenger carried by Q.A.N.T.A.S. (it was not known as 'Qantas' until some years later) was 84 years old. He was Alexander Kennedy, an outback pioneer who had agreed to subscribe some money and join the provisional board of the airline, provided he got passenger ticket number one. His flight was on the Longreach–Winton–McKinlay–Cloncurry section of the inaugural mail service from Charleville to Cloncurry. In 1924 a four-passenger DH-50 with an enclosed cabin was introduced on the Charleville–

Cloncurry run.[22] But mail was still the important cargo; in 1925 only **107** 3663 paying passengers were carried by Australian airlines.

Five years later the number of passengers had risen to more than 90 000, but flying in Australia was still often an ordeal and was to remain so for some years. A variety of small planes, both biplanes and monoplanes, carried passengers. Many were built of wood and fabric, though a few had metal structures. Without pressurised cabins, they flew low and the passengers were often severely shaken by turbulence.

A change came after the second and more enduring Australian National Airways—remembered as ANA—came into being in 1936 as a result of a merger between Holyman Airways and Adelaide Airways. Shareholders included the Orient Line and the Adelaide Steamship Company, of which Adelaide Airways had been a subsidiary. A month before the merger Adelaide Airways had taken control of West Australian Airways. ('Western' became 'West' in 1927.) ANA was the largest airline in Australia with routes that included Sydney–Melbourne and Melbourne–Tasmania and extended across the country to Perth. There were also routes out of Adelaide to Broken Hill, Port Lincoln and Kangaroo Island. The new airline quickly introduced the latest aircraft on its services—DC-2s in its first year and DC-3s in 1938.

Ansett begins with one plane

Another airline began operations in 1936, but on a much smaller scale than that of Australian National Airways. In February of that year, the newly-formed Ansett Airways began a daily service between Hamilton and Melbourne with a six-passenger Fokker Universal. In December its founder, R. M. Ansett, won an air race from Brisbane to Adelaide.

Meanwhile, Qantas had become an international airline and eventually withdrew from flying within Australia. In 1934 it joined with Britain's Imperial Airways to form a new company called Qantas Empire Airways. From April 1935 Qantas began to operate the Brisbane-to-Singapore sector of the Australia–England route using four-engined DH-86 Express biplanes, which took four days to reach Singapore.

As the route developed the DH-86, which carried ten passengers, became too small for the increased volume of mail that was being carried. In 1938 Qantas began flying the route from Sydney with Short Empire flying boats. Besides the mail, they carried 15 passengers. In addition to their normal seating, the passengers had the use of a smoking cabin and a promenade deck and a steward was on board to prepare meals and drinks. For passengers going all the way after transferring to Imperial Airways at Singapore or Penang, the trip to

Famous planes of the 1930s (Sources: Qantas Airways, Ansett Australia)

Passenger air services became established in Australia in the 1930s. Top: the majestic Short Empire Flying Boats flew between Australia and Britain with Qantas Empire Airways flying the leg between Sydney and Singapore or Penang. The trip took nine days, but the flying boats were roomy and for the privileged few the journey was an adventure experienced in comfort (Qantas). Centre: the Douglas DC-3 brought in a new era of reliable, comfortable passenger service on Australian domestic air routes. The picture shows one of the aircraft introduced by ANA in the second half of the 1930s (Ansett Australia). Bottom: R. M. Ansett's first airliner, the six-passenger Ford Universal, with which Ansett Airways began service between Hamilton and Melbourne (Ansett Australia).

Britain took nine days, but the flying boats offered some of the luxury **109**
associated with sea travel. Hudson Fysh, managing director of Qantas at
the time, describes the pleasures of flying boat travel:

> Getting up out of his chair a passenger could walk about and, if he
> had been seated in the main cabin, could stroll along to the
> smoking cabin for a smoke, stopping on the way at the prome-
> nade deck with its high handrail and windows at eye level to gaze
> at the world of cloud and sky outside, and the countryside or sea
> slipping away below at a steady 150 mph [240 km/h] if there was
> no wind. On the promenade deck there was also a practical
> usable space where quoits or even golf were played, and child pas-
> sengers could play. There was even a demand for fishing lines at
> refuelling stops, where both passengers and crew members would
> enjoy the relaxation of dropping a line over the side.[23]

In 1938 Qantas had become a partner in a trans-Tasman service which
was called Tasman Empire Airways Limited or TEAL. Union Airways of
New Zealand had 50 per cent of the shares, Qantas 30 per cent and
Imperial Airways 20 per cent. Service had begun in March 1939 with
Short Empire flying boats between Sydney and Auckland. The flights
connected in Auckland with Pan American Clipper flying boat services
to the west coast of the United States.

By this time Qantas' headquarters were in Sydney. It had moved to
Brisbane in 1929 and Qantas Empire Airways was registered in that city,
but because the flying boats terminated in Sydney it was necessary for it
to have its head office there.

Butler's Bat

The first Qantas flights between Singapore and Brisbane had given yet
another pioneer the opportunity to start an airline that would play a
significant part in the development of Australian aviation. In the 1930s
Arthur Butler, a barnstormer and pilot for Australian Aerial Services,
designed a plane that he called the *Butler Bat*. He took the design to
Britain but no-one was interested in it. However, he became famous on
the way home to Australia by making a record-breaking flight in a little
Comper Swift aircraft.

Butler saw his chance to enter the airline business when arrangements were being made to get the mails from England to Sydney after
they arrived in Brisbane on the Qantas plane from Singapore. The
rather tortuous plan was to take them from Brisbane to Charleville by
Qantas aircraft and transship them to another aircraft for carriage
to Cootamundra, where they would be put aboard an express train
for Sydney. Butler Air Transport was the successful tenderer for the

110 Charleville–Cootamundra sector and operated the service with DH-84 Dragon aircraft for four years.

There were many Australian aviation exploits between the wars and the foundation was laid for a viable airline system. There were other hints of the difference the aeroplane would make to Australia's future tourism industry. In this respect the landing of a little Spartan biplane on a salt pan near Ayers Rock (Uluru) by E. J. (Eddie) Connellan in 1938 should not pass unnoticed. After the war Connellan was to make destinations as remote as the Rock and other parts of the Northern Territory accessible to tourists for the first time.

The hospitality sector moves slowly

In the city

There was not a great deal of change in the big-city hotel scene between the wars. Most of the established hotels were expanded and renovated, and their accommodation and their style changed to keep up with the times. A notable exception was the Grand Central in Adelaide, which had its moment of glory in 1920 when the Prince of Wales was a guest and then in 1926 was turned into a Foy and Gibson department store.

Some new hotels were built. The Hotel Manly in Sydney was erected in the 1920s and a 10-storey tower block was added in 1934. In Perth, the Adelphi was opened in St George's Terrace in 1936 and would play a leading role in the city's social life for more than 30 years.

Two new hotels of note in Melbourne were the Hotel Alexander, lavishly built by James Richardson who had the biggest hotel business in Australia, and the Chevron in St Kilda Road. Richardson intended the Alexander to be the finest and most modern hotel in the country. An unusual feature for 1928 (the year it was opened) was that every bedroom had its own bathroom.[24] The Chevron, which was unlicensed, was built in two stages, the first in 1934 and the second in 1939.

Melbourne's Grand Hotel changed its name. It was renovated in the 1920s and could then accommodate around 300 guests in suites and bedrooms, with room for another 75 above the adjoining Old White Hart hotel. Every suite and double bedroom had its own bathroom. In 1923 the hotel, which had had the Prince of Wales to lunch during his 1920 visit, was renamed the Windsor.[25]

A six-storey extension was added to Menzies in 1922. This enabled the reconstruction of the ballroom, which as a dining-room could seat 500. Three more floors were added to the Australia in Sydney in 1921 and a new wing opening on to Martin Place was completed in 1936. The extension accommodated a new Wintergarden, a banquet hall and **111** buffet, three private dining-rooms and six floors of residential suites and bedrooms all overlooking Martin Place. The hotel then had nearly 500 rooms and suites, most with private bathrooms, and a frontage on three sides—Castlereagh Street, Rowe Street and Martin Place, Sydney's 'Golden Gully'.[26]

In the country
In the 1930s country hotels were much the same as they had been for decades; in fact, most of them had been built in the 1880s or 1890s. They could be freezing cold in winter away from public room fires— usually there was no room heating—and the closest thing to 'private facilities' was a wash stand with a jug and basin. The bathroom and toilet were a walk down a corridor or outside, and often difficult to find in the dark.

> The bed was made of iron, and there was linoleum on the floor but if one was lucky there was a small square of tired carpet by the bed … There was a wardrobe with a mirror on the door and with a bit of luck that wardrobe would contain a few shelves where you could put your clothes. It was the custom to line the shelves with newspaper. (K. Dunstan, *Flag: The First 30 Years*, 1991)[27]

As a sign of things to come, a camping ground was opened at Woodend in Victoria in 1924 to cater for the travelling motorist. More were being laid out in other areas. By 1936 there were 460 camping grounds in Australia. At the Melbourne Motor Show that year eleven different makes of caravans were on display and caravan parks were being built around the country.

To further their tourism interests the Victorian Railways invested in accommodation, buying the Mount Buffalo Chalet, 340 kilometres from Melbourne, in 1924 and the Bungalow on nearby Mount Feathertop in 1928 and assuming the tenancy of the Hotham Heights hostel on Mount Hotham in 1932.[28] The department ran its own motor coaches to and from the resorts to connect with train services.

Elston becomes Surfers Paradise
The Chairman of Commisssioners of the Victorian Railways, Sir Harold Clapp, also influenced tourism in Queensland.

In 1923 a 61-year-old Englishman called James Cavill went to live at a sparsely-populated beach area called Elston, south of Brisbane. Two years later, he built the 16-room Surfers Paradise Hotel.

112   The name 'Surfers Paradise' had been in use since 1917 when two developers had called their subdivision 'Surfer's Paradise Estate'.[29] The name was not instantly popular, but after he had built and named his hotel Cavill came to think the whole area should be called 'Surfer's Paradise'. The local Progress Association thought so, too, and in 1933 'Surfers Paradise' was officially recognised as the postal address instead of 'Elston'.

In 1936 Cavill's hotel was burned down. Downhearted, he was undecided about whether or not he should rebuild. Sir Harold Clapp, who was visiting Surfers Paradise at the time, told Cavill that if he did build a first-class hotel he (Clapp) would

> ... make a package deal with the NSW Railways to carry our Victorian Railway employees free, if they should want to travel here for their annual holidays. We will take them to Albury by our trains, the NSW trains can take them from the border to Murwillumbah, and a bus will bring them to your Surfers Paradise Hotel.

With this assurance, Cavill decided to build another, bigger hotel.[30]

In Australian resorts generally there were few hotels. Guest houses were the more usual form of accommodation for families and others who did not have holiday houses or did not camp or have a caravan. In the Blue Mountains, Katoomba was known as the 'guest house capital',[31] while at St Kilda, the Melbourne beach suburb, holidaymakers had no fewer than 319 guest houses to choose from.[32]

Women and hotels

In the lounge of Melbourne's Windsor Hotel in the 1920s, waitresses wore long black dresses and starched white aprons. They were not permitted to go into the smoking-room where men drank hard liquor, nor did they go into the public bar to collect drink orders. The only liquor they served were cocktails and they picked these up at the still-room servery counter. They did not work in the dining-room unless not enough waiters had shown up for a meal service. Ten shillings was deducted from their pay for meals.[33]

In Adelaide, the Women's Christian Temperance Union continued to campaign to close hotels at noon on Saturdays. A correspondent to the *Register* of 11 August 1925 wrote:

> The Premier told the Rev. D. C. Harris he would not close the hotels at noon on Saturdays, as requested by the reverend gentleman and his party. The Premier did quite right, and voiced the

opinion of a large majority of the State. There are hundreds of **113** men who all the week take no stimulants until they have ended their week's work. They go home, clean, have their dinner, then retire to have a glass or two of beer ... The W.C.T.U. ought to be satisfied. They have 6 o'clock closing, and all have settled down to it. Why bring the matter up again?[34]

However, the W.C.T.U. was not satisfied. It was just as zealous 20 years later. At its annual convention in 1945 there were reports by 'lounge combers', temperance women who went in pairs on 'authorised visits' to hotels and found 'demoralising scenes'. The convention sought the abolition of hotel lounges and drink waitresses.[35]

Eating out

Dining out during these years was a tortuous business for most people compared with today because of the liquor laws. People wanting to have an alcoholic drink had to begin their meal before 6 p.m. Not surprisingly, there was not much choice of sophisticated restaurants. The leading hotels had excellent dining-rooms, of course, but otherwise there was mostly a variety of café-style restaurants.

> These establishments specialised in meals of the steak-and-vegetables variety with Worcestershire sauce and white bread on the table. A cup of tea was normally complimentary with the meal. Cafe-cum-restaurants varied in quality from rough-and-ready establishments to the more refined eateries where some modicumof service could be obtained for a higher charge. (M. Williams, *Australia: We Remember the Twenties and Thirties*, 1988)[36]

Some were fashionable. In Sydney, the place to eat—and be seen—for middle-class women became the Grand Restaurant in the David Jones department store on the corner of Elizabeth and Market Streets after it was completed in 1928. It had individual tables instead of booths, crisp white linen, silverware and uniformed waitresses. At certain times, a small orchestra played.

When one stayed in the average hotel, dining was an average experience, though according to Keith Dunstan breakfast was surprisingly good:

> Dinner, of course was appalling, a deadly roast meal over-cooked. It was served at the nursery hour of 6.30 and if you did not get there by 7.30 p.m. it was 'off'. Yet breakfast, curiously enough,

114   almost everywhere was excellent. It was served in the dining room, white linen, silver toast racks, silver teapot, bacon with splendid country eggs. At some hotels, particularly in the north, breakfast was served with everyone sitting round the one large table. There was no menu and the subtle approach of the waitress was often interesting, particularly to overseas guests. Len Evans, famous vigneron from the Hunter, recalls one country hotel, where the waitress came into the breakfast room, glared at all the guests and shouted: 'O.K. 'Ands up oos for porridge.'[37]

Overall, this picture of staying and eating away from home is not attractive by today's standards, except for the traveller who could afford to stay at the very best hotels. However, expectations were different, and no doubt Australians still found much to enjoy from the hospitality industry of that time. And there were people of enterprise like James Cavill, James Richardson and Sir Harold Clapp who were intent on making the next era of hospitality a better one.

ENDNOTES

[1] Taylor, C., op.cit., p. 45.

[2] Vamplew & McLean, op.cit., p. 168.

[3] John Evans (South Australian Tourism Commission), interview, May 1998.

[4] Sir Harold Clapp, chairman of Commissioners of the Victorian Railways, also urged a national policy for travel and tourism promotion. He was familiar with the methods used by American railways to promote resorts and initiated similar methods in Victoria. See Piesse, R. D. (1966), 'Travel and tourism', in *Yearbook Australia 1966*, Canberra, p. 1160.

[5] Brooke, S. (1984), *Railways in Australia*, Dreamweaver Books, Sydney, p. 157.

[6] Brimson, S. (1988), *The History of Australia's Airlines*, PR Books, Sydney, first published as *Flying the Royal Mail* in 1984 by Dreamweaver Books, Sydney, p. 15.

[7] Pemberton, op.cit., p. 146.

[8] ibid, p. 149.

[9] ibid., p. 127.

[10] Gilltrap & Gilltrap, op.cit., pp. 119, 137 & 151.

[11] Anderson, W. K. (1994), op.cit., p. 60.

[12] ibid., p. 88.

[13] Williams, M. (1988), *Australia: We Remember the Twenties and Thirties*, PR Books, Sydney, p. 49.

[14] RACQ annual report, 1925. Information on the early activities of motoring organisations was supplied by the organisations in the form of annual reports, other printed material and unpublished notes.

[15] In New South Wales, the name was changed to National Roads and Motorists Association (NRMA) in 1923.

[16] Davina Gibb, curator, RACV in a fax dated 20 August 1998.

[17] Spearritt (1987c), p. 119.

[18] Maddock, J. (1992), *The People Movers: A History of Victoria's Private Bus Industry 1910–1912*, Kangaroo Press, Kenthurst, NSW, pp. 142–3. Bill Caffey later held managerial positions in Ansett Pioneer.

[19] The aircraft was taken over during the war by the government, ending Penfold's airline venture. (Interview with Russell Penfold, son of A. R. Penfold, February 1998).

[20] Maddock, op.cit., p. 97 for Ansett's beginnings. Later Ansett, Pioneer and Greyhound activities are related in the next chapter.

[21] The airline suspended operations in June 1931, but late that year it was given approval to fly a Christmas airmail, Australia–England–Australia. This gave Kingsford-Smith and Ulm a last chance to keep the airline together. In terms of that goal, this final desperate venture failed. The plane, carrying more than 50 000 items of mail, the Avro Ten Airliner *Southern Sun* piloted by G. U. Allen, crashed taking off at Alor Star, Malaya. Kingsford-Smith flew there from Darwin in another Avro Ten, *Southern Star*, picked up the mail and flew it to England, arriving on 16 December, in time for a delivery before Christmas. He made the return journey on 7–19 January, completing the first all-Australian airmail flight to and from England, but it was the last venture in which he and Ulm were associated. Kingsford-Smith was knighted in 1932. He presented the *Southern Cross* to the nation in July 1935. In November of that year he and T. J. Pethysbridge disappeared in the *Lady Southern Cross* near Aye Island, off the coast of Burma (Isaacs, op.cit., pp. 331 & 334).

[22] In 1926 Qantas began building the British-designed aircraft under licence. The Qantas-built version was designated the DH-50A.

[23] Cottee, M. (1995), ed., *Beyond the Dawn: A Brief History of Qantas Airways*, Qantas Public Affairs, Sydney, p. 12. Quoted is Hudson Fysh (later Sir Hudson), at the time managing director of Qantas.

[24] Now the Savoy Park Plaza. It was bought by the Nauru Royalties Trust in 1987, refurbished at a cost of $54 million, and reopened in 1991 as a modern 162-room four-star hotel.

[25] The Prince of Wales had been guest of honour at a luncheon given by the Returned Soldiers and Sailors Imperial League of Australia in the hotel in June 1920. Spicer suggests the new name may have been chosen to remind customers of this association with the royal family, or as the management put it: 'The very name of Windsor is inspiring, as it brings to mind the great ancient castle where English royalty have for centuries sought peace and comfort. Just as Windsor Castle is characteristic of the English race, so does the Hotel Windsor typify the dignity of the city of Melbourne' (*Hotel Windsor*, Melbourne: Speciality Press, c. 1924, cited in Spicer, 1993, op.cit., p. 43).

[26] Rühen, op.cit., p. 31.

[27] Dunstan, op.cit., p. 10.

[28] The Mount Feathertop and Mount Hotham buildings were destroyed by bushfires in 1939. The Hotham hostel was partially rebuilt in the same year and sold in 1952 to the Ski Club of Victoria.

[29] McRobbie, op.cit., p. 32. One of the developers was a Brisbane surveyor, Thor Jensen, who was working in the area when he heard a friend say, 'You know, this place is a real surfer's paradise!' This gave him the inspiration for naming the subdivision.

[30] Vader, J. & Lang, F. (1980), *The Gold Coast Book*, Jacaranda Press, Brisbane, p. 57.

[31] Spearritt (1978), op.cit., p. 6

[32] Longmire, A. (1989), *St Kilda: The Show Goes On: The History of St Kilda*, v. III, 1930–38, Hudson Publishing, Melbourne, p. 2.

[33] Spicer, op.cit., p. 47.

[34] Whitelock, op.cit., p. 118.

[35] ibid., p. 118.

[36] Williams, op.cit., p. 76.

[37] Dunstan, op.cit., p. 12. Dunstan was writing of what he called the pre-motel period and the Evans incident probably took place after the Second World War. The pre-motel period, of course, included the years between the wars and the incident described is illustrative of that time as well as the 1940s and 1950s.

Attracting tourists at home and abroad

Beaches, mountains, movies and dancing

For recreation most Australians kept on doing what they had done before the war, but there were a few changes. For holidays, particularly in the summer, they went to the beaches and the mountains as usual. Some went touring by car. However, though this was a significantly new way of spending leisure time, their numbers were still comparatively few. Some holidaymakers took package deals that combined rail connections with river trips on the Murray River steamboats *Gem, Marion* and *Ruby*.

In the cities, there were attractions and events that drew people into them and also entertained their residents. The newest form of entertainment was motion pictures. Making silent films was not expensive and an Australian industry flourished in the 1920s. The demand for these films, as well as for pictures from Hollywood and Britain, was such that spectacular theatres were built for them. Sydney had the Colonial Theatre, which included a child-minding service and an amusement arcade; the Prince Edward Theatre, which had an impressive foyer adorned with numerous vases of fresh flowers; the Capitol, which was designed like a Roman garden with vine-covered walls, pergolas and statues of gods and goddesses; and the State Theatre, 'the great temple of picture-going'.[1]

Among the theatres in Melbourne were the Capitol, designed by American architect Walter Burley Griffin, creator of the national capital

The river boat Marion *(Source: Department of Infrastructure, Victoria)*

The excursion boat Marion *on the Murray River in the 1930s. Packages including rail travel and a trip on the* Marion *or some other river steamer were among the holiday options of the time.*

Canberra; the Regent, where an orchestra played during intermission; and the State, which looked something like an ornate Gothic cathedral. Other cities also were given lavish film palaces: the Winter Garden and Regent in Brisbane, the Ambassadors in Perth and the Regent in Adelaide.

Country people came to town to see these extraordinary theatres and the latest films, but they were also able to see movies closer to home. The early 1920s were the years of the 'picture show men' who travelled around the country and set up each night in a small town, often in the town hall or the showground, and screened a selection of films before moving on. However, their era was a short one. By the end of the decade permanent theatres had been built or converted from existing buildings in all but the smallest population centres and the travelling shows had just about finished.

Royal visits attracted patriotic displays and huge crowds of locals and visitors. The Prince of Wales (later King Edward VIII) toured the country in 1920 and the Duke of York (later King George VI) opened the new Parliament House in Canberra in the course of a tour in 1927.

The opening of the Sydney Harbour Bridge and its consequences

On 19 March 1932 the Sydney Harbour Bridge was opened; it immediately began to change the patterns of people's lives. Whether or not anyone realised it then, this was an event of great tourism significance. In later years the bridge was to become a symbol of Australia that would be used in a great deal of overseas promotion.[2]

One unexpected stimulus to local tourism was the sudden redundancy of some of Sydney's newest and biggest ferries. As a result two of them, the *Koompartoo* and the *Kuttabul*, were modified for excursion work and were so successful that two laid-up vehicular ferries, the *Koondooloo* and the *Kalang*, were converted into showboats.[3] Their services were promoted vigorously to tourists. For example, Sydney Ferries Ltd created a Freedom of Sydney Harbour Pass, which for five shillings (50 cents) permitted tourists to travel to Manly return and to the Taronga Park Zoo return (zoo admission included), to take one showboat cruise and to travel as many times as they liked on the company's ferries for seven days.

Ferry companies also promoted the harbourside resorts that flourished in the inter-war years. Clifton Gardens was one example but the biggest was Manly, which in 1926 had reconstructed baths complete with grandstands and by 1933 could advertise 'the BIG POOL, the largest enclosed bathing area in the world'.[4]

Sydney's Luna Park was also by the harbour. A delegation of councillors from the Bondi area had investigated the value of Melbourne's Luna Park in 1932, but when the Sydney park opened in 1935 it was at North Sydney, on the site of a former engineering workshop.[5]

In the 1930s Sydney's surf beaches began to attract many more people and undermined the popularity of some of the harbourside resorts. Coogee had an ocean pier, opened in 1928; Bondi had reconstructed its beach front in the late 1920s and built a Marine Drive. By the late 1930s Bondi was visited by at least five million surf bathers annually and fourteen million passengers travelled there each year by tram or bus.[6]

Dancing and cruising

The 1920s in Australia were not the 'Roaring Twenties' of American legend, but in the aftermath of war there were changes in social attitudes which affected dress and what people thought of as having a good time. Australians did adopt the Charleston and Black Bottom to add to their more traditional dance repertoire; dancing was very popular and the ballrooms and dance-halls were respectable places for young men and women to meet.

120   In Perth, passengers on the Swan River excursion boats danced and sang to a variety of bands, and in the 1920s these ships were making seven trips per day. In the summer of 1920 Perth tourists had a choice of cruising to Fremantle and on to Rottnest Island or to the Dinghy Club races and the Select Summer Dance at the club's ballroom. On most nights there was a 'grand moonlight excursion' for a shilling or a cruise to the Point where the Perth Concert Band played.[7]

One of the features of certain public holidays in Hobart each year were races between the little steamers *Cartela* (194 tons) and *Togo* (151 tons) on the Derwent. They had started the contest in 1913 and went on until 1931, on a course down the Channel and back to Hobart. Each year they gave three hours of excitement to those watching and the vessels were so evenly matched that the race could be won by a few metres. In 1926 they collided and the *Togo* ended up on the rocks of the Hobart Esplanade. It was refloated and raced again the following year.

The extension of the snowfields

During the 1920s and 1930s skiing became much more popular than it had been before the war on both the New South Wales and the Victorian snowfields. Without lifts most skiing was cross-country, but national championships including downhill events were held regularly from 1930. The Australian National Ski Federation (later the Australian Ski Federation) was formed in 1932. Access to the snowfields was still poor but motor vehicles made it easier to get there, at least for part of the way. Bill Murray was one of the first to drive a bus on to Mount Kosciusko, thus beginning a motor coach tradition. In a later era Murray's Australia would be Australia's biggest coach company.[8]

Skiing was more advanced in New South Wales than in Victoria at the beginning of the period between the wars. In 1924 when the Ski Club of Victoria was formed there was little thought of skiing as a sport. What primitive skiing there was in the Victorian Alpine region was centred on the Mount Buffalo Chalet and club members set out first to explore other areas to find suitable skiing terrain.

> In atrocious weather, these pioneers toured and climbed thousands of feet through the snow lugging heavy packs of food and clothing to cattlemen's shelters seldom meant for winter occupancy.
>
> In so doing, they 'discovered' miles of virgin downhill running, recognised the huge skiing potential and then started to open up the mountains. The areas with easiest access (then still very poor) became the focal points for skiing.

By the 1930s people flocked to Donna Buang and the real enthusiasts ventured to Buller and the Bogong High Plains, including Hotham. (J. M. Lloyd, *Skiing into History, 1924–1984,* 1986)[9]

Organising, promoting and selling tourism overseas

Australia looks abroad

The last two States to set up tourist bureaus did so in the 1920s. Western Australia's Tourist and Publicity Bureau began operations in Perth in August 1921 and Queensland followed by creating a Tourist Bureau in 1926. The other State bureaus expanded, interstate offices were established and the Victorian bureau became the biggest travel agency in the country.

The Australian National Travel Association (ANTA) was set up in 1929 to establish offices overseas to promote tourism to Australia.

Although the world depression had hit and the only way to get there was by ship (Qantas was still confined to Queensland), the far-sighted pioneers behind ANTA foresaw the role tourism could play in developing our future. (B. Atkinson, 'A pat on the back for ATC prophets, *Galah Gazette,* June 1993)[10]

The most determined of those pioneers was Charles Holmes, chairman of the Betterment and Publicity Board of the Victorian Railways.

Tall and distinguished and a Military Cross winner from World War I, he travelled Australia by train, tram, car and even camel in the 1920s preaching the potential and virtues of tourism.[11]

His most important audience was the Associated Chambers of Commerce of Australia. In an address to their annual conference in Hobart in February 1928 he pointed out that tourism provided Canada's third largest source of income, averaging the 'astounding figure' of 38 million pounds a year. South Africa's tourism had increased fourfold since it had begun promotion. If one person in 2000 in the English-speaking world could be persuaded to visit Australia, it would give the country additional income of 21 million pounds in five years. And on top of this benefit there would be others:

• Australia would be better known overseas.
• Its export trade would be developed.
• New capital would be brought into the country for investment.

122
- Money that would otherwise not be available would be circulated among all sections.
- Australia would gain more investor-settlers.

Holmes put forward the proposal that an organisation should be created with headquarters in Australia and offices in London and New York. Appealing for guarantees of support for five years, he told the conference that the scheme already had the financial backing of the Australian railways and other business groups as well as the leading residential hotels in Australia. Implementation of the plan would 'go a long way' towards raising the standard of hotel accommodation throughout the country.

The plan was not only to develop traffic to Australia but also to 'handle [visitors] properly when they arrive'. He also advocated the introduction of 'developmental tours' so Australians would be induced to see more of their country, noting that 'the lack of knowledge of the Commonwealth on the part of Australians generally is claimed to be notorious—and no less than 22,000 persons travel overseas each year.'[12]

Offices open overseas

Holmes' persuasion worked. ANTA was formed the next year; he became its chief executive and remained in that post until 1957. The first ANTA overseas manager left by ship in 1929 to establish an office in London. He was followed a few months later by a manager not for New York, as was originally suggested, but for San Francisco. An office was opened in Wellington in 1934 and another in Bombay in 1938, a year in which 33 480 visitors came to Australia from all parts of the world.

These were bold moves. At that time Australia was part of the British Empire and there was very little in the way of official Australian offices abroad—no embassies, trade or immigration bureaus, marketing boards or other representation as there was to be later; only State Agents-General offices and a small High Commission in London. The ANTA office in San Francisco was the first tourism promotion office of any nation on the west coast of the United States and the one in Bombay was the first on the Asian continent.[13] ANTA's initial annual budget was $35 000, of which the Commonwealth Government contributed $4000.[14]

How travel and tourism was sold

The State bureaus were major agents for travel operators and people bought their railway tickets from them as well as tickets for sightseeing and packaged tours. The biggest of them, the Victorian Government Tourist Bureau, was still part of the Railways Department. It had two offices in Melbourne and opened branches in Sydney, Brisbane, Hobart, Adelaide, Perth (part of a combined Eastern States bureau), Mildura, Bendigo, Ballarat and Geelong. It was equipped to make bookings to any part of the world, but its main business was selling travel within Victoria.[15]

There was no independent travel agency system, although there were a handful of agencies set up just to handle travel. One was the Australian Overseas Travel Service in Melbourne, which promoted group travel to Europe for coach tours. Another was Ask Mr Pickwick in Sydney, established by Roland Hill in the Pickwick Club, a genteel luncheon club in the basement of 60 Hunter Street. Thomas Cook had offices in Sydney and Melbourne and was considered a superior organisation because of the breadth of services it offered.

Most travel between towns and cities was by rail or coastal steamer and the State bureaus were the principal agents for the railways and the coastal steamship companies. Travel overseas, except for the very few, was by ship and so shipping agencies were valued by those who wished to sell travel with a bigger price-tag.

Most of the traffic was to Europe and P&O and Orient Line operated the fastest, most reliable and most comfortable passages to Britain via the Suez Canal. Other companies offered slower, less luxurious voyages via the Cape of Good Hope. Burns, Philp & Co. vessels sailed from Sydney to the Pacific islands and its services to Singapore, Hong Kong and Darwin began in Melbourne. The Matson Line ran a service between Sydney and San Francisco.

Stock agents like Elder Smith, Dalgety's and Goldsbrough Mort arranged overseas travel as a service to their clients. Shipping companies were their customers because of the wool shipments overseas and so the stock agents became passenger agents for those companies with which they did business. Elder Smith were P&O agents in Adelaide, John Sanderson and Co. in Melbourne were agents for the Blue Funnel Line and Dalgety's in Melbourne were Matson Line agents. The stock agents regarded this activity more as a service to their clients than as a serious part of their business; the shipping companies would give them commissions on passenger travel, which they often passed on to their better customers as a discount.

Banks and other organisations

The banks also organised travel for clients but did not receive commissions from the shipping companies. The English, Scottish and Australia

124 Bank (E.S. & A.) had begun to handle travel arrangements for its clients as early as 1904, when it made rail and accommodation bookings for a Western District (Victoria) farmer going to Bradford in England to sell his wool clip. It then decided to offer a travel service to other customers through its correspondence department. In 1934 there was enough travel business for the bank to make travel arranging the sole job of one of its staff, Jack Murrowood, who was perhaps the best known of those in bank travel in its early days.[16] The Bank of New South Wales (later Westpac) began operating in travel in 1934 and the National Bank set up a travel department in 1937.

Burns, Philp & Co., the biggest company in Australia at the time in terms of capitalisation, was not only a ship-owner but was also an agent for other lines, such as P&O. Stewart Moffat, who became one of the most prominent travel agents in Australia after the Second World War, joined Burns, Philp's passenger department in Melbourne in 1933. The department's main task was issuing tickets for the company's extensive services. The staff of six in the Melbourne passenger department were not always busy and in slack times Moffat was seconded to the freight department.

Airline business—on a small scale

Moffat was sent to London for six or seven months in 1935 to learn something of the travel agency business at Dean and Dawson, an agency owned by the London and Northeastern Railway. Burns, Philp's passenger department's activities in Melbourne were less comprehensive than those of a full travel agency. For people going to London, for instance, the department would give them a letter to the Burns, Philp office there rather than attempting to make arrangements itself.

Few people had need of an agent's services because few people travelled long distances. Shipping companies were the most powerful businesses in travel and tourism, as were the airlines in a later period. But although almost all overseas travel was by ship there were only 237 540 temporary departures in the years between 1926 and 1938—an average of fewer than 20 000 a year.[17]

Moffat became the Qantas 'traffic representative' in Melbourne in 1938 with a staff of one. Melbourne supplied more passengers than any other Qantas office, but he had plenty of time to pursue other duties, like procuring spare parts. The reason was that the through seat allocation for Australian-originating passengers was only two per flight on those glamorous flying boats, which left from Rose Bay. The aircraft went to Singapore, and later Penang, to connect with the Imperial Airways flights to Southampton.[18]

Domestic aviation was also small-time business. In 1937 Moffat had worked as a salesman for Ansett Airways, which had not long before taken delivery of three ten-passenger Lockheed Lodestar aircraft. In an unusual exercise in scheduling, the aircraft served three destinations from three markets. One flew from Sydney, another from Melbourne and the third from Adelaide and they all went to Narrandera, where passengers changed to catch flights to the cities the planes had come from. Ansett's original aeroplane, a Fokker Universal, was the airline's reserve aircraft. An Airspeed Envoy, which could carry six passengers, had replaced it on the original Melbourne–Hamilton route.

There was a problem in getting enough passengers; sometimes the planes left with only two or three. Moffat was asked to leave after four months because there was not enough business to justify his employment. Nevertheless, that brief period had historical significance: Moffat was the first airline salesman in Australia.

The shape of things to come in Australian tourism could be seen in the promotion of Australia overseas and the foundation of a sales system at home. Most of these endeavours passed by the average citizen, whose holidays were taken in the traditional way at the beaches and in the mountains. Considering what was to come after the Second World War, the beginnings of an airline sales operation were intriguingly tentative, but nevertheless it was a recognisable thread in the fabric of the modern era of tourism.

ENDNOTES

[1] Williams, op.cit., p. 79.

[2] Among other promotional uses, the Harbour Bridge was usually the icon representing Australia in the early multi-destination tour programs from overseas markets after the Second World War. Later the Opera House was used for this purpose.

[3] After the Second World War, the *Kalang* was rebuilt to accommodate a dance floor of tallow wood. It could carry 1925 passengers and a crew of 25, including catering staff. The vessel ran morning and afternoon cruises on Wednesdays. In 1960 it was renamed the *Sydney Queen* and ran dance and strip shows. It was laid up in 1963.

[4] Spearritt (1978), op.cit., p. 237.

[5] Longmire, op.cit., p. 3; Spearritt (1978), op.cit., p. 233.

[6] Spearritt (1978), op.cit., p. 239.

[7] Pemberton, op.cit., p. 97.

[8] Bill Murray later had his own company, which his son Ron bought after the Second World War. Ron Murray built his company into the biggest coach company in Australia. See Chapter 10.

[9] Lloyd, op.cit., p. xi.

[10] Atkinson, B. (1993), 'A pat on the back for ATC prophets', *Galah Gazette*, June. The *Galah Gazette* is a journal circulated to former ATC staff members.

126

[11] ibid.

[12] Holmes' speech 'Advertising Australia' was printed by the Associated Chambers and circulated to members throughout the country. A copy is the source used here.

[13] Many British people stationed in India visited Australia during their summer break instead of going up into the hills to escape the oppressive heat of Calcutta or New Delhi. Others used Australia as a place for their children to study or go to school; the educational opportunities were promoted by ANTA.

[14] Piesse, op.cit., p. 1160. The original budget would have been in pounds, but Piesse uses dollars. Australia converted to decimal currency in 1966, the year Piesse's work was written. At the time of the change, two dollars was equal to one pound.

[15] Harrison, L. J. (1963), *Victorian Railways to '62*, Victorian Railways Publications and Betterment Board, Melbourne, pp. 166–8.

[16] Ken Lee, former ANZ travel manager, interview, March 1998.

[17] White (1987), op.cit., p. 437. The population in 1933, a census year, was 6 629 839.

[18] More seats could be made available by checking with Imperial Airways in Singapore, if there were passengers to fill them. Melbourne was the major passenger office because the service headquarters were in that city and service personnel were freqent users of international air services at that time. Others included journalists and business people. (Stewart Moffat, interview, May 1998).

The era of mass tourism: after 1945

A S THE NATIONS began to put the pieces back after the Second World War, it became obvious that the attitude to travel had changed. The war had internationalised much of the world as well as force-feeding it technological advancements that made it easier and cheaper to travel. The age of the transport aircraft was on its way and was finally given full expression with the arrival of jet airliners. From the late 1950s, the economy and reliability of these planes brought about a huge increase in medium- and long-distance travel. The Boeing 747 of 1970 and the other wide-bodied aircraft that followed it provided fresh impetus.

Domestic travel was dominated by the motor car. Australians, slower than some people overseas to buy cars on a large scale, made up for lost time. The making and care of roads at last became part of the national agenda. Spending increased until governments accepted that billions of dollars were required each year. Motels spread across the country, as did caravan parks and camping grounds. For most people, the family car was the chosen vehicle for taking holidays and exploring the country.

Although shipping and railway interests were at first set back by the quick ascendancy of the plane and the motor vehicle, they recovered

128 with new roles and new vehicles. Increasingly, they added appealing dimensions to modern tourism. Hotels were built around the world, many of them run by international management chains. Famous-name hotel companies came to Australia, but Australian companies also built up their own brands and chains.

Computers and telecommunications enabled the industry to handle the vastly increased numbers of tourists. They also brought about the globalisation of markets and hastened the internationalisation of the larger components of the travel and tourism industry. At the same time as the numbers of people travelling to and from Australia grew to proportions unimaginable at the beginning of the period, the Australian industry became part of a world industry. Its largest company, Qantas Airways, became a member of a global alliance of airlines; its smallest companies could no longer avoid the influences of the world markets.

Tourism becomes a global business

The war's travel legacy

Travel is a large part of the business of modern war. Huge numbers of people are moved across continents and oceans; the means of moving them are constantly expanded and improved. When the Second World War ended, people were far more conscious of the world outside their national boundaries than they had been before. The transportation companies were quickly back in peacetime business and, with the advances in technology that had resulted from the war, everything was better and faster: the ocean liners, the planes, the trains, the coaches and the cars.

It was not long before the travel and tourism business was booming —unevenly of course, as it always has, because whether a nation's people can travel depends on a number of factors, including the strength of its economy, the distribution of its wealth and the amount of leisure time available. Some Americans who before the war could not have afforded to take an overseas holiday were able to do so soon after it ended because of the strength of the US dollar against other currencies. People from some other well-off countries travelled freely too, but there were also nations whose citizens were forbidden to travel abroad for pleasure because of their countries' adverse balance of payments. Currency restrictions limited overseas travel for Australians for several years after the end of the war.[1] British travel allowance restrictions were not removed until 1970.[2]

Nevertheless, there were 25 million tourist arrivals throughout the world in 1950 and international travel would expand in the next 20

130 years at an annual growth rate of 9.9 per cent, which has never been equalled since.[3]

1950 to 1970

The jets take over from the ships

In the 20 years between 1950 and 1970 there were profound changes, which included the end of scheduled trans-oceanic passenger shipping. In the 1950s the luxury liners were more glamorous than ever. P&O's first post-war liner was the 27 955-ton *Himalaya*, which was launched in 1949 for the Australian run. Other notable vessels that became familiar in Australian waters in the post-war period were the *Oriana* and the 45 500-ton *Canberra*, launched in 1960, which could carry 2250 passengers in style.[4]

On the Atlantic, the passage of the American steamship *United States* was followed by millions of newspaper readers and radio listeners around the world as it sped across the Atlantic to take the Blue Riband in July 1952 with an average speed of 35.6 knots. The biggest liner of them all, the 83 673-ton *Queen Elizabeth*, which had been a troop ship during the war, joined the *Queen Mary* on the glamour run for Cunard.

But in the 1960s the liners were being tied up, their usefulness at an end because they could not compete with jet airliners. P&O and the Orient Line, already linked in ownership, merged businesses and names in 1960. The company first used the combined name P&O-Orient Lines, but eventually it was considered too clumsy and 'Orient' was dropped in 1966. The next year, after the Suez Canal was closed, P&O stopped running a scheduled service between Britain and Australia. In the same year, the *Queen Mary* was removed from service after a thousand Atlantic crossings and taken to Long Beach, California to become a tourist attraction and hotel. In 1968 the *Queen Elizabeth* made its last voyage—to Hong Kong, to become a convention centre under its first new owner and a floating university under its next. It was destined to be neither. Instead it caught fire in Hong Kong Harbour and sank.

The jet airliner had changed the way people travelled long distances. Jets brought Australia into closer contact with the rest of the world and made it possible for it to share significantly in international tourism. Coinciding with rising prosperity, increased leisure time in the advanced-economy countries and the development of inclusive tours, the big jets had introduced a new era of tourism. Ocean-going ships were to have a new role, not so much as transportation between ports but as cruise ships, instruments of holiday pleasure.

Much of the travel and tourism world as we know it had already **131**
begun to take shape in the 1960s: well-equipped airlines offering competitive services; improved roads; cheap cars; motels organised into
marketing chains; and international hotels that conformed to recognisable standards in accommodation, food and beverages and service in
many different countries. Disneyland, the enduring model of the
modern theme park, had opened at Anaheim near Los Angeles in 1955.

The Comets

The first jet transport in commercial service was Britain's de Havilland
Comet 1, first flown by the British Overseas Airways Corporation
(BOAC)—now British Airways—in May 1952. The 36- to 44-passenger
Comet, cruising at 788 kilometres per hour, halved the flying time of
other aircraft on any route and did it with unprecedented smoothness,
operating at 'over the weather' altitudes. However, between May 1953
and April 1954 three Comets broke up in the air, victims of the previously unknown fatiguing effect on metal of constantly increasing and
decreasing the pressure as the aircraft climbed and descended. All
Comet 1 aircraft were withdrawn from service, but jet airliners were
made safer as a result of the lessons learned from these accidents.

The Soviet airline Aeroflot introduced the world's second jet airliner,
the TU-104, in 1956. Carrying up to 50 passengers, it was crude and
uneconomic by Western standards, but it was to remain the only jet airliner flying passengers until 1958. In that year, a pair of redesigned and
larger Comets—designated Comet 4s—were the first jets to carry fare-
paying passengers across the Atlantic.[5] But by that time the Boeing 707,
the first in a line of successful Boeing jet airliners, was entering service.
It was with the larger American aircraft, the Boeing 707, which carried up
to 190 passengers, and the Douglas DC-8, which began carrying passengers in 1959, that the new age of tourism began. New aircraft came
from the factories in rapid progression; in the 1960s at least 26 new
types were flown for the first time or entered service.[6]

Qantas was Australia's participant in the international airline expansion. The Commonwealth Government became sole owner of the airline
in 1947, the year that Qantas took delivery of its first Lockheed
Constellation aircraft and began a regular weekly service to London on
the Kangaroo route.

Cars dominate land travel

The motor car's ascendancy in land travel was soon established in the
years after the war. Factories began pouring out motor vehicles, even in
countries ravaged by war. In West Germany, for instance, there were

132   only 2.4 million motor vehicles of all kinds in 1950, but the total had risen to 16.8 million by 1970. In 1950 the Federal Railways had a 37.5 per cent share of West Germany's passenger travel, which was more than either coaches (29.3 per cent) or private cars (33.1 per cent) had. By 1960 the railways' portion had fallen to 15.6 per cent and by 1970 to 7.8 per cent. Elsewhere the figures differed, but the trends were the same.

The travel market was much bigger than it had ever been before, because people were paid more and they had more holidays with pay. Motoring was cheap and so were charter air services; the trains could no longer capture anything like the proportion of travellers they had once carried. However, as time went on, railway executives realised that a small part of the new, much bigger market was worth more than the premium market they had catered for in earlier eras.

The railways adopted new concepts that favoured speed and regularity to appeal to the broader market. The British were the first to introduce the 'Inter-City' concept, which involved running standard-speed trains to a regular-interval timetable between cities and attracting customers with cheap fares when traffic was low. Continental railways followed suit, sometimes using the 'Inter-City' brand without translation. Most traditional restaurant car services were replaced by self-service or buffet cars. As early as 1962 the Wagons-Lits company could see the modern economics of dining cars working against it and persuaded the railways to take over the vehicles while it provided only the catering services—that is, the provisions and staff.

American railways boomed during the war and in the months after it, encouraging some of the companies to invest in new, streamlined trains. But these were soon making heavy losses as passengers switched to air and road transport. As the losses accumulated, mergers and bankruptcies became common. Even the once-great rivals, the New York Central and the Pennsylvania Railroad, merged and then went under.

New-style accommodation

Tourism required new types of accommodation. The most prolific were motels, which spread throughout the United States and other parts of the world, including Australia, with the rapid increase of car travel. At first they averaged about 25 rooms and were small, individually-owned businesses situated in towns along the highways and on the edges of cities and often run by a husband-and-wife team. But they became bigger—some of them had more than 100 rooms—and began to appear in the business districts of cities as well as along the major roads. They also began to be formed into chains carrying a common brand and sharing a common marketing system. In 1945 there were **133** 15 000 motels in the United States; by 1970 there were 61 000. Half of all the motels then existing had been built in the 1950s.[7]

The growing number of airline passengers had to be catered for as well. Chains of hotels offering recognisable standards in different parts of the world were built. The major airlines went into the hotel business.

> The airline knew what the business traveler wanted and built its hotel business on that understanding. Even in the 1960s and '70s, hotels in some countries were far below the standards that US business travelers expected. A Pan Am hotel provided a comfort zone.[8]

There were other benefits in chain operations—in purchasing, promotion, reservations, financing and personnel. And so the number of chains increased, with or without airline participation: in the United States and Canada there were some 200 by the early 1970s[9] and there were others in Europe and Asia.

Innovation by accident

The credit card, an indispensable part of the modern traveller's equipment, arrived on the scene in 1950 because of a mishap in New York. Businessman Frank McNamara was embarrassed because he had left his wallet at home when he was entertaining guests at a restaurant. As a result he and his lawyer, Ralph Schneider, thought of introducing a charge card that could be used at several dozen restaurants. The Diners Club card was issued that year to 200 people, mainly McNamara's friends, and the idea spread rapidly.[10] American Express issued its first credit card in 1958. It was made from purple cardboard.

A chance meeting in 1953 led to collaboration between American Airlines and IBM to produce the first airline computer reservations system. When C. R. Smith, the founder and chief executive of American Airlines, sat next to another man named Smith on a flight from Los Angeles to New York it was natural that he should talk about the difficulty of handling reservations for a huge airline network and his frustration at not finding a solution.

The other man was Blair Smith, an IBM salesman, and the conversation they had started a long process. It was 1962 before the revolutionary computer system came to life in Westchester County, New York. It not only was able to provide an updated list of seats sold and available on each flight, but also included the name of every reservation holder and his or her telephone number, special meal requirements and rental car or hotel reservation information. It was originally called SABER (for

134   Semi-Automatic Business Environmental Research), but the name was changed to Sabre along the way because someone liked the name of the Buick car, LeSabre.[11]

International organisations

The International Union of Travel Organisations (IUOTO), a European-only organisation when it was formed in 1924, had become truly international after the war. One of its first activities was to work on a definition of 'international tourist' with United Nations agencies. The United Nations Statistical Committee established the concept of the 'international visitor' in 1953 and ten years later the United Nations Conference on International Travel and Tourism in Rome recommended acceptance of a definition of the terms 'visitor', 'tourist' and 'excursionist' proposed by IUOTO; these were subsequently accepted by the UN Statistical Committee in 1968. These definitions then formed the basis for the gathering of international statistics. Among the other matters IUOTO addressed was the impact tourism was making on the social and physical environment, acknowledging the need for conservation measures to prevent irreparable damage.

Following the 1963 meeting in Rome an Australian, Basil Atkinson, was elected to a two-year term as IUOTO president. Atkinson, the 39-year-old general manager of the Australian National Travel Association (ANTA), was the first president from the Asia Pacific region. It was the time of the Cold War and East–West rivalries were reflected in IUOTO, as were those of developed and developing countries. Tourism was pursued as a means of overcoming these rivalries.[12]

The idea of making IUOTO an intergovernmental organisation connected to the United Nations had been discussed for some time. During Atkinson's presidency a working group was established to determine how this might be done. The subject was pursued in subsequent years at special meetings of committees and the IUOTO General Assembly.

ANTA was also an enthusiastic member of another international organisation, the Pacific Area Travel Association (PATA), founded in Honolulu in 1952 by Lorrin P. Thurston, publisher of the *Honolulu Advertiser* and William J. Mullahey, South Pacific regional manager for Pan American World Airways. It was later to become the Pacific Asia Travel Association, but at the time of its founding this was not foreseen. Then the primary target market for the destinations represented was the United States. It was natural therefore that, after a couple of years in Hawaii, the headquarters should be moved to San Francisco.[13]

The members of IUOTO were official tourism organisations; ANTA **135** saw that PATA's strength lay in its being non-official. National tourism organisations were influential members, but PATA was primarily driven by commercial interests.[14]

The year of the tourist

The United Nations General Assembly designated 1967 International Tourist Year. It was also the year of a famous cartoon lampooning the kind of tourism then prevailing. This showed an American after he had arrived on a coach somewhere in Europe where there were cathedrals, museums of art and restaurants that served wine with meals. Dressed in straw hat, Hawaiian shirt and Bermuda shorts, camera hanging around his neck, he staggered off the coach in yet another imposing 'grande place' uttering words that became famous: 'If it's Tuesday, this must be Belgium.'[15]

Travel and tourism from 1970

Jumbo jets

By 1970, when the Boeing 747 began to fly for Pan American World Airways, the number of international arrivals had increased by 664 per cent over the 1950 figure to 166 million. By 1996 the number was 594 million.[16]

The 747—the jumbo jet—played a dominant role in this expansion; in fact, no other single vehicle in history has had such an effect on the scale of movement of people. Yet in the beginning it was not expected to have a long life as a passenger jet. It was originally designed for easy conversion to a freighter because supersonic airliners were being developed and it was thought that airlines and passengers would prefer them.[17] But in the event, the few supersonic airliners that came into service have remained an option for only a privileged minority.[18]

The 747, usually seating about 400 people, offered trans-oceanic flight at a new level of comfort and at a price that attracted more and more travellers. By mid-1993, 747s had carried more than 1.4 billion people: equivalent to about one in four people then living. It and the other wide-bodied airliners of the time, such as the Douglas DC-10 and the Lockheed Tristar, consolidated the concept of mass air transportation.

As the years went on and new types of planes were built, the outward appearance of airliners did not change much from that of the first jets in the late 1950s. But inside there were great differences. Progressively,

136   new technologies were added to aeroplanes until they became virtually flying computers. Instead of the big joystick of the old jets, which required the pilot to have real muscles to move it around, the new planes of the 1990s—like the Boeing 777 and the big Airbuses—were operated with a little 'no-load' joystick. This was connected to a computer, which responded not only to the position of the joystick but also to the plane's orientation and speed, the way it was loaded and many other factors. Other computers helped navigate the plane, checked for other aircraft in the flight path and advised if the aircraft was too close to the ground—among other things. The twin-engined 777 was the first plane designed entirely by computer.

Challenges of competition and technology

The airlines were the dominant companies in world travel and tourism; their performance and decisions influenced the very large distribution systems that had grown up, as well as much of the hospitality industry and other sectors. Setbacks to worldwide airline services such as the fuel crisis of the early 1970s had a very severe effect on much of the rest of the industry.

Competition and technology were constantly challenging the management of airlines and bringing continual change in the way they did business. It was obvious in the 1990s that, for major carriers, being big was better. Events were being driven by such forces as an increased recognition of the importance of tourism and moves towards the privatisation of airlines and the liberalisation and deregulation of air routes.[19]

Airlines could no longer rely on technological improvements in aircraft alone to give them increased economies of operation; nor could they rely on government regulations to protect them from competition. The 1980s and 1990s were decades of relentless pursuit of competitive advantage characterised by cost-cutting, innovation and the formation of alliances.

The development of global distribution systems

The most successful airline computer systems had grown into global distribution systems. This helped to create the new kind of world that the airlines and many other travel and tourism businesses had to understand and try to master.

In 1976 airlines made reservations systems available to travel agents in the United States. The next step was the inclusion of other carriers' reservations information. This presented the systems' owners with a powerful marketing tool for their owner airlines, who could arrange the **137** displays to favour themselves at the expense of their competitors. Regulators stepped in to prevent this. The United States Congress outlawed screen bias in 1984 and the European Commission, the European Civil Aviation Conference and the International Civil Aviation Organization introduced similar regulations soon afterwards. The diversification of ownership of reservations systems in the 1980s also helped eliminate bias; by this time consortia of European and Asian airlines were involved as well as American airlines.

The systems became more than airline reservations systems; they had the ability to make reservations for hotels, rent-a-cars, theatres, sporting events and other items of interest to travellers. They were very powerful instruments, not only for the airline business but also for turning the world into a single market for much of its travel and tourism.[20] Four global distribution systems (GDSs) became part of the Australian distribution system—America's Sabre, Galileo (owned by a European consortium of airlines but with links to United's Apollo), Amadeus (another European system) and Abacus (owned by Asian airlines).

The dependence of the industry on this technology was conveyed in 1991 to a Pacific Telecommunications Council seminar:

> From the standpoint of information technology, the travel industry is a globally dispersed set of immense relational databases containing between thirty to forty million airfares, even more passenger name records and arrival and departure times, millions of room-nights, tens of thousands of rental cars, thousands of carriers—all connected by wide area networks that use the most advanced switching and circuits money can buy. The travel industry is the world's largest consumer of telecommunications services and its demand is growing.[21]

Frequent flyer and yield management programs

Computer reservations systems gave the airlines the means to develop powerful new marketing techniques. In the 1980s, American Airlines made use of its Sabre system to develop the frequent flyer loyalty program and yield management—both now standard systems used by airlines throughout the world.

Early in the decade, American Airlines found that about 40 per cent of its business came from five per cent of its customers, the frequent flyers. Any additional passengers were valuable, but incremental frequent flyers were, on average, nearly ten times as valuable. Sabre was

138   reprogrammed to identify them and they were rewarded for their loyalty to the airline with free travel. The method was derived from Green Stamps, the original brand loyalty program of the retailing trade, the difference being that customers accumulated mileage instead of stamps to qualify for a reward.[22]

Other travel and tourism businesses, including hotels and rent-a-car companies, followed the airlines' lead in database marketing and launched frequent-user programs. The first was Holiday Inns in the United States with its Priority Club in 1982. Loyalty programs quickly spread around the world. Many hotel loyalty schemes had an affinity with credit cards and supplied airline frequent flyer points and other rewards such as car rental or cruises.[23]

Yield management, introduced in 1985, was a pricing strategy aimed at maximising revenue by manipulating demand. It required that different categories of passengers should pay different prices for the same seat on an aeroplane. American Airlines used historical data from Sabre to estimate demand from different types of travellers on each of its flights and worked out a price that would sell for each category of passenger. It held back a reserve of seats for full-fare-paying passengers who would be booking close to the day of departure.

This was so successful that it was followed by other airlines, including Ansett Australia and Qantas Airways. Yield management was also introduced into other businesses, including hotels and restaurants.

Code-sharing

Before the domination of computers, airlines in the United States had come up with an idea to eliminate the aversion of passengers to changing airlines when they changed planes on connecting flights. In the passengers' minds a change of airlines increased the chance of missing connections and losing baggage. To get over this, the same two-letter airline designator code was used for an entire journey, even though two airlines might have been involved. This practice was called code-sharing.

In Europe it was at first considered a subterfuge and banned. But as code-sharing added revenue to airlines and so continued to be adopted, the Europeans relented. International requirements were introduced to ensure that passengers knew what was happening to them. In Australia the government made it mandatory that passengers be told, when they were making their booking, which airline would be operating the flight.

In 1998, 19 airlines code-shared on flights into and out of Australia, accounting for six per cent of capacity on international services. Between them Qantas and Ansett had entered into commercial partnerships with **139** 15 carriers, many of which involved code-sharing.[24]

Airline alliances

Among their responses to operating in an increasingly global environment, airlines found that there were enormous marketing advantages in being big. At first they had achieved greater size by mergers and acquisitions, but in the 1990s they turned to alliances. As of October 1997, the so-called Star Alliance was the biggest in terms of revenue and number of aircraft. The airlines involved were United, Lufthansa, SAS, Air Canada and Thai International. Ansett Australia and Air New Zealand joined in 1999. In scale there was not much between the Star Alliance and the Oneworld combination, which brought together the very big carriers American Airlines and British Airways, as well as Qantas Airways, Iberia, Canadian Airlines, Aerolineas Argentinas and Finnair.

Co-operation between airlines extended beyond their alliance partners: in 1998 Qantas offered no fewer than 22 round-the-world fare combinations in conjunction with 25 airlines.[25]

Changes on land and sea

On land and sea there were changes in the ways tourists travelled that were equally as marked as the changes in the air, though not with the same impact on the industry in general.

The liner *United States'* record across the Atlantic was broken in 1990 by a ship of a vastly different kind. This was the world's biggest catamaran at the time, the Hoverspeed *Great Britain*. Built as a cross-Channel ferry in Hobart by Incat Australia, the 74-metre vessel crossed the Atlantic in 3 days, 7 hours and 54 minutes at an average speed of 36.65 knots in June 1990 to take the Hales Trophy, the prize awarded to the holder of the Blue Riband.[26]

The record stood for eight years until two bigger Incat catamarans broke it in successive months. In June 1998 the 91-metre ferry *Catalonia*, on its way to Barcelona, crossed the Atlantic from New York to Tarifa, averaging 38.88 knots. It also became the first commercial vessel to speed more than 1000 nautical miles in a 24-hour period, covering 1015 nautical miles at an average of 42.3 knots. Then in July *Cat-Link V*, another 91-metre wave-piercing catamaran, broke both records. This ship achieved a 41.284-knot average speed crossing the Atlantic and covered 1018.5 nautical miles in a 24-hour period, despite being diverted in a vain search for a crashed single-engine plane.[27]

140   The *Orient Express* made its last journey in 1977, although it was to be reborn in 1982 as a tourist train running between London and Venice, offering old-style luxury for those with the time and money to indulge in nostalgia. In its first season, May to December 1982, most passengers were British and Americans; one per cent were Australians. The new owner of the name was a London-based division of the American company Sea Containers. By the 1990s it had developed three luxury trains, the *Venice Simplon-Orient-Express*, the *British Pullman* and the *Eastern Oriental Express*, which runs between Singapore and Bangkok. It also operated a chain of Orient Express hotels and a river cruise ship, the *Road to Mandalay*. In 1999 it began operating another luxury tourist train, the *Great South Pacific Express*, which ran between Sydney, Brisbane and Cairns in association with Queensland Rail.

The Wagons-Lits company became part of Accor SA, the French hotel, restaurant and catering conglomerate, which was also to become Australia's biggest hotel operator. While it no longer owned or controlled rolling stock, Wagons-Lits still continued to service sleeping and dining cars on trains all over Europe, including the cross-Channel services. Its distribution arm, which controlled 1100 travel agencies, was combined with the travel agency division of the American company Carlson to form Carlson-Wagonlit Travel in 1994.

In the United States, the government had to step in to save the passenger train service. Amtrak, a public corporation, part-capitalised with Federal funds, was formed in 1971 to operate a network of inter-city passenger trains. Amtrak, using the old rolling stock it had inherited from the independent railways, was able to demonstrate that a section of American travellers still wanted to travel by train. It then began to re-equip with new cars, including bi-level 'superliners' which had sleepers and cafe-lounges for its long routes.

High speed became desirable to compete with aircraft on routes of 600 kilometres or less in Europe and Asia. A number of European countries, including Germany, Spain and France, experimented with very fast trains in the 1960s, but it was the launch of Japan's Shinkansen (New Railway) in October 1964 that set a new standard for high-speed, reliable express train service. The first-generation Shinkansen trains ran on the 515-kilometre route between Tokyo and Osaka at speeds of up to 209 kilometres per hour from dawn to dusk day in and day out. Later on, the Shinkansen ran into its own problems—financial, political and not least environmental—but its inauguration was a milestone in modern railway history.

The Eurostar service through the Channel tunnel was launched in November 1994 to connect London with both Paris and Brussels. In its

The new Orient Express (Source: Colvin Communications)

A famous train reborn. The new Orient Express *winds its way through a European landscape.*

first full year it carried 1.67 million passengers from London to Paris, taking so many passengers from airlines that the Heathrow–Paris air route was no longer the world's busiest international air sector. Numbers flying from Heathrow to Paris' Charles de Gaulle Airport fell by one-third from 2.83 million to 1.97 million.

Electric services such as the French Trains á Grande Vitesse (TGVs) and the Japanese Shinkansen provided standards of speed and comfort rivalling those of airliners. New French high-speed trains reached speeds exceeding more than 500 kilometres per hour and regularly operated at up to 350 kilometres per hour. But the very fast trains could not run on normal tracks at full speed. To reach their highest speeds they needed specially built or 'dedicated' tracks with steeply banked curves. Alternatively, trains could be built with bodies that leaned or tilted as they went around bends. These tilting trains could travel safely on normal tracks at very high speeds.

For shorter trips, motor vehicles were still the favoured means of travel for most people in developed countries. Road systems and specialised accommodation, food and entertainment facilities were all provided. Coach touring was popular in most parts of the world, particularly for younger and older tourists.

142   A prolonged shopping spree by Canadians in the United States in the late 1980s and early 1990s demonstrated the power of the car for tourism. In 1991, 59 million Canadians drove to the United States and returned the same day, as against 20 million Americans making a day-trip to Canada. The balance of trade deficit between Canada and the United States was greatly increased by the Canadians' shopping and it was thought to have been a major cause of an increase in lost jobs (over 4000 in Ontario) and retail bankruptcies in Canada. Among the measures taken to reverse the flow were the introduction of Sunday shopping and the legalisation of gambling in Ontario. A promotional campaign was mounted to encourage Canadians to see more of their own country.[28]

Hotel expansion

The continuing expansion of travel meant that more hotels were built in most parts of the world. By 1995 there were about 307 600 hotels in the world. The highest concentration was on the European and North American continents, but considerable growth was also taking place in regions with developing economies in Asia, the Middle East and South America. The estimated total number of rooms worldwide was 11 333 000, of which 70 per cent were in Europe and North America.[29] The global hotel industry covered a wide range of accommodation from full-service luxury hotels to bed-and-breakfast establishments, motels, inns, suites, resorts, limited service accommodation and economy properties that were owned or managed by independent operators, national and multinational chains, insurance companies, pension funds, governments and other investors.

Transcontinental travel had led to the multinational hotel industry, which began with train travel in the nineteenth century (page 13). In 1994 there were chains with hotels in as many as 61 countries. The leading corporate chain at that time, Hospitality Franchise Systems, had more than 4000 hotels and more than 400 000 rooms. Holiday Inns Worldwide, Best Western International, Accor and Choice Hotels International all had more than 1900 hotels and 200 000 rooms.[30]

The hotel industry was served by worldwide reservations systems of which the largest by far in 1996 was Utel International, headquartered in London. It represented 1 385 800 rooms (6576 hotels). Others were Anasazi Travel Resources (Phoenix, US, 211 000 rooms), Lexington Services Corporation (Irving, Texas, US, 200 000 rooms) and JAL World Hotels (Tokyo, 151 045 rooms).[31]

The Internet

The Internet, which had been around for a quarter of a century and quietly doubling in size each year, came into public view in 1993. This was when it went multi-media via the World Wide Web. Through a combination of special software and a method of connecting documents users could network with pictures, sound and video simply by pointing and clicking a mouse. Suddenly the Internet became more than a way of sending e-mail and downloading the occasional file.[32]

By 1996 it was having a noticeable impact on all sectors of travel and tourism. Being a global medium it had a direct effect on Australia as well as on the rest of the world. Two major travel marketing sites were launched on the Internet in that year and they were both the products of very large American companies.

Travelocity, which appeared in March 1996, was a joint venture of the Sabre global distribution system and the Worldview Systems Corporation, which claimed to be the world's leading publisher of interactive and online destination information. Travelocity included no fewer than 200 000 pages of tourist destination information from Worldview, including 15 000 destinations throughout the world. This information included time-sensitive events such as national and international festivals, art exhibitions, plays and concerts. This was constantly updated. Two hundred and forty-eight Australian destinations were listed.

Travelocity also included countless pages of travel reservations information that allowed instant bookings to be made via Sabre. By linking databases, the two companies had created what was said to be the largest collection of integrated and searchable travel and tourism information on the Internet. It included schedules for more than 700 airlines, reservations and tickets for more than 370 of them, and an automatic search tool for the lowest fare available between multiple cities. Reservation and purchase ability was available for 28 000 hotels and 50 car rental companies.

Eight months after Travelocity became operational Microsoft launched Expedia, which it described as a new-generation electronic travel agent available to the general public. Expedia started with information on 250 destinations, weather conditions and forecasts around the world, a currency converter, a talk facility and travel agent services that included templates for booking flights, hotels and rental cars and a feature called Fare Tracker for updating and calculating airfares. Expedia received commissions from airlines, just as travel agents did,

144　but it did not include net fares, contract rates or local commercial deals that might give travel agents an edge.

Travel and tourism companies and destination marketing organisations from many parts of the world prepared sites. Most of these presented information only, in a variety of formats, but some also offered booking facilities of one kind or another—some direct, some through travel agents—with various payment methods. There was an early problem with security for credit card payments. Although technically this was overcome by 1997, there was still hesitancy on the part of many consumers. Nevertheless, an IBM survey valued commerce over the Internet by North American users in 1996 at $US 5 billion. Half of this was attributable to travel and tourism.[33]

The world's biggest business

Somewhere along the way travel and tourism had become the world's biggest business—bigger than armaments, bigger than petroleum, bigger than automotive manufacture, bigger than anything else.

> Tourism is now the largest industry in the world by virtually any economic measure, including gross output, value added, employment, capital investment and tax contributions. (S. Wheatcroft, *Aviation and Tourism Policies*, 1994)[34]

As such, it was of great importance to nations as well as companies and individuals who made their living from it. At the World Conference on Tourism held in 1980, this importance and its widespread effects were recognised in the Manila Declaration on World Tourism, which stated:

> Tourism is considered an activity essential to the life of nations because of its direct effects on the social, cultural, educational and economic sectors of national societies and in their international relations.[35]

The International Union of Official Travel Organisations (IUOTO) had been replaced by the World Tourism Organization (WTO) in November 1974. WTO became the world's intergovernmental tourism organisation, linked to the United Nations. The first General Assembly of the new body was held in Madrid in 1975. The WTO later moved its headquarters from Geneva to the Spanish capital.[36] The Australian government had opposed the creation of WTO on the basis that it would increase its United Nations costs, and after a few years it ceased to be a member of the organisation.[37]

In 1990 an influential new body came into being. The World Travel **145** and Tourism Council (WTTC) was established with membership open to chief executive officers of companies from all sectors of the industry. Its chief goal was to convince governments of the contribution of travel and tourism to national and world economic development; to this end it regularly produced estimates of the economic impact of world tourism. It also aimed to promote the expansion of travel and tourism markets in harmony with the environment and eliminate barriers to the growth of the industry.[38]

Concern about social and environmental impacts

While the enormous increases in travel and tourism had brought economic benefits in terms of increased national incomes, foreign exchange, employment, wages and salaries and taxation returns to governments, concern grew that these benefits came at a cost. Although IUOTO and others had earlier warned of these dangers, it was only from the 1970s that tourism was widely recognised as a powerful agent for social change at destinations and as something that would have a continuing effect on the environment.

From then on economic, sociocultural and environmental impacts were the areas most extensively examined in academic literature on tourism.[39] Over the years, researchers discovered an enormous variety of impacts, both good and bad, though on the whole non-economic impacts were regarded as negative.[40]

There was some argument over this.[41] It was also pointed out that money earned from tourism might be used to improve the environment and social services; improving the environment could create tourism jobs and therefore enhance social well-being. But there was no doubt that the sustainability of tourism had become a contentious issue of great importance.

The consumer was very much involved. From the mid-1970s there was a change in what many tourists wanted to do. This was quite sudden in the United States: after a couple of seasons of rapid decline, American tour wholesalers reported that escorted 'grand tours' of Europe, their mainstay since the war, had finished. Of course they had not finished altogether, but there had been a significant shift among Americans since the early years of the decade towards travelling individually and making their own plans rather than following the rigid schedules of tour operators.[42]

146   The change was happening in Europe and other markets also. The term 'new tourism' was applied to this trend towards flexibility and more authentic tourism experiences. Consumers were growing more sophisticated and more demanding, and tiring of mass-market tourism products and resorts.[43] New markets, such as those Asian countries that had eased travel restrictions only in the 1980s, were not affected, but it was apparent that as markets matured and travellers within them became more experienced, they were seeking more individualised itineraries.

By the late 1980s there was a consciousness among many tourists of the vulnerability of the planet and a widespread desire to experience natural attractions. From this period ecotourism became a desired form of tourism for some, although it was the broader 'nature tourism' that attracted the large numbers.[44]

The history of travel and tourism in the half century after the Second World War was an extraordinary one. Industry, governments and communities in many parts of the world had to accommodate themselves to a new phenomenon, mass tourism, arising out of an old habit, travel. This took considerable human ingenuity and involved many issues besides those of providing the services that enabled tourism to take place. These issues—economic, social and environmental—were now part of the public agenda in most countries of the world.

ENDNOTES

[1] Having to obtain a tax clearance to go overseas was just as big a hurdle. The Australian National Travel Association played a leading role in having this requirement abolished in the late 1950s.

[2] Feifer, op.cit., p. 223.

[3] WTO figures; see the WTO leaflet *Global Tourism Forecasts to the Year 2000 and Beyond: World* (1993). Average annual growth rate in the years 1990–1995 was 3.2 per cent.

[4] Dean, op.cit., p. 25.

[5] The Comet 4 was designed to carry 58 to 80 passengers over a 4600-kilometre range. In all, 113 Comets were completed before production ended in 1962. The Comet 1s were permanently withdrawn from service after the mid-air blow-ups; Comet 2s were delivered only to RAF Transport Command, apart from one acquired by BOAC for flight trials and crew training; and the Comet 3 was used as a test bed for the long-range Comet 4. Of the 67 Comet 4s, 4Bs and 4Cs that entered airline service between 1958 and 1964, many remained in service for more than 25 years. But they were not suitable competitors for long-range operations against the big American jets (Stewart, 1986, pp. 36–58).

[6] *Air Transport World*, May 1994, p. 5.

[7] Lattin (1990a), p. 295.

[8] Former Pan American World Airways executive Lou Hammond, quoted in *Air Transport World*, September 1993, p. 60. As noted in chapter 5 (page 88), Pan American had started to build hotels before the Second World War. Other airlines around the world followed Pan Am's lead and established or bought international hotel chains. But Pan Am had sold its Inter-Continental Hotels before the airline collapsed and most other airlines (e.g. United, which at one time owned the Hilton International and Westin chains) sold out to concentrate on their core business.

[9] Lattin (1990a), p. 295.

[10] *The Australian Financial Review*, October 1996, p. 9.

[11] Petzinger, Thomas Jr (1996), *Hard Landing: The Epic Contest for Power and Profits that Plunged the Airlines into Chaos*, Times Business, NY, p. 60.

[12] Atkinson, interview, July 1998.

[13] Gee, Chuck Y. & Lurie, M. (1993), eds, *The Story of the Pacific Asia Travel Association*, PATA, San Francisco, pp. 1–12. For its first two years, PATA was called PITA, Pacific Interim Travel Association.

[14] ibid.

[15] Feifer, op.cit. p. 219.

[16] WTO (1998), *Tourism Highlights 1997*, Madrid, p. 5.

[17] Richardson, J. I. (1995), *Marketing Australian Travel and Tourism: Principles and Practice*, Hospitality Press, Melbourne, pp. 23–4.

[18] The first supersonic airliner to fly was the Russian Tu-144, which made its first flight on 26 December 1968. It began passenger service on 1 November 1977 and ceased on 30 May 1978 after an aircraft was lost in flight. The remaining aircraft were stored or scrapped. The Concorde, built jointly by British and French companies, flew for the first time on 2 March 1969 and is still in service with British Airways and Air France. Only 20 were built. (Bond, op.cit., pp. 62–3).

[19] Wheatcroft, S. S. (1994), *Aviation and Tourism Policies*, a WTO Publication, Routledge, London & NY, p. 27.

[20] Not all travel and tourism, of course, impressive as the influence of GDSs is. For example, few people holidaying by car in Australia would have need of a GDS.

[21] Darby, G. E. (1991), 'An overview of information technology for travel agencies', in L. S. Harms (ed.), *Telecommunications and the Travel Industry: Impacts on National and Regional Development, Proceedings of the Pacific Telecommunications Council's Mid-Year Seminar*, Bali, Indonesia, p. 105.

[22] Petzinger, op.cit., pp. 155–7.

[23] Opperman, M. & Cooper, M. (1996), 'Databased marketing in the hospitality industry', in Gary Prosser, ed., *Tourism and Hospitality Research: Australian and International Perspectives, Proceedings from the Australian Tourism and Hospitality Research Conference*, BTR, p. 570.

[24] *The Australian Financial Review*, 16–17 May 1998, The Weekend FIN, p. 3.

[25] ibid.

[26] The catamaran was capable of a top speed of 42 knots, giving it a comfortable theoretical margin over the *United States*, which averaged 35.6 knots on its record trip. However, the catamaran was not driven at maximum speed; it averaged 36.65 knots and arrived with just 10 tonnes of fuel left when it reached Falmouth. The distance timed was the 4500 kilometres between the Ambrose light vessel, *New York*, and Bishop Rock off the Isles of Scilly. The catamaran was called a wave piercer because, as the hulls were very short in comparison to the craft's breadth, they must pierce the waves if pitching was to be controlled (Hawkes, N., 1992, *Man on the Move: Great Journeys by*

148   *Land, Sea and Air*, RD Press, Sydney, pp. 76–9). The 1.22-metre-high Hales Trophy dates from 1934, when it was donated by Harold Hales, an English MP, to be presented to 'the ship which shall for the time being have crossed the Atlantic Ocean at the highest average speed'. (Incat Australia media release dated 10 June 1998).

[27] The *Cat-Link V* and *Catalonia* were built with some differences to suit the requirements of their owners. However, they each could carry between 800 and 900 passengers and more than 200 cars, or a combination of four coaches and cars. (Incat Australia media releases).

[28] Timothy, D. J. & Butler, R. W. (1995), 'Cross-border shopping: A North American perspective', *Annals of Tourism Research*, v. 22(1), pp. 16–34.

[29] International Hotel Association (1996), p. 10.

[30] ibid., p. 29.

[31] Lexington Services Corporation, reprinted from *Hotels*, July 1997.

[32] *The Economist*, 10–16 May 1997, Electronic Commerce Survey, pp. 5–6.

[33] *Traveltrade*, 15 October 1997, p. 4.

[34] Wheatcroft, op.cit., p. 28.

[35] WTO (1995), *Technical Manual No. 2: Collection of Tourism Expenditure Statistics*, Madrid, p. 1.

[36] WTO document '1961 to 1975: steps leading to the establishment of the World Tourism Organization'. The WTO supplied the relevant extract by facsimile to the author.

[37] Atkinson interview.

[38] *WTTC Progress and Priorities—1993*, title page and pp. 17–22.

[39] Pearce, D. (1989), *Tourism Development*, Longman Scientific & Technical, Harlow, UK, p. 15.

[40] Lindberg, K. & Johnson, R. L. (1997), 'The economic values of tourism's social impacts', *Annals of Tourism Research*, v. 24(1), p. 91.

[41] Allcock, J. B. (1994) 'Sociology of tourism', in Witt, S. F. & Moutinho, L., eds, *Tourism Marketing and Management Handbook*, 2nd edn, Prentice Hall International (UK) Ltd, Hemel Hempstead, UK, pp. 73–81. Allcock argues that there was an acute danger of over-generalisation of results in early studies. Recent researchers were more sensitive to the fact that they were documenting local rather than universal consequences of tourism development.

[42] This is the author's own observation. Based in New York at the time, he was in contact with leading American wholesalers. Academic writers tend to suggest 'new tourism' started in the 1980s.

[43] Poon, A. (1994), 'The "new tourism" revolution', *Travel Management*, v. 15(2), p. 91.

[44] Ecotourism is a form of nature tourism. There are a variety of definitions; that used in the National Tourism Strategy (1994) is 'nature-based tourism that involves education and interpretation of the natural environment and is managed to be ecologically sustainable' (p. 3). According to Hvenegaard, Ceballos-Lascurain may have been the first to use the term in 1987 (Hvenegaard, G. T., 1994, 'Ecotourism: A status report and conceptual framework', *Journal of Tourism Studies*, v. 5(2), December, p. 24.

Post-war expansion in Australia

Early changes: immigration and the motor car

The war had changed Australia profoundly. During the conflict its people had acquired different attitudes, and different needs and wants.

Immigration, which started soon after the war, ensured that change would not only continue but would also accelerate. For the first time in Australian history, the Commonwealth Government deliberately sought large numbers of migrants of non-British origin. This was to have a direct impact on the travel and tourism industry in a number of ways. In a few years it would help launch a travel agency system, change preferred outbound destinations and add new dimensions to the Australian hospitality sector.

The first concern of Australians after the war was housing; what they wanted next was a car. Within a few years Australia was building its own—the Holden. The first model, known as the 48-215, came off the production line in 1948. It was so popular that two years later there was a waiting list of almost 100 000, and by the time the FC model appeared in 1958 Holdens accounted for half the Australian car market.[1] Cars were affordable, not because they were cheap but because they could be bought on hire purchase. The motor car quickly became the preferred vehicle for leisure travel. So many cars were to come on to the roads in the next 30 or so years that by the mid-1980s Australia had more cars than dwellings.[2]

Australians used cars for their holidays by the sea or in the mountains, or for discovering more of their country. Often they towed a caravan behind. Matching their needs was a growth in facilities and services

150 provided for them by a vigorous private sector. Australia was being changed by the enterprise of individuals who were building companies that provided new forms of accommodation, transport and attractions.

Nothing seemed impossible. Areas once so remote they were thought to be inaccessible except by specialised parties became part of the regular tourism scene. For more than a decade after the first graded track was made in 1948, Ayers Rock (Uluru) had only a trickle of visitors. Then, in 1961 and 1962, two coach companies began to take tourists there. Two years later nineteen companies were involved in Ayers Rock touring.[3]

The Snowy Mountains Authority built access roads in Kosciusko National Park and helped open up the New South Wales snowfields. Thredbo got its first lift in 1957 and by the next year seventeen buildings were completed. The construction of roads into Alpine forests and the Kiewa hydro development basin did the same for the snowfields in Victoria. The building of ski lifts in both States made regular downhill skiing possible. With access and increasing facilities, the popularity of the sport rose dramatically. Accommodation and facilities would be added over the years until by the 1990s some two million people were visiting the snowfields each year. Growth was boosted by the introduction of snowboarding in the 1980s.[4]

The domestic airlines, Ansett and Trans Australia Airlines (TAA), acquired resort islands off the Queensland coast. They developed large wholesaling departments that offered attractive packages to these resorts and to many other places in Australia.

Overseas travel became cheaper and cheaper as the decades followed each other and was promoted forcefully and with great skill by fiercely competing airlines and tour wholesalers. From a few thousand in the immediate post-war years, the number of Australians travelling overseas each year rose to three million in the late 1990s.

And so it proceeded. Travel and tourism in Australia kept on expanding. Companies struggled, many failed, some found their niches and prospered and a few became household names; the majority did not, but they became part of that fabric of small businesses characteristic of travel and tourism.

Following the pattern in other industrialised countries, planes as well as cars dominated post-war travel. Ships and trains were nowhere near as important as in earlier eras, although in time they found new roles. Travelling by car was the ultimate in flexibility; the ability to come and go as one pleased was the biggest reason for owning one. Millions belonged to motoring organisations, but the attempts of those organisations to influence their members as to where they should go **151** and what they should do were modest. Not so with the airlines. They set out to persuade people to go where they wanted their planes to go, and in doing so changed the way Australians thought of holidays in their own country and elsewhere.

As the years went on the use of cars in Australia declined for longer journeys—those that included one or more overnight stays. Surveys showed that cars were used for 86 per cent of all such trips in 1973–74, 82 per cent in 1978–79, 78 per cent in 1992–93 and 66.4 per cent in 1994–5.[5] The decline in the 1990s to a large extent reflected the increased use of planes for longer-distance travel as the result of deregulation. The percentage of overnight trips by plane in 1984–85 was 7.6 per cent; in 1994–95 it was 10.6 per cent.[6]

The watershed years

The 1980s were a watershed for Australian travel and tourism. International tourism became big business in the second half of the decade and tourists became part of the scene in cities and other destination areas—in sightseeing spots, on the roads, at the airports and in the hotels and restaurants. The increase was accompanied by unprecedented investment in hotels and resorts and raised as never before the public consciousness of tourism as an economic engine.

The 1980s was also the decade in which Australia celebrated its Bicentennial, though perhaps not with the same sense of national wonder as it had celebrated the Centennial 100 years earlier. However, there were appropriate and lavish celebrations—and additional travel to and within the country. And 1988 had its great exhibition: this time it was the Brisbane Expo. Whereas the Centennial had emphasised that Australia was now a nation in its own right, albeit part of a benevolent Empire, the Bicentennial came at a time when communications were making Australia part of an integrating world in which, among other things, tourism markets were on their way to globalisation.

Australia itself was changing rapidly under these influences and in ways that Australians of a century before would have found impossible to foresee. The 1980s were notable for Australia's engagement with Asia. In 1981 and 1986 migrants from Asia made up the biggest increase in Australians born overseas[7] and Asians constituted a growing proportion of our overseas visitors. People in travel and tourism businesses began learning new languages. Australians began visiting Asian countries in much larger numbers.

152 The 1990s

The 1990s were years of fluctuating fortunes for Australian travel and tourism. The decade started in recession and, while numbers of overseas visitors were up, yields were not. In 1991 and 1992 international tourism increased by 7 per cent and 9.8 per cent respectively when measured in terms of arrivals. However, the effect was illusory for many in the industry, because in both years the number of visitor nights was lower than in the previous year, and so was overall expenditure.[8]

This was not the only unpleasant fact that Australian operators were learning to deal with as tourism increased rapidly. Another major issue was competition from Asian inbound operators working in Australia who cut margins below normal profitable levels, or even worked for shopping commissions only. There were calls for regulation and the Commonwealth Government responded in 1998 with a promise to work with the States and Territories to enforce legislation governing inbound tour operators.[9] Time and again lessons about yield were driven home. In an attempt to keep numbers from falling in a price-driven market, Japanese tour operators cut tour costs within Australia, which meant that some services were dispensed with and some small businesses had to downsize as a result. A bed tax in Sydney, introduced in 1997, prompted a rearrangement of itineraries, with the result that less time was spent in that city.

The domestic market was sluggish during the 1990s, failing to reach even the modestly increased levels that had been predicted. Both the inbound market and the investment climate improved in the middle of the decade, but the financial crisis in a number of Asian countries, which began in 1997, caused some formerly high-growth markets to fall apart. The effect on sections of the industry was severe, although it varied greatly. Forecasts of international visitor traffic for future years were adjusted downward.

Nevertheless, Australian travel and tourism was operating on a much larger scale than ever before and the industry was recognised as an essential part of national, state and regional economies. Studies 22 years apart showed how substantial growth had been. In 1973–74 travel and tourism was estimated to have contributed 2.6 per cent of Gross Domestic Product (GDP); in 1995–96 the figure was 6.23 per cent directly contributed with another 4.3 per cent indirectly contributed. The industry employed 118 000 people in 1973–74; 22 years later it gave jobs to 694 000 people directly and 334 000 indirectly. The total of 1 028 000 represented 12.4 per cent of the workforce. In 1995–96 tourism expenditure was estimated to have been $60 350 million.[10]

Australia had become a major player in world tourism. Although it was a long way from the top 20 in terms of numbers of international arrivals, in 1990 it ranked fourteenth in the world in terms of receipts from international tourism and by 1997 was ninth.[11]

International travel

Overseas travel became progressively more affordable for Australians after the war. In 1945, it took someone on an average wage 130 weeks to earn enough to pay for the lowest Sydney-to-London return airfare. By 1965 that figure was down to 21 weeks; by 1985 it was five weeks and in 1995 it was 3.5 weeks.[12]

Most Australians wanted to travel overseas. In 1977, the Gallup organisation polled 9000 people in 58 countries, asking: 'If you had the time, money and opportunity, would you travel to other nations in the world or not?' Australians, together with the French and the Scandinavians, had the highest affirmative rate: 84 per cent.[13]

Between 1963 and 1975 the number of short-term departures increased from 112 427 to 911 815 at a remarkable annual average rate of 19 per cent. In 1950, 31.5 per cent of Australian international travellers went to Britain. However, destination choices were to change, partly as a result of migration. By 1965 the proportion travelling to Britain was down to 10.6 per cent and by 1970 it was 7.3 per cent. On the other hand travel to Italy, the source of the second biggest ethnic group in the country, rose from 5.4 per cent in 1950 to 8.3 per cent in 1965. By 1970 it had dropped, but by then the big migration from Italy was over.

Other factors besides ethnic origin were also important. Promotion was one of them. Airlines and wholesale tour operators presented attractively priced products, luring Australians overseas. National tourism organisations provided stimulus to the travel sellers and infor-mation for consumers. During the 1970s the amount of money spent on tourism messages to the Australian public grew at about 17 per cent per year and most of it seemed to be devoted to promoting international destinations.[14] New Zealand was the favourite destination of the 1960s and 1970s. In the latter period Britain and Ireland were again among the leaders and so was the United States. Australians started travelling in considerable numbers to Asian destinations like Singapore and Hong Kong in the 1970s.

Although the average rate of growth declined over the next quarter of a century—in the ten years to 1996 it was 5.9 per cent—the numbers of short-term departures kept rising so that by 1997 the total had reached

154 2 932 800.[15] Australians were sought-after travellers, providing the biggest market for New Zealand and significant markets for the United States, the United Kingdom and Singapore. By 1996 Asian countries were the prime destinations for 36 per cent of Australian overseas travellers.

Inbound tourism and the travel gap

Throughout the 1950s and 1960s there had been more overseas visitors to Australia than there were Australians leaving on short-term trips. However, the high growth rate in Australian overseas travel in the 1960s and early 1970s had its effect and from 1972 on the situation was reversed. By 1975 the imbalance was quite noticeable.

In 1972, 426 402 overseas visitors arrived in Australia and short-term resident departures numbered 504 519—a difference of 78 117. In 1975 the 'travel gap' had reached nearly 400 000 (visitor arrivals 516 023, Australian departures 911 815).[16] This was regarded with alarm by some people, who called for increased promotion overseas and a campaign to persuade Australians to holiday at home. Others said that a comparison of the figures did not matter and that there was no reason to talk of a gap.[17]

It was not until 1987 that the situation was reversed once more and visitor arrivals exceeded resident departures. In that year, 1 784 900 visitors arrived and 1 622 300 residents departed on short-term trips. In 1997 the figures were 4 317 000 visitor arrivals and 2 932 800 resident departures.

Japan leads the inbound growth

The big increase in inbound tourism had begun in the mid-1980s. At the beginning of the decade growth was slow, averaging less than 3 per cent annually in the years 1981 to 1984, but the latter year was a notable one. It was the first year in Australia's history when more than a million visitors arrived here. It took only four more years to reach two million —annual growth rates from 1985 to 1988 were 12.8, 25.1, 24.9 and 26.1 per cent respectively.

The driving force behind this sudden surge was the Japanese market. Two factors contributed to make the price-driven Japanese suddenly interested in Australia. One was lower airfares for tour operators, following a hiatus brought about by the fuel crisis of the 1970s,[18] and the other was a much more favourable exchange rate. In March 1980 it had taken 270 yen to buy an Australian dollar, but in 1985 it required only 165 yen. Japanese tourism began to move fast. In 1985 there were 197 590 arrivals in Australia and by 1989 the total had reached 349 500.[19]

With much more airline capacity, competitive fares and a greater **155** variety of destination areas than in earlier eras, Japanese travel to Australia continued to expand rapidly in the early 1990s. This was helped by a falling dollar against the yen; the exchange rate went from 120 yen to the dollar in 1990 to as low as 60 in 1995. In that year there were 782 700 Japanese arrivals in Australia—21 per cent of total tourist arrivals.

Other Asian countries had also made their contributions. Tourism from Singapore grew almost six times in the decade 1985–95, again helped by a favourable movement in the exchange rate. The markets in South Korea, Taiwan, Malaysia, Thailand and Indonesia all grew very quickly during this period and there were solid gains from New Zealand, Germany and the United Kingdom.

1997 saw a check to this growth, due to the currency crises already referred to, problems with the Japanese economy and increased competition. At the same time there were expectations from emerging markets in China, India, Eastern Europe and South America.

The entrepreneurs

Although much of the Australian industry had a corporate look about it after 1980, up till then it had been shaped largely by individuals. Among these were Alan Greenway (motels and hotels), Oliver Shaul (hotels and restaurants), Keith Williams (Sea World and Hamilton Island), John Haddad (hotel-casinos), Geoff McGeary and Mayer Page (coach touring), Ron Murray (tours and coach charters), Trevor Haworth (Sydney Harbour cruises) and Eric McIllree and Bob Ansett (rent-a-cars). Sir Sydney Williams was managing director of Bush Pilots Airlines in this period, helped found Lizard Island Resort and Cape York Wilderness Lodge and also ensured that Far North Queensland had a place at the national tourism table at a time when few others could see its coming eminence. Those who helped give form to the early travel agency business included Frank Johnson of Sydney, Stewart Moffat of Melbourne and Roy King of Adelaide.

Perhaps no single person had more influence on the development of Australia's travel and tourism in that period than Sir Reginald Myles Ansett. As has been mentioned before (pages 104 and 105), he started in travel before the war with a second-hand Studebaker car running between Victorian cities. When the Victorian government put him out of business because he was taking customers from the railways, he started a one-plane air service.

156   After the war, he developed the country's largest coach operation and eventually controlled one of the two major domestic airlines. He built and bought tourist hotels for his coach and plane passengers—so many of them that by 1948 his company, Ansett Transport Industries, was the biggest hotel operator in Australia. He helped popularise the snow-fields. He saw the possibilities of Queensland as a winter getaway for people from the south and built the first true Australian resort, the Royal Hayman Hotel, which opened in 1950 on Hayman Island in the Whitsundays. He added glamour to the northern experience by running a fleet of flying boats from Sydney's Rose Bay to Queensland ports as far north as Cairns, as well as to Lord Howe Island.

He was knighted and became one of Australia's most influential business figures, his name a household word, his company one of the most powerful in Australian travel and tourism. But there were many points on his way when he wondered if he would be in business the next day. His career was characterised by vision and considerable inge-nuity—also by a staying power that few others have matched.[20] In each sector of the industry there were men and women who were pioneers and innovators, with vision in their own fields and considerable fortitude.

The Gold Coast

Nowhere was the new spirit of post-war tourism adventure so notice-able or so stridently proclaimed as on the Gold Coast. That was not its name at the beginning of the post-war period. It was given the unglamorous title of the Town of South Coast when the resorts along the Queensland coast between Southport and Coolangatta were incorporated in the one local government area in 1948.

This was no hindrance to development. Wartime building restric-tions were lifted in 1952 and investors from the southern States as well as Queensland poured millions into accommodation projects. Between 1951 and 1955 the population increased 150 per cent, more than half the new residents coming from New South Wales and Victoria. Bernie Elsey, Stanley Korman and other developers built accommodation for tourists. Korman's Chevron Hotel, completed in the early 1960s, her-alded a new style for Australia with large areas of glass and an indoor beer garden with a cabaret.[21]

In 1958 South Coast Town became Gold Coast Town and the next year it received its charter as a city. 'Gold Coast' had come into use in the mid-1950s after a *Brisbane Courier-Mail* reporter had written about a land sale in what he said 'must be the golden half-mile on the South

Birds galore at Currumbin (Source: Currumbin Sanctuary)

Wild rainbow lorikeets have been gathering at Currumbin Sanctuary for more than half a century, and they continue to arrive in masses twice daily for a supplementary meal to the great interest of visitors to the Sanctuary, the Gold Coast's oldest attraction. This 1950s picture shows Alex Griffiths, the beekeeper and flower grower who founded the Sanctuary in 1947, with plenty of birds and visitors.

Coast'. The pictorial editor shortened this to 'Gold Coast' for a caption on a photograph, and after that used the term regularly.[22] As development continued, the population increased and tourism boomed, the use of the name was extended to include the whole 32-kilometre strip. In Queensland and the southern States, Gold Coast land was promoted, apartments in high-rise buildings were promoted and tourism was promoted, all with a fervour unknown in Australia up to that time.

Gold bikinis helped make the resort famous. In 1965 bikinis were frowned upon on Sydney and Melbourne beaches, but Meter Maids wore a gold version when they first appeared on Surfers Paradise streets. It had been felt that the introduction of parking meters would create bad publicity, especially when the motorists fined were visitors. So the Progress Association countered with Meter Maids, who carried bags of coins to insert in 'expired' meters. The Meter Maids happened to be attractive young women in gold bikinis, so the publicity the parking meter issue created was anything but bad for Gold Coast tourism, and it was nation-wide.

158   No-one used publicity devices better than Sir Bruce Small, who had accumulated a fortune making Malvern Star bicycles,[23] retired to live on the Gold Coast in 1958, developed the Isle of Capri as a 'hobby', and became Gold Coast mayor and a passionate promoter. He was a controversial person of great energy who led Gold Coast promotions to all the major tourism markets in Australia.

Entrepreneurs created glamorous attractions. Keith Williams developed a water-skiing show at Surfers Paradise Gardens and in 1965 staged the World Water Ski Championships there—the first time an international sporting event had been held on the Gold Coast. In 1971 Williams moved his ski show from Surfers Paradise Gardens to a new location on the Spit that he called Ski-Land. The next year he changed the name to Sea World and added performing dolphins, marine displays, a replica sailing ship, a licensed restaurant and other facilities so that families could spend the whole day there. Later he added sophisticated amusement park rides and Sea World became the outstanding theme park in Australia.

The Gold Coast, long a favourite with New Zealanders, began attracting other overseas tourists in considerable numbers as Japanese tourism increased in the early 1980s and planes from Tokyo began landing at Brisbane Airport. Some of the Gold Coast's first hotels had been built on the strata-title principle,[24] financed by numbers of individual investors because of the difficulty of attracting enough capital from financial institutions to construct large, high-rise buildings. However, the Japanese investment boom of the 1980s had the Gold Coast as one of its targets. This resulted in a number of new first-class hotels as well as apartment houses and other facilities.

With a guaranteed tourism flow, a number of high-cost theme parks were developed to join Sea World: Dreamworld (1981), Wet 'n' Wild Waterworld (called Cade's County when it opened in 1985) and Warner Bros. Movie World (1991). Other attractions included Jupiters Casino and Pacific Fair Shopping Centre, which especially catered for visitors.

The Gold Coast's oldest attraction, dating from 1947, was still going strong. This was the Currumbin Sanctuary, best known for the colourful lorikeets that visited twice daily. Its 27 hectares of landscaped grounds were home to more than 1250 Australian native birds and animals. The sanctuary had been started by Alex Griffiths, a beekeeper and flower grower, who had originally fed the wild rainbow lorikeets to keep them off his flowers. He later gave the park to the National Trust of Queensland.

The past as an attraction

Many relics of the past, as described in earlier chapters, continued to fascinate Australians and visitors and were preserved or re-created as part of the modern tourism experience. Museums of old vehicles were popular in many parts of Australia. Steamboats chugged along the Murray carrying tourists, as did steam trains on a number of lines, some of which were preserved only for tourism.

Echuca's old port was a big tourist attraction. So was the Pioneer Settlement on the banks of the Murray at Swan Hill, an imaginative recreation of life in other eras. The first days of white settlement were brought to life at Sydney's Old Sydney Town and Ballarat's Sovereign Hill was a living reminder of the boisterous, prosperous days of the Victorian gold rush. The sea-going past was remembered around the country—in Sydney and Melbourne and at the Flagstaff Hill Maritime Museum at Warrnambool, the South Australian Maritime Museum at Port Adelaide and the Western Australian Maritime Museum at Fremantle.

The National Maritime Museum was at Darling Harbour, an old Sydney dockland area that had been converted into a glossy tourism precinct which included hotels, restaurants, the Star City Casino, the Sydney Convention and Exhibition Centre, the Sydney Aquarium and numerous other attractions, including extensive shopping facilities. The Queen opened Darling Harbour during the Bicentennial celebrations in 1988 and by 1997 the State government had spent one billion dollars and private enterprise three billion on development projects.[25]

The Polly Woodside Maritime Museum in Melbourne was somewhat isolated along the southern bank of the Yarra River until the Melbourne Exhibition Centre was opened alongside it in 1996. It then became part of the new tourism precinct, which swept more than a kilometre along the Yarra bank from Princes Bridge and encompassed the Southgate leisure complex and Crown Casino.

The small Tasmanian town of Sheffield decided to put its past on its walls to attract tourists. Murals depicting scenes from the history of the area were painted on the walls of buildings around the town. The first was on the back of the toilet block because the town had long been regarded as nothing more than a toilet stop for tourists on their way to Lake Barrington or Cradle Mountain. No more. Scenes like The Smithy at Work, The Mail Coach, Amelia Morse's Kitchen, Frank Slater's Wireless Studio and The Missed Opportunity created so much interest that in the late 1990s three new motels and six other new businesses had been created.[26]

160 Protecting the environment

From the 1970s governments, individuals, the conservation movement and the industry showed increasing concern about potential damage to physical and social environments by tourism. Steps were taken to protect Australia's two best-known natural attractions, the Great Barrier Reef and Ayers Rock (Uluru). The Great Barrier Reef Marine Park Authority was established in 1976 and the Reef was inscribed on the World Heritage List in 1981. Tourist facilities near Ayers Rock, which were causing considerable environmental damage, were moved to the Yulara tourist village, later called the Ayers Rock Resort, in 1983–84. The resort, designed to exist in a fragile environment, was placed 20 kilometres from Ayers Rock. The Uluru-Kata Tjuta National Park, in which the Rock was situated, was placed on the World Heritage List in 1987.

Elements of the industry responded directly to the environmental challenge. For example, the SPHC hotel group developed expertise in operating hotels in environmentally sensitive areas such as Kakadu National Park, which was another World Heritage Area. Australian Pacific Tours was the first Australian company to introduce coaches designed to minimise environmental impact, with features that included an improved engine design to reduce exhaust and noise emissions and air-conditioning units that used environment-friendly gas. Murrays Australia was another large company that produced vehicles which limited environmental impact.

The Ecotourism Association of Australia was formed in 1991, growing out of an international conference titled 'Ecotourism Incorporating the Global Classroom' at the University of Queensland that year. Its membership in 1998 was about 450, half of whom were tourism operators and the other half a mix of academics, students and representatives of government agencies and conservation bodies.

Government agencies and associations like the Pacific Asia Travel Association and Tourism Council Australia (and its predecessor the Australian Tourism Industry Association) also took action. PATA and ATIA issued environmental guidelines for tourism operators and in 1992 a PATA 'Think Tank' in Australia produced a discussion paper on the subject of 'a profitable industry in a sustainable environment' titled 'Endemic Tourism'.

The Commonwealth Department of Tourism published a National Ecotourism Strategy in 1994 and later produced several guides on environmental best practice. The State and Territory organisations prepared declarations of policy with respect to the environment and tourism; progress reports were issued regularly. Tasmania changed its **161** positioning statement from 'Tasmania—Australia's Best Holiday State' to 'Tasmania. Discover Your Natural State'.[27]

It was not only tourism that impacted on the environment, of course. In the 1960s there had been well-publicised environmental controversies about such issues as the flooding of Lake Pedder in Tasmania and oil drilling and limestone mining on the Great Barrier Reef. The States legislated to protect the environment in the early 1970s and the Commonwealth followed suit in 1974. Legislation included provision for Environmental Impact Assessment (EIA) if there were reason to believe that any matter might impact significantly on the environment. In 1992 the Commonwealth, States and Territories agreed on a national approach to EIA.[28] Though not specifically aimed at tourism, these measures were to have their effects on tourism development.

Tourism in Australia was perceived as having a mixed social impact. On the one hand there might be benefits such as a greater diversity of restaurants, the growth of local cultural events and increased interest in preserving historic buildings. But there were negatives, too. Usually these were the result of congestion and pollution. However, other issues surfaced as well, such as possible increases in crime and the loss of low-cost accommodation when land prices rose as a result of tourism. In 1989 the Cairns Social Planning Group claimed that tourism had changed the nature of Cairns 'by creating an atmosphere of transience and poorly developed family support systems'.[29] The Social Impact Assessment (SIA) became part of the tourism development format.

Some of the conflicts

Considerable conflict occurred over tourism developments; three examples are given here.

1 In 1994 the French leisure group Club Méditerranée SA decided not to proceed with a proposal to enlarge Byron Bay Beach resort and convert it to a Club Med resort, following a bitter campaign against it by a group of residents and activists as far away as Sydney and Melbourne. Club Med had bought the 90-hectare beachfront property in Byron Bay, on the north coast of New South Wales, in 1991. The proposal was approved by the Byron Bay Chamber of Commerce and eventually, in 1993, by the Byron Bay Council. However, a deter-mined public opposition campaign was mounted which included marches, letters of protest to authorities, approaches to politicians

including the Prime Minister and a well-orchestrated and successful press program, involving capital city as well as local media.

The main point of the protest was that a Club Med resort would change the character of Byron Bay and its lifestyle—the way that people there did things. When Club Med came, others would follow and Byron Bay would become another King's Cross or Fortitude Valley.

There was plenty of drama. Roadside signs read 'Better dead than Club Med' and death threats were reported in the local press. When the Land and Environment Court voided approval for the project in 1994 on a technical point—a flora impact statement had not been filed—Club Med had had enough. The proposal was shelved.[30]

2 Environmental problems, mainly one of noise pollution, dogged Sydney Airport after a third runway was opened in 1994, leading to protest marches, airport blockades and political controversy. Some 31 000 households as well as schools, hospitals and nursing homes were said to be under the new flight path. One report claimed that the values of houses there had fallen by up to 16 per cent.[31] The Commonwealth Government gave those affected $190 million in compensation and new take-off schedules were introduced in a bid to alleviate the noise problem. A proposal to build a second airport for Sydney at Badgerys Creek also proved controversial; interest groups rejected environmental impact studies as inadequate. It was estimated that 50 000 people would be subjected to noise and other environmental problems, including air pollution from the airport. The issue was: to what degree?[32]

3 Protests on environmental grounds had already stalled a resort development at Port Hinchinbrook near Cardwell on Queensland's far north coast for four years when a Senate inquiry was told by the environmental manager of the Great Barrier Reef Park Authority in August 1998 that much of the cost and anguish could have been avoided if an environmental impact study had been carried out at the start of the project. On the other hand the developer, Keith Williams, said that under an agreement he had signed with the Commonwealth Government he had had to satisfy even stricter environmental conditions than would have been stipulated as the result of such a study. He estimated that in the past four years the project had cost taxpayers six million dollars, including funding for government reports, independent studies and the legal costs incurred by conservationists fighting the development. The Great Barrier Reef Marine Park Authority said its costs alone were at least $120 000 a year.[33]

Indigenous tourism

One of the expressions of the 'new tourism' (see chapter 8, pages 145–6) was a growing interest in the cultures of indigenous peoples. About 557 000 international visitors, or 15 per cent of the total, visited indigenous sites and attractions in Australia in 1996.[34] Aboriginal people and Torres Strait Islanders had been involved in various ways as tourism had grown. These included cultural activities such as dance and arts and crafts as well as tour operations, investment in tourism enterprises and other business activities.

Clark and Larrieu have postulated that indigenous involvement in tourism has a long, rich heritage. They point to some nineteenth-century activities as precursors of contemporary forms of tourism:

- tour guiding: escorting European explorers, sojourners and other travellers through their territories and provided them with interpretation
- hospitality: staging 'diplomacy festivals' such as Tanderrum, in which strangers were given 'freedom of the bush'. The Tanderrum Aboriginal Cultural Ceremony has now become one of the major cultural events in Victoria
- event tourism: staging what may be called annual harvest festivals in which non-local people were invited to participate (examples included eeling and emu-hunting)
- the handicraft industry, though some of this was involuntary when nineteenth-century collectors appropriated Aboriginal cultural material
- sports tourism, through Aboriginal people showcasing their skills in such activities as boomerang-throwing, wrestling, steeplechase riding and playing cricket.[35]

Even so, as tourism began to grow after the Second World War attitudes towards the involvement of Aboriginal people and Torres Strait Islanders were cautious. In the 1970s the Australian Tourist Commission was circumspect about promoting anything that might appear exploitive or reflect adversely on the dignity of indigenous peoples. However, in 1997 the Aboriginal and Torres Strait Islander Commission (ATSIC) and the National Office of Tourism published a tourism strategy for Aboriginal people and Torres Strait Islanders designed to increase that involvement. This acknowledged the role indigenous tourism could play in the overall industry, while at the same time fostering economic independence and cultural preservation

164   for the peoples concerned.[36] The strategy aimed to promote the 'considerable diversity of regional cultures' through marketing and educational activities.

Indigenous tourism had not progressed far, according to the strategy. It accounted for only about 200 businesses, with total revenues of some $5 million. On the other hand, indigenous arts and crafts were estimated to be worth about $200 million a year, with about half the sales occurring through tourism. Aboriginal people owned mainstream tourism operations worth about $20 to $30 million, mainly in accommodation and transport.

Several Aboriginal communities conducted cultural tours, including day tours from Adelaide, and there were a number of successful cultural centres and dance theatres. The enterprising Tiwi people, who live on Bathurst and Melville Islands 80 kilometres north of Darwin, ran nine businesses in the 1990s ranging from buffalo exports to a pearl farm. The Tiwi Land Council owned Tiwi Tours, which operated day trips and two-day camping tours from Darwin. Seventy per cent of its custom came from overseas, primarily Europe.[37]

The Cape York Wilderness Lodge, at the top of Cape York, was owned by the Pajinka people. It was opened in 1982 by a group that included the managing director of Bush Pilots Airlines, Sir Sydney Williams, and was bought by TAA when it acquired the airline and Lizard Island in 1985. The local Aboriginal community later bought the lodge.

One of the best-known indigenous attractions was the Tjapukai Aboriginal Cultural Park near Cairns. The Tjapukai people owned a majority share in the 10.5-hectare park, which was the home of the Tjapukai Dance Theatre and was situated next to the Skyrail Rainforest Cableway. The dance company was started in 1987 at Kuranda by Don and Judy Freeman, Americans who had settled in Queensland, and six young Tjapukai men. In its first decade it won 16 major tourism, art and cultural awards and was listed in the Guinness Book of Records for having the longest-running play in Australia. One of its plays, a historical musical about the region, had a cast of 70. The theme park, to which the company moved in 1996, combined theatrics and technology with interactive experiences involving Aboriginal people.[38]

The internationalisation of the industry

The EMDG scheme

In the early 1970s the Australian industry had problems overseas with reservations. Companies could advertise in ATC and other publications,

Indigenous tourism (Source: Tjapukai Aboriginal Cultural Park)

Top: dancers bring tourists a taste of Aboriginal culture at the Tjapukai Aboriginal Cultural Park near Cairns. Bottom: The Creation Theatre, which stages productions illustrating the spiritual beliefs of the Tjapukai people.

166 but international telecommunications—telephone; not everybody had telex—were expensive and mail took too long. Only a few Australian companies had representation overseas. Many companies wasted money on advertisements or other promotions. Interest was generated, but faded when travel agents overseas found making a reservation for an Australian tourism product more difficult or expensive compared with making reservations for other destinations.

The Commonwealth Government's Export Market Development Grants scheme was applied to the travel and tourism industry in 1978. Grants were paid in proportion to eligible expenditure in marketing services overseas, enabling members of the industry to organise better communications and in some cases set up representation. This had a significant effect on the reservations problem as well as generally increasing overseas marketing. The EMDG scheme was to continue to play a part in internationalising the Australian industry, although its on-again-off-again application to travel and tourism was, in the words of Laurie Stroud, 'a clear message that tourism was not understood by the bureaucrats in Canberra and the industry lacked political clout'.[39]

The scheme had been introduced to Australian business generally in 1974, but it was four more years before the travel and tourism industry was admitted. The industry was taken out of the scheme in 1985 and admitted again on a restricted basis in 1990. It was not until July 1997 that it was again placed on an equal footing with other industries. Even though computer reservations systems and greatly improved telecommunications went a long way to overcoming the reservations problem, there was still concern in the 1990s that the Australian industry was not converting all the opportunities created for it by ATC awareness advertising and other promotions; lack of continuity in respect to the EMDG scheme had been partly to blame.[40]

Moves towards globalisation

Nevertheless, the larger elements of the Australian travel and tourism industry had become enmeshed in the trend towards globalisation; in terms of international connections the Australian travel and tourism industry was scarcely recognisable in 1998 compared with where it had been 20 years before.

The two major carriers, Qantas Airways and Ansett Australia, were partly foreign-owned and were members of international alliances. The two biggest Australian-based hotel companies, Accor Asia Pacific and the SPHC Group, were not only foreign-owned and part of worldwide systems; in their own right they were substantially involved in the Asia-

Pacific region. Many of the world's major hotel management companies were operating in Australia. The successor to the original Australian motel marketing group was now branded as Best Western, part of the international group with headquarters in the United States.

In some areas Australian and New Zealand interests were routinely entwined: aviation, accommodation and distribution. Ansett New Zealand was owned by Australian companies and Australian hotel companies and travel agent marketing groups were part of the New Zealand industry. Air New Zealand owned half of Ansett Australia and all of Jetset Tours and the New Zealand company Helicopter Line owned World Travel Headquarters and other Australian tour wholesalers.

The above are but examples. Internationalisation of the industry was advanced in many different ways. The reservations and accounting functions of many companies operating in Australia were integrated into regional or worldwide systems; departmental executives as well as chief executive officers often reported to someone outside the country or had outsiders report to them. When travel agents operated their computer reservations systems they used codes that were understood around the world and that had helped standardise business procedures.

Globalisation was by no means complete by the last years of the 1990s, but the Australian travel and tourism industry was to a large extent part of the international industry.

ENDNOTES

[1] *Sunday Herald Sun*, 26 July 1998, p. 49. Ford challenged Holden in 1960 with the Falcon, its Australian-designed car, but it was not until the 1980s that the Falcon passed the Holden as Australia's best-selling car.

[2] Spearritt, P. (1987c), 'Cars for the people' in *Australians from 1939*, ed. A. Curthoys, A. W. Martin, T. Rowse, Australians: A Historical Library series, Fairfax, Syme & Weldon Associates, Sydney, p. 129.

[3] Richardson, J. I. (1996), *Marketing Australian Travel and Tourism: Principles and Practice*, Hospitality Press, Melbourne, p. 31.

[4] The Victorian figures illustrate the huge expansion of snow sports after the war. In 1947 the skiing population was estimated to be 3000–5000 (Lloyd, op.cit., p. 93). In 1991 the total number of visits to Victorian Alpine resorts was estimated to be 807 000 and the net economic impact of the Alpine industry in the State was said to be almost $200 000 000, with an associated 5700 jobs created (Centre for South Australian Economic Studies, 1993, *The Economic Significance of Alpine Resorts*, Adelaide, pp. ii–iii).

[5] 1973–74 and 1978–79 figures from Leiper (1980), op.cit., p. 74 and later figures from the Domestic Tourism Monitor. A 'trip' is a journey of at least 40 kilometres from home and includes a stay away of at least one night.

[6] Domestic Tourism Monitor 1984–85.

168

[7] The increase was 244 000 and Asians made up about two-thirds. However, the actual number of Asians in Australia at the time of the 1986 census was about 500 000, or three per cent of the population (ABS).

[8] Richardson (1995), op.cit., p. 44.

[9] Office of National Tourism, *Ticket to the 21st Century: National Action Plan*, p. 3.

[10] Bureau of Industry Economics (1979), Research Report No. 4, *Economic Significance of Tourism in Australia*, AGPS, Canberra, p. 70. The estimates are at 1968–69 prices. O'Dea, D. (1997), BTR Research Paper No. 3, 'Tourism's direct economic contribution 1995–96', BTR, Canberra, pp. 6–24.

[11] WTO (1998), op.cit., p. 4.

[12] Australian Bureau of Statistics and Qantas Airways, based on the lowest basic Qantas airfare on the route at the time and average weekly earnings for full-time work, excluding overtime. In 1995 the airfare was $2249 and average weekly earnings were $646.10.

[13] Leiper (1980), op.cit., p. 67. The study had been conducted for the Kettering Foundation.

[14] ibid., p. 61.

[15] The number of departures is not the same as the number of people travelling overseas, of course, because many people travel more than once. Leiper (1980) used figures from surveys to find that in 1973–74 those travelling abroad made on average 1.44 trips abroad. In 1978–79 the survey figure for Australians flying with Qantas was an average of 1.94 trips (p. 76).

[16] Vamplew & McLean, op.cit., p. 180.

[17] The Bureau of Industry Economics put the economic argument in its report 'Economic significance of tourism in Australia', op.cit., p. 18: 'The ability to attract tourists is often regarded as a symbol of national pride and prestige. This can be expressed in terms of a desire to reduce a travel deficit in an attempt to balance the account or even achieve a surplus. This may result in the pursuit of a policy objective of "closing the travel gap". However, there is unlikely to be any justification in the government intervening, by means of discriminatory assistance measures, in the pursuit of such an objective. Countries engage in international trade in goods and services in order to export those goods and services which they produce relatively inefficiently and import those products which they cannot produce at all or only relatively inefficiently. The only constraint is that overall the balance of payments should be in long term equilibrium. Within that constraint it is to be expected that different sections of the overall account will record deficits or surpluses. These will tend to occur in accordance with a country's comparative advantage.'

[18] Tour-basing fares were a hot issue between Australia and Japan several years before they were introduced. After high-level discussions in Tokyo on the issue, the author reported to the ATC and others that Japan Airlines would not consider the reduced fares until it could put new aircraft on the Tokyo–Sydney run; it nominated a date some two years ahead. The airline was adopting a cautious re-equipment program following the fuel crisis of the early 1970s. There had been so much talk in Australia of the imminence of the new fares that the report on the Tokyo discussions was widely discounted. Tour-basing fares were introduced in the month forecast by the Japanese to the author two years earlier.

[19] Exchange rates are as at June of the year quoted, except where specified otherwise. The source is the Balance of Payments section of the Australian Bureau of Statistics. Arrival figures from the ABS.

[20] 'Not even R. M. Ansett's enemies would deny that he was a fighter; in fact he would continue to fight long after others would have conceded defeat, if it affected his company

in any way.' (Maddock, op.cit, p. 99). **169**

21 Korman lost interest in the hotel company during the credit squeeze of 1961–62 but remained in Surfers Paradise as a developer.

22 Vader & Lang, op.cit., p. 83.

23 Malvern Star bicycles were ridden in Australia and Europe by the most famous Australian cyclist of all time, Sir Hubert Opperman. Small was knighted in 1975.

24 Greg Graham, a former fighter pilot, moved to the Gold Coast in 1954 and built the Eldorado, the first American-style motel, on the Gold Coast. In 1970 he formed Quality Inns Pty Ltd with the idea of managing investment and accommodation. The Iluka Quality Inn, opened in 1971, was a 112-room high-rise resort hotel, the first built under his new plan. The owners of the 48 one-bedroom and 32 two-bedroom units formed a company, leasing their units under the management of Quality Inns.

25 Darling Harbour Authority, annual report 1996–97, p. 4.

26 *Sunday Herald Sun* magazine, 9 August 1998, pp. 20–23.

27 Richardson, op.cit., p. 169. The slogan was changed to 'Tasmania. More than you imagine' in 1998, as part of a new emphasis on 'proximity/diversity', positioning Tasmania as a place with a diversity of attractions which were easy to access.

28 Thomas, I. G. (1996), *Environmental Impact Assessment in Australia: Theory and Practice*, The Federation Press, Annandale, NSW, pp. 81–113.

29 Industries Assistance Commission (1989), Report No. 423, Travel and Tourism, AGPS, Canberra, p. 184.

30 This account was written from briefings by Associate Professor Graham Brown, of Southern Cross University, and Warren Treasure, of Byron Bay Resort, during Southern Cross University's Tourism Executive Development Course in June 1998.

31 *The Weekend Australian*, 13–14 May 1995, p. 11.

32 *Herald Sun*, 22 December 1997, p. 23.

33 *Weekend Australian*, 1–2 August 1998, p. 8.

34 This was a 45 per cent increase on the previous year, according to the Office of National Tourism (*Tourism Facts*, no. 11, June 1998).

35 Clark, I. & Larrieu, L. (1998), Indigenous tourism in Victoria: Products, markets and futures, paper presented at 'Symbolic Souvenirs', a one-day conference on cultural tourism at the Centre for Cross-Cultural Research, Australian National University, p. 5.

36 ATSIC and National Office of Tourism (1997), National Aboriginal and Torres Strait Islander Tourism Industry Strategy, Canberra, p. iii.

37 Commonwealth Department of Tourism (1993), *A Talent for Tourism: Stories about Indigenous People in Tourism*, Canberra, pp. 25–7.

38 Information from Mia Lacy, Tjapukai Aboriginal Cultural Park, faxed, 18 August 1998.

39 Laurie Stroud, former Assistant Secretary, Department of Tourism, interview August 1998. He is now a consultant on tourism matters in Canberra.

40 ibid.

More revolutions on the ground

The love affair with cars

During the war petrol rationing and restrictions on car production restrained motoring. But after the war Australians did not hesitate; as soon as they possibly could they took to the roads. Some cars were imported ready for the road and others came from Australian factories. The Ford Motor Company, which had been in Australia since 1925, began assembling civilian cars again in 1946. First came the American Ford V8s and Mercury V8s and then the English-designed Prefects, Anglias and Ford Pilots.[1] As has already been noted in chapter 9, General Motors began production of Australian-designed Holdens in 1948.

Incomes increased, as did the credit available for buying cars by hire purchase. Car ownership in Australia numbered 522 000 in 1946 and over a million by 1952. One commentator illustrated the Australian love of the motor car by pointing out that 208 000 cars were registered in 1954 as against 202 000 babies born.[2] In 1959, according to the RACV, 50 000 motorists from southern States visited New South Wales and Queensland. The NRMA reported that 85 000 of its members travelled interstate each year.[3]

The love affair continued through the decades. By 1980, 80 per cent of Australian households had at least one car and one-third had two or more. The next year car registrations passed the six million mark.

Acquiring a licence and a car has become the most important ritual in the transition from childhood to adulthood in our society. Men and women who do not or cannot pass this basic test are thought to be weak and dependent. (P. Spearritt, in *Australians:* **171** *From 1939,* 1987)[4]

More than 11 million Australians held licences in the mid-1990s and passenger vehicle ownership per head had risen to 0.46 vehicles per person—up from 0.37 per cent in 1976. In short, there were nearly half as many passenger vehicles as there were people in the country.[5]

The impact of the motor car on tourism has already been commented on. Although use of the car had been declining, it was still the chosen vehicle for two-thirds of long trips taken in Australia in the late 1990s. It had fostered new forms of accommodation, such as motels and caravan parks, and new kinds of food outlets.

More than six million Australians belonged to motoring organisations in 1995. There were seven of these, one in every State and one in the Northern Territory. They had an important influence on where people stayed, because they administered an accommodation ratings system which required the inspection of 14 000 properties a year. They published an accommodation guide and they distributed some eight million maps and itineraries a year.[6]

Despite the increase in the number of cars, road construction was slow to start after the war. The road system had been extended to cope with wartime needs. More than 5800 kilometres of new roads had been built; one of the major projects had been the reconstruction of the Stuart Highway from Darwin to Port Augusta. Nevertheless, Australia's roads on the whole had deteriorated badly and when the war ended governments had to do something about them in order to cope with so many more vehicles.

Early agreements between the Commonwealth and the States were scrapped in 1947 and a new Commonwealth Aid Roads and Works Act became law. In 1950 this was replaced by the Commonwealth Roads Act and by Acts of the same name in 1954 and every five years thereafter until 1974. In that year the Commonwealth government introduced the National Highway System, under which it assumed full financial responsibility for the construction and maintenance of the roads that linked Australia's capital cities and major provincial centres. These totalled 18 400 kilometres in 1996. In 1994–95 the three levels of government spent a total of $5707 million on roads.

The new era had got under way in the mid-1950s, when work began on new kinds of roads—the urban multi-lane freeways, bypasses and flyovers. In the 1960s inter-urban freeway routes began to appear; in the 1970s road-building technology moved into the computer age with the introduction of automated equipment. From the mid-1980s

172   improved construction technology made new roads smoother, which not only allowed for more comfortable car travel but also resulted in less wear and tear on the vehicles and saved fuel.

In the late 1990s Australia had 800 000 kilometres of roads—further in combined distance than a trip to the moon and back. For each kilometre of road there were approximately 23 people, compared with 41 in the United States, 154 in Britain and 1123 in China. More than 300 000 kilometres, or 37.5 per cent, of Australia's roads had a bituminous or concrete sealed surface.[7] About 1000 kilometres of freeways had been built. In Victoria alone there were some 640 kilometres, including the Hume Highway between Wodonga and the outskirts of Melbourne.[8]

Coach touring

Ansett leads

R. M. Ansett was the leader in developing long-distance coach travel after the war. During the conflict tour operations were banned as non-essential to the war effort, but Ansett had an eye to the future when he bought Withers' Pioneer Tourist Coaches Pty Ltd in 1944—the year before the war ended—even though at the time it was inactive and no vehicles were involved in the sale. But Pioneer had been a major tour operator throughout Australia. When the war was over, Ansett moved quickly to exploit that fact—so quickly that by 1948 Pioneer was operating 150 tourist coaches on more than 200 routes in all States except Western Australia.

Ansair, another Ansett company, was producing coaches in the latest designs and yet another company, Pioneer Tourist Hotels Pty Ltd, was managing 28 hotels which had been upgraded to cater for the new wave of travellers. Drivers were trained under the eye of a former RAAF group captain, Hal Harding, who insisted that no-one should be allowed to 'go solo' until he had learned each route under a senior driver. Harding called his drivers 'coach captains'. This term was picked up by other companies and became standard usage.[9]

In the 1950s, 1960s and 1970s, Pioneer expanded its network by acquiring smaller coach companies in different parts of Australia. As motels became plentiful it lost interest in providing accommodation for coach travellers, but on the road it was dominant. It ran express services between cities and its touring coaches helped open up much of Australia for tourists. In the 1960s it was said to have had 90 per cent of the express market and 60 per cent of the tour market.[10] It was a leader in vehicle selection and in imaginative tourism marketing, which included vigorous promotion in overseas markets.[11]

Rivalry from Greyhound

Pioneer's chief rival was to be Greyhound Coaches of Brisbane, with its well-marketed express network. The Greyhound name came on the Australian travel and tourism scene at about the end of the war. A. R. (Russ) Penfold, who had started running service cars from Toowoomba in 1928 (see chapter 6, page 105), adopted the name and the racing greyhound emblem for the cream-coloured KB International chara-bancs he had acquired to run between Brisbane and Toowoomba and on other relatively short routes.[12]

The company expanded slowly. It shed the wartime vehicles which were fuelled by gas producers, first for buses built on the chassis of army ambulances and then for modern purpose-built vehicles. It was not until 1968, a few months before its founder's death, that Greyhound was ready to take on long-distance express services. The first was from Brisbane to Sydney, followed by a Brisbane-to-Cairns service.

Under the direction of Russ Penfold's son, who was also named Russell, it then set out to cover the main express routes in the country. This required some acquisitions, but the network was built up largely on the basis of agreements with other operators to work long-distance routes under the Greyhound name. The Greyhound company provided the marketing, including a computerised reservations system, but the individual operators supplied the terminals, workshops and coaches—and ran them.

In 1979, when Sir Peter Abeles and Rupert Murdoch took control of Ansett Transport Industries, Greyhound coaches were covering more kilometres a week than those of Ansett Pioneer.[13] With new owners at Ansett there was immediate speculation about the future of Ansett Pioneer. The company was big—it had nearly 200 coaches—but road passenger services represented only two per cent of group assets. In 1981 Ron King and John Sinclair, Victorian coach operators who had acquired Matilda Tours in Darwin and Legion Trailways in Alice Springs, took over the Northern Territory operation of Ansett Pioneer as a franchise. The name of their operation became Ansett Trailways. Five years later a consortium led by King and Sinclair, and including Greyhound Coaches, took over Ansett Pioneer itself.

By that time the interstate express business was at the midpoint of a period of intense competition. A procession of companies came and went in the 1980s. VIP Express, Redline and Sunliner were among those names that became familiar on interstate routes, succeeded in diluting the market share of the established companies, and then failed finan-cially. Perhaps the best known of these was De Luxe Express, which began by offering the same low fare to everybody—25 dollars—

174 between Adelaide and Sydney using hired coaches. From this single route it expanded very quickly in both routes and services until it was rivalling Pioneer and Greyhound in numbers of passengers carried. But by the end of the decade it, too, was gone. One company that was expanding in the 1980s and continued to flourish into the 1990s was McCafferty's of Toowoomba.

The decline of the coach companies

In 1988 Pioneer Express (the Ansett name had reverted to the airline) was absorbed into Greyhound Coaches. Pioneer Tours became the principal activity of Pioneer Trailways.[14] However, by the next year both Greyhound Coaches and Pioneer Trailways were out of business.

Greyhound Coaches was a sudden and totally unexpected victim of Brisbane's Expo of 1988. The company had taken over a number of coaches from Pioneer at about the time Pioneer Trailways had taken over the touring role. These had been used for a greatly increased service between the Gold Coast and Brisbane during the exposition.[15] But when Expo was over, coach traffic with Brisbane connections became a trickle. Greyhound's revenue fell by 20 per cent, some trade debtors (other coach companies) failed to pay, and the company was unable to meet a bank debt on time. Administrators took over and the name and assets were sold. The undercapitalised Pioneer Trailways went into liquidation some months later.

The Greyhound and Pioneer names lived on in Greyhound Pioneer Australia Ltd, which became Australia's biggest express coach company. This came about as the result of a series of complex corporate arrangements in 1992 and 1993, in the process of which a single company acquired the organisations using the Greyhound and Pioneer names plus the Western Australia-based Bus Australia. After a period during which the three were run as separate entities, they were combined into a unified structure. The company was listed on the Australian Stock Exchange in 1992, originally under the name Australian Coachline Holdings Ltd; later it became Greyhound Pioneer Australia Ltd.

Tour operators, big and small

While this battle of the titans of the express routes was fought and lost, other companies had been started or had grown all over the country, operating express routes, sightseeing schedules, charter and school services and tours. A little company could be operating school buses most of the year and turn into a tour operator on long weekends and on holidays. Suburban operators learned to market through associations that represented common interests, like sport, or catered for people with the time to take trips, like the elderly.

Ron King's brother Bill went to the Northern Territory in the 1970s to run a coach service and developed a genuine affection for the outback. He had an unusual ability to communicate this to others; he developed a safari business using customised vehicles and marketed it in the United States and Europe as well as in Australia.

In 1967 two young men, Geoff McGeary and Mayer Page, sons of Melbourne suburban bus operators, pooled resources with a third operator, Cliff Quince, to form Australian Pacific Coaches. Quince soon dropped out and McGeary and Page went on to build up a company that would play a significant part in Australian touring. They started with school contracts, organised tours during school holidays and then took to the outback over primitive roads in SB Bedford coaches, with the rear seat removed to stow camping gear, roof racks for luggage and small side-lockers to store food.

By 1976 the company had progressed sufficiently to design its own coach, a 42-seater that towed a trailer for supplies. Australian Pacific had gone overseas to attract customers; it was marketing tours in New Zealand, the United States and Europe. As it expanded, it began day tours in Melbourne and Sydney, acquired an interest in a New Zealand operator and a motor inn in Hobart and opened offices in the United States and Britain.

In 1983 AAT Coach Holidays approached Australian Pacific Tours with the idea of taking over the company. AAT was a major touring company started in 1973 by the airline TAA and road freight company Mayne Nickless to compete with Ansett Pioneer Tours. Page and McGeary did not give the offer much thought but countered by saying, in effect, 'Why don't we buy you?' And so AAT became part of the Page-McGeary group, which decided to continue to operate it as a separate company rather than merge it into its own operations. Outwardly the business continued to operate in its own right, with its own board, but some rationalisation was carried out. Reporting systems were made to conform with APT practice, older coaches were phased out, the head office moved out of the city to West Melbourne and parallel tour itineraries were changed.

One of the biggest problems within AAT was that the company had taken over Bill King's Outback Tours and Clyde Harding's Grand Central Tours and there were still unnecessary duplications of business functions and depots. As part of their rationalisation program, the

176   company changed its name to AAT-King's to make use of Bill King's high profile in outback touring.

In 1993 Geoff McGeary and Mayer Page decided to divide their business interests. The principal effect of this was that McGeary took over ownership of Australian Pacific Tours and Page took control of AAT-King's. From that point the two became locked in a fierce competitive battle, although to some extent they diverged, Australian Pacific Tours concentrating on the longer escorted tours while AAT-King's decided to make a speciality of the short-break tours. In 1998 the latter company's 'bread and butter' was three-day tours including Alice Springs, Ayers Rock and King's Canyon.

In 1997 AAT-King's was sold to Travel Corporation, a company with headquarters in Bermuda. Travel Corporation owned a number of tour companies operating in Australia, including Trafalgar Tours, Contiki Holidays for 18 to 35s, Creative Holidays, Insight International Tours and New Horizons Holidays. Like the chief executives of those companies the general manager of AAT-King's, Dallas Newton, then reported to Mike Ness of Travel Corporation, who in earlier days had been the first chief executive of AAT Coach Holidays.

Murrays, the Australian experience

The biggest coach company in Australia in 1998 was Murrays Australia, which operated some 350 coaches from depots in Sydney, Melbourne, Brisbane, Canberra, the Gold Coast and Cairns. Through a subsidiary, Canberra Cruises and Tours Pty Ltd, it also operated the Gundaroo Pub, Burbong Sheep Station and cruises and a restaurant on Lake Burley Griffin.

The history of the company started in the Australian Capital Territory—or just outside it, because it was in Queanbeyan that Ron Murray became a travel agent in 1966 at the age of 19. Two years later he also went into his father's Canberra-based coach company and in 1970 bought the company.

As a travel agent Murray had created experiences with an Australian flavour for overseas visitors; taking them to a property just outside Canberra where they could sample Australian country life, see sheep shorn, throw a boomerang and eat damper. Murray was no stranger to the outdoors. His great-grandparents had run a store and mill at Jindabyne and taken pack-horses over the mountains. His father was an expert horseman and Ron himself had ridden bulls in rodeos—his father considered this was less dangerous than riding bucking horses. Ron Murray also played the didgeridoo and was a member of the Monaro Folk Music Association.

So he bought the Gundaroo Pub and made it part of the tourist circuit, where visitors from overseas could hear traditional Australian songs and Banjo Paterson's verse. He played the didgeridoo and he hired musicians from the Monaro Folk Music Association to take part in sessions at the pub. After buying the coach company he continued as a travel agent, inbound tour operator and entertainer. His company also had the ground handling contract for East-West Airlines and at one time he represented Airlines of New South Wales as well.

Among those companies who chartered his coaches in the ACT was Thomas Cook. In 1978 Cook's persuaded Murray to expand his business to Sydney because of dissatisfaction with the six coach operators that were handling inbound business in that city at the time. They were operating as a cartel and doing things their way. For example they liked to work out rosters a month ahead, whereas Japanese tour operators wanted to book a few days ahead.

In 1988 Murrays moved to the Gold Coast during the Brisbane Expo and stayed to continue charter work in both cities. The company was also able to help Japanese operators co-ordinate their tour movements during that period by making available software and hardware support through its mainframe computer in Canberra.

The business expanded in the next two years with the opening of depots in Melbourne and then Cairns. Each time the moves were made as the result of requests from Japanese tour operators and there was enough business coming from them to make the move feasible. The company, tightly controlled through its management systems, was able to grow without overstretching. As a result, Ron Murray was able to say:

> It is interesting what happens if you do your work well. I have 70 per cent of the Japanese market and I have never made a sales mission to Japan.[16]

Car rentals

McIllree's rent-a-car vision

Rent-a-car companies operated in Australia before and during the war and by the early 1950s there were local companies around the country. One operator was Eric McIllree, an aviator with a colourful history who not only ran car rental companies such as AAA Rent-a-Car and Sydney-Drive-Yourself after the war, but also had a business selling ex-wartime aircraft. An inveterate traveller, he could see that international travel was expanding in North America and Europe and that the day would come when Australia was also a tourism destination. When that

178   happened, success in the car rental business would require an international connection.

On a visit to the United States he began negotiations with Hertz, but the executives he talked to had little knowledge of Australia and less interest. So he turned to Avis. The reception was much more enthusiastic and he arrived back in Sydney with a licence from Avis on extremely favourable terms. In 1955 he set about launching Avis Australia-wide, beginning operations with 150 FJ Holdens stationed at nine airports.[17]

When Hertz did discover Australia, the company was not pleased at what had happened, particularly when they found that McIllree had registered its business name in this country, effectively blocking it out. Negotiations led to a deal: McIllree would sell Hertz back the right to its name for one shilling (10 cents) provided the company stayed out of Australia for three years. With this agreement as a protection from competition from the world's biggest rent-a-car company, McIllree set out to make the most of those three years, negotiating business arrangements with airlines, railways and hotels. He also negotiated exclusive airport rights—vitally important because most users of airlines and rent-a-cars were business travellers. McIllree had registered the names of two other American rent-a-car companies, Budget and National. He used National at a few service stations and there were other National licensees afterwards, but the brand was slow to make an impact in Australia outside Queensland.[18]

In 1965 McIllree started a new company under the Budget brand, focusing on the downtown walk-in-walk-out market, to complement but not compete with Avis and its airport monopoly. It *was* designed to compete with Kay's Rent-a-Car, an Australian company that had been McIllree's most formidable rival in his early years. Kay's was run by Alex Katranski, who had come from New Zealand in 1956. Katranski was quite willing to compete with McIlree in pricing, the traditional weapon in car rental wars.

The Hertz name became a major force in Australia after Doug Wootton, a former Avis executive, and John Murphy bought Kay's Rent-a-Car from a subsidiary of Ansett Transport Industries in the late 1970s. At the time Hertz was a small corporate operation, but Wootton and Murphy bought the master licence and so Kay's became Hertz for Australia and New Zealand.

The Ansetts: the battle between father and son

Some months after starting Budget McIllree made Bob Ansett, Sir Reginald Ansett's son, chief executive. Ansett had only recently returned

to Australia from the United States, where he had been educated and **179**
spent his early working life after serving in the US Army during the
Korean War.[19]

His beginnings in the rent-a-car business were far from grand. He had
a small fume-filled office in a garage in La Trobe Street, Melbourne,[20]
one employee and 20 cars. He also had ambition, energy and an instinc-
tive marketing flair and he began to put Budget into all the main cities
and tourism areas. When McIllree died in 1973 Ansett was already well
known through his personal style of marketing. The following year he
and Australian Guarantee Corporation bought the company.

Immediately he launched a widely-publicised attack on Avis'
monopolistic grip on the airport business, focusing attention with a
'Freedom of Choice' campaign on television. The issue became big
news when his father's company, Ansett Transport Industries, bought
Avis in 1978 and TAA and Mayne Nickless bought Hertz. Thus Bob
Ansett was pictured as a David up against two Goliaths, with the added
piquancy that one of the Goliaths was David's own father.

While this battle of the media was going on, Bob Ansett continued to
build up Budget, extending the number of outlets by franchising, which
was new ground for rent-a-car companies at the time. The enormous
publicity generated by the various moves in the car rental business, the
drama of father pitched against son, and the image of a small company
battling two giants and the Commonwealth government had a huge
impact on the industry as a whole. The car rental industry's penetration
of the market increased from 5 per cent of the adult population using a
rent-a-car to 20 per cent—higher than in the United States.[21]

Budget's campaign against the airport monopoly lasted five years. In
1978 the Commonwealth government announced that two rent-a-car
companies would be awarded airport contracts following a tender
process. This was increased to three after Bob Ansett spoke to the Prime
Minister, Malcolm Fraser. The specification was that there would be two
contracts awarded nationally and that the third contract would be on
an airport-to-airport basis.

In the tendering process, Hertz was awarded the first national contract and Budget the second, the latter having bid $3.15 million to Avis'
$3.1 million. In tendering on an airport-to-airport basis, Avis secured
contracts for only 11 out of 56 airports, a devastating result for a company that previously had held a monopoly. Budget took over $17 mil-
lion worth of Avis' business within six months, was market leader in
1980 and ultimately grew to control 50 per cent of the market.[22]

In 1989 Budget was in financial difficulties, experiencing severe cash
flow problems exacerbated by the pilots' strike of that year. The

180 company went into provisional liquidation and was later taken over by the US Budget Corporation. Bob Ansett disappeared from the rent-a-car scene.

New forces in the market

Avis had earlier come under the ownership of its parent company in the United States. Ansett Transport Industries sold the Australian company in 1980 to a joint venture of Avis Inc. and Burns, Philp & Co. Avis Inc. bought Burns, Philp's share in 1986, making the Australian company a wholly-owned subsidiary. The Hertz Corporation also took over the Australian company that bore its name from TAA and Mayne Nickless.

New forces came into the market. Thrifty Car Rental was first established in Australia in 1977 but played a relatively minor role until the 1990s, when it began to grow rapidly under new ownership. By the late 1990s it was the third biggest rent-a-car operator in Australia after Avis and Hertz, servicing more than 260 locations including all major and most minor airports. It was operated by Kingmill Australia Pty Ltd, a company formed in 1990 with Mitsubishi Motors Australia and Thrifty Rent A Car—USA as its shareholders. In this period, Budget occupied fourth spot among car rental operators.

The biggest off-airport car rental operation was Australian-owned. Delta Car Rentals dated back to 1981, but its major expansion was under the ownership of Mario Salvo who bought it in 1988. Salvo was born in Sicily and arrived in Australia when he was four. He was the second youngest of eight children, and it is said that his childhood struggles helped give him the drive and determination to succeed in his various business enterprises.[23] By 1998 Delta was operating from 60 locations and was positioned as one of the top five players in the industry.

Recreational vehicles

As interest in off-the-beaten-track touring grew in the 1980s with the increased availability of off-road and recreational vehicles, the rent-a-car companies moved to meet the demand, adding to their fleets four wheel drive vehicles, campervans and motorhomes. Specialist companies also appeared, some appealing strongly to inbound markets. Brits:Australia Rentals, the largest of these operators in 1998, regarded continental Europe as its main market.

Touring in remote areas had also resulted in the formation of another kind of company. Aussie Outback Tours was established by a Melbourne academic, Lloyd Junor, in 1987 to escort convoys of caravanners and others in recreational vehicles into areas where the inexperienced adventurer could not only get into trouble but through frustration or ignorance could also miss the real attractions.

Outback tourism (Source: Aussie Outback Tours)

Outback touring was a growth area of Australian tourism. It required careful preparation and the right equipment. The camper being towed in this picture was designed to go (almost) anywhere in the outback.

The railways

The railways' post-war decline

The war had exhausted the railways. They had carried huge numbers of military personnel and vast amounts of equipment and supplies, particularly on the east coast between Melbourne and Brisbane. But when the war was over they did not get the investment that was needed to revitalise them. Instead, they were faced with competition they could never have contemplated in the 1930s. This came from a road transport industry that used an enlarged road system and war-surplus vehicles and an aviation industry that was equipped with some of the thousands of DC-3s built for war service. In the 1950s the railways generally went into a decline as the new services flourished. Nevertheless, there was some progress.

In Queensland, the government legislated to prevent road transport from competing against the railways on the Brisbane–Cairns route and invested in new rolling stock for new passenger trains. One of these, the *Sunlander*, had modern air-conditioned carriages hauled by a diesel-

182 electric locomotive which took 41 hours on the journey from Brisbane to Cairns.

Tasmania had been the first to introduce the cleaner and more powerful diesel-electric locomotives in 1950 and the other systems were soon to follow. Victorian Railways added a steam engine to its fleet in 1951 but it was the last—the age of steam was on its way out.

One line links major cities

The vexatious problem of gauges was raised again in the mid-1950s and a Commonwealth Parliamentary Committee recommended a sustained program of conversion to the standard gauge. A 'sustained program' was too much to tackle at the time, but in 1957 work was started on a standard-gauge line from Albury to Melbourne and this was completed early in 1962. Thus Melbourne and Sydney were connected by one line at last. The bogies of the *Spirit of Progress* were changed to allow it to run on the new tracks and the *Southern Aurora*, a new luxury train, was built for the service as a joint venture between the New South Wales and Victorian railway systems.

The Commonwealth Railways had a busy couple of decades. Trains were able to run all the way from Sydney to Perth when the standard-gauge line from Broken Hill was extended to Port Pirie. Here it was linked with the transcontinental railway and another standard-gauge link was built at the other end between Kalgoorlie and Perth. A new train, the *Indian-Pacific*, made its first run between the capitals on opposite coasts in 1970. A standard-gauge line was built from the transcontinental track at Tarcoola to Alice Springs. In 1980 a smart new *Ghan* gave passengers a much improved and faster service than the old train, which had plodded its way through the desert with second-hand carriages on poorly-maintained tracks.

The Commonwealth Railways took over the railways of some State systems. In Tasmania it was a complete takeover in 1974, and the last passenger service ran in Tasmania in 1978. In South Australia, the Commonwealth took over all railway services except for the suburban Adelaide lines in 1975. The *Overland*, the Melbourne–Adelaide express, became a joint venture between the Victorian Railways and the Australian National Railways (the name adopted by Commonwealth Railways) in 1975.

The XPT: the start of a new era

The first sign of a revival of the railways in the overseas style came in 1982, when the New South Wales State Rail Authority introduced the XPT (Xpress Passenger Train) on the Sydney–Dubbo run. This high-speed train, with its comfortable airline-style seating, was based on the **183** British HST (High Speed Diesel Train). The limitations of the New South Wales track restricted its normal operating speed to a maximum of 160 kilometres per hour, although it did set an Australian record by reaching 193 kilometres per hour in September 1992. In 1990 the XPT service was extended to the Sydney–Brisbane run and from 1993, the year new cars were delivered, it provided regular services between Sydney and Melbourne. Configured in five- or seven-car trains, the XPT offered first class and economy seating and sleeping cars on the longer journeys between Sydney and Melbourne, Sydney and Brisbane and Sydney and Murwillumbah.

Only two country passenger trains were being operated in the 1990s by Westrail, as the government railways in Western Australia were then known, but they are worth noting. They were quality railcar services run at high speed, though on different gauges. The 1435-millimetre gauge *Prospector* service to Kalgoorlie operated at 140 kilometres per hour and the 1067-millimetre gauge *Australind* to Bunbury travelled at 120 kilometres per hour.

Queensland Rail introduced a 160 kilometre-per-hour train, running between Brisbane and Rockhampton, in late 1998. It was known as the Tilt Train because its cars were tilted by compressed air as it went around curves, allowing speed to be increased by up to 25 per cent. The angle of tilt was controlled by on-board computers. Passengers were accommodated in six cars, one business class and the others economy. This was a modern train in many ways, with features that included pay-telephones, a fax machine, a passenger information system providing details of speed and expected time of arrival, and a 'driver perspective system' that enabled passengers to see what the driver could see.

By the 1990s trains were a potent part of Queensland's attraction as a tourism destination, with international travellers providing some 30 per cent of its passengers.[24] Queensland Rail developed a number of themed trains designed to reflect the character and landscape through which they travelled, grouping them in three categories: coastal, scenic and outback. They included the *Queenslander*, an all-first-class train with sleeping berths which ran up the coast from Brisbane to Cairns, a journey of nearly 31 hours; the Kuranda scenic railway which wound its way along 34 kilometres of original track constructed in 1882 from Cairns through rainforest to Kuranda, 328 metres above sea level; and the *Spirit of the Outback* (a new version of the *Midlander*), which linked Brisbane with the growing destination area of Longreach, home of the Stockman's Hall of Fame.

Luxury train travel (Source: Colvin Communications)

Vintage luxury Australian style. The Great Southern Express, *which runs between Sydney and Cairns, was created as a modern tourist train in the luxury style of another era. The train was a joint venture by Queensland Rail and Venice Simplon-Orient-Express.*

Queensland Rail launched its most ambitious project in 1999, the *Great South Pacific Express*. It operated the train in association with Venice Simplon-Orient-Express, the London-based division of the American company that had revived the tradition of the *Orient Express* with a train bearing that name in Europe as well as other trains in the grand old style in Britain and Asia. The *Great South Pacific Express* was not only designed to bring travellers the sumptuous ambience and service of other eras, but was also the first to make the 3000-kilometre journey between Sydney and Cairns.[25]

Meanwhile, the *Indian-Pacific* was running on its 4352-kilometre trip between Sydney and Perth under a new owner. A private company, Great Southern Railway Ltd, took over the passenger services of the Australian National Line in November 1997, thus becoming the opera-tor of the *Ghan* and the *Overland* as well as the *Indian-Pacific*. The inter-ests behind the new venture included two British companies (a

specialist passenger rail operator and a large facilities management
group), an American freight rail operator and an Australian investment
bank. The new company extended *Ghan* services to include Melbourne
and Sydney, adjusted timetables, increased frequency and improved
on-board services. The *Overland* was refurbished.

A high-speed Canberra–Sydney link

In August 1998 the Commonwealth government announced that a
VHST (Very High Speed Train) link would be built between Sydney and
Canberra using French TGV technology, and was expected to begin
operating by the end of 2003. With speeds of up to 300 kilometres per
hour, its travel time between the two cities would be 81 minutes. The
$3.5 billion development by the Speedrail consortium, a joint venture
between France's GEC Alsthom and Leighton Contractors Pty Ltd,
would require the construction of a new line and new stations and
would be Australia's biggest transport infrastructure project. Speedrail
would own and operate the system for 30 years, after which it would
revert to public ownership.[26] There were proposals to extend the line
from Canberra to Melbourne and for other high-speed train services
between Melbourne and Darwin and Alice Springs and Darwin.

The twentieth century was ending with more optimism about the
future for Australian railways than had been evident for 50 years. They
would never regain the dominance in land travel they had held
between the wars, but the fast train services were already proving competitive with airliners and coaches and the expansion of the luxury
tourist train sector—the hotels on wheels—had created a major tourist
attraction.

ENDNOTES

[1] Adrian Ryan, Ford Motor Company consultant archivist, interview, August 1998.

[2] Gilltrap & Gilltrap, op.cit., p. 161.

[3] Davis, V. C. (1959), *Let's Talk Motels: Motel Guide for Australia*, 2nd edn, The Australian
Motel Magazine Company, Sydney, p. 7.

[4] Spearritt (1987c), op.cit., p. 128.

[5] Austroads (1997), *Roadfacts '96*, pp. 15 & 30.

[6] Richardson (1996), op.cit., pp. 81–2.

[7] Austroads, op.cit., pp. 6, 7 & 17.

[8] Lay, M. G. (1996), 'Roads and roadmaking' in *The Australian Encyclopaedia*, 6th edn,
Australian Geographic Pty Ltd, Terrey Hills, NSW, v. 7, p. 2594. Freeways are technically
defined as roads with separate carriageways for each direction of traffic, no intersections and no side access other than via the entry ramps provided at grade-separated
interchanges.

[9] Maddock, op.cit., pp. 97–116, a chapter titled 'Rise and fall of Ansett'. Maddock cites Colin MacDonald for some of his information, including that on Harding. MacDonald joined Ansett as a driver in 1934 and went on to be executive director of the whole road transport division of Ansett Transport Industries.

[10] ibid., p. 112.

[11] Its overseas marketing manager was Jack Long, who took part in travel missions organised by the ATC in the United States in 1975 and 1977, as well as maintaining a network of contacts in the major overseas markets. The national marketing manager was Brian Milnes, who in 1997 was given a Victorian Tourism Award for an outstanding contribution by an individual. He was then sales manager for the Brits group.

[12] These vehicles, which carried 14–20 passengers, had a line of doors on the left-hand side leading to bench seats. Much later Greyhound Coaches Pty Ltd, as the company became known, negotiated reciprocal representation rights with the Greyhound Corporation of the United States. Ansett Pioneer also represented the US company for a period. The greyhound emblems (stylised dogs) of the US and Australian Greyhound companies were not exactly the same. There is little documentation of Greyhound Coaches' history. (Russell Penfold, managing director of Greyhound for some 20 years up to 1989, interview, February 1998).

[13] ibid.

[14] Maddock, op.cit., p. 114.

[15] During Expo Greyhound ran 18 services a day between the Gold Coast and Brisbane, both ways.

[16] Ron Murray, interview, August 1998.

[17] Avis Australia Fact Sheet, 1998.

[18] The American company recovered the licence and in the late 1990s was seeking to acquire an established Australian company with the idea of bidding for airport licences. Competing for licences changed with the sale of airport leases by the Commonwealth Government. Each airport management company could set its own terms for car rental licences. There could be no national negotiations as there had been when airports were administered by Commonwealth Government agencies.

[19] McIllree said to Don Hamence, Avis' Melbourne manager at the time, 'I've had Reg on the phone. He wants a job for his son Bob but he hasn't got a position himself. Politically, it might be wise for me to put him on. Have you got a job for him? What about sales manager?' Hamence said he already had a sales manager. 'Better not rock the boat then,' said McIllree. 'I've just started Budget. Bob might do well as manager there' (Don Hamence, interview, March 1998). Hamence had a long and distinguished career in the rent-a-car industry. Besides his service with Avis he was also deputy managing director of Hertz Australia. He later became Travel Commissioner in the Australian Capital Territory. In 1999 he was a director and national franchise manager of Sargent Rent A Car Systems (Australia) Pty Ltd. He is the source of much of the information in this section.

[20] 'Fume-filled'—author's personal observation at the time.

[21] Bob Ansett's figures confirmed by Hamence, interviews, March 1998.

[22] Bob Ansett, interview, July 1998.

[23] Notes from Delta Car Rental supplied to author, May 1998.

[24] Queensland Rail brochure 'Queensland Rail's Traveltrain', issued 1998.

[25] Queensland Rail's chief executive, Vince O'Rourke, conceived the idea of creating 'the world's most beautiful train', not only in fulfilment of a grand vision, but also to keep his workshop staff in employment. He brought in Venice Simplon-Orient-Express to contribute its name, ideas and marketing experience, and to operate the train. Denise

Corcoran, an Adelaide-based designer, who had previously worked on designs for the *Ghan* and the *Queenslander*, was chosen to head the design team and ensure that the décor was authentically Australian. The late Victorian and early Edwardian eras were chosen as the design basis because their decorative styles, elegant and ornate, exemplified the style of Venice Simplon-Orient-Express products (notes from Colvin Communications International).

[26] *The Australian Financial Review*, 5 August 1998, pp. 1–2.

More revolutions in the air

Government involvement in the airlines

Immediately after the war, the Commonwealth government tried to nationalise the airline industry in Australia but was thwarted by court action. So it did two things:

1 It took over Qantas Empire Airways by a normal commercial process. First it bought the 50 per cent held by the British Overseas Airways Corporation, the successor to Imperial Airways, and then in 1947 the shares held by Queensland and Northern Territory Aerial Services Limited.
2 It set up Trans Australia Airlines to operate within Australia, equipping it with twelve former Royal Australian Air Force DC-3s. TAA commenced regular flights in November 1946. Within four weeks its aircraft were flying all the trunk routes between the Australian capital cities.[1]

Australian international services

Qantas had been radically affected by the war. Of the Short Empire flying boats it had in 1939, only one remained at the end of the conflict.[2] From June 1943 to July 1945 the airline had maintained part of the Australia–Britain air link by using Catalina flying boats between Perth and Ceylon (now Sri Lanka), where they connected with flights to Britain by BOAC.[3] After the war the Catalinas, which had been supplied by the British Air Ministry, were scuttled at sea under the lend-lease agreement with the US government. To stay in business, Qantas had to **189** quickly acquire aircraft to fly on a variety of routes. It got them, and they were a mixed bag.

Seven Catalinas were taken over from the RAAF and used for services in New Guinea and to New Caledonia, the New Hebrides (now Vanuatu), Fiji and Lord Howe Island. They were also used in New Guinea. DC-3s were introduced on the Australia–New Guinea, New Guinea internal and Queensland routes.[4] Short Sandringham flying boats were added to the Catalina fleet for South Pacific services.

On the Qantas sectors of the Australia–Britain route which connected with BOAC flights, converted bombers—at first American Liberators and then British Lancastrians, a civil version of the Lancaster—were used between Sydney and Karachi. These were not liked by the passengers, who had to sit on one side of the fuselage and look out through windows on the other side.[5] More comfortable were the Short Hythe flying boats, a larger and more luxurious version of the pre-war Empire class, which Qantas flew between Sydney and Singapore.

An exciting new aircraft had been ordered in 1946. Qantas had received government permission to buy four Lockheed Constellations for $A5.5 million at a time when strict wartime currency restraints were still in force. The Constellations were a big improvement on planes that Qantas had flown before, because they were true pressurised long-range airliners. The delivery of the first of these aircraft was taken in November 1947.

Qantas continued to expand its route structure. In 1949 it introduced the DC-4 on new services to Hong Kong and Japan. In 1953 it began flying to Johannesburg, South Africa and secured an agreement that allowed it to fly to North America instead of British Commonwealth Pacific Airlines, which the Australian airline eventually absorbed.[6] Qantas opened its Australia–United States–Canada service with Super Constellations in May 1954, flying between Sydney, San Francisco and Vancouver via Fiji, Canton Island (now Gwangdung) and Hawaii. It also operated four royal flights that year, carrying the Queen and Duke of Edinburgh on their Australian tour.

By 1956 Qantas had a fleet of 34 propeller-driven aircraft, including Super Constellations. In that year it carried a record number of passengers to the Olympic Games in Melbourne. It brought the Olympic flame into the Southern Hemisphere for the first time on its longest-ever trip: from Athens to Darwin, a total of 13 800 kilometres.

Intercontinental travel in style (Source: Qantas Airways)

Qantas introduced Lockheed Constellations on its transoceanic routes in 1947. These were a big advance on the land planes Qantas had flown previously because they were not converted bombers and they were pressurised. The airline promoted the new service with this striking poster.

This was also the year the airline ordered its first jets, seven Boeing **191**
707s, at a cost of $A28 million. It took delivery of these aircraft between
July and September 1959, putting the 707 into service ahead of every
other airline outside the United States. It was also high in the list of airlines that chose to fly the Boeing 747, placing orders for four in August
1967; its first jumbo went into service four years later. In the same year
it was renamed Qantas Airways Limited.

In 1974 Qantas evacuated 673 people on a single 747—a world
record at the time—from Darwin after the city had been devastated by
Cyclone Tracy. Qantas operated 747s exclusively from 1979 to 1985,
when Boeing 767s were introduced on New Zealand, Asian and Pacific
routes. In 1979 it was the first airline to introduce business class.

By 1996 Qantas was operating more than 250 international flights a
week to 40 destinations in 26 countries. Forty-four other airlines also
flew to and from Australia. The tyranny of distance was well and truly
conquered.

By the beginning of the 1990s, fundamental changes in the airline
industry around the world were affecting the Australian airlines' view of
the future and how they might exist in an era of globalisation. The
bilateral regulatory system that had fostered a nationally-based airline
industry since the war was now going through profound change.[7]
Qantas could not compete in this changing environment while it was
under government ownership which, for one thing, prevented it from
raising the capital necessary for re-equipping. It was clear, too, that
Qantas had to be free to make commercial alliances of one kind or
another with other international carriers.

Ownership changes

The ownership changes began in 1992 when Qantas bought Australian
Airlines for $400 million. The next year British Airways (successor to
BOAC) bought 25 per cent of Qantas for $665 million. The rest of the
shares in the airline were sold to the public, to financial institutions
and to foreign investors in an Australian Stock Exchange float in July
1995. Total foreign ownership was restricted to 49 per cent.

In the early 1990s British Airways was expected to lead the way to an
era of transnational mega-carriers. After some shuffling among major
airlines, what had actually emerged by the late 1990s were alliances
among the airlines rather than takeovers or increased equity purchases.
Qantas was part of the powerful **One**world alliance that included
British Airways and American Airlines.

192 Ansett International begins service

In 1993 Qantas had, for the first time, direct competition on some routes from another Australian carrier, Ansett International Airlines, which began services to Asian ports in September 1993. Ansett had recognised that the forces of change, referred to in chapter 8 (page 136), could also affect its chances of survival in the long run. Ansett International was formed as part of Ansett Australia but in 1996, when Air New Zealand bought a half share in the company, 51 per cent of Ansett International was sold to Australian institutional investors to protect its designation as an Australian carrier and its regional route approvals. However, Ansett International operated as a division of Ansett Australia Holdings under the brand name of Ansett Australia.

Ansett International set out to build up a network in the Asia-Pacific region. By 1997 it had flights from various Australian cities to Indonesia (Bali and Jakarta), Hong Kong, Japan, Taiwan, Malaysia, New Zealand, Korea and China. It also had code-share arrangements with other airlines in the region. The Asian financial crisis that began in 1997 was a severe blow to Ansett International, which was forced to cut back on its Asian network, but unlike Qantas did not have other routes to which it could divert its efforts.

The origins of Air New Zealand went back to TEAL, the consortium carrier formed before the war by Qantas, Union Airways of New Zealand and Imperial Airways. After the war it continued to take flying boats across the Tasman and expanded its services to the South Pacific islands north of New Zealand.

BOAC withdrew from the partnership in 1953, leaving Australia and New Zealand owning half of TEAL each. The airline re-equipped with Lockheed Electra prop-jets in 1959, a decision forced on it by the Australian government because Qantas was flying that type on some routes. The decision was not popular with New Zealanders, who wanted to re-equip with pure jets. Their resentment prompted the New Zealand government to negotiate the purchase of Australia's 50 per cent interest in the company in 1961, making it New Zealand's official international airline. Its name was changed to Air New Zealand.[8]

In 1960 Australian domestic airlines began to operate services between Australia and Papua New Guinea. They also began to fly within Papua New Guinea: TAA took over services within Papua New Guinea previously operated by Qantas and Ansett bought Mandated Airlines from W. R. Carpenter and Co., which had operated there since 1938. On 1 November 1973 Air Niugini was formed to take over the Papua New Guinea services operated by TAA and Ansett. After Papua

New Guinea became independent in 1975 the new government owned   **193**
the majority shareholding in Air Niugini.

TAA's domestic challenge

When the newly-formed government airline Trans Australia Airlines
first flew in 1946 with DC-3 aircraft, its main private enterprise competition was from ANA, which introduced the larger four-engined
Douglas DC-4 Skymaster in February of that year. TAA responded; its
first DC-4 went into service ten months later. Ansett Airlines, which had
prospered during the war on American military contracts, was not a
major competitor; it flew only in south-eastern Australia and did not
compete directly with the two major airlines on trunk routes. It
achieved this by not flying directly between capitals—Sydney to
Melbourne and Melbourne to Adelaide—but by always including an
intermediate country destination. Ansett also introduced economy
fares, which were very popular.

ANA's managing director, Ivan Holyman, had pursued a policy of
expansion by taking over smaller airlines to build a route network
which in 1946 extended from Perth to the tip of Cape York. However,
ANA's standard of service had deteriorated, affecting its punctuality and
customer service. Once again competition was the spur to better things.
When TAA began operations there were 'sudden and miraculous
improvements' in ANA's service and punctuality.[9]

From 1946 to 1950 TAA established a good reputation, particularly
after it introduced pressurised Convair aircraft, while ANA's reputation
suffered from three crashes which killed a total of 15 people, forcing it
to drop its slogan 'ANA—Australia's most experienced airline'.[10]

In 1952 the government felt it necessary to stabilise the airline
industry and did so by promulgating the Civil Aviation Agreement Act.
Under this Act, air mail and government business would be shared
equally between TAA and ANA, air navigation charges would be
reduced and both carriers would be given government assistance to re-
equip their fleets.

ANA continued to perform badly, however. This was partly due to
TAA's again introducing superior aircraft: the prop-jet Vickers Viscount.
Eventually, in 1957, after the death of Sir Ivan Holyman (he was
knighted the year he died) and months of discussion in government
and business circles about the economics of the domestic airlines,
R. M. Ansett offered to buy ANA. The offer was first rejected by the
ANA board as 'rude' and 'unwarranted'.[11] The directors refused to take

194   Ansett's offer seriously; his airline was just one of the small carriers they had once tried to take over. But after more months of negotiation they concluded that Ansett's offer represented the only means of getting back some of their investment. They accepted it. Ansett paid £3 300 000 for the faltering ANA and a new carrier, Ansett-ANA, came into being.

The origins of the Two Airlines Policy

That was not the end of it. The airline system was still unstable because of uneven profitability on trunk routes and heavy losses for operators of DC-3 aircraft on developmental routes subsidised by the government.[12] The government introduced what became known as the 'Two Airlines Policy', embodied in the Airline Equipment Act 1958 which was amended in 1959. This made sure that there was little difference between the two airlines—significantly in aircraft types and seating capacity on each route.

The airlines also flew to the same schedules, which passengers found particularly irritating; some ports might not have a flight for a day, but the next day two flights might leave within five minutes of each other. TAA had the better planes, particularly its Vickers Viscount turbo-props,[13] but it was forced to exchange some of them for Ansett-ANA's less attractive Douglas DC-6s. From then on, the government decided what new aircraft the airlines could order, ending TAA's hopes of introducing the pure-jet French Caravelle.

In fact, when the Two Airlines Agreement was extended to 1977 by the Airlines Agreement Act 1961, the legislation stipulated that neither airline was permitted to introduce jet aircraft before 1 July 1964. Any new aircraft had to be ordered by both airlines at the same time, arrive in Australia at the same time and enter service at the same time. Boeing 727s were put into service in 1964, followed by Douglas DC-9s in 1967. The next year Ansett-ANA dropped the 'ANA' and the airline became Ansett Airlines of Australia. In the meantime, R. M. Ansett had already embarked on an expansion program by taking over the principal intrastate airline operations Butler Air Transport, Guinea Airways and MacRobertson Miller Airlines.

Butler Air Transport was the largest and most successful airline operating in New South Wales, serving all major ports except Tamworth. The company also owned Queensland Air Lines, which serviced towns between Brisbane and Gladstone. Ansett took over Butler in 1958 and later renamed it Airlines of New South Wales. Guinea Airways had been confined to internal routes in South Australia since the Commonwealth Government had deprived it of New Guinea and Northern Territory routes. It was taken over by Ansett in 1959 and became Airlines of South Australia. It was another ten years before MacRobertson Miller became a wholly-owned Ansett subsidiary and it was not until 1981 that the name was changed to Airlines of Western Australia.[14]

East-West Airlines remained independent. It had been formed in 1946 to operate the Tamworth–Sydney route and then developed a network of services using Fokker F-27 Friendships. It had attracted notice in the 1970s with innovations such as cut-price fares from Sydney to the Gold Coast and Maroochydore; the possibility of its becoming the third trunk carrier was widely canvassed.[15]

In 1979 East-West took over Connair—formerly Connellan Airways—and established Northern Airlines to operate Northern Territory services from June 1980. The new company ceased flying after only seven months and Ansett Airlines of Northern Australia took over the service. Connellan Airways had been formed after the war by pioneer aviator Eddie Connellan, who had not only inaugurated air services to Ayers Rock and elsewhere in the Northern Territory but had been a great promoter of Northern Territory and Australian tourism (see page 110).[16]

In the early 1980s there was takeover speculation about East-West Airlines, which included approaches by Bob Ansett, Sir Reginald Ansett's son. However, it was Bryan Grey, a former Ansett executive, who gained control of the airline and established cut-price services on routes between Sydney and Canberra and Sydney and Melbourne via Albury. In late 1983 the company was sold to the Western Australian charter operator Skywest, but in 1987 it entered the Ansett fold at last, bought by TNT and News Limited, which by that time had been owners of Ansett Transport Industries for eight years.

Abeles and Murdoch take over

The moves to wrest control of Ansett Transport Industries from Sir Reginald Ansett had started in the 1970s, with Sir Reginald characteristically fighting back although he was of retiring age. At first, the main players bidding for the airline and associated companies were Sir Peter Abeles, of TNT Ltd, and Robert Holmes à Court, head of the Bell Group. Eventually, in 1979, Sir Peter Abeles was joined by Rupert

196   Murdoch, the head of News Limited, and they prevailed in a last-minute flurry of share-buying with TNT and News Limited each buying 50 per cent of ATI; Abeles and Murdoch became joint managing directors.

They brought fresh thinking to the airline and, as TAA was forced for follow suit, to the domestic airline business as a whole. They not only changed the look of Ansett with new livery and other imagery; they changed its concept of service with new passenger terminals and improved in-flight service.

> For the first time in decades passengers were treated as though they were important. (S. Brimson, *Ansett: The Story of an Airline*, 1987)[17]

The Two Airlines Policy was not yet dead, but the airlines were now free to choose their own aircraft. This resulted in differing fleets; TAA ordered Airbus 300s and Ansett decided on Boeing 767s and 737s (the latter to replace the DC-9s).

In 1986 under a new managing director, James Strong, TAA went through a change of image and of operating culture as profound as that which Ansett had undergone a few years earlier. This included a new name—Australian Airlines—and was part of the preparation for a new era of competition. The writing had been on the wall for some time. In 1987 the government announced that the Two Airlines Policy would end in 1990. Ansett and Australian Airlines had already begun spending large sums in preparation for all-out competition, buying new planes and improving terminals and ground support facilities. In the six years from 1986 to 1992 each spent about $2.5 billion.

But before deregulation could take place there was an event that traumatised the system. In July 1989 the Australian Federation of Airline Pilots (AFAP), representing 1645 pilots, lodged a claim for a 29.5 per cent pay increase which the airlines rejected. Eventually the pilots resigned en masse and the airlines struggled to keep the system going, leasing foreign aircraft and recruiting replacement pilots from overseas. They were helped by the government, which contributed RAAF transport aircraft.

The dispute lasted from August 1989 to May 1990. Although the number of passengers carried fell markedly during this period and the strike was costly to the airlines, it also helped them prepare for deregulation and its new competitive forces. The number of pilots was reduced by 25 per cent and their hours at the controls increased by 25 per cent.

Deregulation and the two Compasses

On 4 October 1990 Ansett announced another name change—to Ansett Australia—and a new livery. Four weeks later, on 31 October, the government withdrew from economic regulation of aircraft imports, capacity, airfares and routes. The skies were open for competition and the wait was not long: on 1 December 1990 Compass Airlines began operating on the Melbourne–Sydney–Brisbane route.

There were to be two airlines flying under the Compass name and they both failed commercially. The first, headed by Bryan Grey, flew 288-seat Airbus A300 aircraft. It lasted just over a year, until December 1991. The second, operated by Southern Cross Airlines, used much smaller planes, 142-seat MD-80s. It lasted only half as long as its predecessor, beginning service in August 1992 and ceasing in March 1993.

Both new entrants were undercapitalised for a battle with Australian Airlines and Ansett Australia, which was fought largely on price; although schedules, destinations (Cairns and Perth were beneficiaries of the first challenge) and other factors such as terminal access had their place among the issues that decided the outcome of the contest. Australian and Ansett had much greater experience, an established customer base and industry alliances. They also had greater resources, could dictate the tactical moves and could withstand competition for a longer period, even if it meant accepting losses. The Compasses were not the only casualties. East-West Airlines, which for most of this period was positioned as a holiday airline, also went out of business.

Price competition continued and the result was a period of the fastest growth in domestic airline history. Apart from 1988, the Bicentennial year, the 1980s had shown little growth in domestic airline patronage on trunk routes. In 1982 there were 11 006 000 passengers on the major airlines and in 1986 there were 12 345 000. In 1989, the year before deregulation, the figure was down to 10 445 000 because of the pilots' strike. In 1991, the first full year without regulations, the number of passengers reached 17 304 000 and in 1994 21 200 000.[18] Much of the growth was in a recession, although in every previous recession airlines had lost business. There was a general decline in airfares after deregulation in both real and nominal terms.[19] In a six-month period in 1994 Qantas sold 3.5 million discounted domestic airfares.

The industry continued to undergo change. After lengthy negotiations Air New Zealand bought TNT's 50 per cent share of Ansett for $325 million in August 1996, agreeing also to inject a further $150 million as part of a $200 million capital increase. Early in 1990

198   Singapore Airlines announced a bid for News Limited's 50 per cent of the company.

The rise of regional airlines

In the late 1990s there were some 50 regional airlines in Australia; a regional airline being defined for statistical purposes as one that flies scheduled services with planes carrying fewer than 39 passenger seats or a payload of less than 4200 kilograms. Regional airlines flew to country cities and towns and fed into the capital cities.[20]

The regional system had its genesis in 1966 following the withdrawal of Ansett-ANA and TAA from 'supplementary services'. The Department of Civil Aviation decided to allow carriers using smaller aircraft to fly scheduled services on approved routes to country centres that had limited airport facilities and insufficient traffic potential for development by the major airlines.

Progress was rapid. In 1972 regional airlines carried 122 742 passengers. By 1992 the figure had reached two million. From 1972 to 1992 the annual growth rate in passengers carried averaged 16.1 per cent, compared to the major domestic airlines' 5.3 per cent.

Qantas and Ansett played a major part in the regional system. Qantas' regional subsidiaries in 1998 were Airlink, Eastern Australia Airlines, Southern Australia Airlines and Sunstate Airlines. Ansett had ownership links with Aeropelican Airlines, Kendell Airlines and Skywest Airlines. Its former state-based subsidiaries had been absorbed into Ansett Australia.

The hard changes that airlines were having to make in the late 1990s in the face of globalisation and the resultant competition included a closer matching of the economics of aircraft types to markets. In 1998 Ansett announced that it was withdrawing Boeing 737 services from some Tasmanian and regional routes and that these would be taken over by regional airlines using smaller aircraft. Thus, 32 years after it began, the regional airline system was still evolving, its role continuing to grow in importance.

ENDNOTES

[1] Brimson (1988), op.cit., pp. 110–17.
[2] Brimson (1988, op.cit.) says that Qantas had six Short Empire flying boats in 1941 (p. 108). Cottee (op.cit.) says that Qantas had operated ten of the aircraft. By March 1942 three had been destroyed by enemy action and another two lost in accidents

resulting from wartime service. The flying boats were recalled to Australia. Qantas continued a Brisbane–Darwin service and a handful of minor Queensland routes, but overseas passenger services were curtailed until the end of the war. More than half the fleet of flying boats were commissioned for war service by the Australian government. There were some famous wartime incidents. Twice Captain Aub Koch was flying aircraft that were destroyed. Japanese Zero fighters shot down his flying boat while he was evacuating women and children from Surabaya. Shot through the arm and leg, he swam eight kilometres to shore. On the other occasion, when his aircraft was lost near Port Moresby, he gave his life-belt to a passenger and swam unaided for 19 hours. Cottee's book has a picture of a flying boat taking off after a bombing of Darwin Harbour. Near the aircraft a long column of black smoke is coming from the 11 000-ton munitions ship *Neptuna*. Moments after the flying boat took off, the *Neptuna* exploded with such force that the stern landed at the other side of the wharf (p. 13).

[3] The weight of fuel required limited the *Catalina*'s load to only three passengers and 69 kilograms of diplomatic and armed forces mail. The single Indian Ocean flight of 5652 kilometres was the longest non-stop regular passenger flight in the world at the time. Celestial navigation had to be used so that radio silence was maintained over waters patrolled by enemy aircraft. The flying boats travelled at about 200 kilometres per hour, taking an average of 28 hours for the journey. When the winds were unfavourable they could take more than 32 hours (Cottee, op.cit., p. 14). Flying boats had a minor role in post-war aviation. They were outperformed by long-range, land-based aircraft developed during the war. And in most parts of the world, as the result of wartime needs, there was no shortage of concrete airstrips.

[4] Qantas services to Papua New Guinea, Norfolk Island, Lord Howe Island and other Australasian areas, together with its Queensland operations, were later handed over to other Australian airlines and Qantas became a purely international airline.

[5] However, they were fast for that time. Passengers could get to London from Sydney in 47 hours.

[6] British Commonwealth Pacific Airlines was 50 per cent owned by Australia, 30 per cent by New Zealand and 20 per cent by Britain. It had been formed in 1944 because Pan American World Airways held a monopoly on most of the Pacific route. BCPA had no aircraft. ANA was contracted to operate the route—Sydney, Auckland, Fiji, Canton Island, Honolulu, San Francisco, Vancouver—using Douglas DC-4s.

[7] Wheatcroft, op.cit., p. 27.

[8] Brimson (1988), op.cit., p. 165.

[9] ibid., p. 129.

[10] On 26 June 1950 ANA's and Australia's worst air accident occurred when the DC-4 *Amana* crashed near Perth. Basil Atkinson, later general manager of the ATC, was a young reporter who was first on the scene. He broke the story in the middle of the night and helped carry out one survivor, who subsequently died.

[11] Brimson, S. (1987), *Ansett: The Story of an Airline*, Dreamweaver Books, Sydney, pp. 80–2.

[12] ibid., p 113.

[13] The image of the Viscounts was tarnished, however, by four crashes, including the first aircraft delivered to TAA in 1954, which crashed on a training flight at Mangalore, Victoria.

[14] Guinea Airways was established in the late 1920s by the mining company Guinea Gold to fly freight and passengers from the Papua New Guinea coast to the company's gold mines at Bulolo. A flight of about 30 minutes replaced a journey of more than 10 days on foot. MacRobertson Miller Aviation Company Limited began in 1927 after Horrie

Miller, a wartime pilot, met MacPherson Robertson, founder of MacRobertson's confectionery business. Miller was looking for someone to finance a new airline and Robertson not only had the money but was also interested in aviation. The two became partners in the new venture and their first aircraft, a de Havilland DH61, was called *Old Gold* after the best-selling MacRobertson's chocolates which had helped make MMA possible.

[15] Brimson (1988), op.cit., p. 208.

[16] Connellan was chosen as the industry spokesman for the first all-Australian travel trade mission to the US and Canada, organised and led by the ATC in 1975. When he was unable to make the trip, Bill King, another Northern Territory tourism pioneer, was selected to replace him.

[17] Brimson (1987), op.cit., p. 149.

[18] From July 1993, the Department of Transport began the practice of including in its domestic count passengers travelling on Qantas international flights between Australian domestic airports. On that basis the 1994 figure is 22 660 000. The 1994 figure given in the text is compatible with those of earlier years.

[19] A study by the Bureau of Industry Economics in 1994 concluded that Australia's domestic airfares were among the cheapest available in the world, rivalled only by a few Asian routes and by discount fares in North America.

[20] It was unclear in early 1990 what difference would be made to classifications following the introduction of 50-seat aircraft by Kendell Airlines to fly between Melbourne and Hobart—previously regarded as a trunk route. Kendell was taking over some routes previously flown by Ansett with B737s.

More revolutions on the water

An end to coastal passenger services

The ships came home from the war. The splendid motor ships had all served—the *Manunda* had been a hospital ship and the *Duntroon*, *Westralia*, *Manoora* and *Kanimbla* had been armed merchant cruisers and landing ships. Immediately after the war they had been engaged in bringing troops home, but in 1949 and 1950 they were refitted and ready to resume their peacetime trade.

The trade was no longer there, most of it lost to air, road and rail services. Some of the steamships that had maintained the interstate trade during the war had already been sold to foreign ship-owners. There were no longer enough ships to provide a regular passenger service and the expense of building more did not justify the commercial risk.

Only six vessels were engaged on the mainland passenger service after the war as against ten in 1939, and this had dropped to two in 1960. Intending passengers could wait weeks for a sailing at a time when aeroplanes were flying around the country every day. The railways had a tired look after the war but there was no lack of trains. Express coach services were linking major cities by road and people were driving longer distances on better roads than those they had driven on before the war. One by one the ships left Australian waters—the oldest and smallest first. The *Manunda* was sold in 1956 and the *Westralia* in 1959. The *Manoora*, *Duntroon* and *Kanimbla* were set to cruising in the Pacific and to Tasmania and Japan, but the return was not sufficient and they were withdrawn. The *Duntroon* was sold in 1960 and the other two in 1961.

202   There was still some passenger capacity on the Western Australian coast. The State Shipping Service, founded in 1912 by the Western Australian government, was operating five vessels to the State's north-west in the 1960s, each taking from 34 to 94 passengers on long voyages whose primary purpose was to carry a great variety of cargoes, not people. However, passenger calls were made at Geraldton, Onslow, Point Samson, Port Hedland, Broome, Derby, Yampi, Wyndham and Darwin. By the end of the decade the trade was changing so radically that the ships were no longer considered suitable for it, and in 1971 they were replaced by vessels that did not carry passengers.

Changes in Bass Strait

At the end of the war the *Nairana*, owned by Tasmanian Steamers, was the sole ship providing the ferry service across Bass Strait and it was get-ting old and worn. The *Taroona* was refitted after its wartime trooping duties, a process which changed the way it looked. Its two funnels became one: the aft funnel was removed and part of it was used to make the forward funnel taller.

The *Taroona* joined the *Nairana* on the Bass Strait run, but there was now much stronger competition from the airlines and, worst of all, the shipping company had lost the mail contract to them. The worn-out *Nairana* was taken out of service in 1948 and anchored in Hobsons Bay, near Melbourne. It met an unfortunate end in February 1951 when it dragged its anchor in a gale and was washed ashore on Port Melbourne beach. The ship could not be refloated and was broken up where it lay.

In the meantime the *Taroona* had continued the service alone to northern Tasmanian ports. The route became less and less profitable and a Commonwealth subsidy was needed to keep it going. Eventually the ship became too old and expensive to retain. In 1959 it was sold to an overseas company and a new kind of ferry, the roll-on-roll-off *Princess of Tasmania*, built in Australia, replaced it.

The *Princess* was an entirely new concept. Its owners, the Commonwealth Government's Australian Coastal Shipping Commis-sion, which traded as the Australian National Line, recognised that the market had changed and the *Princess* was designed to cater for it. The *Taroona* could carry about 40 cars, which had to be swung aboard by derrick. The *Princess*, a slightly smaller vessel at 3981 tons, could carry 100 cars plus mail and road transports, all of which were driven on through a stern doorway. Loading was swift and efficient. The service was called Searoad.

The *Princess* carried up to 334 passengers who ate at a cafeteria **203** counter, not in a gracious dining-room. There were no spacious public rooms and not everybody had cabins. Some passengers dozed the night away in reclining chairs in a forward lounge. This was a utilitarian way to travel and it was cheap.

The Australian Coastal Shipping Commission put two other ships on the Bass Strait run. In 1965, it revived the Sydney–Tasmania route with the *Empress of Australia*, at 8750 tons a much larger vessel than the *Princess*, and in 1969 added the *Australian Trader*, which made three separate voyages a week out of Melbourne to Burnie, Devonport and Bell Bay.

The *Empress of Australia* was a conventional motor ship, which could carry 250 passengers, with public rooms that had the space and comfort of the old style of ship. It served Hobart and northern Tasmanian ports on a twice-fortnightly schedule. The *Australian Trader* was a 7005-ton roll-on-roll-off ship that was designed to carry semi-trailers and containers as well as passengers' cars. It had accommodation for 200. For some three years there was a six-day-a-week service to Tasmania from Melbourne in addition to the sailings from Sydney by the *Empress of Australia*.

This period ended with the selling of the *Princess of Tasmania* in 1972. It had been a success in its early years, but rising costs in the 1960s had made it unprofitable. The *Empress*, its public rooms stripped of their luxury fittings and fitted with reclining chairs for sit-up passengers, took over the Melbourne–Devonport run and the *Australian Trader* was assigned to the *Empress'* Sydney–Tasmania schedule. The *Australian Trader* was laid up in 1976 and later sold to the Royal Australian Navy. The *Empress* kept up the Bass Strait service, but the Tasmanian government was not satisfied. With tourism in mind, it wanted something not only bigger and better, but also quite different in style. The government formed its own TT Line, bought and refurbished a German-built European ferry and named it the *Abel Tasman*. It started operations in 1985.

At 20 000 tons this ship was large by previous Bass Strait standards and properly equipped for its task, which entailed transporting vehicles as well as people. Motorists could drive their cars on and off the ship, as they had been able to do on the Australian-built roll-on-roll-off vessels, but the utilitarian style was gone. Restaurants offered quality food and wine and everyone was given a bed for the night.

The new standards were welcomed by the travellers of the day but, as is the nature of tourism, the time came to upgrade. The 31 000-ton

204 *Spirit of Tasmania*, which replaced the *Abel Tasman* in 1993, was also a German-built ferry that had plied the Baltic before its acquisition by TT Line. It cost the Tasmanian government $175 million and was part of an ambitious plan to increase the numbers of passengers crossing to Tasmania by 30 per cent. Not only was it much bigger than the *Abel Tasman*, with a berth capacity for 1225 as against the *Abel Tasman*'s 707, and capacity for 360 cars—100 more than its predecessor—but it also represented a step up in quality and facilities.

Besides five levels of accommodation, ranging from suites to hostel-type accommodation with shared facilities, there were three restaurants on the *Spirit of Tasmania*, a lounge-bar with a pianist, another bar with audio-visual entertainment, a gaming area, a teenage entertainment centre, a toddlers' area and a gymnasium with a swimming pool and sauna. This was a tourist ship—the public areas had been designed to create a holiday experience rather than make passengers feel they were using public transport.[1]

In December 1990, six months after the big catamaran *Hoverspeed Great Britain* broke the record for crossing the Atlantic, a similar vessel began racing across Bass Strait from Launceston to Port Welshpool in Gippsland. This was the *SeaCat Tasmania*, built by Hobart's Incat and operated by Tasmanian Ferry Services. It ran for three summer seasons, carrying up to 350 passengers and 84 cars, but did not return for the 1993–94 season. The announcement was made shortly before the *Spirit of Tasmania* commenced service. The reason given was that the service had been uneconomical.

However, the big catamarans did return to the Bass Strait run. The *TasCat* made a trial run in July 1997 and then the 91-metre *Devil Cat*, with capacity for 900 passengers and 240 cars, ran the full December–April summer season under charter to TT Line in 1997–98 and 1998–99.

South Australia: the Gulf Trip and catamarans

At the end of the war, passenger ships were still running on local routes in South Australia on the Gulf Trip, across the mouths of both Spencer Gulf and Gulf St Vincent to Port Lincoln, then north to Port Augusta. The Gulf Trip had great appeal, because it was a long drive to Eyre Peninsula by road around the head of Spencer Gulf.

Nevertheless, as highways were improved road transports began to take more and more of the goods previously shipped on the Gulf Trip.

Passengers enjoyed the leisurely voyage, which could take almost a **205** week, but as the cargo trade declined the route became uneconomical. The Gulf ships *Moonta* and *Morialta* had been sold by the Adelaide Steamship Company by 1957, although the ferry *Minnipa* remained in service between Port Adelaide and Port Lincoln until 1960, when it too was sold. Meanwhile, Coastal Steamships' ageing *Karatta*, 553 tons and built in 1907, maintained the sea link with Kangaroo Island until the Adelaide Steamship Company introduced the modern roll-on-roll-off ferry *Troubridge* in 1961.[2]

The Adelaide Steamship Company had owned 92 large trading steamers over the years, but its time as a ship-owner was nearing its end. It merged with Associated Steamships at the end of 1963 and the *Troubridge* was its only vessel. It lost money. As a result the company cut out a service to Port Lincoln, restricting the ferry to the route between Adelaide and Kingscote on Kangaroo Island. There was such an outcry that the South Australian government stepped in, bought the vessel and restored full service.

The *Troubridge* was replaced in 1987 by another roll-on-roll-off ship, the *Island Seaway*, which made a fortnightly voyage to Port Lincoln besides maintaining a more frequent service to Kingscote from Adelaide. However, the Port Lincoln service was cut out after all— not so much because of economics this time but because the *Island Seaway* rolled excessively when it caught the swell of the Southern Ocean side-on, as it did for most of the crossing to Port Lincoln.[3] It was decommissioned in 1995.

Kangaroo Island still had a service, however, which suited tourists. A series of vessels called *Philanderer* had been operating between Cape Jervis and Kangaroo Island ports since 1982, carrying passengers and cars. When the *Island Seaway* was taken out of service, *Philanderer 3*, a catamaran with a capacity for 200 passengers and 30 cars, was making up to five trips a day between Cape Jervis and Tenneshaw, which was the shortest route. The private service had been started by the March family of Kangaroo Island. They were bought out in 1989 by K.I. Sealink, a company owned by Malaysian interests. In 1997 the business changed hands again when a group of South Australian investors bought the company.

In September 1998 a larger catamaran, the *Sealion 2000*, which had been purpose-built for the route in Fremantle, took over from *Philanderer 3*. Carrying up to 350 passengers and up to 60 cars, it could make the crossing in 40 minutes.

206 Cruising from Australian ports

Ocean cruising from Australian ports resumed in the 1950s, when migrant ships began to arrive from Europe. These were often employed in short Pacific cruises before they returned to Europe. They included the P&O vessels *Himalaya*, *Iberia* and *Arcadia* and the Orient Line ships *Orsova* and *Orcades*. The 1960s saw a surge of cruising in the Pacific. The new and bigger ships *Oriana* and *Canberra* arrived in the early years of the decade, and there were others.

> The 1960s were the salad days of year-round South Pacific cruising and P&O-Orient ships—such as *Arcadia*, *Iberia*, *Orsova* and *Orcades*—were household names.
>
> In those days these grand ladies of the sea were two-class—first and tourist.
>
> First-class was exactly that and dress was formal every evening except on sailing day and days in ports, and passengers gathered on deck at sunset with pink gins to join the Green Flash Club. (H. Hutcheon, 'Can P&O recapture its former glory?, *Travelweek*, 18 June 1997)[4]

But the sun was already setting on the Green Flash Club and two-class cruising. Thus the *Orcades*, which could accommodate 773 first class and 772 tourist class passengers when it served as a floating hotel during the Olympic Games in Melbourne in 1956, was refitted in 1964 to take 1635 tourist passengers.[5] Other ships were also being converted to one-class vessels and this was to become the normal configuration for cruising.

In the mid-1970s there was a check to cruising because of the international fuel crisis. Some shipping lines withdrew from the Pacific; others reduced their number of cruises. P&O reduced the time in ports. All this affected the economies of the Pacific countries that benefited from the spending of cruise passengers.

Among the more popular ships at the time were the Sitmar vessels *Fairsky* and *Fairstar*. They had been working to schedules combining voyages to and from Europe with Pacific cruising. An Italian company, Sitmar (Societa Italiana Marittimi S.p.A.) originally started sending its ships to Australia in1953 in fulfilment of a contract to carry migrants,[6] but it also saw an opportunity to fill its berths on the return voyage and opened an office to market to young Australians who were anxious to see Europe before settling down.

For many now middle-aged Australians the six week trip to
Europe on a ship remains their fondest memory, filled with
romance, freedom, continuous parties, dashing Italian crew,
cramped cabins, strange ports and eventual arrival in England
absolutely exhausted. (N. Douglas & N. Douglas, 'P&O's Pacific',
Journal of Tourism Studies, 1996)[7]

'The Funship'

Sitmar captured the same mood on its cruises and in 1974 abandoned
regular voyaging to Europe to concentrate on cruising. The *Fairstar*,
launched on the Clyde in 1957 as a British troop ship, had first arrived
in Australia as a migrant ship in 1964. Now it was marketed as 'the
Funship' and budget-priced. In the years ahead it was to become the
most consistently popular cruise ship in the South Pacific.

P&O took over the American Princess Lines in 1974 and introduced
its ships *Pacific Princess* (the Love Boat of the television series) and
Island Princess on to the Pacific cruise market soon afterwards. These
were smaller, luxurious vessels, that came to the Pacific in the northern
hemisphere winter until the early 1990s. P&O also maintained cruising
schedules for ships from its European fleet. Thus the *Oriana* was
engaged in an annual three-month cruise season out of Sydney from
1973 to the 1980s.

With fuel problems now in the past, the 1980s saw Pacific cruising
reach new heights of popularity. By the middle of the decade about
100 000 Australians a year were cruising in the Pacific on the *Fairstar*,
the *Oriana*, the *Canberra* and 'the Russians'—more than twice as many
as had sailed in the second half of the 1990s.[8]

Australians were going elsewhere to cruise, too, taking fly/cruise
packages to more distant waters such as the Caribbean, the
Mediterranean and the fiords of Europe and Alaska. They were also
turning to Asia for cruising experiences. Australia-based ships began to
include Asian as well as Pacific itineraries in their yearly schedules and
in the 1990s cruising from Singapore and from Indonesian ports
attracted many Australians. However, the vast majority taking cruises
continued to do so from Australian ports.

P&O still set the pace for cruising from Australia. It bought Sitmar in
1988 and continued to market the 24 000-ton *Fairstar* as the 'Funship',
although it tried to change this positioning when research showed that
many Australians would not go on the cruise because of their perception
of the behaviour of its party-going young passengers. The *Fairstar*'s

208   program in the 1990s included a series of Asian cruises, which operated every second year. It was retired in early 1997, having sailed out of Sydney Harbour on 575 cruises.

It was replaced with the 25 000-ton *Fair Princess* which, although eight months older than the *Fairstar*, had been completely rebuilt from the hull up in 1971 and refurbished in the mid-1980s. Slightly larger than the *Fairstar*, the *Fair Princess* had three swimming pools to *Fairstar*'s one and a bathroom with every cabin—a feature lacking in the *Fairstar*. The pricing structure was similar to the *Fairstar*'s, although the ship was said to be more upmarket. The *Fair Princess* achieved 94 per cent load factor in its first cruising season.

While the *Fairstar* was becoming a legend and P&O was prospering, other companies had been in the Pacific and gone. When the Italian company Starlauro Cruises withdrew its vessel *Achille Lauro* in May 1992, it left P&O with just two competitors sailing out of Australia. These were both former Soviet lines, CTC (Charter Travel Company) Cruise Line and Pacific Cruise Company (PCC), and both aimed at the over-50s market. CTC had been operating out of Australia since the early 1970s; PCC began in 1991.

CTC had been cruising to the South Pacific from east coast ports until it decided to position one of its two ships, the *Azerbaydzhan*, in Fremantle in late 1992 and offer a program of cruises to Asia. The company provided subsidised airfares and travel on the *Indian Pacific* train for passengers from other States to join the cruises.

CTC had problems with ships. Its flagship *Belorussiya* was damaged in a Singapore dockyard in 1992 and it was more than three years before a replacement could be found and sailed to Sydney. From then on ships seemed to come and go until in March 1997 the single remaining vessel operating from Australia, the *Kareliya*, was arrested in Noumea over the alleged non-payment of a debt to a German dockyard incurred by the ship's owners, the Black Sea Shipping Company of the Ukraine.[9] Passengers were flown back to Sydney. Two months later CTC Cruise Line went into liquidation, having operated in Australia for 25 years.

PCC operated two ships, the *Mikhail Sholokhov* and the *Russ*. Apart from its cruises to Asia and the Pacific, the company offered special event cruises—to Melbourne for the Melbourne Cup and *Phantom of the Opera* and to Adelaide for the Formula 1 Grand Prix. PCC tried to find new markets by operating from ports other than Sydney and scheduling some cruises out of Brisbane and Newcastle. However, it found the competition too strong and withdrew from Australia in late 1995. According to P&O figures from that year, the *Fairstar* alone had 70.2 per cent of the Australian cruise market while CTC had 14.9 per cent, PCC **209** 10.3 per cent and others 4.5 per cent.[10]

The *Crown Monarch* and a new market

A competitor seeking a different market from that of the *Fairstar* and the Russian lines arrived at its Sydney base in late 1993. This was Cunard's upmarket *Crown Monarch*, rated by the Berlitz *Complete Guide to Cruising and Cruise Ships* at four stars plus.[11] Rates were higher than on other Australian-based ships and marketing was aimed at overseas as well as domestic passengers. In quality and style its offering was more akin to Caribbean vacation-style cruising than had been usual out of Australian ports.

The *Crown Monarch* operated at an average 70 per cent loading but the ship was withdrawn in October 1994 by its owners, the Scandinavian ferry operator Effjohn, after 11 months, seven months short of fulfilling its brochured program. The decision was not made by Cunard but by Effjohn, which decided it could make more money chartering the vessel to Singapore interests.

Sarina Bratton, the Cunard executive who had overseen the *Crown Monarch* experience, later resigned from the company to start her own cruise company, Norwegian Capricorn Line, in which the US company Norwegian Cruise Line had a 50 per cent shareholding. Its ship, the 28 000-ton *Norwegian Star*, began operations from Sydney in late 1998. The vessel, the former *Royal Viking Sea*, was built in 1973 for 90-day world cruising. It was refurbished in 1997.

Cunard, which had a considerable marketing presence in Australia, had five ships in its fleet, all graded five-star by Berlitz. The company's 70 000-ton flagship, the *QE2*, made yearly visits to Australia in the 1990s on its world cruise. Of Cunard's other ships, the *Royal Viking Sun* and *Vistafjord* also visited Australian ports in 1998.

Other ships that came to Australia in the 1990s during longer cruises included P&O vessels bearing famous names from the past. One of them was the new *Oriana*, a 67 000-ton 'superliner' built in a German shipyard at a cost of $425 million. One of its features was an atrium rising through four decks, highlighted by a 'huge waterfall that descends through the atrium like a vast, shimmering curtain, an illusion achieved by running tiny rivulets of water down extremely fine strands of thread.'[12] The ship called at two Australian ports, Sydney and Brisbane, in February 1996 on its 23-port maiden world voyage. Australians made up about one-third of the passengers.[13]

The QE2, *symbol of post-war cruising (Source: Cunard)*

The QE2, *perhaps the best known of the twentieth-century cruise ships, in the Mediterranean. In the 1990s the 70 000-ton vessel called at Australian ports during an annual round-the-world cruise.*

There was also a new *Arcadia*. This 63 000-ton ship, which started life in 1989 with P&O as the *Star Princess*, was renamed *Arcadia* to take over the round-the-world cruising role of the 45 000-ton *Canberra*, which paid its last visit to Australia in early 1997. When the *Arcadia* was refitted for its new task, some memorabilia from the *Canberra* were added, including a room with photographs of incidents in the *Canberra*'s long service, including its involvement in the Falklands War.

It was not just the big ships with famous names that visited Australia in the 1990s. The 164-passenger *Frontier Spirit*, operated by SeaQuest Cruises, made voyages to Antarctica from Hobart during several summers and cruised from Port Moresby to Hobart and back in 1992–93.

Reef, harbour and inland cruising

In November 1995 the 3000-ton *Reef Endeavour*, a vessel jointly owned by Captain Cook Cruises and Qantas Airways, began operating a series of three- and four-night Great Barrier Reef cruises from Cairns. It had been purpose-built in a Fiji shipyard to carry 168 passengers in 75 cabins on Reef cruises in ocean-going style. The largest ship so far operated by Captain Cook Cruises, it replaced the *Reef Escape*, which was assigned to cruising in Fijian waters.[14]

Captain Cook Cruises started in 1970 when Captain Trevor Haworth, who had been retired from the sea for ten years, began offering 'coffee cruises' on Sydney Harbour in a 28-year-old converted Second World War Fairmile launch, which he had named *Captain Cook*. The concept prospered; indeed, the format for the coffee cruise was not to alter over the years.

Captain Haworth decided to make his marketing appeal mainly to overseas visitors from the start, at a time when there were fewer than 350 000 visitors to Australia a year. In the beginning, Captain Haworth and his wife Geraldine were their own marketers. They maintained a vigorous campaign with inbound operators, travel agents and accommodation houses in Australia and also went on missions to the major markets overseas. They got results: business prospered.

As time went on, new vessels were added and other cruises were developed with particular market segments in mind—the one-hour mini-cruise, the businessman's luncheon, the candlelight dinner cruise—all aimed at clearly-defined markets. The dinner cruise, offering fine food and a romantic atmosphere, was designed to compete with the *John Cadman Cruising Restaurant*, a converted harbour ferry that had been operating on Sydney Harbour during the 1970s.

In 1984 Captain Cook Cruises, with the Japanese market in mind, eliminated the competition by buying the *John Cadman* and its operation. Two more vessels bearing the John Cadman name were built later to work also as cruising restaurants. By 1998 Captain Cook Cruises had ten boats operating on Sydney Harbour, including the 700-passenger *Sydney 2000*.

Competition grows

There had always been other boats for charter and sightseeing on Sydney Harbour, but in the 1980s more formidable competition began to appear. Brian Grey had started his business with luncheon cruises in Broken Bay in 1978; in 1980 he launched a floating restaurant, the *Pittwater Princess*, on Sydney Harbour. He followed this up with two showboats, suitable for restaurants and entertainment. These were purpose-built paddle-wheelers, stable and with some attractive features Grey had specified—he wanted his guests to be able to walk around the vessels on the outside despite the big superstructure, and he wanted enough windows for everybody to see outside. They were spectacular craft, styled after Mississippi River stern-wheelers. *Sydney Showboat 1* could seat 240 and *Showboat 2* could accommodate 360. Grey floated his company, Blue Line Cruises, on the Stock Exchange in 1987 and in 1996 it was bought by Accor Asia Pacific. The company later added

212 another craft, the *Majestic*, a catamaran that could carry up to 60 people on corporate charters.

Matilda Cruises, the brainchild of Tim and Jillian Lloyd, began operations from Darling Harbour in mid-1981 with a 19.9-metre catamaran called the *Matilda*, which could take up to 200 passengers. Success and the prospect of the 1988 Bicentennial celebrations led to several more *Matildas* appearing later. All were catamarans. In the 1980s the company acquired the topsail schooner *Solway Lass* for harbour cruises. Built in 1902, this ship had had an eventful history that included having been sunk and refloated during the Second World War. Tim Lloyd saw it as a run-down island trader in the Ellice Islands (now Tuvalu), brought it to Sydney and had it thoroughly restored. It was the official tall ship host for visiting sailing ships during the Bicentennial year.

Amalgamated Holdings bought Matilda Cruises in 1996 and a few months later also bought Sail Venture Cruises with four sailing catamarans. This gave it a fleet of 14 vessels, the largest on the harbour. All were catamarans. Five of them were 'Rocket' ferries, sleek craft that could carry 120 to 150 passengers on a regular service between Circular Quay and Darling Harbour, where Matilda Cruises was based. The others ran regular daily cruises and were engaged in charter work.

The Harbour cruise market had its problems in 1998. Following the takeovers by conglomerates, it was hit not only by the Asian financial crisis but also by the Sydney bed tax. As a result, price competition was fierce. All companies were faced with the problem of finding mooring space on the Harbour for the servicing of their vessels.

On the rivers

Cruising on the Murray started soon after the war. Murray Valley Coaches bought the veteran paddle-steamer *Murrumbidgee* in 1946 and converted it to a cruise vessel. It began operating cruises and charter trips out of Echuca in 1947, but the following year it caught fire and its career ended. Murray Valley Coaches replaced it in 1950 with the *Coonawarra*, which had accommodation for 44 passengers in 21 cabins. It operated first from Echuca and later from Mildura. By then another cruise boat, the *Wanera*, was also operating from that port. In 1960, after Murray Valley Coaches had been wound up, the *Coonawarra* was moved to Murray Bridge.

In the mid-1970s a paddle-wheeler of a different dimension was to bring a new quality to Murray River cruising. Keith Veenstra, a Dutch migrant, and Bill Green, a motel owner, had built an excursion boat unlike anything that had previously been seen on the river. Designed by Veenstra, the vessel, named the *Murray River Queen*, had 44 two-berth cabins, all fitted with private bathrooms, and a large lounge-dining room and was fully air-conditioned. It left Goolwa on its first cruise in March 1974.

The company that owned it, Murray River Cruises, put into service a second boat, the *Murray Explorer*, in 1979. It had been inspired by the modern European river boats and had twin propellers. The *Proud Mary*, which began cruising out of Murray Bridge in 1981, also had twin propellers but had a stern-wheel as well, which turned with the forward motion of the boat.

And then in 1986 the largest boat ever seen on the Murray began cruising out of Renmark. This was the 1700-ton *Murray Princess*, which was based on the design of the Mississippi stern-wheelers of the previous century. It was built entirely of steel, could accommodate 120 passengers and had lifts connecting the decks. The stern-wheel was as high as a three-storey building. With its arrival there was too much capacity for the market and the *Murray Explorer* was moved to the Brisbane River, with the new name *Brisbane Explorer*, in time for the 1988 Expo.

In 1988 Trevor Haworth, of Captain Cook Cruises, bought Murray River Developments, which owned three vessels. Two of them, on the Murray River, were the paddle-wheelers Murray Princess and Murray River *Queen*. The other, the conventionally-driven *Brisbane Explorer*, was on the Brisbane River. Captain Cook Cruises moved the *Murray Princess* to Mannum, from which town it continued a regular accommodated cruise program. The *Murray River Queen* was chartered to Keith Veenstra's son Jock and tied up at Goolwa as a floating motel. The *Brisbane Explorer* became *Captain Cook's Explorer* and was used for functions on Sydney Harbour.

The *Proud Mary* continued to operate from Murray Bridge and the *Emmy Lou*, a relatively new paddle-steamer in the old style, also offered accommodated cruises sailing from Echuca. There were also excursion boats, which ran from a number of Murray River ports.

Boats galore

Tourism existed on Australia's waterways in many different ways in many different kinds of craft. Visitors could not only cruise the Murray for several days, or take an excursion for a few hours; they could spend a lazy holiday by themselves on a houseboat. There were plenty of houseboats, particularly between Wellington and Renmark and at Mildura.

214   Melbourne's Yarra River, its tourism potential neglected for so long, became abuzz with sightseeing craft, ferries and water taxis in the years following the opening of the Southgate Arts and Leisure Complex in 1992. In Western Australia long, lean craft sailed down the Swan River and then out to Rottnest Island, while Quicksilver Connections' wave-piercing catamarans sped up the Queensland coast from Cairns to Port Douglas and then out to the Reef.

Cairns was a centre for water activity—sightseeing craft, Reef cruises, big game fishing. A number of different companies offered yachting cruises in the Whitsundays. In fact, most places where there was water offered some kind of tourism experience.

It had been a long time since the days when the sea was considered Australia's ring road, with its coastal and inland waters furnishing the arteries that connected its settlements and allowed its trade to develop. Yet there was more activity than ever around the coasts, on the bays and lakes and in the rivers, and the main driver of growth was tourism.

ENDNOTES

[1] *Traveltrade*, 28 October 1995, p. 23.

[2] Coastal Steamships was wound up in 1966.

[3] Greg Burk, manager, Patrick Sleigh Shipping Agencies Pty Ltd, Port Adelaide, interview, August 1998.

[4] Hutcheon, H. (1997), 'Can P&O recapture its former glory?', *Travelweek*, 18 June 1997, p. 4. The 'Green Flash' is a split-second phenomenon that is reputed to occur on the horizon at the moment that the sun sets.

[5] The *Orcades* was then a P&O-Orient Lines ship. P&O and Orient Line merged businesses and names in 1960. The combined name P&O-Orient Lines was considered too clumsy and 'Orient' was dropped in 1966.

[6] Other Italian lines servicing Australia at the time included Lloyd Triestino, which had been in the Australian trade since the 1930s and Cogedar, which entered the migrant trade in 1952. The Greek Chandris Line started bringing migrants in 1962 (Pemberton, op.cit., p. 13).

[7] Douglas & Douglas, op.cit., p. 7.

[8] *Traveltrade*, 12 November 1997, p. 24. The figures were quoted by Sarina Bratton, managing director of the Norwegian Capricorn Line, who told the Seatrade Pacific Cruise Convention that in the 1990s the *Fair Princess*, 'sole survivor', carried fewer than 40 000 passengers a year.

[9] There was some confusion about ownership at the time. Although the debt was reported to have been incurred by the Black Sea Shipping Company and it had employed the crew, it claimed to have sold the ship in 1995. The *Kareliya* was managed by Silver Line of London and chartered by CTC. Although the incident precipitated the end of CTC Cruises, passengers did not lose money. Because of the complicated web of owners, agencies and charterers involved with CTC ships, the Travel Compensation Fund had required CTC to lodge a $500 000 bank guarantee and additionally to keep

pre-paid passage money in a trust account. The *Kareliya* was released by authorities in Noumea in early June 1997, but did not return to Australia.

[10] *Traveltrade*, 13 December 1995, p. 10.

[11] ibid. It was not rated five-star because it did not have single-seating dining.

[12] Stephen Berry, 'The new Oriana: second to none', *Traveltrade*, 27 July 1994, p. 14.

[13] *Travelweek*, 28 February 1996, p. 2.

[14] In 1998 Captain Cook Cruises had four vessels operating Fijian cruises out of Denerau marina. Besides the *Reef Escape* there was the *Lady Geraldine* and two sailing ships, the *Rama Rama* and the *Spirit of the Pacific*. The company also owned the island of Tavu.

Accommodation: keeping up with the times

The travel liberation

Affordable and plentiful cars liberated the ordinary Australian just as in an earlier era the railways had enabled the ordinary Briton for the first time to visit places beyond a day's walk from home. The new mobility created a demand for accommodation in different forms, most notably motels. This did not happen overnight, although once the idea took root expansion was rapid. By the end of the 1950s there were still only 80 motels in the country, but another 80 were already being built and by 1964 the number in operation was approaching 700.[1] Also there were motor-hotels (like hotels but catering mainly for motor travellers), guest houses, chalets and lodges (indistinguishable except for location), serviced apartments or flats, caravan parks, hostels and camping grounds. And of course there were hotels—new ones as well as old, in resorts as well as in cities and towns.

The new accommodation brought exciting differences for the Australian traveller. The first visit to a motel was a revelation to someone accustomed to the strange ways of Australian country and suburban hotels.

> The luxury of having your very own bathroom, placed right there near your bed, plus your very own lavatory, not having to go outside, nor walking down the corridor, this was a luxury beyond belief. Then what ingenious things you could do. You could order breakfast for any time you wished. No demand to be present at

7 a.m. Why, you wrote on a piece of paper the night before what you **217** wanted for breakfast, then they would deliver it to you at, say, 6.30 a.m., 7.30 a.m. or if you were sleepy, nine o'clock. (K. Dunstan, *Flag: The First 30 Years*, 1991)[2]

This seems routine to us now, but the hotels the average Australian traveller stayed at before there were motels were, in the words of Keith Dunstan, 'so bad some of us always travelled with a survival kit'. This included a 100-watt electric light globe, because usually the light was so dim in a hotel room it was impossible to read; a torch for the long walk to the bathroom and lavatory; a hot water bottle, because vintage hotels provided neither heating nor cooling; a hook with a suction pad, because there was never a place to hang pyjamas and dressing gown; a towel, because those supplied were tissue-thin; and ear plugs, because country hotels were eerie places.[3]

The proliferation of motels

Australia's first motel was opened at Pirate's Bay, Eaglehawk Neck, Tasmania in January 1949. Named the Penzance Motel, it was built by Donald C. Richardson, a former naval officer, and modelled on the scattered-unit style of some American motels. The fact that it was a resort property may have confused some people, because there were arguments in the mid-1950s about what could be called a motel. The Motel Federation of Australia, the first body of motel owners, defined a motel as having at least ten rooms, each equipped with its own toilet facilities. But what if its units were separated or were in two storeys, or if there was no off-street parking? What if it was in a resort area where people might stay a few days? Were not motels for travellers in transit? Modern definitions include all these circumstances, the single defining criterion being that they should cater for motor travellers.

> A motel is difficult to define precisely. It can be small or large, simple or elegant, located in the city or the country, and be under individual or corporate ownership. The distinguishing feature is that it is built for, and caters to, the convenience and informality of motor travel. (G. W. Lattin, in *Collier's Encyclopaedia*, 1991)[4]

Don Richardson and his wife Nancy were to run city motels, including the prominently-placed Panorama in Hobart, but that first imaginative enterprise at Eaglehawk Neck was a retreat that took motorists away from highway bustle.

218   The motels that came next fitted the more conventional view of the day—that of the transit motel. These were the Bathurst Motor Inn, which opened in February 1954, and the Jolly Swagman in Taree, which opened later in the same year.[5] Other early motels were in Gosford, Dubbo, Orange (all in New South Wales), Canberra (in the ACT), Mildura and Oakleigh (in Victoria).[6]

One of the first to realise the potential of the motel business was Alan Greenway, who after demobilisation from the Royal Australian Navy had first worked in a used car dealership and then run two country hotels—but always with bigger things in view. His next step, in 1957, was operating a primitive motel in Goulburn. He was soon convinced that his future lay in providing accommodation for the new motor traveller, but this accommodation went beyond a single structure. After all, motorists did not go only to one place; if they could be assured of a standard of comfort and service by seeking a motel name they already knew and trusted at their next stop, then they were likely to prefer it to a motel they knew nothing about.

Greenway persuaded others to join him in the enterprise that was taking shape in his mind. They formed a company and built a motel at Gundagai, all within a few months. But it was only a start. The motel was opened on a Saturday in December 1958 and on the Sunday Greenway called a meeting of his fellow directors. They agreed to his suggestion that they expand.

Greenway had his hands full. He travelled widely on his search for more sites and a local woman filled in for him at the Gundagai motel while he was away.[7] Being motel manager also meant being yardman, maintenance man, reservation clerk, gardener, receptionist and reserve housemaid as well. In a few years, the larger vision that was driving him took him from filling all those roles in a small New South Wales country town to sitting in boardrooms in the United States and Britain as well as in Australia, mixing on equal terms with some of the world's most powerful people in the accommodation business.

In its first seven years his company grew 300 times; by the end of 1965 it was operating 6000 rooms. A public company, it was first called Motels of Australia Ltd, but along the way it acquired the name TraveLodge.[8] Eventually Greenway was to lead the consortium which took over the much larger company of that name in the United States. TraveLodge also spread its interests to New Zealand and Fiji. When Greenway left the company after its takeover by Southern Pacific Properties in 1975, it had become more than just a motel operator; its properties now included the upmarket Parkroyal group, high-rise city

TraveLodge motor hotels of more than 200 rooms and the four-star **219** Boulevard Hotel in Sydney.

In the early days of motels, others also had seen the need to provide motor travellers with an assurance of quality, but they did not have a single company with a single brand. So in 1957 thirteen motel owners grouped together in the Motel Federation of Australia under a common brand that guaranteed standards and provided a directory. Lou Pimblett, who had one of the first motels in Australia at Gosford, was the first president and Alan Greenway was the second.

Greenway took Motels of Australia Ltd out of the organisation in 1961, feeling it was overly concerned with boosting its membership numbers at the expense of quality. On the other hand, single motel owners were suspicious of a large group like Motels of Australia Ltd, doubting that it would cross-promote to the membership in total.[9] The Motel Federation of Australia became Homestead Motor Inns in 1975 and affiliated with the American chain Best Western International in 1981, fully adopting its brand in 1989.

Its formidable competitor, Flag Motels, began with a meeting of 26 moteliers at the Chevron Hotel, Melbourne in October 1961. They adopted the name 'Flag' at that meeting and it proved one of the best brand names devised in Australian travel and tourism. But finding a name was one of the last items on a long agenda and no-one remembered later who had suggested it. The convenor was another unusual person in the history of Australian travel and tourism: Angus Taylor, who was not only part owner of a motel but at the time also a chief petty officer in the Royal Australian Navy.

One of the principal motivations for forming Flag was a perceived lack of promotion by the Motel Federation of Australia. The Flag members instituted not only a book-ahead reservation service—referral from one motel to another—but also a promotion which has stood the test of time: the giving of a free night's accommodation to people who stayed seven nights at Flag motels. The company eventually became Flag International Ltd and its name and pennant logo were associated with some 500 motor inns, hotels, resorts and apartment hotels in Australia, New Zealand, Papua New Guinea and Fiji.

In 1998 Flag took a new direction by combining with Choice Hotels International, a US-based—and also the world's second largest—hotel franchisor, to launch Flag Choice Hotels Limited as the largest accommodation franchising company in Australia. Flag Choice Hotels was established as a wholly-owned subsidiary of Flag International, and acquired a 20-year Australian Master Franchise to use the Choice

220 brands Clarion, Quality and Comfort. The new franchise company comprised some 500 properties, representing 26 000 rooms. Choice contributed 17 properties in Australia. A number of Flag properties were re-branded with the Choice Hotel brands that best served their market segments.[10]

The Budget Motel Chain was the third of the big motel chains to be formed and in 1998 it was the biggest in Australia in numbers of properties. It had more than 500 member motels in this country and in New Zealand, having begun in April 1978 with 40 members. The idea was to build a low-cost, clean, basic referral chain similar to the Budget Motel 6 concept in the United States. Budget continued to live up to its name; 20 years after its founding it had a head office staff of six and no central booking office. It not only expected its members to make onward bookings; it expected them to do so by telephone. It even saved on what most people would consider an essential in the 1990s—a computer system. The chain's philosophy was to keep overheads low and subscriptions at a minimum so that customers knew they could get the lowest possible rates.[11]

The old, grand hotels go

For some years after the war the city hotel scene looked as though it might continue much as it had in the scores of years preceding the conflict. Dunstan, writing of the 'good accommodation' in the capitals at that time—what he called the 'pre-m' (pre-motel) days—named as examples Usher's and the original Wentworth in Sydney, Menzies, the Windsor, Scott's and the Australia in Melbourne, Lennon's and the Bellevue in Brisbane, the South Australian in Adelaide and the Esplanade in Perth.[12] Most had been built before the First World War.

Certainly they had been worn down by the Second World War and they needed refurbishing; tastes were changing and alterations were needed to cater to new expectations. But the continuance of the grand old hotels, with names and styles that were part of their cities' character, seemed assured—at first.

The Australia, in Sydney, underwent a massive renovation over three years in the mid-1950s. This involved most of the bedrooms, which then had their own bathrooms, and the creation of a number of de luxe suites. In Melbourne, the Windsor was renovated in the 1950s and 1960s and extended by taking in the Old White Hart hotel site,[13] stretching a new wing to Bourke Street. Additions were made to other venerable hotels, including the Palace in Perth.

Change was coming, and not only in the buildings themselves. In **221** 1954 the waiters in the lounge and restaurant at Sydney's Australia threatened to walk out unless recently engaged female staff were replaced by men. However, management refused to back down and the affair blew over.[14]

By the 1960s the old hotels were having to contend not only with new preferences and new competition but also with something even more deadly: escalating land prices, which made the land they stood on more valuable than the hotels themselves.

Sydney, Australia's pre-eminent gateway city, was benefiting from tourism and new hotels began to rise in response—for example Menzies, the Town House, the Chevron Hilton and the new Wentworth. The Australia was finding it hard to compete with the newcomers. Despite all the rebuilding and refurbishing, it was still an old hotel: the floorboards creaked in the corridors, the kitchens were antediluvian and the boilers were coal-fired.

When Frank Christie, one of the new breed of young hotel managers, was brought in as general manager of the Australia at the end of 1966 after a period at the Chevron, he put in a contemporary bar to attract the 'new crowd'—mainly young business people—but this was only fiddling with the problem. He recognised that the hotel no longer had the capacity to generate enough revenue to compete with the new hotels and left after a year.[15] In fact, the writing had been on the wall for a number of years: the new travellers were staying at the new hotels and motels and, with land prices soaring, the economic argument against the Australia's continuation was compelling. The old hotel was closed on 30 June 1971 and was soon demolished.

Other famous hotels had already gone, two of them in Melbourne. Scott's, beloved by graziers and racehorse owners, was one of the first, demolished in 1961. Menzies, more than a century old and in its early years said by the English novelist Anthony Trollope to be the best hotel he had stayed in anywhere, followed in 1969. In Perth, demolition of the relatively young Adelphi had begun on Christmas Eve 1968 to make way for a new hotel, the Parmelia.

The wreckers were busy all over the country in the 1970s. In Adelaide, the South Australian was demolished in 1971; the Oriental, the Occidental and the Federal in Melbourne had all been levelled by 1972; in Sydney the Metropole was removed in 1972 and Petty's in 1975; while in Perth the Esplanade was gone by 1972.

In Brisbane the decision to demolish the Bellevue Hotel caused a political crisis. There was opposition to knocking down the historic

222   hotel from a large proportion of Brisbane's population, including National Trust representatives, architects, church leaders and politicians. After the demolition, which began under police protection after midnight on the morning of 21 April 1979, there were protests in the Queensland parliament. A motion that 'this House condemns the precipitate and unannounced way the demolition of the Bellevue Hotel was commenced' was lost by only 11 votes.[16]

By that time Lennons had been reborn. The old hotel in George Street had found fame during the Second World War when it had been requisitioned for use by the American Commander of Allied Forces in the South-West Pacific, General Douglas MacArthur. But 25 years after the war the Brisbane City Council was not interested in historical sentiment: it wanted the land the hotel stood on for an administration building and gave its owners two years to vacate. A new, smaller hotel was built in Queen Street and the move was made in 1972.[17]

Part of Perth's Palace Hotel remained. When the Bond Corporation built an office tower—at the time the second tallest in Australia—on the corner of St George's Terrace and William Street in the early 1980s, a portion of the Palace, which had occupied part of the site, was retained and restored to its original architectural style. The building had been declared a historic monument by the National Trust.

Hobart's Hadley's Hotel escaped the fate of most of the old hotels, although its latter history was fraught with financial difficulty. Twice it was in the hands of receivers and in the 1950s its then owner, Arthur Drysdale, put it up as a prize in a raffle. The winner took the alternative prize—$400 000 in cash.[18] The Australian Tourism Group's Country Comfort hotel chain took over the management of the hotel in 1993 and it began trading as Country Comfort Hadley's Hotel. An extensive refurbishment program was undertaken, resulting in its rating being raised from three to four stars. One of the features of the first stage of refurbishment was the renovation of the hotel's facade, in which the original leadlight glass in the hotel's awning was reinstated.

The most spectacular survivor was the Windsor in Melbourne. In the 1970s it was under threat from the familiar pressure of new hotels and rising land prices. Its owner, Windsor Hotel Ltd, prepared a plan for a 38-storey flat-topped glass tower on the Bourke Street corner, which would have reduced the number of bedrooms by half but would have increased revenue from bars, function rooms and office space. This met with widepread opposition, not least from the government, because it was thought that the tower would ruin the view from Parliament House, which was diagonally opposite across Spring Street. Eventually the hotel was sold to the government in 1977 and Federal Hotels became the management company.

In 1980 Oberoi International, an Indian company that operated a chain of prestige hotels in India and in other parts of the world, took over the lease.[19] Then followed years of restoration to the Windsor's nineteenth-century magnificence—a work of art in itself, which cost more than three times the original budget.[20] While the Windsor was converted into a modern hotel functionally, its restoration was faithful in style to its nineteenth-century origins. The restored Windsor was officially reopened on 24 February 1983, about a hundred years after construction had started on the original Grand Hotel.

The international breed

Some resort hotels had been built in the 1950s—for example, R. M. Ansett's Lufra Hotel at Eaglehawk Neck in Tasmania and Lennons Broadbeach Hotel on the Gold Coast—but it was not until the next decade that big new residential hotels would begin to appear in the cities.

Developer Stanley Korman's Chevron Hilton opened in Sydney's Potts Point in 1960 with Hilton International as the operator, the first of the international management companies to come to Australia. But Hilton did not stay long; it left the Chevron—and Australia—in 1961. It was to return in December 1974 to open the Melbourne Hilton and, a few months later, the Sydney Hilton. The company later expanded its operations to other cities and became a permanent part of the Australian hotel scene.

In the meantime, Melbourne had acquired an international operator, Inter-Continental Hotels, with its five-star Southern Cross, which opened in August 1962. Inter-Continental Hotels was then owned by Pan American World Airways.

Other notable hotels built in Australia in the 1960s included the Hotel Menzies in Sydney (later the All Seasons Premier Menzies), the Hotel Australia, Adelaide (the Hotel Adelaide) and the Hotel Rex (the Canberra Rex). Qantas built the 450-room Wentworth Hotel next to its Sydney headquarters and this was opened in December 1966. It was later operated by the Sheraton group and in 1998 was being managed by Rydges Hotels.

In the bigger cities, a steady stream of international hotels was built in the decades that followed the 1960s. They were not all five-star; there was a conscious attempt to produce hotels for particular market segments with differentiation in prices and facilities. When Hilton

224 came back in the 1970s it was accompanied by other famous-name hotel management companies, such as Hyatt and Sheraton. Others— such as Regent, Marriott, ANA, Ritz-Carlton and Park Plaza—were to follow. Australian hotel chains grew up to join Southern Pacific, Federal and the international chains in competing for management of hotels and resorts. Among these were Rydges, All Seasons, Metro and the biggest of them all, Accor Asia Pacific.

Around the coasts of Queensland, New South Wales and Western Australia new resorts appeared. Some of them were in the international class—for example, the Sheraton Mirages in Port Douglas and Surfers Paradise, the Hyatt Coolum on the Sunshine Coast and the new Hayman Island resort.

Some city hotels built in the 1980s and 1990s incorporated significant elements of the past. In Melbourne the new Menzies Rialto Hotel, later Le Meridien, was largely fashioned from buildings that were part of the famous Rialto precinct. In Sydney the Hotel Inter-Continental incorporated the old Treasury building in Macquarie Street; the Ritz-Carlton Hotel partly occupied the former New South Wales Board of Health building, also in Macquarie Street; and an old warehouse and several terrace houses were incorporated in the All Seasons Harbour Rocks Hotel in Harrington Street.[21]

The hotel investors

In the 1980s, as inbound tourism increased rapidly and new destination areas began to open up, it became apparent that attention had to be given to future capacity if growth in the flow of visitors was to be maintained. Hotels were the main problem; they were expensive to build and their profitability could be volatile because of seasonality, competition and other fickle variables as weather and fashion. Also hotels required a long lead time from conception to opening, and successful investors had to consider future demand carefully. The evidence of the 1990s suggested that Australian investors were influenced more by what had happened the month before than by what might happen three years in the future.

In the second half of the 1980s, just when it was needed, there was an unprecedented burst of investment in hotels and resorts. Two major factors were responsible: the removal of government controls over a large area of financial activity and a new interest in Australia's tourism future from Japan, because it was Japanese tourism that was leading the inbound growth. The five biggest investors were AGC/Westpac,

Beneficial Finance/State Bank of South Australia, Tricontinental/State Bank of Victoria, the Long Term Credit Bank of Japan and Daikyo. Between them they spent $7 billion on hotels.[22]

The exuberance did not last into the 1990s. In the early years of that decade Australia was in recession and there was a severe downturn in the Japanese lending market. Some of the Australian institutions that had invested in hotels went out of business. The Japanese retreated, having lost billions.[23] Developers defaulted by the dozen. By mid-1993 there were so many of these that one in ten of Australia's top-level hotel rooms was in the hands of the banks or receivers: almost 11 000 rooms in 68 hotels rating three, four and five stars.[24]

This situation attracted a new wave of offshore investors who were not interested in building, but in buying at bargain prices what others had lost. These came mainly from Singapore, Malaysia, Hong Kong and Indonesia and they moved so quickly that by the end of 1993 two-thirds of the hundred or so hotels with 165 rooms or more under management agreements were owned by overseas investors.[25]

Some came to stay. The biggest buyer at the time was Singapore's Thakral group, which bought eight hotels from the Westpac bank and then raised $74 million on the Australian Stock Exchange to help pay for the deal. The Thakral Property Trust later expanded its hotel inventory —by 1997 it owned 15 properties—and bought the All Seasons management group.

The boom-and-bust sequence had destroyed the interest of the financial community in hotel developments, at least for the short term. When a function was held in 1991 to bring financiers and government officials together to discuss investment in accommodation and other tourism projects, no representatives of banks or financial institutions bothered to turn up.[26]

The problems of the early 1990s had also exposed marketing issues. Inbound tourism had continued to rise in the first years of the decade when the country was in recession. However, a proportion of the new traffic was low-yielding, leading to cries of profitless volume. In policy terms, there was a tug-of-war between the need for existing hotels to produce better returns on investment and the need to provide competition for them by building more hotels to meet future demand.

No immediate solutions were forthcoming. By 1994 there were predictions of accommodation shortages in most capital cities, the Gold Coast and Cairns—and they were imminent.[27] By 1995 the predictions were being borne out, overseas business was being turned away and significant revenue lost because of room shortages.[28]

226   In 1994 the Commonwealth Government created the Tourism Forecasting Council, with the aim of providing investors with reliable predictions of tourism demand. It also encouraged the Australian Stock Exchange to introduce a Tourism and Leisure Index. The purpose of this was to provide investors with a mechanism for tracking the performance of tourism stocks included in the index in relation to the rest of the stock market. The expectation was that this would give investors more confidence in the travel and tourism industry.

In 1995 the outlook for investors was brighter. Occupancies, room rates and yields were all rising. Earnings of hotels and motels in Australia increased 10 per cent in 1995–96, according to Australian Bureau of Statistics figures. By the December quarter of 1996 the average occupancy rate in Australia, 59.9 per cent, was the highest since the ABS had begun its Accommodation Survey in 1975. This had been achieved without cutting prices; earnings were up 8 per cent on the same quarter in the previous year; there had been a 2.4 per cent increase in the number of rooms and the average room rate had risen from $94 to $99 a night.[29]

In 1996 confidence had returned. A new wave of investment in Queensland tourism projects worth almost $1 billion was reported[30] and there were three floats on the Australian Stock Exchange in the year—Bankers Trust's BT Hotel Group for $284 million (the Sydney Inter-Continental, the Brisbane Sheraton Hotel and Towers and the Canberra Parkroyal), the Grand Hotel Group for $203 million (50 per cent of the Grand Hyatt, Melbourne and 100 per cent of the Hyatt Regency in Perth) and the $145 million Tourism Asset Holdings (Accor Asia Pacific's hotel assets).

Two years later institutional lenders were again suffering from cold feet. Inbound traffic had declined slightly as the result of Asian economic problems and the domestic market remained sluggish. A survey conducted in February 1998 by Horwath Asia Pacific showed that 67 per cent of respondents rated hotels as 'unattractive investments' compared with 7 per cent in 1997. Only 15 per cent of respondents perceived hotels as better investments than commercial, industrial or retail property, compared with 56 per cent in 1997.[31]

The operators

In the early post-war period, the main focus of excitement in the hotel industry was provided by Federal Hotels under the leadership of Oliver Shaul, who joined the company as managing director when it was in financial trouble in 1947. Two years later Shaul made the first step in **227** taking the one-hotel operation (Hotel Federal) to market leader by buying the Alexander in Melbourne and renaming it the Savoy Plaza.

Over the next dozen or so years he expanded the company to an unprecedented extent by Australian standards, buying hotels in four States—Menzies in Melbourne, Wrest Point in Hobart, Usher's and Hampton Court in Sydney and Lennons in Toowoomba, Brisbane and Broadbeach. Federal also participated in the early stages of the new hotel era by helping design and then operate under management contract the new Menzies in Sydney. Shaul left the company in late 1962 to start a new career as a restaurateur.[32]

In the 1960s and 1970s the TraveLodge group (which became Southern Pacific Hotels in 1975) expanded in the cities and at Melbourne Airport. Federal Hotels sold off some of its older hotels, including the Federal, Menzies and Usher's, for demolition and in 1968 embarked on a five-year project to create the country's first hotel-casino at Wrest Point in Hobart. Overseas operators, Inter-Continental, Hilton and Sheraton, became established in the premium market.

The 1980s saw an explosion. As expensive luxury hotels appeared in cities and resort areas, the number of overseas operators in Australia kept growing; by the 1990s most five-star hotels bore international names like Hyatt, Sheraton, Regent, Inter-Continental, Oberoi, Ritz-Carlton, Hilton, Marriott, Renaissance and Nikko. However, there had also been a rise of enterprising Australian operators.

Southern Pacific Hotels had more rooms under management than any other hotel company in Australia in the mid-1990s, having developed three levels of hotels under different brands: the luxury Parkroyal, the mid-range Centra and the budget Travelodge. Close to it in size, but soon to take the lead, was Accor Asia Pacific, which operated four brands: Sofitel, Novotel, Ibis and Mercure. Third was Rydges Hotels and fourth the All Seasons group. Rydges (1988), All Seasons (1982) and another leading Australian company, the Australian Tourism Group (1986), had all started in the 1980s. Accor Asia Pacific was produced in 1993 by a merger between Quality Pacific and Accor SA, a French-based company, said to be the largest hotel and tourism operator in the world.[33]

Accor Asia Pacific was listed on the Australian and Hong Kong stock exchanges and expanded quickly in Asia as well as in Australia. The Asian expansion was to cause some difficulties when the currency crisis hit a number of countries in 1997. By then Accor Asia Pacific was operating some 70 hotels in Asia. In December of that year Accor SA offered

228

The harbinger: Novotel, Darling Harbour (Accor Asia Pacific)

In 1991, when Accor opened its first hotel in Australia—the Novotel, Darling Harbour—few could have foreseen the corporate twists ahead, or expected that within a few years Accor Asia Pacific would become Australia's biggest hotel chain.

$295 million for the 74 per cent of the Australian company it did not own; at the time the French company had a market capitalisation of $9.96 billion and a network of 2465 hotels.[34] When the offer was taken up, Accor Asia Pacific was no longer listed on the Australian Stock Exchange. It operated as a division of Accor, to the same system that the company employed in other parts of the world.

Although hard hit in Asia, Accor Asia Pacific continued to expand in Australia and by July 1998 had 8851 rooms in 56 hotels under management. Judging by the measure of rooms managed, it was by then well in front of the SPHC Group (5550), Rydges (3969) and All Seasons (3500).

The name of Southern Pacific Hotel Corporation had become an acronym in 1997, to be known thenceforth as SPHC. The SPHC Group operated more hotels outside Australia than within, its overall tally in 1998 being 69 hotels with 12 763 rooms in 13 countries in the Asia Pacific region. The company had been owned since 1988 by the American Pritzker family, who had paid $540 million for it. The Pritzkers, who also owned the much larger Hyatt group, were reported in 1998 to have dedicated $100 million to giving the SPHC Group's

oldest brand, Travelodge, a fresh look; the first of a new generation of **229**
two-star 120-room Travelodges opened in Sydney late in 1998. About 50
were to be built in Australia and New Zealand, located near clubs or
restaurants that also offered room service. The hotels themselves would
serve only breakfasts, though rooms would have kitchenettes with
microwave ovens. They would also be equipped with entertainment
channels on television and a computer data link.[35]

Rydges Hotels was a subsidiary of Amalgamated Holdings Ltd, a
company listed on the Australian Stock Exchange, which also operated
Greater Union Theatres, the Bobby McGee's themed restaurants in
Sydney and Melbourne, the Featherdale Wildlife Park in western
Sydney, and Matilda Cruises on Sydney Harbour. Its first three hotels
were branded Noah's. As the company expanded, it became the practice
to call them by their individual names. In 1995 the brand name Rydges
was adopted.[36] In 1998 Rydges operated 28 hotels and resorts in
Australia and a number of other properties in New Zealand. Its flagship
hotel was the Wentworth in Sydney and its resort portfolio included
Thredbo Alpine Village.

All Seasons was started in Perth in 1982 by David Connors and
David Price. By 1998 David Connors had died and David Price had
handed management of the 27-property group to Peter Frawley, a
former Sheraton executive. The company was bought by Thakral
Property Trust in 1994 and in 1998 it was managing five of Thakral's 15
properties, including All Seasons Premier Menzies in Sydney.

The history of the Australian Tourism Group began when a syndicate
of investors led by Darryl Courtney-O'Connor took over the Country
Comfort motel chain owned by the Lend Lease Group. In 1976 Lend
Lease had put one of its executives, John Hagley, in charge of five AM
Motor Lodges it owned, with instructions to make something of them or
get the company out of the motel business. Hagley changed the name to
Country Comfort, took the group out of the Homestead referral chain in
favour of running his own reservations system and expanded it to
about a dozen motels. Courtney-O'Connor, then employed by Lend
Lease, bought them in 1986 with the help of a number of investors.

He then built the group to become the largest owned chain of
motels and hotels in Australia, consisting of mainly three-to-four-star
properties from Adelaide to Cairns. It was listed as the Australian
Tourism Group in 1994, with Touraust Hotels as its operating arm. In
1997 it announced its diversification into a multi-brand chain; the
Country Comfort brand was to be positioned against Flag and Best
Western and a new 4.5-star Chifley range of hotels was to be

230 introduced, with eight planned by 2000. It would develop the Australis brand as its premier leisure and destination product.

International companies like ITT Sheraton and Hilton were managing hotels with room totals of between 2500 and 3000 with much fewer properties than most of the Australian chains, for the obvious reason that their hotels were much bigger. By the late 1990s they seemed to have stabilised and had hotels in the major cities.

On the other hand, Bass Hotels & Resorts was continuing to expand its Holiday Inn chain, announcing the purchase of four hotels in one month—January 1998—and its intention to become a market leader in Australia. By then it owned, managed or franchised 14 hotels with 2464 rooms. Bass Hotels & Resorts had changed its corporate name from Holiday Hospitality in keeping with the identity of its parent, Bass PLC, the British-based hospitality, leisure and branded drinks company. Among the Bass Hotels & Resorts brands was Inter-Continental, which was also represented in Australia.

Hotels and casinos

Wrest Point hotel-casino, the first of its kind in Australia, broke new ground in a number of ways when it opened in Hobart in February 1973. Driven by the imagination of its managing director, John Haddad,[37] Federal Hotels overcame a number of taboos to bring a new level of entertainment and service in a hotel complex, making it a year-round attraction in itself. It offered not only the casino, but also a 24-hour coffee shop and international shows of a style and lavishness that were new to Australia at the time.

Importantly for the future, Federal wrote casino rules that answered Australian concerns. They were different from those in place overseas and were so successful they were adopted in other parts of Australia years later, when other casinos under other managements were introduced. Their aim was to ensure that the 'rorts, rip-offs and shady practices' that existed in other countries did not happen in Australia.[38] The rules included government participation in the counting of proceeds and a prohibition against tipping staff from winnings.

Federal continued to manage a few top-ranking hotels into the 1990s, including the Windsor and Menzies Rialto (later Le Meridien), but following the success of Wrest Point it specialised as a hotel-casino operator. After opening the Don Casino in Darwin under a temporary licence from 1979, it helped design—and then operated—the Alice

Springs Casino (1981), the Country Club Casino (Launceston 1982) **231**
and the Mindil Beach Casino (Darwin 1983), all of which had quality
hotel facilities as well as casinos.

The Mindil Beach and Alice Springs Casinos were expropriated in
1984 by the Northern Territory government in controversial circumstances.[39] This followed a disagreement with Federal Hotels about a
proposed new development in Darwin to which the government
required the casino licence to be transferred. When Federal Hotels
resisted, the government took over its two casinos in the Northern
Territory. In the event, the proposed development did not proceed.

Wrest Point had been designed to attract visitors year-round to help
Tasmania get over its traditional seasonality problem, which caused
tourists to stay away during the colder months. Besides the casino it
offered stage shows, spacious and well-equipped convention venues
and special gambling facilities for those visitors who played for high
stakes: the high-rollers and the premium players. The casinos that followed usually attracted a large local market but also were designed to
appeal to visitors, especially convention delegates. Three were opened in
1985—the Adelaide Casino, the Burswood Resort and Casino in Perth
and Jupiters at the Conrad Hilton International at Broadbeach on the
Gold Coast.

The Adelaide Casino varied from the others in that it occupied an
old building: a converted railway station originally built in 1929. It was
given the opulent look of another time; this helped the marketers differentiate it from its interstate rivals. The Hyatt Regency hotel was in the
same development precinct, as was the Adelaide Convention Centre.

The Sheraton Breakwater Casino-Hotel in Townsville, opened in
1986, was the last casino to be built in the 1980s. However, there were
more to come—the Casino Canberra in 1992 and in 1996 another two
in Queensland: the Reef Hotel Casino in Cairns and the Conrad
International Treasury Casino in Brisbane, which incorporated a heritage
building. In 1997 two very large complexes were built, replacing temporary casinos in Sydney and Melbourne. These were entertainment
centres on a scale never seen in Australia before, incorporating not only
large casinos but also hotels, theatres, cinemas, spas, shopping arcades,
restaurants and nightclubs.

The $876 million Star City on Sydney's Darling Harbour had a 352-
room, five-star hotel as its centrepiece and also 139 serviced apartments, ranging from one to three bedrooms. Melbourne's vast $2.2
billion Crown Entertainment Complex, occupying the equivalent of
two entire city blocks on the banks of the Yarra River, opened with the

Changes at Wrest Point (Source: Wrest Point Hotel Casino)

Casino gambling was not thought of as a Tasmanian attraction in 1941 when this advertisement for Hobart's Wrest Point Riviera Hotel was published in the Mercury (above). The copywriters were not modest about the hotel's drawing power, however. Wrest Point took on a different shape in more ways than one in 1973 when it became Australia's first hotel-casino. A recent photograph (top right) shows the distinctive tower and conference complex on the banks of the Derwent.

500-room Crown Towers and deferred the planned construction of a second 500-room tower when the Asian financial crisis affected its business in 1997–98.

Caravans, camps and hostels

As Australians took to the roads after the war, more and more of them saw the logic of taking their accommodation with them. Caravanning boomed in the 1960s and 1970s, both in the number of caravans registered and in the number of caravan parks set up to cater for them. In later decades there was a slump, partly because of the rise in the cost of developing parks and, in some cases, because of the limited return on investment.

Nevertheless, the industry in the late 1990s was a major part of the accommodation sector, accounting for up to 25 per cent of all visitor nights in Australia per year. The statistics were impressive: more than 350 000 caravans throughout the country, 2700 short-term caravan parks, employment for some 15 000 people and revenues of $1.5 billion.[40] Many motor travellers who did not have their own caravans saw a caravan park with on-site vans or park cabins as an economical alternative to other commercial accommodation. Besides 176 416 caravan sites, parks had 8743 on-site vans and 11 356 cabins and flats in 1997.[41]

The popularity of recreational vehicles was reflected by the formation of the Campervan and Motorhome Club of Australia in 1986. In

1998 the organisation had more than 7300 active memberships representing more than 14 000 individuals. Most were from Australia, but there were also members from New Zealand, Britain, the US and other countries.

Camping had always been popular with some Australians, not only when they were touring from place to place but also when they went on regular holidays to the same place each year. Camping areas at popular beach resorts often attracted the same groups from year to year, forming stable communities for the holiday period. Touring camping increased from the 1980s with the development of campervans and other recreational vehicles.

The Australian Camping Association was incorporated in Melbourne in 1983 to foster the use of bunkhouse and cabin accommodation, mainly by school groups. Facilities were often provided by churches or community organisations like the YMCA. While school groups accounted for 90 per cent of the use of some camps, the remaining clientele was remarkably diverse. The Youth Hostels Association, formed in 1939 in Victoria and based on a European model, grew steadily after the war until by the 1990s there were 140 hostels in Australia. The hostels were well placed to participate in the growth of backpacking, which had quickened in the 1980s.

In response to the growing demand, other accommodation was also provided for backpackers in popular resort areas, particularly in the north, and in the cities. Specialised travel centres were established to help backpackers make their travel arrangements; thus the Youth Hostels Association operated a travel agency for members and Backpackers Travel Centre, founded in 1993, had offices in Melbourne, Sydney, the Gold Coast, Brisbane and Alice Springs five years later.

A ratings guide for backpacker accommodation was introduced in 1995. This ranked establishments assessed by the Australian Automobile Association on a one-to-five 'backpack' system: one 'backpack' indicating clean, simple, basic facilities and five 'backpacks' indicating a superior standard.[42]

The international market for backpackers caught the attention of the industry after research showed that backpackers not only stayed three times as long as the average tourist, but also spent twice as much. They were said to have a preference for budget accommodation, to travel on an independently organised and flexible schedule, and to like informal and participatory holiday activities.[43] Between 200 000 and 300 000 international backpackers a year visited Australia in the mid-1990s.

Tourists in the home

Some farmers had seen the possibility of attracting tourists to their properties in the 1970s; the first overseas promotion of farm holidays took place in that decade. The idea was that visitors would be able to see the farm in action as well as mix with the family. The Victorian Host Farms Association was formed in 1977 during a period of development and expansion of farm tourism ventures in Europe. Organisations in other States followed some years later and in 1988 a national organisation, Australian Farm and Country Tourism, came into being.

The number of properties involved built up gradually over the years, the pace of increase depending on the economic climate. Accommodation included self-contained cottages, rooms in homesteads and shearers' quarters. Guests were given the opportunity to observe or participate in farm activities. By 1998 the number of farms belonging to the State organisations was about 500. Member farms were inspected by the Australian Automobile Association and given a star rating. Victoria had introduced an accreditation program, which was concerned with risk management as well as standards generally.

It was not only farmers who had guests in their homes, of course. There was a growing number of bed-and-breakfast establishments in Australia—perhaps as many as 5000.[44] These could be ordinary houses, farms (there was some overlap with Host Farms), cottages, self-contained apartments or something different again. The style of accommodation was not so important; the main criteria were that the host or hostess should be there to offer the personal touch and that breakfast should be available. The Australian Bed and Breakfast Council was formed in 1992; State organisations, for the most part, came later.

Bed-and-breakfast establishments were not necessarily cheap; in fact, there had been a tendency as the 1990s wore on to go upmarket. Size and style varied greatly. The Victorian Bed and Breakfast Council put the range at 1 to 16 rooms, each sleeping 1 to 4 persons. The norm was two bedrooms with a double bed in each.

The bed-and-breakfast phenomenon—and it was that—was indicative of the interest that tourism created in so many Australians in the 1980s and 1990s. They seized the opportunity to participate as business people without large capital expenditure. Collectively, they made a valuable addition to Australia's accommodation stock and helped provide different experiences for those tourists who were turning away from standardised touring.

236   As a whole, the Australian accommodation industry had learned to segment its market very well and had developed a range of hotels, resorts, motels, holiday apartments, camping grounds, caravan parks, host farms, 'B&Bs' and backpacker and youth hostels to cater for every traveller. That is not to say that everything was perfect—far from it—but in diversity of accommodation it was a very different picture from the situation in Australia immediately after the Second World War when, apart from the few grand hotels in the major cities, we only had pubs and guest houses and the odd caravan park and camping ground.

ENDNOTES

[1] *The Motel Guide for Australia*, 2nd edn (1959), said 80 motels were operating in Australia in December 1959. The *NRMA Accommodation Guide* listed 675 motels for 1964 (Harris, Kerr, Forster & Co. and Stanton Robbins & Co. Inc., 1966, *Australia's Travel and Tourist Industry, 1965*, ANTA, Melbourne, p. 155).

[2] Dunstan, op.cit., p. 9.

[3] ibid., p. 11.

[4] Lattin, G.W. (1990b), p. 586.

[5] *The Western Magazine*, 16 June 1975, p. 9. There has been considerable confusion about the first motels. V. C. Davis, secretary of the Motel Federation of Australia, acknowledges the Penzance and Bathurst motels as the first two in an article in the *Motel Guide for Australia* in 1959, as does the *Western Magazine* article. Davis mentions the Jolly Swagman but does not put a date on its opening.

[6] Alan Greenway in a fax from San Diego to the author dated 21 May 1998: 'I can't take issue with the claim for Don Richardson's property—I knew him well as a fellow member of the Board of the Motel Federation of Australia . . . The Bathurst Motor Inn was created by Rex Bray, and it was first in a chain which included the Club Motel at Wagga. The Jolly Swagman was created by Eric Sebire. Both Rex and Eric were foundation members of the Board of MFA . . . which organisation was created by Lou Pimblett. Another pioneer, still around, is Hugh McCarron.'

[7] Greenway drove a Chevrolet utility on winding two-lane roads at a speed which was the stuff of legends. A man of many interests, he later became a rally driver. His biographer, Richard Brett, notes his early 'passion for fast driving' and this author can testify that it had not diminished when Greenway drove him in 1976 on a particularly tortuous section of the Pacific Coast Highway between Los Angeles and San Francisco in an attempt to reach Big Sur by sunset. Brett's book was still under preparation at the time of writing and publication details were unknown. Richard Brett made available part of the manuscript for preparation of the section on Alan Greenway and the early days of Travelodge.

[8] It was spelt with the capital 'L' at this stage, although later the present spelling of 'Travelodge' was adopted.

[9] Brett, op.cit., p. 37.

[10] Flag media release, 16 June 1998.

[11] A number of people went to considerable trouble to find information for this section. The author is particularly grateful to Nancy Richardson, Alan Greenway, Tony Major

(Bathurst Motor Inn) and John McKirnan.

[12] Dunstan, op.cit., p. 10.

[13] The Old White Hart Hotel had been built on the corner of 'Great Bourke' and Spring Streets about 1846. In 1920 it was sold to the Melbourne Hotels Company, which owned the Grand (later the Windsor). It gradually lost its identity and by the 1950s was known as the Windsor Annexe. From 1932 until its demolition in 1959 its dining-room housed Ricco's, one of Melbourne's best-known Italian restaurants. The Old White Hart was demolished so that a new Annexe could be built to provide new bar and banquet room facilities and accommodation for another 100 guests. In the 1990s part of this space was given over to the Hard Rock Cafe.

[14] Rühen, op.cit., p. 37.

[15] Interview with Frank Christie, June 1998.

[16] Fitzgerald, op.cit., p. 546.

[17] Leon La Roche, Lennons concierge, interview June 1998.

[18] Larkins, J. (1973), *Australian Pubs*, Rigby Limited, Adelaide, p. 144.

[19] The Windsor was not Oberoi's first Australian hotel. The Oberoi company was part of a consortium that had bought the Australia Hotel in Adelaide a few years previously. It was while Rai Bahadur Oberoi, the chain's founder, was in Adelaide on an inspection tour with his son that they saw the Victorian government's advertisements calling for tenders to operate the Windsor.

[20] The Oberoi group's restoration budget went from $2.5 million to more than $8 million. The Public Works Department spent another $3 million on exterior works and fire protection (Spicer, op.cit., p. 102).

[21] Simpson, M. (1995), *Old Sydney Buildings: A Social History*, Kangaroo Press, Sydney, pp. 33, 34–8 & 92. The Inter-Continental was opened in 1985, the Harbour Rocks conversion took place in 1987 and the Ritz-Carlton was opened in 1990.

[22] Richardson (1995), op.cit., p. 129.

[23] The six leading Japanese developers spent about $7 billion on projects, including tourism developments, and lost about half in the bail-out. (Richardson, 1995, op.cit., p. 140).

[24] ibid., p. 135.

[25] ibid., p. 141.

[26] ibid., p. 8.

[27] A sample of newspaper headlines at the time indicates the concern: 'Queensland needs hotels urgently' (*Weekend Australian*, 15–16 October 1994, p. 8), 'Room shortage risks restricting tourism gains' (*The Australian*, 9 November 1994, p. 9), 'New plea for hotel incentives' (*Australian Financial Review*, 30 May 1995, p. 45), 'States urged to help over-come shortage of hotel accommodation' (*Australian Financial Review*, 21 June 1995), 'Perth needs a new hotel a year' (*Australian Financial Review*, 26 July 1995, p. 36).

[28] Jon Hutchison, managing director of the Australian Tourist Commission, quoted in the *Australian Financial Review*, 29 August 1995, p. 8. He said the Japanese industry had indicated that 5 to 15 per cent more tourists could have been sent to Australia in the peak season if sufficient accommodation had been available.

[29] *The Australian Financial Review*, 1 April 1997, p. 35.

[30] *The Australian Financial Review*, 11 October 1996, p. 63.

[31] *The Australian Financial Review*, 27 March 1998, p. 67.

[32] Oliver Shaul interview, August 1998. Some aspects of his restaurant career are dis-cussed in the next chapter. Shaul was also a member of the board of the Australian Tourist Commission when it was set up in 1967. In 1998 he was working as a consul-tant as well as serving as chairman of the companies controlling the Summit restaurant

238

and Blue Line Cruises and chairman of the board of the Northern Institute of TAFE.

[33] The first Accor hotel, the Darling Harbour Novotel, Sydney, preceded the merger—it had opened in 1991.

[34] *Weekend Australian* Financial Review, 6–7 December 1997, p. 13.

[35] SPHC media releases and the *Australian Financial Review*, 12 December 1996, p. 32. The Pritzkers were said to be the fifteenth richest family in the world, with a net worth of between $US 4.4 billion and $US 6 billion.

[36] The chairman of Amalgamated Holdings was Alan Rydge and his father, Sir Norman Rydge, had been chairman of the company that owned Usher's Hotel in Sydney before Federal Hotels bought it.

[37] Haddad later held a number of senior industry positions and was chairman of the Australian Tourist Commission from 1985 to 1995.

[38] Glaser, W. (1988), 'A guide to casinos in Australia', *Tempo Australia*, v. 6(25), p. 54.

[39] In 1998 the Mindil Beach hotel-casino was called the MGM Grand and the Alice Springs hotel-casino was called Lasseter's. The Darwin property was bought by the US gambling company MGM in 1995, re-christened MGM Grand Darwin and given a $25 million refurbishment. MGM owns the 5000-room MGM hotel and casino in Las Vegas.

[40] Gerry Ryan, chairman of the Caravan Industry Australia, speaking at the CIA's conference in Canberra, January 1998 (Office of National Tourism, *Talking Tourism*, March 1998, p. 3.)

[41] ABS, Cat 8634.0, p. 6.

[42] Department of Tourism, *Talking Tourism*, September 1995, p. 1.

[43] ibid., November–December 1994, p. 10.

[44] Lynne Peterkin, chairman, Australian Bed and Breakfast Council, interview, August 1998. Research was being undertaken at the time of the interview with the aim of establishing an accurate figure.

A *culinary renaissance*

From desert to abundance

It was often difficult to find somewhere to eat if you were away from home in Australia in the early 1950s. Restaurants and cafés were few by standards of later eras and travellers were unlucky if they were in a city on a Sunday night without knowing precisely where they would have their next meal. Indeed the hearts of Australian cities were desolate, lifeless places on a Sunday night and not much better on a Saturday afternoon.

During the working day there were restaurants for shoppers and workers. Those for the former were rather genteel places serving light food or meat and vegetables in the English style. Some cafés—a typical one might have uncomfortable booths down one side and tables and chairs filling the rest of the space—could offer something different because their proprietors came from Italy or Greece. There were a few restaurants similar to what we would later call bistros; usually there were two or three in a city's business district.

Strange liquor laws emptied the hotels at six o'clock in most States. Even in a fine restaurant—whether in a hotel or not—there were sometimes problems if you wanted to drink alcohol. There was a limited range of excellent dining for those who could afford it, much of it in the hands of hospitable Italians. Australians dining out expensively were accustomed to eating three courses at least. Clubs were fashionable for those who were eligible because they avoided the more restrictive drinking laws. Some of the best and most innovative restaurants were not licensed and operated outside the law by allowing the

240 consumption of liquor. A few were in grand old houses and there was something furtive and exciting about eating and drinking luxuriously in them.

The migrant influence varied from city to city. Hobart did not even have a restaurant representing one of our longest-established ethnic groups, the Chinese. In other places it was considered self-indulgent fun to go to a Chinese restaurant carrying pots and pans to collect food; the restaurants did not supply cartons for takeaways. The most popular takeaway was the fish-and-chip shop.

But new influences were making themselves felt, at least to a few. In the 1950s the French chef Paul Harbulot arrived to take charge of the kitchen of the new Johnnie Walker Bistro in Sydney and Georges Mora landed in Australia from Paris; he went on to create the Café Balzac in Melbourne and won for himself the reputation of being the first modern restaurateur in the country. In 1960 a Swiss chef, Hermann Schneider, opened Two Faces in the Melbourne suburb of South Yarra.[1]

The Italians, who had given Melbourne such restaurants as the Florentino, the Latin, the Society and Molina's, were a growing force in the food and culture scene in the cities. In the 1950s an Italian migrant family established a restaurant named Gambaro in Brisbane. It became known for its preparation of seafood, particularly oysters and mud crabs, and was to be a popular social and eating venue over the next four decades. In 1954 a young Italian, Gino Di Santo, installed Melbourne's first Cimbali single-piston espresso machine in the Lexington Café and inaugurated Melbourne's café life, which flourished in and around Lygon Street in the inner-city suburb of Carlton.[2] The first espresso in Adelaide may have been poured a couple of years earlier, probably at the Mocca Bar in Hindley Street, from an old Gaggia with a pump handle.

> This event marked the beginnings of civilised culinary life in Adelaide, even though the only decent Italian cooking in the city was in the boarding houses where the young Italian migrants lived. (N. Hopkins, 'South Australia: Tradition with a twist' in J. McCallum (ed.), *Australia: A Gourmet's Paradise*, 1995)[3]

Other migrants of that era who made their mark in the kitchens included Greeks, Austrians, Hungarians, Lebanese and Yugoslavs.

From the mid-1960s, small BYOs (bring your own bottle) appeared, usually serving French provincial food. Among them were Juillet's in Potts Point, Sydney. Patric Juillet opened other restaurants later that featured southern French cooking with traces from Asia.

Stephanie Alexander, originally trained as a librarian, had studied **241** French cooking while working as an au pair in France. However, her first restaurant, Jamaica House, which opened in Melbourne in the 1960s, served authentic Jamaican food that included curries. In the mid-1970s she opened Stephanie's in Brunswick Street, Fitzroy, and then put the skills she had learned in France to good purpose. Her mother had been a cook and Stephanie revived some of her traditional recipes cooked in her own style. Dur-é Dara, a musician who started as a waitress at Stephanie's a year after it opened, later became the restaurant's manager and then Stephanie's partner in the business. She describes the cuisine there as 'a sum of all the parts'—contemporary, relying on fresh Australian ingredients and carrying influences such as Stephanie's French training and her mother's culinary legacy.[4]

A culinary event of importance in Sydney was the opening in 1974 of the Bon Gout by Tony and Gay Bilson.

Born in a scruffy corner of East Sydney, Bon Gout became a benchmark, a body and soul affair that with its freshly inventive soups and dishes such as saddle of hare, canard au cerises and ambrosial French pastries, developed along nouvelle lines. Bon Gout was seen to be parallel with, and then encouraged by, the lightening and liberating of food in France when rule-breaking was sanctioned. The Bilsons were the first Australian-born chefs to become celebrities. (A. Williams, 'Influences: Tastes of Australia', in J. McCallum, op.cit.)[5]

In 1977 the Bilsons opened the Berowra Waters Inn on a cliff at the northern reaches of Sydney, 'a culinary lighthouse'. As a schoolboy Tony Bilson had run an account at the Balzac in Melbourne and on Georges Mora's recommendation had been apprenticed to Paul Harbulot in Sydney.

In the 1970s Mietta O'Donnell and Tony Knox opened 'a coffee-house salon of Italian Asian flavour' in the inner Melbourne suburb of North Fitzroy, but when they moved to a city restaurant they 'fell for the wine culture and therefore French cuisine.'[6] They were an important influence in Melbourne's restaurant life.

The restaurant as a tourist attraction

Although many Australians relished the new influences on their food, others were not about to change their tastes quickly. When Oliver Shaul

242 took over the catering of the newly-opened Sydney Opera House in 1973, open sandwiches were offered in one area—paté, smoked salmon and underdone fillet of beef. However, as Shaul later said, 'We couldn't give them away. They would be fine now but our tastes are evolutionary, not revolutionary. We went back to selling corned beef and pickles.'[7]

A few restaurateurs were thinking seriously about attracting tourists. Wolfie Pizem and Joe Malek opened the Coachmen restaurant in 1960 in a house in the Sydney suburb of Redfern. The house had been built in 1826 for Thomas Campbell, the famous pioneer merchant who was a founder of the Bank of New South Wales.[8] The restaurant soon attracted the attention of inbound tour operators and airline sales people.

In 1975, as tourism expanded, Pizem participated in the first Australian Tourist Commission travel trade mission to North America, fastidiously setting up his booth as an elegant restaurant table before each business session. He forged relationships with prominent American tour operators that were to serve him well over the years as he opened more restaurants: the Waterfront (1978), the Italian Village (1987) and Wolfie's (1992).

In 1968 Oliver Shaul opened the Summit restaurant on top of the Australia Square Tower. It was the biggest revolving restaurant in the world and offered superb views of Sydney, taking an hour and three quarters to make a full revolution.[9] It became a tourism landmark. At Doyle's fish restaurant on the harbour at Watson's Bay, tourists could sit in the sun and watch a world of colour and movement on the water against a splendid city backdrop.

The 1980s were years of fundamental change in the culinary world, just as they were in so many other aspects of Australian life. The liberalisation of licensing laws meant that wine, in particular, could be enjoyed much more widely than before. By that time Australians were sophisticated drinkers of a varied bounty of excellent wines. The increase in the number of international hotel companies helped add depth to Australia's food choices. Asian migration made a huge impact on Australia's already eclectic restaurant scene. We were accustomed to various Chinese cuisines and to superb restaurants like the Flower Drum in Melbourne, but now there were Thai, Indian, Malaysian, Indonesian, Japanese and Vietnamese as well. In the 1990s some 45 different ethnic cuisines could be counted in Melbourne, and it was a similar story elsewhere.

The 1980s were also the time for a change of heart among Australia's leading chefs which was to have an effect in restaurant kitchens all over the country. One of those who influenced this new movement was Anders Ousbäch, who opened a small café in Sydney after a period with Hermann Schneider at Melbourne's Two Faces. Among the restaurants he was to run later was the Wharf at the Sydney Theatre Company's headquarters on Walsh Bay. Besides working on food at Two Faces, Ousbäch had also studied wine for three years under an expert, Len Evans.

From the beginning of the change, food was presented in a simpler style, without the distraction of garnishes. International influences such as nouvelle cuisine and cuisine minceur were put aside as chefs experimented with Australia's wealth of ingredients to produce something distinctive. This new style often bore flavours inspired by the tastes of a multicultural population.[10] The creation of a distinctive style was noticed overseas and Australian chefs began to travel the world demonstrating it.

Andrew Mirosch, owner-chef of Brisbane's About Face, typified the new approach. He wove ideas around 'the unique and distinctive produce of the state, with just a hint of knowledge and exotica that has come from elsewhere in the world'.[11] He was widely respected for his work with game meats, red deer venison and low-fat kangaroo cuts from Queensland's outback, serving them with braised Asian vegetables grown in the south-east of the State. Mirosch liked to catch his own fish on his days off.

Another who brought originality to food preparation was Cheong Liew, who had come to Australia from Kuala Lumpur in 1973 as an engineering student but dropped out to become a chef in Adelaide. He began as the grill chef at a Greek restaurant, then quickly moved to a couple of other restaurants before opening his own, with a partner, in 1975. It was called Neddy's. Cheong drew inspiration from a variety of cuisines—Malaysian, Indian, French, Greek and, most of all, Chinese. He read avidly, his inspiration including a cookery book by Salvador Dali, whose decorative presentation appealed to him.

In the words of N. Hopkins, he took 'a multitude of cuisines with an Australian ingredient to create a perfect multicultural blend' in what may be regarded as one of the starting-points of Australia's new cuisine.[12] His dishes included kangaroo marinated in wine and vinegar, served with mustard and a fennel bulb poached in milk; octopus fried in olive oil with avocado and quail egg salad; pot-roasted pigeon fin-

244 ished with parmesan and breadcrumbs; and pork hocks served with wood fungus and yellow ginger-flower rice.

The fundamental Asian influence

The Asian influence had a fundamental impact on contemporary Australian cuisine. John Dunham, writing in the Restaurant and Catering Association of Victoria's newsletter in 1994, regarded it as part of a broader change that had seen

> ... the dethronement of French *haute cuisine* and its replacement by a new respect for cooking which uses more fresh seasonal ingredients, less saturated fats and oils, faster cooking techniques, and aims at creating dishes in which flavours are not disguised. These are dishes which are less complicated, more readily understandable. And while the notion that presentation is still important persists it avoids the minimalist artistry of the so called *nouvelle cuisine*.[13]

The change in cuisine was accompanied by a change in customer preference for lighter, cheaper meals in informal surroundings. Cafés even moved outdoors, especially in Melbourne—tables and chairs were placed on the pavements with or without traffic guard rails. And there was plenty of choice: at the end of June 1992 there were 8700 restaurants and cafés operating in Australia.[14] In part, the change was brought about by the recession, which caused people to think more about how they spent their money. Eating out by this time was ingrained in Australians as part of their way of life. They wanted to keep going to restaurants and cafés during the recession, but money was tight and they wanted value for it. They also wanted larger serves of fresher, better produce, cooked more lightly. Asian and Mediterranean cuisines were better able to meet these requirements than food in the classical French style.

> The old hierarchies have been disturbed, if not permanently dismantled. No longer are the haute cuisine and controlled ambience of the fine dining rooms of the five-star, internationally-managed hotels at the heart of the city as assured of their place at the top of the hierarchy as they might have been a decade ago. Similarly, the formerly unpretentious casa linga and sparely decorated suburban cafe has been re-valued upwards and judged by many as worthy of a more inclusive patronage. There has been a deliberate avoidance by the industry's professionals of the once

standard categories of 'restaurant' and 'cafe' and an enthusiastic employment of a multitude of less formal and more exotic stylings reflected in such names as brasserie, bistro (or bistrot?), taverna, diner, deli, inn, tearoom, bakehouse, grill, and even fishcaf. (J. Dunham in *What's Cooking*, 1994)[15]

In the 1990s there was still some of the old along with the new, however. Beppi's in East Sydney had been going since 1956; in Melbourne there was still a Maxim's and a Florentino. In Brisbane Gambaro was not only prospering as a restaurant but had become Queensland's largest wholesale supplier of oysters, mud crabs and most other seafood. But restaurateurs and chefs move on. Peter Doyle opened a new restaurant called the Cicada in Potts Point while his brother Greg did something different with the Pier at Rose Bay. Hermann Schneider left South Yarra for a restaurant at Arthur's Seat on the Mornington Peninsula.

Regional food differences

When people travelled in Australia in the 1950s and 1960s they noticed the regional differences. Seafood was excellent, then as always, in Tasmania, and it could be cooked well even in a small seaside pub. For those who thought the only good fish were those caught in cold waters, the first taste of a Reef fish somewhere north of Brisbane was a time to revise opinions. And Queensland had delicious fruits not seen in southern markets.

In the 1980s Tasmanians began to farm fish, the delicious Atlantic salmon, and this was so successful that ten years later 3000 tonnes were being harvested annually. By then Tasmanian and King Island cheeses had also won a reputation throughout the country. Queensland was supplying southern markets regularly with exotic fruits—indeed, what was grown in the north of the State was largely dictated by the food revolution in Sydney and Melbourne. Pawpaws and mangoes were as familiar in the south as bananas and the Queensland growers were cultivating fruits with names that were decidedly unfamiliar, such as jackfruit, mangosteens, rambutans, rolinas, carimbolas and soursops. These were but two examples of the way the range of quality foods available to chefs had widened. One chef remembered that there were three varieties of potatoes in the 1970s: pink, white and dirty. Twenty years later she could count 27.[16]

Travellers in Australia were sometimes surprised at the variety of foods on offer. At Miss Daisy's restaurant in Alice Springs they could eat emu, kangaroo, buffalo and witchetty grubs prepared with a French

246   influence. At Scotty's, in the same city, the menu included Flutter and
Hop (emu and kangaroo), Wallow and Hump (buffalo and camel),
Hop and Hump (kangaroo and camel) and Bait and Bite (barramundi
and camel).

Feeling hungry as they strolled through the Mindil Beach market in
Darwin, they could be tempted to the food stalls by

> ... tropical vegetables, herbs, spices, fruits, ices, steamed mud
> crab, Arafura prawns, grilled barramundi, crocodile, buffalo and
> green paw paw salad ... as well as a variety of styles including
> Malay, Filipino, Chinese, Japanese, Portuguese, Indian, Lebanese,
> Creole, Greek, Spanish and Thai. (J. Hirst, 'Northern Territory—
> an ancient land', in McCallum, op.cit.)[17]

By contrast Alan Fabregues, owner-chef at The Loose Box, one of
Western Australia's leading restaurants, cooked in the classical French
style. He was awarded the Meilleur Ouvrier de France in 1991, a high
honour for a chef. His was a French cuisine with a local flavour and he
used some of the State's unique foods, such as marron (freshwater cray-
fish) combined with herbs and vegetables grown in the restaurant's
garden. The Loose Box was at Mundaring, 30 kilometres east of Perth.[18]

In the 1990s travellers in Australia were spending about $4 billion a
year on food and drink,[19] and clearly enjoying it. In 1996 restaurants
rated highest as a cultural and entertainment drawcard, according to
the 1996 International Visitor Survey, with 3.5 million visitors patron-
ising restaurants, cafés and other food outlets—an increase of 14 per
cent over 1995. Some 390 000 visited a winery.[20]

However, there was more to it than that. The rise of the restaurant
and catering industry from those glum post-war days was also an indication of the enthusiasm for eating in public that has become part of
the Australian culture. It had not always been so; there was a time when
Australians ate out only when they had to or on special celebratory
occasions.

In other areas, huge advances were brought about in the last half
century by developments in technology. In this field, however, it was
the Australian people who have changed their way of life. It has been
their desire for quality and value, their preferences in terms of cuisine
and ambience and their demand for a relaxation of legislative restraints
that have been the principal forces for change. The tourism industry has
been a major beneficiary.

ENDNOTES

[1] Williams, A., 'The influences: Tastes of Australia', in McCallum, J. (1995), *Australia: A Gourmet's Paradise*, Focus Publishing, Sydney, p. 14.

[2] Durack, T.: 'Victoria: Rich and cosmopolitan', in McCallum, op.cit., p. 134..

[3] Hopkins, N., 'South Australia: Tradition with a twist', in McCallum, op.cit., p. 159.

[4] Dur-é Dara, interview December 1998.

[5] Williams, A., 'Influences: Tastes of Australia', in McCallum, op.cit., p. 15–17.

[6] Williams, A., 'Chefs & heroes: Celebrating rare talent', in McCallum, op.cit., p. 49.

[7] Oliver Shaul, interview, August 1998.

[8] In 1998 it was the Russian Coachmen. Pizem still owned the restaurant but leased it to others.

[9] Revolving restaurants move at 1.2 metres a minute.

[10] Interview with Michael Foulkes, director of operations Accor Asia Pacific Tourism Leisure, formerly executive chef, Sydney Opera House, August 1998.

[11] Hart, B., 'Queensland: Exotic by nature', in McCallum, op.cit., p. 81.

[12] Hopkins, N., 'South Australia: Tradition with a twist', in McCallum, op.cit., p. 164.

[13] Dunham, J. (1994), 'Development and changes within the Victorian restaurant and catering industry over the past decade', in *What's Cooking*, July issue, p. 7. Dunham was a former academic who owned three restaurants.

[14] An Australian Bureau of Statistics figure. At the time of writing the ABS's last survey was in 1991–92. This survey also listed 4300 pubs, bars and taverns and 3800 licensed clubs.

[15] Dunham, op.cit., p. 6.

[16] Campbell, J., Introduction, McCallum, op.cit., p. 10.

[17] Hirst, J., 'Northern Territory: An ancient land', in McCallum, op.cit., p. 64.

[18] Powell, G. D., 'Western Australia: A different time and space', in McCallum, op.cit., p. 181.

[19] Richardson (1996), op.cit., p. 289.

[20] Office of National Tourism, *Talking Tourism*, October 1997, p. 1.

Distribution: people and electronics

The post-war years

The new era of travel that came after the war required a more elaborate and sophisticated distribution system than any that had been known before in Australia. However, this was not put in place immediately. In the meantime, in the first few years after the war's end, companies that were to make a mark on the Australian travel scene had started business—among them King's Travel in Adelaide, Stewart Moffat Travel in Melbourne and World Travel Headquarters in Sydney. The early work was not in selling travel out of Australia, but in selling it into the country—the migrant trade. Agents made travel arrangements for prospective immigrants, usually from Italy and Greece, after being approached by their relatives in Australia.

When the migrant trade dried up in the 1960s, the agents turned to more conventional retailing: selling travel to Australians. There was hardly any wholesaling at first, though all the agents mentioned above would be creating tours as well as selling travel within a few years.

Frank Johnson had started his career in 1945 as an office boy in Sydney with the tourism development section of the New Zealand Government Offices. He went to TAA as an office junior in 1946 and it was there that he met John Webb. They became a team, transferring first to Roland Hill's travel business where they worked in the migrant trade before joining Orbit Travel, an offshoot of the short-lived New Holland Airways.

In 1951 Johnson was persuaded to open a branch of World Travel Headquarters in Sydney. The company had been started by Noel

Harrison-Bourke at a desk in Lennons Hotel, Brisbane. John Webb **249** joined Johnson and soon afterwards they found themselves running the business. Harrison-Bourke was a tall, dark and handsome man who was generally referred to in the business as 'Buster Bourke'. He was a romantic and went off to live in Tahiti, where he was later killed in a car crash. In 1956 Johnson and Webb and the other shareholders took in Australian Consolidated Press as an equal shareholder.[1] In 1971 the shareholding was split evenly three ways between the original group, Australian Consolidated Press and P&O.

These three companies had already been in business together in the 1960s promoting and operating the Women's Weekly Discovery Tour, one of the most successful operations in Australian tourism history. The combination of the press (the *Australian Women's Weekly* was an Australian Consolidated Press publication), a powerful shipping company and an expert travel operator and retailer was a potent recipe for success when certain social regulations presented them with an opportunity.

At the time the tour operated, people applying for the pension were means-tested for assets. If they had too much money to qualify for the pension, it was common for them to spend the excess before settling down. The Women's Weekly Discovery Tour benefited from this arrangement. The biggest number in a year to take the five-month world tour was 1200.

Among other Sydney agents working in the early post-war years were John Kemnitz, a New Zealander who set up Universal Travel, and Nevin Paxton, whose Paxton's Travel became one of the first successful inbound operators. Paxton's Travel had been started by Nevin's father as an adjunct to his real estate business. In Adelaide, Roy King was one of the first to go into wholesaling, beginning with tours to Kangaroo Island and then to Fiji.

The formation of AFTA

In Melbourne, Stewart Moffat returned to Qantas briefly after the war and then spent time in the migrant trade, both as a representative for an Italian airline and with shipping agencies. As business in this area wound down, he converted to general travel agent and tour operator. He already had a Melbourne office. He added others in London, Sydney, Perth and Adelaide between 1953 and 1962.

In 1952 he began sending Australians on coach tours of Europe and in 1953 opened a London office to handle the operations.[2] Ten years later he became the managing agent in Perth and Adelaide for the

250 Chandris Line, which in the 1960s was the biggest passenger-carrying shipping company in the world. He was also general sales agent for the Overseas Visitors' Club, which offered reasonably-priced accommodation in London for young Australians, who were then flocking to London on working holidays. Chandris offered special deals, which included an introductory stay at the Overseas Visitors' Club, and Moffat's business benefited. In 1963 he began to develop the tour market to Port Vila and Noumea from Australia—and did well enough to be given allocations of hotel and aircraft space from 1966 on.

Moffat, Johnson and King were all founding members of the Australian Federation of Travel Agents, which came into being in 1957 with 12 members. By the time of the first convention held on the Gold Coast the following year, the total membership was 45 and 31 attended. In 1965 AFTA still had only 130 active members,[3] but as air travel grew in importance so did the travel agency system. By 1993 the number of AFTA agents was 1504. There were many more travel agents—perhaps twice as many—who were not members of AFTA.[4]

AFTA has never represented all agents; the ratio has usually been reckoned at about one in three. Many who did not join were smaller agents of doubtful viability,[5] but later on major companies, including the Flight Centre chain, refused to join because they disagreed with AFTA policies. Others have left the organisation or have threatened to do so.[6] Nevertheless, in 1998 AFTA represented 1900 retail outlets out of about 4700 in Australia.[7]

The specialists break away

The foundation members of AFTA included tour operators, though some of these had retail agencies as well. The first presidents—Frank Johnson of Sydney and Stewart Moffat of Melbourne—became leading wholesale tour operators as well as travel agents. As Moffat said, 'The lines between wholesale and retail were ill defined and often the same personnel were involved in both aspects of the business.'[8] However, as more retail agents joined, there were complaints that the executive committee was dominated by tour operators. As annual meetings were an opportunity for airing complaints against principals, wholesalers as well as carriers came in for criticism.

In 1964, fifteen wholesalers formed a division of AFTA known as the Australian Council of Tour Operators. Later it was called the Australian Council of Tour Wholesalers. It retained formal links with AFTA, although from 1999 it was no longer represented on the AFTA board.

The Australian Incoming Tour Operators Association (AITOA) was
also formed as a division of AFTA. The reason for this was that representatives from large travel agencies involved in inbound travel were among the twelve agents who attended the founding meeting in 1957. AITOA was to remain attached to AFTA for thirteen years, but in that time many changes occurred.

In the 1970s AITOA was dying—by 1971 its membership had dropped to five. A meeting of influential non-AITOA inbound operators discussed forming a new group, partly because of AITOA's links with AFTA. However, a peace meeting was organised and the 'rebels' decided to join AITOA. With the ranks increased to seventeen, the organisation decided to change its name to Inbound Tour Operators Association and institute an annual ITOA symposium, which was to become a fixture on the Australian tourism management and promotional calendar. The first symposium was held in Sydney in 1978 and its theme was 'Does Australia Really Want Inbound Tourism?'

Whatever the answer was to that question, inbound tourism increased and it was for that reason, five years later, that the AFTA executive engaged in an examination of the changing roles of AFTA and ITOA and concluded that they were 'totally divorced'.[9] The executive started proceedings to separate.

This took time, however. It was in December 1984, thirteen months after ITOA's decision was announced, that the AFTA executive resolved that ITOA be released as a division. There was an immediate surge in ITOA membership: an increase of 55 per cent to 114 in the first year. ITOA changed its name to Inbound Tourism Organisation of Australia, retaining the acronym, in 1986. The new title was intended to convey a broader role for the organisation, help increase the organisation's public and private sector profile and drive recruitment. In April 1998 membership was 668.

The wholesalers

As has been mentioned above (page 250), pioneer travel agents such as Stewart Moffat Travel and World Travel Headquarters included wholesaling as a normal part of their activities, just as some of them produced confidential tariffs for overseas operators sending clients to Australia. In other words, they were wholesalers, retailers and inbound operators.

252   However, as time went on and the markets became bigger, specialists developed either as separate companies or as subsidiaries or divisions of large ones. Many suppliers turned to wholesaling to increase sales of their own products. Among these were Qantas, the domestic airlines and regional airlines; hotels and motel chains; coach companies and restaurants.

Thus the Ansett group packaged air travel from Sydney by flying boat with accommodation at Hayman Island in the 1950s. The flights worked on a weekly back-to-back basis, flying up to Hayman in the middle of the night and returning to Sydney mostly in darkness.

The Australian National Line turned to wholesaling in the 1970s, packaging voyages on the Bass Strait ferry *Empress of Australia* with the ingredients of a holiday in Tasmania. This had great success for a first venture. Occupancy for the *Empress* was 90 per cent during the financial year November 1976 to June 1977 when the packages were operative.[10]

Coach tour operators like Australian Pacific Tours and AAT-King's wholesaled their own tours. Ansett Airlines' Holiday Division grew out of the activities of the group's Pioneer coach division in the late 1950s when packages were produced combining air and coach travel.

Trans Australia Airlines quickly matched what Ansett was doing. By the late 1960s both airlines had wholesaling divisions packaging tours to Tasmania, the Gold Coast, the Whitsunday holiday islands, Alice Springs, Ayers Rock, Cairns (just starting) and Papua-New Guinea. They hired attractive hostesses as tour guides and promoters.

The airlines had a stranglehold on the domestic wholesaling of packages including air travel, simply because they would not give others a tour-basing fare. They discounted fares for their own holidays by 15 per cent if the tour was for seven days or more. It was not until 1980 that they succumbed to industry pressure and extended tour-basing fares to other operators.

The 1970s was a period of high growth for airline packages. The holiday designers became more creative, increasing the range of their packages to include such activities as white water rafting, abseiling, bare boat sailing charters, windsurfing and campervanning. Some of this was new. The concept of bare boat yachting had to be explained. The first campervans were made in Tasmania, using one-tonne trucks.

The opening of the Wrest Point Hotel-Casino in 1973 brought a demand for the first short-break packages. Packages that included a full airfare and two nights' accommodation for around $400 were big sellers. Ansett alone sold more than 10 000 weekend packages to Wrest Point in 1975–76.[11]

When Qantas took over Australian Airlines (formerly TAA) in 1993 it **253** absorbed its wholesaling division into Qantas Holidays, branding its domestic product as Qantas Australian Holidays. Ansett Holidays went on to become the biggest domestic wholesaler.

Government tourism organisations also produced tours, most notably Tourism Tasmania (Tasmania's Temptations), which entered wholesaling in the 1960s, and the Queensland Tourist and Travel Corporation, which set up Sunlover Holidays in the late 1970s. Sunlover, one of the biggest domestic wholesalers, was unusual in that it offered a huge range of Queensland products—some 750—but did not generally package them with transport.

Other government organisations contracted their wholesaling or had some other arrangement with one or more wholesalers to increase the product range for their State or Territory. When the Western Australian Tourism Commission closed down Westours, its wholesaling division, in 1984 the product manager, Brian Bowater, began his own company, Great Aussie Holidays. Jac Eerbeck left the Commission's Los Angeles office to join him a year later. In the next ten years or so they built their company into one of the biggest domestic wholesalers, partly by developing products under contract to government organisations but also by finding niches not filled by others and pricing aggressively.

Outbound operators

In 1972 a consortium that included Stewart Moffat Travel, World Travel Headquarters, American Express and Qantas was formed to organise tours to Asia and the West Coast of the United States. These were inclusive tour charters (ITCs) and were designed to make use of Qantas 707s, which were becoming surplus with the introduction of Boeing 747s. When the 707s were sold, the airline decided to continue to organise group travel on regular scheduled flights using GIT (Group Inclusive Tour) fares. This occurred in 1976 and Peter Archer, a Qantas executive who had been brought back from the United States into the fledgling holiday department the year before, was put in charge. The organisation was called QH Holidays and its brand was Jetabout.

In the decades to come Jetabout was to get bigger and bigger, buying up other prominent brands such as Viva! Holidays and Travelscene to increase its range of offerings. It also became an inbound operator by setting up or buying operations in the United Kingdom, North America, Singapore and Fiji. Jetabout and the other brands were dropped in 1996 and packages were offered under the Qantas Holidays brand,

254 which by that time was also the name of the company. By the mid-1990s Qantas Holidays was the largest Australian wholesaler, ranked by the number of outbound, domestic and inbound customers—about 750 000 annually.

The outbound market was to become very competitive. Jetset entered it in the early 1970s when Peter Windsor set up Jetset Tours. It was soon a major player, notable for its flamboyant product launches. Jetset was an early proponent of Asian holidays and went on to develop a full destinational menu. American Express produced a Red Book featuring European holidays in a program linked to Qantas. Other major wholesalers in the 1970s and 1980s included Viva!, Venture Holidays and the Japan Tourist Bureau. Prominent Western Australian programs came from VI Holidays and New Horizons Holidays. In the later 1990s Qantas Holidays, Venture Holidays and Creative Holidays were among the leading mainstream wholesalers.

Overseas companies established Australian branches. One was Trafalgar Tours, which opened an office in Sydney in 1976 and became the biggest wholesaler of coach tours to Britain and Europe. Its long-serving managing director, Peter Elkins, had been sales manager of Avis when Trafalgar appointed him as its Australian chief executive in 1980. In the 1990s Trafalgar's passengers were mostly between 44 and 64 and its major competitors were Insight International Tours and Globus Cosmos.[12]

Most wholesalers specialised, either in terms of demographic segments (for example Contiki Holidays for 18 to 35s), destinations (Guthreys Pacific and Kirra Tours New Zealand Holidays) or purposes (Peregrine Adventures and Alpine Tours International). An Adelaide wholesaler, Expanding Horizons, produced tours solely for coach companies—about 200 of them.

Inbound operators

The early inbound operators were part of other concerns. The New Zealand company Atlantic and Pacific set up a Sydney operation in 1968 because travel to Australia was combined with travel to New Zealand, Fiji and other Pacific islands in tour packages from North America. But it was also interested in sending Australians to New Zealand. Stewart Moffat Travel in Melbourne set up a major inbound operation under the SM Tours brand in 1968 and was the first to publish a confidential tariff for wholesalers and retailers in the United States. The tariff was labelled 'South Pacific' and included Australia, New Zealand, Fiji, Noumea, the New Hebrides and Papua New Guinea.

The principal inbound operator in Sydney in the 1960s was World Travel Headquarters (Margaret Taylor). Others included Paxton's (Ruth Zukerman) and Globetrotters (Len Taylor). The first 'pure' inbound operators were established in 1973—ID Tours, created by Bill Wright, and General Travel, started by John Coplestone, who had previously been with Atlantic and Pacific. They were to endure into the 1990s.

Thomas Cook was one of the earliest into the Japanese market, which was to lead the inbound boom of the 1980s. With the increase in tourism from Asia, Asian operators set up business in Australia. First came the principal Japanese wholesalers, who established inbound operations for their own clients. They were followed by operators who began business in the other markets. These included Australian Tourism Management (ATM) in Melbourne and the Sydney operators Jade Express and Trans-Global Tours.

AFTA and the banks

The banks were seen as the main threat to independent travel agencies when AFTA was formed. One of the four major platforms on which the organisation was launched was 'to declare war on the intrusion of Trading Banks into the field of travel'.[13]

Whether their actions in 1957 were an 'intrusion' is debatable. As we have seen, bank travel had begun in a small way as far back as 1904 and the banks had reformed travel departments after the war. The best-known bank travel man of pre-war days, Jack Murrowood, had gone on war service in 1939. When he returned to the E.S. & A. Bank in 1946, he headed a travel department. He had as an assistant Sam Loxton, better known later as a Test cricketer and a member of the Victorian parliament.[14]

None of this history impressed AFTA, at least not favourably. No sooner was AFTA formed than a committee was put to work to investigate the banks' activities. Vice-president John Kemnitz told the first convention that, as more evidence came before the committee, he 'became appalled that any Australian institution could sink to the depths that certain banks have done in building up the volume of business of their Travel departments.'[15]

The banks were not paid commissions, however. They claimed that they were entitled to them but as former AFTA president, Jim Russell reports, the airlines 'rejected the suggestion out of hand' and wholesaler members of AFTA 'rejected the suggestion of banks receiving commissions under any circumstances whatever.'[16]

256   AFTA mounted a well-planned campaign. When it produced a newspaper called *Travel* in 1958, the front page lead story in its first issue was headed 'Banks Threaten Travel Agents' Extinction'. AFTA wrote to airline investigation boards and the headquarters of the International Air Transport Association in Montreal suggesting that licences to banks be withdrawn. Leading shipping lines received letters urging them to cancel their agency agreements with banks. An issue was made of the Bank of New South Wales supposedly giving a customer an airline ticket when it was not an accredited agent. A Mrs Douglas made a statutory declaration in support of the AFTA case and copies were sent to influential parties.

But behind the scenes business people were urging AFTA executives, including Stewart Moffat, who was then president, to think again. They all had to live with the banks, whether or not they were in travel. In March 1959 Charles ('Chuck') Henry, chief executive of Pan American World Airways in Australia and a strong supporter of AFTA, also urged the executive committee to quit its campaign, suggesting that AFTA would be greatly strengthened if the banks joined the organisation. All this must have taken some swallowing at first, but the pressure was persuasive. In May the executive committee wrote to a number of banks inviting them to become allied members, in August the AFTA constitution was altered to allow banks to become active (full) members and in October the resolution of a previous meeting precluding members from paying commissions to banks on packages was rescinded.

The banks were now accepted by airlines, shipping companies and AFTA. To seal the new sense of fellowship, Yoland ('Yol') Burrows of the Commercial Bank of Australia was appointed to the AFTA executive committee in 1960.

However, opposition to banks did not go away. There were still complaints that they used unfair tactics—such as offering overdrafts—to 'steal' business. The banks, of course, denied doing any such thing, but the conflict smouldered on until 1973 when a meeting between an AFTA committee and bank travel general managers set ethical guidelines as to how the banks should act. Even after this, some AFTA meetings would degenerate into attacks on banks to the point where little other business was conducted.

The banks became a major force in retailing, building up substantial chains of outlets by the 1990s. But as the 1990s began, they decided to get out of travel on the basis that it was not their core business. Their travel interests were sold off progressively, the last going in 1994. Travelstrength, the Commonwealth Bank's brand name, continued to exist under its new owner, the New Zealand-based Tek Travel, for

another two years. But when Tek sold Travelstrength to Traveland in **257**
1996, the name was phased out. Bank travel became part of history.

Consumer protection

Protection of consumers from the financial collapse of travel agents
had long been a matter of contention in Australia before anything was
done about it. The subject was raised at the second meeting of the
AFTA executive committee in 1957.

Thus travel agents themselves recognised the need for a fund to protect travellers who might become stranded as the result of an agency
collapse. However, they were apprehensive that a single State government would introduce licensing of travel agents when they wanted a
Commonwealth-wide scheme. They began lobbying the Commonwealth Government to introduce a bonding scheme in the early 1970s.
Eventually, in 1975 a Bill to license travel agents was presented in the
House of Representatives and was awaiting the second reading when
that Government fell. The new Government decided not to proceed
because of the cost of administering the Act.

In the meantime, the situation agents had feared had come about. A
single State, New South Wales, had begun to register and license agents
in 1973 without waiting for the Commonwealth or other States to act.
There were murmurings about the need for licensing from others following some large company collapses, but it was not until February
1987 that Victoria, South Australia and Western Australia introduced
their licensing systems. Queensland, Tasmania and the Australian
Capital Territory followed.

The introduction of an Australia-wide travellers' protection scheme
was similarly protracted. New South Wales had its own fund to accom-
pany its licensing system. An AFTA–IATA plan of the early 1980s for a
wider scheme met opposition from large travel companies with
numerous locations. However, when other States introduced licensing
a few years later, the scope of the New South Wales compensation fund
was adjusted to accommodate them. This became the Travel
Compensation Fund (TCF) and all States and the ACT made reference
to it in their legislation, requiring agents to contribute to it before they
could be licensed. The fund, operated by a trust, was used to compen-
sate travellers disadvantaged by the financial collapse of licensed travel
agents.

The Northern Territory government allowed agents a choice.
They could participate in the TCF or in a Territory-owned consumer
protection scheme organised by Zueillig Insurance Brokers and FAI

258 Insurance. Under this plan, each agent was assessed on individual risk and paid for a policy to protect its clients against its default. Advocates of the indemnity scheme said it was fairer because agents were responsible for their own risk but had no financial obligation with regard to other agents.

The rise of agency groups

While agency grouping had begun in the 1970s, from about the mid-1980s the movement accelerated so that by the mid-1990s more than 60 per cent of travel agency outlets either were owned by a single company or were in a franchised or buying group. Those that had emerged as the 'Big Six' in the late 1990s were Jetset, Flight Centre, UTAG, Harvey World Travel, American Express and Traveland. Other important groups were Thomas Cook, ATAC, National World Travel, the Community Travel Group and STA Travel. They represented a mix of organisational structures.

Flight Centre's, Thomas Cook's and STA Travel's agencies were wholly owned. Some of Traveland's and American Express' agencies were owned and some representative. Traveland was wholly owned by Ansett Australia.

Some of Jetset's agencies were owned by the company, some were franchised and some were part of a marketing or buying group. Jetset was owned by Air New Zealand. Of the others, Harvey World Travel was a franchise operation; National World Travel was a tight franchise; UTAG was a marketing and buying group; ATAC was a buying group with some joint marketing; and the Community Travel Group was a buying group with no joint marketing.

American Express

American Express, the world's biggest travel retailer, had been a force in Australian distribution since the 1950s, but made a big leap forward in 1994 with major acquisitions—75 retail outlets from the National Bank and Westpac plus 20 Thomas Cook corporate outlets (20 business units and 10 'implants', which were on-site offices at its customers' premises). Soon afterwards it had 96 owned and 117 representative offices, but the network required rationalisation because of competing agencies and some unprofitable business. By mid-1996 the owned locations had been reduced to 9 business centres, 37 retail offices and 20 implants.[17]

American Express representatives were not franchises in the accepted retail travel sense, but were existing agencies that paid a fee. In 1994 the company defined its worldwide strategy as growing its credit card and **259** travel business with the primary focus on business travel.[18] All offices— owned and representative—benefited from the promotional power of the American Express family of credit cards. A membership loyalty program was part of an overall marketing package built around the card and 'Membership Miles' was launched in Australia in 1992. In 1996 the American Express–Qantas co-brand corporate card was instituted.

ATAC

The Australian Travel Agents Co-operative (ATAC) was a trading co-operative, which required its members to invest $1000 in shares on joining. The shares earned a yearly dividend—10.5 per cent in 1997— and bonuses came from the incentives and management fees paid by preferred suppliers. ATAC, which had about 100 members in 1998, began when 16 agencies in Victoria broke away from UTAG in 1987 and formed Travel Agents Co-operative Victoria Ltd (TAC) as a buying group. They did not want a brand name for their new venture because they did not intend to compromise their individual identities.

Discussions with co-operatives in other States began in 1995 because suppliers—airlines and wholesalers—made it clear that they preferred to deal with a single, national body. Talks with Community Travel in Perth were discontinued over a disagreement about where the headquarters of a unified body should be but, following the removal of a legal impediment, TAC absorbed a small New South Wales co-operative in late 1997. The name was changed to ATAC and a new chief executive was appointed—Peter Watson, who had been responsible previously for the Jetset Travel network.

The group organised some advertising on a test basis, though some members argued that ATAC should be a buying group only and should not advertise at all. Others thought some marketing was necessary, but agreed it should be funded by participants on a 'user pays' basis rather from a central fund created by a marketing levy.

The Community Travel Group

The Community Travel Group was started in 1978 in Western Australia by 'fiercely independent' agents who nevertheless felt the need to associate to get the deals from principals that only come with scale of purchase. They did not advertise as a group. The group's motto was 'Collective strength, individual expression'. In 1998 Community Travel had 54 member agencies located in Western Australia, South Australia, New South Wales and the Australian Capital Territory.

260 The group was administered through a Perth-based company in which the members were shareholders. Besides having competitive product-buying rates and support from preferred suppliers, members benefited financially from rebates on individual and group sales performance and from company dividends. The group's corporate documents described a co-operative as 'an autonomous association of persons united voluntarily to meet their common economic, social, and cultural needs and aspirations through a jointly-owned and democratically-controlled enterprise.'[19]

Flight Centre

Flight Centre in 1998 had more than 400 retail outlets, most of them in Australia, although it also had moved into travel retailing in New Zealand, the United Kingdom, Canada and South Africa. The company, which was listed on the Australian Stock Exchange, owned all its agencies and was thus Australia's biggest owned retail chain, with a turnover in 1998 exceeding $1.4 billion.

The origins of Flight Centre go back to 1973 when Graham Turner, an Australian veterinary surgeon, decided to switch to travel after finding an old double-decker bus in a field in Yorkshire. It gave him an idea. With economist Bill James, another Australian, he founded Top Deck Travel in London and used old double-deckers for cheap travel in distant lands. By 1981 they had 50 buses operating overland routes in Central and Eastern Europe and the United States, and a London-to-Sydney route via Kathmandu and Perth. In that year they sold out and returned to Australia.

In London they had met Geoff Harris, a Melbourne marketing man, and the three decided to open a travel agency chain in Australia, focusing on discount airfares to differentiate it from other retail operations. The new venture was financed with a $6000 loan. Each of the directors lived in a different city, which explains why the first Flight Centre opened in Sydney in November 1981 and the next two started in Melbourne and Brisbane in early 1982.

Price advantage on airfares was the main marketing weapon. The company constantly repeated the statement that its aim was to beat, not match, fares and to never lose a booking over price.[20] Despite this continuing emphasis on price advantage, Flight Centre was a high-yield operation by travel agency standards.

The company developed its own distinctive set of corporate philosophies, which were manifested in its lean management structure of three layers: the board, the company or state leader and the shop teams. The support staff-to-consultant ratio never exceeded seven per cent and **261** everybody worked in small teams. There were no secretaries or individual offices.

All staff members' salary packages were made up of one-third to one-half incentives. When the company was floated on the Stock Exchange in 1995, about half the staff bought shares at 85 cents (95 cents for the general public). The $15.1 million public float was oversubscribed two weeks ahead of schedule and Flight Centre exceeded its prospectus forecast of profit in its first year as a public company. In April 1999 shares were being traded at $6.25.

Harvey World Travel

The Harvey World Travel name, which became one of the best-known in Australian travel and tourism, goes back to the early days of post-war retailing. The first Harvey World Travel office was opened in 1951 as an adjunct to the Harvey Real Estate company in the Sydney suburb of Cronulla.

By the time it had expanded by opening the USA World Travel Service in central Sydney in 1978, Harvey World Travel was recognised as one of the largest (if not the largest) privately-owned travel agencies in Australia. But it was clear that to compete with the banks and the large multi-outlet organisations it would have to increase its number of outlets.

American franchising operations supplied the inspiration, and the first franchise outlet was opened in 1979 in West Gosford, followed quickly by Earlwood, Miranda, Yagoona and Rose Bay. Since 1981 the franchisees have owned the company and the rights to the Harvey World Travel name. The company grew rapidly from the mid-1980s and in late 1997 had 370 outlets in all States and Territories of Australia and New Zealand.

Jetset

Jetset Tours began as a single agency in Sunshine, a Melbourne suburb, and grew to become Australia's biggest travel distribution company. Its founder was Isi Liebler, who entered the travel agency business in 1963 as the result of a loan to a friend, Bono Weiner, who was seeking accreditation from the International Air Transport Association (IATA) for Sunshine Travel Service.

Liebler was an innovator. Once the agency was accredited he experimented with airline ticket distribution, arousing the ire of Qantas. The ensuing conflict, which for a time threatened to prevent Liebler from

262   issuing international tickets, energised him and he moved the agency into the city and renamed it Astronaut Travel. He saw opportunity in the difficulty agencies had in acquiring the right to write and issue international tickets. IATA would grant accreditation only after a period of probation lasting several years, during which period agents could not claim commission on the tickets they wrote.

Liebler bought Oakleigh Travel, an IATA-accredited agency, and then proceeded to write tickets for non-IATA agents, thus beginning the practice of consolidation. Oakleigh Travel was renamed Midtown Travel and in 1984 became Jetset Fares and Ticketing. The 'Jetset' name had come into use in 1975 for the newly-formed wholesaling arm, Jetset Tours.

Liebler had begun to build his own retail network in the 1970s and by 1982 some 200 travel outlets were involved, trading as Jetset Tours agencies. Growth was promoted by the introduction of Equity Participation Offices or EPOs. Under this system, Jetset helped finance agencies. At first it owned 90 per cent and the eventual owners 10 per cent, but the idea was that the position would be reversed in ten years.

By 1987 no fewer than 900 travel agencies were associated with Jetset in a variety of relationships.[21] In that year another new concept was launched: the Jetset Travel Centre Network, which was initially made up of 270 agents already associated with the company. In 1992 this chain was turned into the Jetset franchise network and agencies traded under the 'Jetset Travel' name. More than 600 other agents still remained associated with Jetset, benefiting from its buying power with principals but not publicly identified with the company.

The company reached the peak of its expansion in the early 1990s. It was then involved in more than 20 per cent of the travel agency system, initiated about 25 per cent of the domestic package tour market and sold about 40 per cent of international air tickets from Australia. It had 33 offices overseas.

However, over several years in the mid-1990s Jetset posted substantial losses, due in part to its investment of money and energy in technology. From the 1980s Jetset had developed Worldmaster, its own industry-wide computer reservations system, which included a unique electronic payments system. Liebler had remained chairman of the company, but had left the day-to-day management to an executive team. In 1995 he came back as chief executive and progressively dismissed or replaced most of the senior executives.

Among the resultant changes was the selling of the technologies into a joint venture with Telstra Atlas and the Amadeus global distribution

system. Jetset made other radical changes, cutting the range of its holi- **263**
day packages by two-thirds and forming the National Association of
Independent Travel Agents (NAITA) as a buying group within the Jetset
organisational structure. Most of Jetset's overseas businesses were
closed.

In June 1997 Air New Zealand, which had bought half the company
in 1985, acquired the other half from the Liebler family. It appointed a
new chief executive, Peter Lacaze, whose background was in the automotive and packing industries.[22] Saying that he believed the company
had tried to do too many things, he quickly repositioned Jetset Retail
Travel as the company's core business.

National World Travel

National World Travel was closer to the McDonald's type of franchise
than other travel agency groups because the company retained total
control of the brand, product and marketing. In most agency franchising a brand name is franchised, usually to an existing agency, along
with branded materials such as signage and uniforms, and the fran-
chisee obtains marketing, products, training, technology and so on
from the franchisor.

National went further. It chose the location, the style of building and
the presentation, including a tightly controlled fit-out covering telephones, computers, desks, brochures and stationery. The concept was
the brainchild of David Robinson, developed when he was chief executive of UTAG, and he had meant it to become a top-level franchised tier
of that organisation. But when Robinson sold his interest in the UTAG
management company in 1994 he decided to devote his time to
National as a separate entity. He saw it as a complete turnkey operation, from carpet to paint and from computers to paper clips. National
was the only travel company that registered and trademarked all its
working documents.

Most new members were new to the industry. Almost all of the 50 or
so agencies operating in 1998 were start-ups; there had been only three
conversions. National aimed to recruit people into the industry—
people who had knowledge of administration and financial management—and then teach them about the travel agency business.

STA Travel

The formal origins of STA Travel in Australia went back to the 1970s,
when Australian Union of Students travel services appeared on university campuses to cater for the adventurous students of the day.

264 However, there was an earlier starting-point in the 1960s when Sammy Heifitz, of World Travel Service, set up sales desks and offices in university campuses around the country. The first was a desk outside the cafeteria in the Students' Union at the University of Melbourne.

Heifitz, born in Egypt of Austrian and Russian parents, had sold travel in Cairo after the war, much of it to American missionaries going to Africa. He became BOAC's top agent and the airline gave him an educational visit to Australia in 1949. He never went back. He worked for General Motors in Adelaide and tried his hand at the chicken business before going to Melbourne. By this time he had organised residency with the immigration authorities and made arrangements for his family to join him.

He worked for Stewart Moffat Travel for two years and then created his own company, World Travel Service, in an office in William Street, Melbourne—or rather, half an office: the other half sold ties. The main business was inward—Italian and Greek migrant traffic—and this led him to open a branch office in Carlton, not far from Melbourne University. Before long he set up an implant at the University to service students. The migrant business faded and Heifitz extended into a number of different types of travel, including an expansion of his student business to other campuses. But this was not his main business; apart from general sales of travel he had big corporate accounts, including the Melbourne University account for academic and staff travel.

Gregor Macaulay, a science student at Melbourne University, was president of the Australian Union of Students in 1970. He became interested in travel and promoted it to students on behalf of the Union, with World Travel Service handling the operations. But Macaulay had ambitions to develop products for student travel along the same lines that he had observed in Europe. As a result, AUS Travel Operations came into being in February 1971, headquartered in North Melbourne and operating in universities throughout Australia. In 1973 it took over the campus implants set up by Sammy Heifitz.

AUS Travel began by organising a charter program to Asia, in association with Qantas, in the summer of 1971. This program grew each summer so that by 1975 one hundred charter flights were made to Indonesia, Singapore, Malaysia, Thailand, Hong Kong, New Zealand and London in three months. Besides its Australian offices it had others in London, Singapore, Malaysia and Thailand.

But AUS Travel had grown too big too quickly. By August 1977 it was in financial difficulties. Eventually it was bought by Edward Keller

Holding, a long-established Swiss trading company that had already **265** bought Stewart Moffat Travel in 1970 and World Travel Service in 1974. The Swiss company had no particular interest in travel. Eventually it sold off Stewart Moffat Travel and World Travel Service to Australian companies, but decided to develop student travel internationally.

Under the STA (Student Travel Australia) brand, the company that had begun as AUS Travel was said in 1988 to be the largest youth travel specialist in the world, with more than 180 wholly-owned outlets. These included more than 50 wholly-owned branches in Australia and 10 in New Zealand. It specialised in travel for young people in general, not just students.

Thomas Cook Limited

Thomas Cook had a longer history in Australia than any other group, having operated in the country since 1910. In 1998 the company had about 70 agencies in Australia, concentrating on holiday and VFR travel following the sale of its corporate business to American Express in 1994.

The company differentiated itself from other travel sellers by emphasising its expertise in currency exchanges. Thus there was a 'cage' in each Thomas Cook outlet in which foreign currency or traveller's cheques could be bought; a Thomas Cook agency was a one-stop shop for both travel and currency needs. The company also had some 30 stand-alone exchange bureaus in Australia, including bureaus in all major airports except those in Brisbane and Cairns.

Thomas Cook was the largest retailer of European train travel in Australia. It also sold tickets for shows in London, Paris, New York and Las Vegas to the travel industry and the public. The company was one of the largest Australian inbound operators and organised conferences and incentive travel through a separate division.

The headquarters of Thomas Cook was in London, but the group was owned by Germany's third largest bank, Westdeutsche Landesbank. The Australian operation was wholly owned by the group, a 49 per cent shareholding having been bought by Qantas in 1993.

In 1981 Thomas Cook signed an agreement with MasterCard International to increase worldwide acceptability of its traveller's cheques. MasterCard cardholders could receive emergency assistance through Thomas Cook offices. The company also had a partner relationship with Visa International and distributed the Visa TravelMoney disposable card, which allowed travellers instant access to cash at Visa machines internationally.

266 Traveland

Traveland was founded by Steven Rich in 1968. Its first outlet was in the David Jones store in Sydney; David Jones and the Fairfax newspaper group were part-owners of the new venture. Traveland quickly expanded as a wholly-owned chain and in 1974 began to franchise agencies as well. In 1982 it bought Grace Bros. Travel—the biggest retailer in New South Wales at the time—to become the largest wholly-owned retail travel chain in Australia.

In 1987 it was bought by Ansett Transport Industries to enlarge the airline's distribution network. As part of this strategy, Coles Myer Ansett Travel (CMAT) was established soon afterwards. CMAT acquired the Grace Bros. stores from Traveland and in 1990 bought ANZ Travel. All this became part of the Traveland group in 1992, when it took over the combined CMAT–ANZ group, which by that time included Stewart Moffat Travel.

Acquisitions continued. In 1995 the Sydney-based corporate travel specialist, Travellers, was bought and in 1996 it took over the high-profile Newcastle-based retailer, Jayes Travel Service, with 11 outlets throughout the Newcastle and Hunter region, and Travelstrength's 28 retail leisure outlets.

In 1996 Traveland entered the Fly Buys loyalty marketing program, backing the decision with a major consumer advertising campaign the purpose of which was to make Traveland a household name throughout Australia. It was the seventeenth company to offer Fly Buys points, but the only travel retailer to do so. It was claimed that the company had emerged as a clear preference for those redeeming points, accounting for 80 per cent of all rewards. By September 1997, Traveland was reporting that almost one in four of its bookings was being made by customers who were using a Fly Buys card, with more than 70 000 purchases registered.[23]

At the beginning of 1998 Traveland had 260 franchises and 93 wholly-owned travel centres around Australia and later in the year it joined with the motoring associations, NRMA and the RACV, to run travel services under a co-branding operation. The agreement affected NRMA Travel's 23 agencies in New South Wales and the 18 RACV Travel outlets in Melbourne and Geelong. This brought the Traveland name to a total of 390 outlets. Traveland chose not to operate the RACV's ten regional outlets because these locations clashed with existing Traveland franchised agencies. The RACV decided to withdraw travel services from these outlets.

UTAG

The beginnings of UTAG—the United Travel Agents Group—were in 1975 when Len Sparrow, an Australian businessman who was not a travel agent, came back from the United States impressed with the Ask Mr Foster agency franchise system he had seen there. So he did a simple name change and introduced Ask Mr Travel to Australia. This was not financially successful. It was taken over by Summerland Travel a few years later and built into a chain of 36 agencies over some ten years. The group was managed under the name of United Franchises Ltd from 1983 and operated as a co-operative buying group. But two years later it was falling apart. The number of agencies had declined to twelve, of which two belonged to David Robinson, who had begun his career with Qantas and later had a diverse career as an innovative travel operator in a number of countries.

Under his guidance, United Franchises Ltd was replaced with United Travel Agents Co. Ltd, an unlisted public company, and the group began to slowly rebuild. Travelscene, a well-known wholesaler and retailer at the time, became a preferred supplier of tours to Bali and Robinson invited Bob Steel, managing director of Travelscene, to join the board. In 1987 Steel bought a share of United Services Pty Ltd, the management company that operated UTAG on behalf of the public company, the shareholding of which was held by participating agents. Steel became non-executive chairman. In 1994 Robinson sold his share of the management company and Steel became its sole owner.

The UTAG brand name was first used in 1988 when the group had about 40 members. It grew steadily in the next ten years, reaching 375 members in 1998 with a turnover of $1.2 billion. The organisation was a buying and marketing group rather than a conventional franchise operation.[24]

The consolidators

Consolidation—the writing of airline tickets by one agent for others who were not qualified themselves or did not want to do so—had become a big part of the distribution business since Isi Liebler began the practice (see page 262).

Concorde International Travel was the biggest consolidator in Australia in 1998. It had already passed Jetset Fares and Ticketing some years before it acquired the rival Metro Travel in 1997. The combined

268   international ticketing turnover of Concorde and Metro was probably between $800 million and $900 million, as against Jetset Fares and Ticketing's $400 million to $500 million and Consolidated Travel's $150 million to $200 million.[25] Consolidated was the only independent operator among them. Concorde-Metro was half owned by British Airways and Jetset was wholly owned by Air New Zealand.

Concorde's founder, Agostino Pistorino, began with the Peloro Travel Agency in the Melbourne suburb of Footscray, working as a shipping agent with the Italian community to bring people from Italy to Australia. He expanded, taking in partners Eddy Baldachino and Henri Crusi. In 1972 when they decided to change the company's name they settled on 'Concorde'. They had not been able to agree on a name— then somebody said they needed *concordia*, meaning they had to agree, because lunchtime was approaching. And so Concorde the company became. In 1977 Leslie Cassar joined to establish World Aviation Systems, the General Sales Agents arm of the company, which represents 40 carriers. Pistorino, Baldachino, Crusi and Cassar still owned half of Concorde in 1998. British Airways bought the other half in 1987.

The founder of Consolidated Travel, Spiros Alysandratos, migrated to Melbourne in 1959 and was a wedding photographer before he started a travel agency in 1967. By 1971 he had obtained IATA accreditation and began to write tickets for non-IATA agents, splitting the commission. By the time the boom years of 1977 to 1980 came along, he was in a position to take advantage of the increase in air traffic.

Commissions and service fees

The second half of the 1990s saw the beginning of changes in the way travel agents did business. Part of this was brought on by the electronic distribution revolution and part by a change in relationship with principals as airlines tried to contain rising distribution costs.

In the United States, major carriers imposed caps on commissions. These limited American agents to a commission of $US50 on return fares of $US500 or more and $US25 for one-way fares of $US250 or more. Before the cap, commissions had been based on face value and volume and agents earned an average 10 per cent on domestic sales and 14.9 per cent on international sales.[26] In the months that followed the commission caps put many agents out of business.[27]

There was no immediate flow-on to the Australian retail industry, but Qantas and Ansett did refer frequently and ominously to the cost of distribution. Then in March 1997 Ansett announced that it would cut

commission rates by 20 per cent from 1 May. It claimed that the new
commission rates—4 per cent on point-to-point ticketing and 8 per
cent for holiday travel—were part of a program to cut costs. This followed losses by the airline that had caused Ansett's value to deteriorate
by about $60 million in a four-month period in 1996.[28]

AFTA's response included cancelling its annual convention in New
Delhi (later reinstated), calling a crisis conference in Sydney and sending
an urgent questionnaire to 3879 travel agents aimed at showing how
much agencies would suffer if Qantas also cut commissions. Not only
AFTA but also the big groups put pressure on Qantas to not follow
Ansett. Flight Centre, the major independent Ansett-aligned chain, said
it would switch its business to Qantas if it did not follow Ansett and
Ansett-owned Traveland sought to persuade Ansett to change its mind.[29]

Qantas supported the Ansett view that distribution costs were too
high, but did not follow its rival in cutting commissions. Eventually,
Ansett backed down and the immediate crisis was over. But the airline's
executive chairman, Rod Eddington, later said that distribution
accounted for 15 to 20 per cent of airline costs and Ansett could not
afford to leave them untouched. Technological advances would not
make agents irrelevant, but he thought a 'user charge' system was likely
to emerge as their means of remuneration.[30]

AFTA responded with an Australian guide to service fees in 1998. It
proposed three possible service-fee methods for Australian agents. The
first was a deposit or booking fee, with the client being charged an initial fee—say $100—which was later taken off the sale balance. The
second phase involved the introduction of a fee schedule. This would see
clients billed various amounts for cancellations, amendments, visa fees,
cheque bouncing and so on. The third phase was a professional consul-
tation fee, which could take two forms: either an agent could charge a flat
fee per person for processing domestic ($5) and international ($10)
fares; or they could charge an hourly rate for constructing complex
itineraries where add-ons were a major booking component.[31]

Electronic distribution

There is a long and involved history of systems for recording airline
reservations and cancellations—of books and pencils, blackboards and
chalk, index cards, electric light boards and even a huge contraption
made of cylinders representing individual flights in which marbles
were either subtracted or added by electrical signal. Each marble represented an unsold seat. Removing one meant that a seat had been
reserved; adding one meant that a reservation had been cancelled.[32]

270   As has been noted earlier (pages 133–4), the first computerised reservations system (CRS) was Sabre, introduced by American Airlines in 1962 initially for its own staff. In 1976 Sabre and United Airlines' Apollo systems were made available to travel agents in the United States.

In the 1970s the Australian airlines developed their own CRSs, which allowed their staffs to check availability and automatically sell or cancel seats. In 1978 Qantas, TAA and Ansett began developing the multi-access Travel Industry Automated Systems (TIAS), with which the user could switch into any one of the three airline systems. This did not meet with the immediate approval of travel agents, not only because of the delays in the system and the cost, but also because there was a feeling that the airlines were trying to rewrite the rules and conditions of distribution.[33]

In the early 1980s there was a flirtation with videotext systems. AFTA announced plans to develop an 'industry owned' reservations system in 1983 (AFTEL) and in 1984 Telecom (now Telstra) entered the arena with its own VIATEL system; one of the results was that the AFTEL venture did not proceed. However, videotext could not stand the competition of advancing technology and VIATEL was almost forgotten by the time Telstra buried it in 1996.

The TIAS system had its drawbacks. The principal one was that it required agents to become familiar with the often complex commands and codes of three different systems. In effect, this was three times as difficult as working with a single-access CRS like Sabre or Apollo.

But moving to a single-access system sparked a bitter dispute between the airlines. Qantas decided to work with American Airlines and Japan Airlines to develop an Asia Pacific version of Sabre. Ansett chose the then British Airways-controlled Galileo, claiming it offered superior technology even though it was not fully operational. Australian Airlines (formerly TAA) surprised the industry by deciding to work with Ansett, leaving Qantas with the development cost of Fantasia, whose name had been suggested by Japan Airlines as the Asia Pacific version of Sabre.

By this time the major systems had come to be called global distribution systems (GDSs). They were no longer the property of a single airline to do with as it wished; certain regulations had to be obeyed to prevent unfair advantage to the particular carriers. Thus it was as GDSs that Galileo and Sabre were launched in Australia. However, adjustment was necessary. The competition led to a price war and that, plus the high cost of maintaining and marketing the systems, soon had the two distribution companies in financial difficulties. By 1991 it was clear that the Australian market could not sustain both systems in their existing forms and the airlines, the owners of TIAS, discussed ways of ensuring the continued viability of both Fantasia and Southern Cross, the company that marketed the Galileo system in Australia.

Under a new arrangement, the two companies continued to operate in competition, but TIAS provided on a non-competitive basis administrative, corporate finance and technical support to both, creating significant cost efficiencies. An agreement with the Trade Practices Commission involved a code of conduct to ensure that there was competition between the Sabre and Galileo systems.

In 1995, when a fourth GDS came on the Australian scene, Fantasia and Galileo had about 90 per cent of the market. Abacus, the Singapore-based system owned by nine Asian airlines and the US-owned Worldspan Global Travel Information Services, had the other 10 per cent. The newcomer was the European system Amadeus, which was to be distributed in Australia by Telstra through its Telstra Atlas division. At that time 93 per cent of Australian travel agencies were linked to some form of CRS[34]—market share had to come from a competitor.

TIAS had its own products including LeisureNet, a protocol or connector that allowed access to land content databases such as Telstra Atlas and to operators' systems, including the databases of Greyhound Pioneer Australia, Sunlover Holidays, Ansett Holidays and Tasmania's Temptations.

Ticketless travel

Both domestic airlines introduced electronic ticketing in the 1990s. Ansett was first in November 1996. By March 1998 one million passengers had travelled on the airline using electronic tickets. At first they were restricted to those booking direct with the airlines, but in August 1997 Ansett began issuing them through travel agents. Qantas introduced its Express Ticket electronic ticketing service at the end of July 1997.

The electronic ticket was a ticket image held in the airline's computer system. It was there anyway, whether or not the customer was issued with a paper ticket. The airline might give the passenger a piece of paper—such as a receipt, itinerary or statement of conditions for record purposes—but this was not needed to collect a boarding pass; all the customer had to produce at the check-in was a form of acceptable

272   identification, such as a driver's licence. The procedure was simple compared with the process involving a paper ticket. As Tony Bracy says:

> What we did in the past was get people to queue up to collect a piece of paper and then get in another queue at the airport to hand it back to us.[35]

Electronic ticketing for long-haul international flights was introduced in Australia by Cathay Pacific in March 1998.

Online travel agencies

Australia's first online travel agency appeared on the Internet in 1996. Named 'The Travel Specialists', it won the Telstra/Australian Financial Review award for the best electronic site in Australia. The Travel Specialists site included contract and net rates and listed a large number of special offers from airlines and wholesalers to various destinations. Flyers released by airlines and wholesalers were scanned into the site and indexed. Its 'Farefinder' listed up to 12 000 flights from Australia. Reservations were by e-mail. It was reported in its first year that most people used the Travel Specialists site for information, though after 18 months the company said it was doing 24 per cent of its business through the Internet.[36]

Other agents were less impressed. One, former Qantas executive Bob Hardie, scaled down his site when he found that people were e-mailing him from places he had never heard of, seeking information that took hours to collate, but that his booking rate was only about 1 per cent.[37]

The Australian Tourist Commission established a comprehensive site in 1996. The States and Territories all had sites or were planning them. These varied from providing an entry point for the State, with connections to relevant information already on the Internet, to a full description of the State, Territory or region and its attractions, touring opportunities and tourism services. Regional centres also had sites.

Australian suppliers—airlines, hotels, attractions, tour operators and so on—were not slow to put their wares on the Internet. The smaller suppliers often acted in association with a destination marketing organisation or a private provider offering an indexed guide to travelling in Australia. But some preferred their own sites—and for a relatively low cost they could achieve a reach far beyond that of traditional media. This sometimes had unexpected results. Within a few weeks of his establishing his Aussie Outback Tours site on the Internet, Lloyd Junor found himself making the land arrangements for a group of German fliers who were planning to come to Australia in a fleet of light aircraft and organising the tour of a Turkish television crew.

But whatever their success—or lack of it—with the Internet, everybody knew in the last years of the century that it was only the beginning. No-one could predict with confidence what the future with the Internet would be like. However, there was little doubt that it would continue to change the way tourism information and products were distributed and that the effect would be increasingly significant, until the time arrived when the Internet—or its successor—would dominate.

ENDNOTES

[1] The other areholders were Mark Hill-Smith and Walter McGrath.

[2] Moffat had contact with the British nobility when he worked in Dean and Dawson's Piccadilly office in 1935. When he opened his own London office next to Purdee's Gun Shop in South Audley Street in 1953, one of his salespeople was Viscountess Tarbet. The London office negotiated hotel contracts and coach hire, and supplied couriers and the like for the Stewart Moffat European tours. It was closed in 1960.

[3] Piesse, op.cit., p. 1168. Active members were those appointed by principals or conferences of principals such as the Australian Passenger Agents Conference (APAC) or the International Air Transport Association (IATA). There were also 31 associate members of AFTA in 1965 (travel agents who did not qualify as active members) and 45 allied members (such as hotels, motels and car rental companies).

[4] Rutledge, J. L. & Hunter, J. F. (1996), 'Relation, by States, between population and number of travel agencies', *Journal of Travel Research*, Spring, pp. 73–6. The authors say the best estimate they could get suggests that about one-third of agents belong to AFTA.

[5] 'A retail travel agency is not an easy way to make a living in any part of the world,' Harris, Kerr, Forster (op.cit.) wrote three decades ago (p. 93).

[6] Traveland and Harvey World Travel in 1998.

[7] Official AFTA figures. Total membership was 2400, including associate members (principals like airlines and coach companies) and non-resident members.

[8] Russell, J. (1982), *The First 25 Years: A History of the Australian Federation of Travel Agents Ltd*, AFTA, Sydney, p. 6. The author, Jim Russell, was not only a former AFTA president, but was also a leading tennis official and a cartoonist known nationwide for 'The Potts'.

[9] Inbound Tourism Organisation of Australia (1997), *ITOA: 25 Years Serving Inbound Tourism 1971–1996*, Sydney, p. 5.

[10] Cox, op.cit., p. 179.

[11] Nick Hill, formerly of Ansett Holidays, and in 1999 Associate Director Sales and Marketing, AAT-King's, interview, June 1998.

[12] Trafalgar and Insight had the same owner, Travel Corporation, with headquarters in Bermuda. That did not affect their competitive position in the Australian market. Elkins had a high industry profile. He was national president of the Skal Clubs of Australia in the 1990s.

[13] Russell (1982), op.cit., p. 17. The other platforms were (a) to strive for adequate commissions; (b) to bring orderly marketing into the industry; (c) to establish a code of ethics.

274   [14] Murrowood died in 1967, two weeks before he was due to retire. His place was taken by Ken Lee, who had joined the E.S. & A. travel department in 1956. He remained in charge after the E.S. & A. Bank and the ANZ Bank were merged in 1970. He retired from the bank in 1988 and turned to work as a travel agent and tourism educator.

[15] Russell (1982), op.cit., p. 17.

[16] ibid.

[17] *Traveltrade*, 10 July 1996, p. 2.

[18] ibid., 1 June 1994, p. 1.

[19] Appendix to Community Travel Group membership application booklet, 1998.

[20] Graham Turner, managing director, in *Travelweek*, 23 April 1997, p. 6.

[21] When Peter Watson joined Jetset in 1982 he was told, 'Your job is to build a larger network.' He did. After heading a number of divisions, he was General Manager Distribution when he resigned in 1996.

[22] Asked why he thought he was selected for the job, Mr Lacaze referred to his branded products background. 'Understanding how to deal with an icon brand is really important. Understanding how to deal with a big network is also important and I've had a lot of experience with this.' (*Travelweek*, 27 January 1998, p. 2).

[23] *Traveltrade*, 17 September 1997, p. 15.

[24] 'I don't know what it is,' Steel said in an interview in March 1998. He thought UTAG best described as a buying/marketing group. It could be thought of as a 'loose franchise', though it was not a true one because UTAG agents did not have exclusive rights to an area; there could be another UTAG agent across the road.

[25] *Travelweek*, 15 January 1997, p. 1.

[26] *Traveltrade*, 8 March 1995, p. 1.

[27] According to *Traveltrade*, 6 March 1996, p. 7, 1559 full-service agencies closed their doors during the first year of the cap, as against 1020 voluntary closures in 1994: an increase of 53 per cent. However, six months later, *Traveltrade* reported that the top 50 US agencies had increased their sales significantly in the previous year, despite the commission cap. American Express was the top agency with gross sales of $US8700 million and Carlson Wagonlit Travel was next with sales of $US4500 million (*Traveltrade*, 18 September 1996, p. 16).

[28] *Traveltrade*, 19 March 1997, pp. 1 & 3.

[29] *Travelweek*, 26 March 1997, p. 1.

[30] ibid., 7 May 1997, p. 1.

[31] *Traveltrade*, 28 January 1997, p. 4.

[32] This was designed and used by American Airlines (Petzinger, 1996, pp. 58–9).

[33] Daniele, R. & Inbakaran, R. J. (1996), An overview of the evolution of electronic distribution of travel and tourism in Australia, working paper submitted for the Australian Tourism & Hospitality Research Conference, p. 4.

[34] Access Research (1994), cited by Daniele & Inbakaran, op.cit., p. 6.

[35] Tony Bracy, Manager Business Systems, Ansett, interview March 1998.

[36] *The Weekend Australian*, 7–8 December 1996, Syte 6, *Travelweek*, 27 August 1997, p. 8.

[37] *Travelweek*, 4 February 1998, p. 8.

Co-ordinating and planning

The early days: no-one was listening

When Australians went on their holidays in the years after the war and began to explore more of their big country in their new cars, most of them did not think of themselves as engaging in tourism. 'Tourism' was not a word in frequent use. There was the 'tourist trade', but that was something the average man and woman thought happened elsewhere — the Riviera perhaps, or some place where palm trees waved in a balmy breeze.

However, over the years the use of the word 'tourism' would change, reflecting the changing perceptions of what tourism was. The early organisations often preferred 'travel', rather than 'tourism', in their titles. The Australian National Travel Association (ANTA) and the International Union of Official Travel Organisations (IUOTO) are two examples. And when the word 'travel' was first dropped, it was in favour of 'tourist' rather than 'tourism'. Thus we have the Australian Tourist Commission, which was named in 1967.[1] The State bureaus were 'tourist' rather than 'tourism' bureaus, with an apparent emphasis on the individual and his or her needs instead of on the business of tourism.

The States were keen to get down to collective business soon after the war. A Commonwealth–State Tourist Officers' Conference, held in Canberra on 1 March 1946, resolved among other things 'that all Federal and State Departments should be enlisted to co-operate actively in forwarding the interests of the tourist industry.'[2]

276   A big influx of overseas visitors was expected. This was:

> ... because of the bond which exists between Britain and Australia as English speaking peoples (Australia having a 99 per cent. population of British origin); because of the huge spending power accumulated during the war and the holiday hunger which now exists; because of the desire of American parents to visit Australia where their sons fought; there will be a large tourist traffic to Australia as soon as transport and accommodation are available. (Queensland Tourist Development Board, 1947)[3]

Expectations turned out to be premature on more than one count, not only as to the expected rush of visitors from overseas but also in terms of interest and co-operation from governments, namely the politicians and their treasury departments. The recommendations of the conference were quietly buried. The meeting had heard that the Commonwealth Department of Information maintained 'an experienced tourist officer' in its London office with the task of keeping in contact with travel agencies in Britain, but in fact the Commonwealth government had no real interest in tourism at the time.

ANTA was so short of funds that its chief executive, Charles Holmes, restarted the organisation in a borrowed room on the second floor of the Victorian Railways building in Flinders Street, Melbourne. It was not until 1954 that the Commonwealth government granted it 20 000 pounds and it was able to assemble its forces to promote Australia overseas. In 1961, however, there was a balance of payments crisis and it suddenly occurred to the government that tourism might help solve it. ANTA agreed that tourism could bring in overseas currency, but not overnight.[4] So began the long process that resulted in the formation of the Australian Tourist Commission.

The bureaus corporatise

The State governments' tourism organisations started in the post-war period as 'tourist bureaus' with the basic function of selling travel and tourism within their own borders, although they also sold travel to any destination.

They were influential. They maintained interstate sales and promotion offices in other States as well as those within their territories. They operated their own sightseeing tours and longer packaged trips, as well as selling tours for commercial operators. They encouraged the development of tourism facilities, usually by making grants to local

Cultural tourism (Source: State Library of South Australia. By permission of the copyright owners Adelaide Festival of Arts)

This poster is a reference point for cultural tourism in Australia. It was produced for the first Adelaide Festival of Arts in 1960. Since then it has become common for people from overseas and within this country to travel in large numbers to attend Australian cultural events of different kinds, such as arts festivals, exhibitions and theatrical performances. Tickets for such events are frequently packaged with travel and accommodation.

278   government authorities or by matching funds on projects such as tourist roads, caravan parks and the like. They maintained publicity departments. However, their promotion, research and planning capabilities were not highly developed and they were hampered by being part of a government system.[5]

Nevertheless, change was on the way. Tasmania was the first to take aggressive promotional action in the 1960s. Then in the 1970s there were changes in the 'tourist bureau' culture when business executives were brought in to run the Western Australian and Queensland organisations.

Thus the State and Territory tourism organisations altered the emphasis of their activities and became oriented to promotion and development rather than to sales. Some got out of selling to the public altogether, leaving it to the travel agency network. The State and Territory tourism organisations competed for the domestic market— valued at $41.9 billion in 1995–96—as well as maintaining more than 40 offices overseas between them.[6]

Victoria was the first to corporatise in 1977 when an Act of Parliament provided for a body that was not part of the public service but was run by a board instead. This was to be the pattern of the future, though Victoria was not satisfied with its first effort and had changed the Act twice by 1992. However, Queensland had followed in 1978 and the Northern Territory by 1980. Western Australia, South Australia and New South Wales also made the change and the last two—Tasmania and the Australian Capital Territory—eventually joined the others in 1997. Structure did make a difference to the way functions were carried out and sometimes led to success or failure on a major scale. Three examples—from Tasmania, Western Australia and Queensland—are given below.

The Tasmanian 'push'

In the early 1960s the Tasmanian Government Tourist and Immigration Department decided that it had to 'push its own barrow' rather than depend on industry or anyone else. The problem was that Tasmania was an island and had a severe seasonality problem. The airlines and coach companies made their money servicing the destination in the warmer six months of the year. They shifted their interest and much of their equipment when it became colder, and felt no obligation to try to solve the winter problem.

The Tasmanian Department began wholesaling coach and fly/drive tours itself, first in the off-peak season and then, as this became suc-

cessful, all the year round. By the late 1970s it had become the dominant **279**
wholesaler of Tasmanian travel, but was uncomfortable with this success
for two reasons. For one thing, the airlines no longer felt the need to
market Tasmania vigorously because the government body was doing it
for them. Secondly, other ground operators were protesting at the
Department's dominance.

Consequently, in the early 1980s it de-emphasised its wholesaling
role to focus more on carrier relations. However, it continued to look
after its own interests in other fields. Its mainland travel bureaus had
become extremely busy, running travel agency networks as well as selling Tasmanian products over the counter. In the mid-1980s the
Melbourne bureau alone had 56 people taking calls, serving the public
directly and processing documents. Tasmania's retail figures became
benchmarks against which some other State and Territory organisations
set their own targets.[7]

But again Tasmania was becoming too successful—its travel centres
could not meet demand and the Department, constrained by government policy, could not cope. The 56 people in Melbourne were processing documents laboriously by hand, yet the Queensland Tourist
and Travel Corporation and the Northern Territory Tourist Commission were already using computers to handle reservations and print
tickets. The crisis point came in mid-1985 when a new Bass Strait ferry,
the *Abel Tasman*, was on its way from Europe. The Department wanted
more staff and more telephones to cope with demand in Melbourne,
but the government had decided to cut public service expenditure by
10 per cent 'across the board'. There were no exceptions.

So there were no more staff and no more telephones. As a result, a
massive blockage developed in the system. People found it so difficult to
make bookings, or simply had to wait so long, that many gave up.
Tasmania lost a considerable amount of business. Next the Department
decided to install a computerised reservations and processing system,
but committed itself to developing this system from scratch instead of
adapting an existing one. This turned out to be the wrong decision:
costly in terms of money and of time. Tasmania recovered from all this
later, but at the time it had fallen from its perch as a leader in State and
Territory government tourism.[8]

Western Australia's stance

The Western Australian government tourism organisation was known
as the Tourist and Publicity Bureau from its founding in 1921 until
1958. The following year the government created the Tourist

280 Development Authority comprising eight members, charged with the promotion and development of the State's tourism industry and with recommending to the government payments from the Tourist Fund. Two types of grants were made: one towards the cost of new or improved tourism facilities and the other to support country tourist bureaus. The Authority opened new interstate offices in Sydney, Adelaide and Melbourne.

In 1972 the name 'Tourist and Publicity Bureau' was dropped and replaced by 'Western Australian Government Travel Centre'. In 1974 there was another organisational change and the Tourist Development Authority was replaced by the Western Australian Department of Tourism. The organisation had a new leader, Noel Semmens, an oil company executive to whom competition was the natural order of things. Travel 'officers' became 'consultants', sitting behind desks to receive their customers just like travel agents rather than receiving them at a counter like the public servants of the time. Semmens did not like it when tour operators treated his organisation as the 'government' with a 'duty' to display and sell their tours without payment. If they were not prepared to pay a commission, their brochures were taken from the shelves.

Western Australia appointed a tourist manager in London in 1978 and continued to expand its overseas representation in the early 1980s. There had been an unwritten understanding that the States and Territories were to leave overseas promotion to the ATC, but the Western Australian view was that geography forced upon it an individualistic approach. The New South Wales Department of Tourism also began opening overseas offices in 1978.

Western Australia was often visualised as an island, with ocean on one side and desert separating it from the rest of Australia on the other. It was not part of the international air route system that served the east coast. It was conscious of its proximity to parts of South-East Asia and developed links that would help its tourism in future years.

In 1984 the Western Australian Tourism Commission replaced the Department; it was a statutory authority in the mould that was becoming standard for State and Territory tourism organisations. In 1987 the Commission closed its New York office and opened offices in Kuala Lumpur and Hong Kong as a sign of its commitment to Asia. It closed its Hong Kong and Los Angeles offices in 1993 to concentrate resources on South-East Asia and reported the next year that it was receiving a third of Australia's visitors from Indonesia, although overall it attracted only 10 per cent of international visitors. Jakarta, three-and-a-half hours' flying time from Perth, is in the same time zone.[9]

Promotion 1990s style (Source: Western Australian Tourism Commission)

The cover of a Mandarin-language brochure produced by the Western
Australian Tourism Commission in 1998. Mandarin was one of a number of
Asian and European languages in which Australian destination marketing
organisations printed brochures in the 1990s. The cover picture was taken at
the Pinnacles, north of Perth.

The America's Cup, the event that started a system (Source: Western Australian Tourism Commission)

There is nothing new about event tourism, but the modern emphasis on it— the bidding for notable events, especially those with extensive international television coverage, and the conscious creation of events to attract visitors from interstate and overseas—is relatively recent, dating from the 1980s in Australia. The America's Cup off Fremantle in 1987 was the catalyst for the formation of Eventscorp, a division of the Western Australian Tourism Commission, to develop, attract and manage events of economic benefit to the State. All States and Territories now have event units of one kind or another to carry out these functions. The picture shows the scene in Fremantle Harbour during the America's Cup.

Queensland's destination development strategy

When Frank Moore (later Sir Frank) was appointed chairman of the Queensland Tourist and Travel Corporation in 1978, he found it difficult to come to terms with the way things were done among the various tourism organisations. He even kept away from meetings of State and Territory tourism directors with agendas of items for co-operation, which he found soporific.

A successful and highly competitive businessman, he was accustomed to setting goals and devising means of achieving them. He

believed Queensland was ready for a shake-up. Apart from the Great **283**
Barrier Reef, its attractions were not well known outside the country. Its
tourism plant had been dictated by the needs of the domestic market
and its single international airport, at Brisbane, catered for less than
five per cent of the capacity of the aircraft flying to Australia. Moore
was convinced that Queensland had to become an international
destination.

But first he had to establish a new kind of organisation that could
co-ordinate a series of functions—in broad terms, the development of
tourism plant, access and marketing. The QTTC was set up as a 'half-
way house' between government and industry. It received funds from
the government each year, but it was a statutory authority, independent
of the public service. Policy-making was the responsibility of a board,
which was made up mostly of business people. Queensland had great
assets in its beaches, islands and sunshine, but without international
resorts it would not be possible to persuade the big overseas operators
and airlines to take notice of the State. The QTTC established a research
department and one of its duties was to provide growth forecasts on
which investors could rely.

Moore's strategy was to turn Queensland into an international destination in the following ways: by developing warm-water resorts; by
providing access to them from overseas; and by designing a marketing
system that provided appropriate products for selected markets and
positioned Queensland's attractions as assets of international quality.

The QTTC dealt directly with potential developers and sometimes its
methods were controversial. Parliament gave it jurisdiction over certain
Crown lands, which it was able to sell or contribute to joint ventures
with developers. The $183 million Sheraton Mirage Resort at Port
Douglas, which opened in 1987, was one example. The QTTC contribution to the project of Crown land was paid for by $10 million in
shares and these were later sold for $13.5 million.[10]

The issue of access was focused on international gateways. On the
wall of Sir Frank Moore's office was a world map with lines joining
major overseas markets with four gateways to Queensland: Coolangatta,
Brisbane, Townsville and Cairns. He kept a chart showing how many
hours an Australian had to work to pay for airfares between Queensland
airports and Australian and overseas cities. In the period between 1965
and 1988 the Brisbane–London route showed the sharpest decline in
required working hours; the one with the lowest decline was the
Melbourne–Gold Coast route. When he left that office in 1990, three of
the four gateways designated on his wall were international airports

Resort planning Queensland style (Source: Sheraton Mirage)

The opening of the Sheraton Mirage at Port Douglas in 1987 was the result of a plan to develop Queensland tourism around warm-water resorts of international standing. This picture was taken soon after the opening.

(the odd one out was Coolangatta) and Queensland was firmly on the world map as a destination in its own right.

Along the way he had conducted a war of words with Qantas over its reluctance to use Townsville Airport after it was internationalised. This was at a time when it was rare for Qantas to be publicly challenged, such was its perceived power in Australian travel and tourism. In the Townsville case, Qantas at first refused to use the airport for international flights but it was forced to change its mind.

Sir Frank Moore applied the pressure. He and the Queensland Premier, Sir Joh Bjelke-Petersen, appeared on television with Sir Peter Abeles and Rupert Murdoch, joint managing directors of Ansett Australia, to discuss the impact of international access to North Queensland. The implication was that Ansett would use Qantas' lack of interest in Townsville as a reason for going international. At this news, Qantas suddenly announced that it would begin international services to and from Townsville.

To improve the sales of Queensland tourism products, the QTTC revamped the retail system it had inherited from the old Department. It also established Sunlover Holidays, a wholesaler with a difference because Sunlover did not package tour elements but offered a huge range of Queensland products for travel agents and travellers to choose from. Besides being represented interstate, the QTTC set up a network of overseas offices.

The QTTC was very successful in achieving its goals for all the ele- **285** ments of its strategy in a co-ordinated fashion—the first time in Australia that such an attempt had been made by a government tourism organisation. One of the key elements in that success was the close relationship Sir Frank Moore had with the government, which listened to the Corporation and acted on its advice.

Also, there was a spirit of enterprise in Queensland which responded to the direction and facilitation provided by the QTTC. Some of the aspirations and schemes pre-dated the QTTC, but they fitted into the plan. Cairns had along aspired to having an international airport and it was during this period that it got it. In 1981 the Cairns Port Authority took over the airport under the Commonwealth's Airport Local Ownership Plan and began turning it into an international airport capable of taking the largest passenger jets. Stage 1 was completed in 1984 and tourism to Cairns—and Far North Queensland generally—began to climb rapidly.

Before 1978 Queensland had received a small proportion of the tourists who visited Australia from overseas. The main pattern of travel for overseas visitors up to that time had been the 'triangle'—Sydney, Canberra and Melbourne. In 1978 the number of overseas visitors was 630 600. In 1990, when Sir Frank Moore stepped down as QTTC chairman, the number was 2 215 000, Queensland was second only to New South Wales among the States and Territories in attracting visitors from overseas and the pattern of tourism in Australia had been emphatically changed.[11]

Regional tourism

When tourism began to develop after the war, New South Wales was in a position to capitalise on both domestic and international traffic. Sydney was a tremendous drawcard. It was the biggest destination area with a constantly growing tourism plant and it was overwhelmingly the major international gateway. The States with the next biggest populations, Victoria and Queensland, were on either side; so New South Wales was placed to get transit traffic between the two as well as to draw their travellers to its own attractions.

However, in the mid-1990s, just when tourism seemed to be going well, there was a problem. Sydney might have been the country's most popular destination area for international visitors, but they were not going anywhere else much in New South Wales. The statistics showed that, while 76 per cent of domestic visitor nights in New South Wales

286 were spent outside Sydney, the figure for international visitor nights was only 18 per cent.[12]

Tourism New South Wales launched a new strategy in 1995, with the idea of focusing development on all levels of tourism. It divided the State into 17 areas, each with a regional tourism organisation to oversee development. Funding and management assistance were provided. Later in the 1990s some of these regions were able to organise funding to mount multi-million-dollar campaigns in major markets.

Regional tourism was well established in some other States. Queensland grouped its regional tourism organisations into zones. Some of its regional bodies—for instance, those representing the Gold Coast, Far North Queensland, the Whitsundays and Townsville—developed sophisticated approaches to marketing. Another big State, Western Australia, had divided its territory into nine tourism regions and appointed regional managers to them between 1982 and 1985. South Australia's regional system in 1993–94 consisted of 13 regional tourism associations with nearly 2000 members and operating budgets totalling $2 300 000.[13]

Although systems differed, by the late 1990s the States and the Northern Territory between them were administering an aggregation of 75 regions. Regional development was also on the Commonwealth government's agenda and successive governments provided funds for it.

Promotion overseas: the formation of the ATC

The Australian Tourist Commission was formed in 1967 by the Commonwealth government to promote Australia overseas. This was in response to recommendations in a report by American consultants Harris, Kerr, Forster & Company and Stanton Robbins & Co., Inc., which was presented to the Australian National Travel Association in 1965 and published in 1966.

ANTA had pressed for the change and organised the study of the Australian industry and its prospects. ANTA executives took over the key roles in the ATC. The first chairman was John Bates,[14] chief executive of P&O Australia, the deputy chairman was Alan Greenway, founder of TraveLodge who had joined the ANTA board in 1958,[15] and the general manager was Basil Atkinson.

Atkinson, a young Perth journalist at the time, had formed a passion for tourism in Britain as a Kemsley Scholar in journalism from 1952 to 1954. Impressed by the way Britain had used tourism to help its post-war economic recovery, he was critical of Australia's lack of action. On his return to Australia, he sought out Charles Holmes and was encouraged **287** to apply for the post of ANTA's first post-war overseas manager. He was chosen from 131 applicants and at the end of 1956 was sent to San Francisco. A few months later, he was back in Melbourne—Holmes had decided to retire and Atkinson had been selected to succeed him.

It was a time of continuing discussions with the Commonwealth government. At first the aim was financial support, which the government agreed to on the condition that all the States accept that ANTA could speak overseas for Australia as a whole. The States accepted and appointed representatives to the ANTA board. Additional offices were opened in London and New York and ANTA took over an office in Auckland from the States.

In 1965–66 ANTA had a budget of $1 021 425, of which the Commonwealth government contributed $734 748, State governments $36 400 and 421 members and contributors $247 277. The formula on which the Commonwealth government contribution was established was a base grant of $462 000 and a dollar-for-dollar subsidy matching contributions from other sources.[16]

However, the ANTA leaders were not satisfied. They felt their organisation needed to be a part of the government for financial stability, but did not want it to be part of the public service. A statutory authority with an independent board was the preferred option.

> We realised that ANTA could not do it. My Board had the same view that I had; the last thing we wanted was a Department of Tourism; we had to do it through some form of statutory body . . .
>
> Experience around the world shows Departments of Tourism are bureaucratic, red tape is considerable, they do not attract industry people to work closely with them. We needed people who know about business to sit on our Board and to build a team of specialists. With a Department you always run the risk of a person seeking a job then, when he is trained, moving off to another Department in the public service. (Basil Atkinson, 1998)[17]

An outsider's view was considered essential to convince the government and other influential Australians and so a report by the American consulting firms was commissioned in 1964. The consultants travelled 25 000 unduplicated miles and interviewed some 300 people, delivering their report *Australia's Travel and Tourist Industry 1965* to ANTA in

288 October 1965. The report gave a detailed picture of the Australian tourism product and the industry—and indicated the potential of both. It called for the Commonwealth government to establish:

> an authority, board, commission, or corporation for the purpose of co-ordinating the planning and development of the Travel and Tourist industry of Australia and the promotion of travel from overseas.

The report recommended that the authority have two operating divisions:

1 *Internal Development Division*, with the necessary staff for research, planning and other co-ordinating activities . . .

2 *Overseas Promotion Division* to execute the overseas travel promotion programme and to administer the necessary staff therefor in Australia and abroad.[18]

The Commonwealth government responded in 1967 with an Act 'to establish an Australian Tourist Commission for the purpose of the encouragement of visits to Australia, and travel in Australia, by people from other Countries'. Functionally, only half the recommendation had been accepted.

Although the proposal to give the new body a role in developing the travel and tourism industry was denied it, the ATC's first management structure included the position of a director of development and work was done, among other things, on Ayers Rock and the Great Barrier Reef.[19] An end was put to this activity by a change of government in 1972, which resulted in the formation of a Department of Tourism and Recreation. Its stated purpose was to relate 'to the policy aspects and development aspects of Tourism—all aspects in fact except promotion of Tourism which is the responsibility of the Australian Tourist Commission'.[20]

The ATC's early years were difficult in more ways than one. The government's allocation did not keep pace with inflation and with the increase in world tourism. By reducing its overheads—cutting staff and closing offices—the Commission was able to increase its operational expenditure marginally, in money terms, from $1.19 million in 1967–68 to $1.28 million in 1976–77. Leiper commented in 1980:

> But when that operational expenditure is indexed against the global tourist market . . . it is apparent that in real terms the net effect over those nine years was a two thirds reduction in relative expenditure.[21]

In the North American market of 1974 Australia ranked forty-first, in **289** terms of expenditure, among countries promoting tourism—on a par with Bulgaria and Tunisia.[22]

The organisation was under critical scrutiny from within the bureaucracy from the time of its creation. The Coombs Report on Government Administration in the early 1970s recommended that it be wound up to save the government money; it was only after a stiff battle on the part of the ATC board and others that this recommendation was dropped.

> It was touch and go whether or not the Commission would survive. As far as the bureaucrats were concerned it was gone. I went to the Prime Minister [Gough Whitlam] and put the case for the ATC as strongly as I could. He listened sympathetically and in the end he prevailed over the bureaucrats. But they did not give up easily. Whenever I think of that time I think of what Wellington said after Waterloo: it was a near-run thing. (Alan Greenway, 1998)[23]

In the 1979 Budget there was a change of attitude: the Fraser government 'reversed its tourism policies'.[24] The ATC's budget for 1979–80 was increased to $8.2 million, well over double what it had been receiving during the 1970s. It was not only the ATC that benefited from the new policy. Tax deductibility for depreciation of buildings used for tourist accommodation was announced as well as money for tourism promotion under the Export Market Development Grants Scheme. Fees for Australia to join the World Tourism Organization and several million dollars for the development of attractions and facilities at Port Arthur, Ayers Rock and Kakadu were also included in the government's tourism program.

The government's more favourable attitude followed the report of the House of Representatives' Select Committee on Tourism, chaired by David Jull, which had held hearings in 1977 and 1978. This had urged greater governmental support for the ATC and recommended that its responsibilities include domestic tourism. Also, for the first time, the government had a report on the economic significance of tourism in Australia. This had been prepared by the Bureau of Industry Economics.[25]

In 1986 the Kennedy Committee—the Australian Government Inquiry into Tourism—made recommendations that resulted in the ATC's headquarters being moved from Melbourne to Sydney, shedding many experienced staff members in the process. In the following year the government introduced a new Act of Parliament that further con-

290 strained the ATC's operations, even to the point of requiring the Minister to approve its corporate objectives each year. According to the Act, the 'principal objects' of the Commission were:

(a) to increase the number of visitors to Australia from overseas;

(b) to maximise the benefits to Australia from overseas visitors; and

(c) to ensure that Australia [was] protected from adverse environmental and social impacts of international tourism.[26]

In 1988–89 the ATC was again under threat of extinction. The Industry Assistance Commission, in a draft report on travel and tourism, recommended that Commonwealth funding be gradually withdrawn from the ATC and its functions handed over to industry. The industry reacted strongly, 'universally challenging' the draft report. It argued that, without a government-supported ATC, marketing would be so inadequate that it would 'adversely affect the efficiency and growth of the Australian economy'. The Commission thought 'it would be imprudent to disregard those views' and reversed its earlier decision.[27]

Nevertheless, the ATC was still losing functions. It had lost part of its research role with the establishment of the Bureau of Tourism Research in 1987 and more with the formation of the Tourism Forecasting Council in 1994.

> . . . the development function left us, it was taken away; then after that the research function left us and was taken away. Now some of us knew that was a mistake because you can't really market effectively unless your research and development are hand in glove. (Basil Atkinson)[28]

On the other hand, the ATC's budgets were increased substantially from the early 1980s.

ATC operations

The ATC took over existing ANTA offices overseas—in Auckland, San Francisco, New York and London—and opened offices in Frankfurt and Tokyo. Its work in the late 1960s and 1970s was mainly with the industries served by those offices, creating awareness of Australian travel opportunities with travel agents, tour operators and airlines. It also provided information services for intending travellers. In North America it worked with other South Pacific countries to attract large audiences of travel agents' clients in a series of 'Destination South Pacific' theatrical and film promotions. Spectacular as events like these were, the weight of the work at the time was with the industry.[29]

The ATC had to work with small budgets, but in any case its view was **291** that it was essential to position Australia in new markets with the travel trade before, or at least at the same time as, the consumer. This required building up influential relationships with airlines, key travel agents and wholesale tour operators and this activity, although time-consuming and requiring initiative, was not costly.

Airlines controlled the relevant tour packaging in Europe. Until the ATC went to work, Australia was included only fleetingly in round-the-world tours because the airlines sold routes, not destinations. The tale was similar in North America. Tours that included Australia were sold from a brochure with a young Tahitian woman on the cover. The first packages offered were 'South West Pacific' tours. These were renamed

Australia as a place in the South Pacific (Source: Stewart Moffat)

In the 1960s, when the first tour programs from North America to this region were produced, Australia was promoted not in its own right but rather as a part of the South Pacific. This was still the case in the early 1970s, when this map was included in a confidential tariff produced for overseas operators by Stewart Moffat's SM Tours. The map shows the South Pacific destinations for which the tariff offered quotes for ground arrangements. Note that Australia is not named on the map, which may imply that the mapmaker thought it would be easily recognised by the overseas operators.

292 'South Pacific' tours when the musical of that name became famous. They included stopovers in South Pacific islands as well as in Australia and New Zealand. In the early 1970s the ATC abandoned the South Pacific consortium to concentrate on building the Australia brand. To this end, it ran an extensive advertising campaign in US magazines in the early 1970s.

Markets like Germany and Japan were developed with painstaking deliberation. Some operators were encouraged; others were not. In Germany in 1970 the ATC chose first to work with a single operator, Helmut Voss, who ran a specialist travel agency which was producing a variety of 'adventure and experience' tours to destinations that included Britain and Ireland.

Voss liked the ideas put to him by the ATC; his first tours sold and other operators, with the help of ATC publicity, took notice. Within a few years the ATC and the Australian industry were working with some 40 German operators. But the big mass producers of German tourism had not been included, because there were doubts about the capacity of the Australian tourism plant at the time to handle large charter groups going to the one destination, and because their clients were low-yield.[30]

In New Zealand the ATC promoted to travel agents throughout the country, co-ordinating visits by State and Territory representatives and working with airlines and wholesalers. It also mounted consumer campaigns at little cost. One example was the expenditure of $25 000 to provide a theme advertisement on 22 radio stations controlled by Radio New Zealand; station managers sold product ads to travel agents in their districts or towns. This near-saturation campaign was followed by consumer promotions involving films and lectures, audiences for which were provided by travel agents from their clients.[31]

Ensuring that the Australian industry was linked with the overseas industries was, of course, a priority, achieved by personal contacts and by organising Australian participation at trade shows like ITB in Berlin and events like the American Society of Travel Agents annual conference. With Qantas' help, the ATC introduced overseas agents to the domestic business exchange Talkabout in the 1970s and in 1979 chose the Gold Coast for its first Destination Australia Marketplace, a business exchange exclusively for overseas buyers (travel agents and tour operators) and Australian sellers (suppliers of travel and tourism services). This was the forerunner of the Australian Tourism Exchange (ATE).

The ATC conducted a domestic tourism campaign in 1974 titled 'Australia—Land of Things to Do' and aimed at young people.[32] The centrepoint of the program was a booklet of the same title, which had 'things to do' for Australians who were young or young at heart. The

ATC was to conduct other domestic campaigns at irregular intervals; the most elaborate, in 1985, included television commercials that featured Paul Hogan urging Australians to see their own country. Called 'Fare Go', the program also included a book of Australian holidays, some two million copies of which were distributed as an insert in the *Australian Women's Weekly* and through travel agents.

Ups and downs in overseas promotion

The 1980s were the beginning of a topsy-turvy period in the ATC's history. Its co-operative marketing activities with the Australian industry were comprehensive and effective. It had begun taking Australian industry groups into markets to meet and do business with overseas industry people in the 1970s: Japan in 1971, North America in 1975 and 1977 and the UK and Europe in 1979. In the 1980s and 1990s trade missions to emerging markets were a regular occurrence.

As time went on, the ATC built up a large and varied co-operative program, offering the industry advertising opportunities in overseas markets and access to the Internet and to huge databases of trade and consumer prospects. It organised industry participation in more than a dozen trade shows and business exchanges throughout the world each year. The yearly Australian Tourism Exchange, held in an Australian city each year, came to be recognised as one of the world's great tourism business exchanges. It also offered Australian suppliers the opportunity to participate in its large-scale and demonstrably effective Visiting Journalists Program.

In January 1994 the ATC launched Partnership Australia. This was a co-operative marketing venture with the State and Territory tourism organisations and the industry. It aimed at cutting out wasteful duplication in the markets and helping the industry develop and market a greater variety of product and improve distribution to travel agents and wholesalers. As a result of its participation in the ATC programs, by 1997 the industry was contributing more than $30 million a year to its budget.[33]

The Commission was less successful in some of its other activities. In 1983 it launched a multi-million-dollar television campaign in the United States featuring Paul Hogan commercials. It was really a series of campaigns, first aired on the West Coast and later extended to the East. Two commercials were used, both featuring Hogan, and the one that is remembered as the 'shrimp on the barbie' advertisement was much more successful in creating awareness than the other. There were follow-on campaigns in subsequent years.

294   The ATC's head office insisted that almost all the budget be spent on advertising, at the expense of support material and promotional activity with the US industry—the latter, of course, had the task of selling the travel that the advertising encouraged. In 1985, two years after the campaign began, there was still a problem.

> The advertising was almost a turn-off. People responded to the commercials, but when they couldn't get information they wanted on Australian travel, they said 'To hell with it, we'll go somewhere else'.[34]

In the decade that followed, when the campaign's effect might have been expected to show up in arrival figures, growth from the United States in fact lagged behind that of every other major market. From 1985 to 1995 arrivals from Japan increased 296 per cent and from Singapore 473 per cent. From the United Kingdom they increased 130 per cent, from Germany 233 per cent and from New Zealand 120 per cent. The figure for the United States was 55 per cent.[35]

> North Americans want to visit Australia more than any other country thanks to Hoges, according to ATC research. The only trouble is, according to the managing director of the ATC, Mr Jon Hutchison, that desire is not translating into American bottoms on trans-Pacific aeroplane seats. (*Weekend Australian*)[36]

This turned out to be a familiar story in the years that followed. The ATC experience in a number of markets demonstrated the limitations of expensive awareness advertising campaigns. The ATC's advertising budget was increased to the point where it became one of the biggest consumer advertisers among national tourism organisations.[37] Tracking showed that the advertising made Australia a preferred destination in a number of important markets. But this often occurred in markets where Australia made little headway, measured by arrivals, or lost market share.[38] There were critics of the advertising approach.

> The trend towards advertising fundamentalism (at the expense of commitment to research) among tourism agencies in Australia is therefore inconsistent with the development of the strategic marketing approach and will be counter-productive in the longer-term. (H. W. Faulkner, 1994)[39]

The ATC also had problems in managing the new Asian markets, notably Taiwan and South Korea. The governments of these two countries relaxed restrictions on leisure travel in the late 1980s and their citizens did not waste time in taking advantage of the new situation. In

South Korea, for example, the number of leisure travellers going overseas increased from 3000 in 1986 to 449 000 in 1989 and by 1991 the total was more than 650 000.[40]

Australian inbound operators and suppliers scrambled for customers with Korean outbound operators. One experienced observer described the results as 'shovelling them in'.[41] This concern for numbers rather than the customers they represented was to have serious consequences.

The ATC was late on the scene. The decision to 'take the ATC into South Korea' was not made until 1991,[42] when it launched an advertising campaign with golfer Greg Norman and a Korean actor. 'The results were immediate with tourist visa issuances to Australia rising a record 128.9 per cent that year.'[43]

But the ATC was addressing the wrong problem. It was not the ease or difficulty of attracting numbers of visitors; it was the fact that Australia had already been positioned as a low-cost destination and that, from the Australian suppliers' point of view, the South Korean market was low-yield. The early 1990s were years of 'profitless volume' for accommodation and other suppliers;[44] later Korean visitors were turned away by some hotels, despite having bookings, because better-paying customers were available. On the other side, a survey by James Cook University in 1994 found that 90 per cent of South Korean visitors surveyed did not want to come back to Australia because of disappointing sights, poor service and high prices.[45]

In 1996 the ATC recognised as a major problem the fact that Australia was not seen as a premium product in Taiwan and South Korea:

> The root of these issues is the value put on Australia as a destination . . .
> If it is sold too cheaply it means it is not valued by the industry and in turn the customer. (*Weekend Australian*, 12–13 October 1996, p. 2)[46]

Following the lessons of the early 1990s, yield had become a big issue for the ATC later in the decade, particularly when deciding how to deal with emerging markets:

> More importantly, India has the potential to be an extremely high yield market. That is the real attraction of the market itself. Yield is far more important to us than the numbers.
> So the challenge is to develop the market so we can protect and build the yield. (Bill Calderwood, deputy managing director of the ATC, August 1997)[47]

296 Commonwealth departments of tourism

The Australian Tourist Commission was established under the Department of Overseas Trade, 'indicative of the purpose of its formation'.[48] The Coalition government was concerned at Australia's balance of payments position and believed that the promotion of tourism would help. With the election of a Labor government in 1972, the Department of Tourism and Recreation was formed. A different philosophy was at work.

> From the outset the Department has conceived its responsibilities as encompassing the total leisure environment—to help ensure that Australians have access to opportunities to enable them to enjoy and enrich their growing hours of leisure.[49]

The differences narrowed over the years, as Labor governments also tended to favour the business view of tourism rather than the leisure view. However, they also favoured a separate department, whereas the Coalition preferred tourism to be handled by a division of a larger department.

The first department claimed that its role related to all aspects of tourism except its promotion, which was the responsibility of the ATC. A later department also emphasised the breadth of its role in its 1993–94 annual report, which included information on a number of marketing activities the department had undertaken, including product development, research and promotion.[50]

In the late 1990s tourism was handled at the departmental level by the Office of National Tourism within the Department of Industry, Science and Tourism. It had three branches: International Tourism & Industry Development, Regional & Environmental Tourism and Tourism Transport & Business Development. Its activities included policy advice and implementation and program delivery.

The department's 1995–96 annual report detailed policy activity relating to the government's overall tourism strategy, the Export Market Developments Grant Scheme, aviation, transport infrastructure, passenger processing issues, the development of accommodation and so on.

It also indicated funding for a range of projects involving the Rural Tourism Program; sustainable tourism projects in forests; accreditation for Victorian tour operators; the Sites of National Tourism Significance Program; the increase of Australia's competitiveness as an ecotourism destination; an ecotourism operators' accreditation scheme; the feasibility of establishing ecotourism business networks in the Flinders

Ranges, the outback and the Blue Mountains; backpacker tourism (21 **297** projects); a training package for cultural tourism; a Heritage and Interpretive Tourism course at the Cairns Institute of TAFE; membership of cultural organisations in North America; and the establishment of a network for major Australian festivals to assist them in international marketing. It also made a grant to Tourism Council Australia to help pay for the National Tourism Awards. Other activities included:

- Marketing. The report stated that the department worked to develop specific market segments, including backpacker, cruise shipping and the MICE sectors. It helped co-ordinate Australia's participation in international expositions.
- Research. The department commissioned or contributed funds for research into the ecotourism market; attitudes of institutional investors to tourism investment (the Tourism Task Force); tourism-related businesses and organisations that marketed their products and services overseas in 1994–95; the international competitiveness of the Australian tourism industry (Tourism Council Australia); and major tourism transport infrastructure needs (the Tourism Task Force).
- Publishing. The department published the following: *Directory of Ecotourism Education, Best Practice Ecotourism—A Guide to Energy and Waste Minimisation, National Backpacker Tourism Strategy, National Cruise Shipping Strategy, National Strategy for the MICE Industry, Tourism Workforce 2003, How Tourism Labour Markets Work,* Tourism *Industry Trends* (twice yearly) and *Impact* (monthly).

Strategic planning

In 1975 the Committee for Economic Development of Australia (CEDA) complained that no long-term objectives for the travel and tourism industry in Australia had been established.

Decisions concerning the adequate provision of trained manpower, the development of different tourist regions in Australia, or the promotion of different types of tourism would benefit greatly if taken in the context of recognised objectives and, within a longer term, a development concept for tourism. These concepts do not yet exist and should be the fruit of concerted research and study, exhaustive discussion and co-ordinated policy by all responsible sectors concerned.[51]

298 The Commonwealth Department of Tourism and Recreation, in a paper commenting on this statement, claimed that an attempt had been made to set down broad objectives as early as 1973; its 1975 paper included a revised set of objectives as well as a detailed formula for drawing up a national plan. However, it was not until 1998 that its successor, the Office of National Tourism, published what it called a national action plan.[52]

In the meantime the States and Territories had learned the value of strategic planning. The New South Wales Department of Tourism began the trend in the late 1970s. Its early plans were comprehensive and sought means of balancing demand with capacity. The problem was that, with changes of government in the 1980s, plans were not always followed—a new government and a new minister would want to alter whatever had been done previously.

By the early 1990s, however, strategic planning was a normal function in the State and Territory organisations. Approaches differed.

The *South Australian Tourism Plan 1991–1993* stated that its intention was to identify the directions the travel and tourism industry should take in order to achieve a stronger position by the end of the century. It was not intended as a 'comprehensive blue-print' but as a framework within which more detailed short- and long-term planning and decision-making could flow.

On the other hand, Tourism Victoria's *Strategic Business Plan 1993* was a 'how-to' book, showing the methodologies of research and planning as well as the results. It even showed how the first year's marketing plan would be derived from the strategic plan.[53] This was followed by the *Strategic Business Plan 1997–2001*, which followed the same principles. These documents broke new ground in Australian strategic tourism planning and provided the guidelines for Tourism Victoria's disciplined approach to tourism development in the period from 1993 to 1998.[54] This was a major factor in the revival of Victorian tourism after years in the doldrums.

Co-ordinating the industry

The Australian National Travel Association continued to exist after the Australian Tourist Commission was formed in 1967 and took away its overseas promotional role. Its name was changed in 1979 to The Australian Tourism Industry Association. Headquartered in Sydney, it at first sought a domestic promotional as well as a lobbying role. Despite its importance as the umbrella industry body representing all sectors, it began to decline in the 1970s, depleting its assets with operating losses over several years. In 1983 operating revenue was under $200 000 and **299** assets, which had been around $250 000 in the 1960s, had dropped to a little over $30 000.

Drastic action was necessary and was taken. A new board was elected with Sir Frank Moore as chairman, Peter O'Clery was appointed chief executive and the headquarters were transferred from Sydney to Canberra. Henceforth it would have a straightforward lobbying role and undertake important industry development tasks.

As an organisation ATIA prospered. Immediately its revenue began to rise and within three years was more than $1 million. In 1989–90 it began the process of installing chapters in every State and the ACT. By the time it was reconstituted as Tourism Council Australia in 1994, it was in a healthy condition with its membership at just under 600, assets of more than $2 000 000 and an operating revenue of $5 260 000.

Sir Frank Moore had stepped down and was no longer its chief spokesperson. That role was taken by Bruce Baird, a former Minister for Tourism in New South Wales, who was appointed managing director.[55] Headquarters moved back to Sydney. TCA saw its chief role as leading the policy debate and to that end its 1997–98 figures indicate the scale of its effort—it made more than 60 submissions to governments and departments, it put out 200 media releases and Baird made more than 150 speeches to various audiences. In that year it also inaugurated a Prime Minister's Lunch.

Other activities included the management of an industry accreditation program, the running of Getaway Holiday Expos (which replaced Holiday and Travel Shows) and the staging of two important annual events: the National Tourism Conference and the Australian Tourism Awards.[56] It also played a leading part in encouraging tourism research and in late 1998 undertook the management of a domestic tourism program.

Another lobbying group was formed in Sydney in 1989 by John Brown, another former Minister for Tourism. Known as the Tourism Task Force, it made public statements on behalf of the industry and was effective in attracting political and public interest.

The organisation was deliberately elitist. Membership was by invitation only and limited to 100 individuals, usually chief executive officers of large companies. Its objectives were (a) to act as a lobby group in matters affecting the viability and profitability of tourism enterprises; (b) to promote investment in viable, profitable and sustainable activities in the tourism industry; and (c) to remain an elite group of senior executives, representing the major players in Australia's tourism industry.[57]

300   Having two organisations speaking on behalf of the industry, however, was confusing. A report to the Minister for Industry, Science and
Tourism in 1997 by Jon Hutchison, managing director of the Sydney
Convention and Visitors Bureau, recommended that the two bodies
merge as soon as possible.[58]

Co-ordinating the MICE sector

The hospitality industry had always catered for meetings of different
kinds, but the HKF Report pointed out that an entire city benefited
from delegate expenditures, not just the hotels. It recommended the
setting-up of city visitor and conference bureaus to attract conferences.
The bureaus should be financed not only by the accommodation
sector, but also by the other businesses that benefited, as well as local
governments. It pointed to the success of such promotional bureaus in
the United States.[59]

As a result of the report, Melbourne hotelier Leon Ress called a meeting of interested parties and the Melbourne Convention Bureau was
formed in 1967 with funding from the Victorian government on a
dollar-for-dollar basis with industry. Its first executive director, Barry
Salgram, started work in January 1968. The Melbourne Convention
Bureau became the first member outside North America of the
International Association of Convention & Visitor Bureaus and was the
first Australian exhibitor at the American Society of Association
Executives Convention.[60] The Sydney Convention and Visitors Bureau
was established in 1969 and other cities soon followed.

The bureaus began to promote incentive travel to their cities as well
as conventions. Eventually exhibitions were added to their responsibilities. Thus from a number of different parts was developed a specialist
business, at first collectively called 'the meetings industry' and in later
years in Australia (though not everywhere else) 'the MICE industry', the
term being an acronym for 'meetings, incentives, conventions and exhibitions'. The MICE Industry Council was the co-ordinating body for
these associations.

In the mid-1990s, the MICE industry in Australia was generating
about $2.4 billion a year in direct expenditure.[61] It was made up of
many parts, including purpose-built centres and hotels providing
venues; professional conference and exhibition organisers; incentive
travel specialists; transportation, accommodation and catering services;
organisers of social programs; and providers of specialised technical
support such as audio-visual services and exhibition facilities for prod-

ucts. The number and variety of different businesses involved was very **301** high; in 1998 the Meetings Industry Association of Australia (MIAA) classified its membership in 50 categories.

Cohesion was achieved through the bureaus and the trade associations, with a peak body for each of the parts of the industry—meetings, incentives and exhibitions. They were also concerned with professional standards.

The incentive trade organisation was formed as the Australian Incentive Association in 1985 and became the AustralAsian Incentive Association in 1995, widening its scope to become the peak body for the Asia Pacific region as a whole. In 1996 it formed the AIA Academy to deliver education to its members and to administer an accreditation program in two categories: Accredited Incentive Practitioner, designated by the initials AIP, and Accredited Incentive Service Provider, designated by AISP. The first category was for those designing and implementing incentive programs and the second was for those who supplied services or products to the incentive industry.

MIAA was formed in late 1975 as the Association of Conference Executives and was renamed in 1990. In the same year it introduced national residential training programs for members and in 1993 an accreditation program for those who reached specified standards, granting them the style of AMIAA (Accredited Member of the Meetings Industry Association of Australia). In 1997 specific accreditation for meetings managers was introduced, with the style AMM (Accredited Meetings Manager).

The convention bureaus—there were 15 major bureaus in 1998—had their own organisation: the Association of Australian Convention Bureaux (AACB), which provided publicity and promotion, information and research, education and lobbying and government liaison.

The first purpose-built convention centre was the Adelaide Convention Centre, opened in 1987, and in the years to 1996 Sydney, Melbourne, Canberra, Brisbane and Cairns also built specialised convention and exhibition facilities; in some cases (such as those of Brisbane and Melbourne) investments of more than $200 million were made. In 1998 the Sydney Convention and Exhibition Centre and the Adelaide Convention Centre were being extended.

The investment of hundreds of millions of dollars in these facilities show how highly conference and exhibition tourism was regarded by State and city authorities; the expansion of facilities suggests previous success. In an earlier era, it was thought that Australia should build one major venue that could compete against the leading convention centres

302   overseas. Because of State and Territory competition, this idea did not find favour. The consequent development of a number of convention centres has led to specialisation in markets and types of conferences.

All elements of the high-yield MICE industry were expanding as the century entered its final years; indeed, they had been steadily expanding since the 1960s. Australia was able to compete internationally—at first, largely because of the eminence of its delegates in areas of science and medicine, but in later years because of its MICE industry expertise.

ENDNOTES

[1] By the 1990s many Australian journalists got it wrong, calling it the Australian 'Tourism' Commission.

[2] Report of the Queensland Tourist Development Board on the Tourist Resources of Queensland and the Requirements for their Development (1947), Brisbane, p. 9.

[3] ibid., p. 10.

[4] Basil Atkinson in Mistilis, N. & Leiper, N. (1998), The Australian Tourist Commission's early years reviewed by former senior managers, submitted for publication, p. 8.

[5] The HKF report noted that their effectiveness would be improved if they were given semi-governmental instrumentality or commission status designed to permit them to function more as business organisations. In particular, they should not be required to accept transfers from other government departments of personnel, most of whom were 'totally inexperienced' in travel and tourism activities (p. 83).

[6] Richardson (1996), op.cit., p. 222. In 1995 the total was 41.

[7] The author recalls the chief executives of both the South Australian and Canberra tourism organisations saying this to him; there may have been others.

[8] Pierre Chaperon, former Tasmanian tourist official, interview, March 1998.

[9] *Australian Financial Review*, 12 October 1994, p. 36. Other sources were the Western Australian Tourism Commission, Brian Bowater and Jac Eerbeck.

[10] Craik, J. (1991), *Resorting to Tourism: Cultural Policies for Tourist Development in Australia*, Allen & Unwin, Sydney, p. 189, cited in Richardson (1995), p. 134.

[11] The author followed most of the Queensland developments at the time and made several visits to the State—and to the QTTC—during the period. Sir Frank Moore supplied anecdotal details.

[12] Tourism New South Wales (1995), *Regional Tourism Strategy*, Sydney, p. 5.

[13] Richardson (1996), op.cit., p. 242.

[14] Later Sir John Bates and Consul-General in New York.

[15] Chairman of the ATC from 1969 to 1977.

[16] Piesse, op.cit., p. 1161.

[17] In Mistilis & Leiper, op.cit., pp. 16–17.

[18] HKF report, op.cit., p. 76.

[19] Some observers consider these first five years of the ATC as its most successful because, although its budget was small, it was able to co-ordinate product development activities and promotion. It was also a period of full co-operation with the States and Territories.

[20] Richardson, J. I. (1986), Submission to Committee of Inquiry into Australian Tourism.

The statement of the Department's role is its own description given to the 1970s Royal **303**
Commission on Australian Government Administration.

21 Leiper (1980), op.cit., p. 204.

22 ibid.

23 Alan Greenway, chairman of the ATC at the time, interview, August 1998.

24 Leiper (1980), op.cit., p. 217.

25 Tourism also had a powerful advocate within the government in the responsible minister, Sir Phillip Lynch, Minister for Industry and Commerce.

26 ATC, Act No.136, 1987.

27 Travel and Tourism, IAC Report No. 423, 29 September 1989, pp. 192–3. The industry rallied to the support of the ATC and persuaded the IAC to 'back off' in its final report. This stated that the Commonwealth funding of the ATC should be maintained for a period of five years 'at which time there should be a review to determine whether continued assistance would be justified' (p. 193). In March 1991 the ATC released the report *Evaluation of the Australian Tourist Commission's Marketing Impact*, prepared in association with the then Department of the Arts, Sport, the Environment, Tourism and Territories and Department of Finance. The report concluded that the ATC had been effective in meeting its marketing objectives and that the impact of ATC marketing, though difficult to quantify, was positive and contributed to the development of the economy. It also concluded that continued government funding of international tourism promotion was justified in conjunction with increased private sector contributions.

28 In Mistilis & Leiper, op.cit., p. 15.

29 Venues like the Chicago Opera House and the New York Town Hall were full for the 1970 promotions. The author was manager, Eastern Region, USA and Canada, for the ATC at the time.

30 Interview with Peter Harding, former ATC manager, Frankfurt, March 1998. Of course, the big German charter operators (often consortiums) did not need the ATC's sanction to come to Australia. They may well have tried to if they had been encouraged by the ATC at the time. Wholesalers encouraged by the ATC at that time, in other markets as well as Germany, usually did perform. There was some interest shown by the German charter operators in the late 1970s in extending Bangkok flights to Sydney, but nothing eventuated.

31 John Brace, ATC Manager, New Zealand, 1973–78 in 'Successful marketing on a shoestring', *Galah Gazette*, August 1998, pp. 4–6.

32 Originally the idea was to progress to other lifestyle segments—families and empty nesters. However, in 1975 there was an election and the new government listened to the protests of the States, which did not want the ATC involved in domestic promotion.

33 Former ATC executives who were interviewed for information on the ATC's history were Basil Atkinson, Don Beresford, Kim Dunstan, Peter Harding, Ian Kennedy, Alan Drew, John Brace, Bill Bostock, Meredith Ryan and Randal Harkin.

34 Bill Bostock, who was assigned to Los Angeles by the ATC in 1985, interview, March 1998.

35 Based on ABS arrival figures.

36 *Weekend Australian*, August 29–30, 1992, p. 3.

37 The ATC had the third biggest marketing budget among all national tourism organisations in 1995, a similar position to the one it held in earlier WTO surveys. Advertising is the single biggest budget item. *Advertising Age* (US) said that Australia was second only to Spain in tourism advertising spending by national governments (excluding States or private business) in 1993 (cited by Rizika, M., 1995). In 1995 the then Minister for Tourism, Michael Lee, announced that the ATC would spend $100 million

over three years on television and print advertising that would reach 500 million people in 10 countries (Melbourne *Herald Sun*, 28 August 1995, p. 9).

[38] *The Age* (25 January 1996, p. 4) quoted ATC market research as showing that Australia was the most popular destination in the US, Britain, Sweden, Switzerland, Korea, Singapore and Indonesia. In Japan 36 per cent nominated Australia as their most preferred destination as against 30 per cent for the United States. (See also ATC annual reports for the 1990s.) In the mid-1990s, according to Japanese departure figures, about six times as many Japanese were visiting the US each year as were visiting Australia. 'Japanese tourists rely on the wholesalers to make their trip especially to Australia because even though Japanese tourism increases annually to Australia, this destination is not as popular as say, USA or Europe. Wholesalers always try to make attractive *package deals* for Japanese tourists by concentrating on cheapness and attractiveness.' (Shin, 1995).

[39] In Theobald, W. (1994), ed., *Global Tourism: The Next Decade*, Butterworth-Heinemann, Oxford, p. 244.

[40] Leisure travellers only—the total number of overseas travellers in 1991 from South Korea was 1 856 000 (Korean 1996 *Annual Statistical Report on Tourism*, p. 53).

[41] Russell Windebank, then Manager Asia for General Travel Australia, who was in South Korea at the beginning of tourist traffic to Australia (conversation with the author, May 1996).

[42] Tony Thirlwell, former ATC managing director, *The Australian*, 13 September 1994, p. 60.

[43] ibid.

[44] Sir Frank Moore, as president of the Australian Tourism Industry Association at the time, was perhaps the most prominent user of the term 'profitless volume'. He said he meant it to describe the situation in the early 1990s when room rates were so low that even when rooms were filled hotels could not make a profit. This had come about after the enormous growth in the 1980s, followed by the pilots' strike which began in mid-1989 and a rise in interest rates in a year on some properties from 12% to 24%. Operators were desperate to get a trickle of money and reduced rates to fill rooms. This put them at the mercy of packagers, particularly those from Asia. 'It was not only accommodation operators who suffered. The industry was using numbers of visitors as its measure of success. We did get the volume, but measured by profits the situation was disastrous' (Sir Frank Moore, interview, December 1998).

[45] *The Australian*, 18 September 1994, p. 60.

[46] Jon Hutchison, the ATC managing director, was quoted as saying that while South Korea and Taiwan continued to be the star performers in terms of tourism growth, poor profitability had led to some Australian operators abandoning them. In the following week, Hutchison held discussions with industry leaders in Taipei and Seoul to discuss ways of increasing profitability from the South Korean and Taiwanese markets.

[47] Bill Calderwood, in a keynote address to a seminar on the Indian market in Melbourne, August 1997.

[48] Leiper (1980), op.cit., p. 144.

[49] Department of Tourism and Recreation (1974), p. 1.

[50] Richardson (1996), op.cit., p. 206.

[51] Department of Tourism and Recreation (1975), unpublished paper entitled 'General Review of Australian Tourism', Canberra, pp. 3–4.

[52] The Commonwealth Department of Tourism published a series of national 'strategies' in the 1990s, including a National Tourism Strategy in 1992. Excellent documents though these were in terms of research of their subjects, they were usually not full plans with statements of achievable objectives. The National Tourism Strategy, titled *Tourism*.

Australia's Passport to Growth, discussed an appropriate range of issues, but no objectives were stated and its so-called strategies were put in such broad terms that they were not specific guides to actions. Its value was as a resource document; it was not a blueprint for action.

[53] Despite their names, the Victorian plans were not 'business' plans in the usual sense of the term, which relates to a plan for the business itself—not only what it will do in terms of production, marketing etc.—but also in respect to its management, staff and finances and other matters relevant to its future.

[54] It was ongoing when this was written.

[55] Baird announced his resignation in August 1998 and was later elected to Federal Parliament. His successor was Phil Young, formerly of P&O Holidays.

[56] Annual Report 1997 and information sheet Year in Review, 1997–1998.

[57] Tourism Task Force information sheet.

[58] Hutchison said, 'There is only one national industry representative body, the TCA', pointing out that the Travel Task Force did not see itself as having a national representative role. However, it was a 'highly respected and active lobbying body, with good access to government'. (Hutchison, J., 1997, *Tourism: Getting it Right for the Millennium*, a report to the Hon. John Moore, MP, Minister for Industry, Science and Tourism, providing industry input to the development of a National Tourism Plan, Canberra, p. 47)

[59] Harris, Kerr, Forster, op.cit., pp. 168–9.

[60] Barry Salgram, interview, August 1998. Salgram resigned from the Melbourne Convention Bureau in 1975 and his successor was Sue Calwell. She expanded it into the Melbourne Tourism Authority and was its head for 20 years. It was later the Melbourne Convention and Marketing Bureau.

[61] Office of National Tourism, *Meetings, Incentives, Conventions and Exhibitions*, Tourism Facts No. 4, May 1997.

Tracking and teaching tourism

Research

The system of collecting statistics on people leaving and entering Australia for periods of less than twelve months was changed for air travellers in 1948. From then on passengers were required to fill in a card; up till then details had been compiled from passenger lists. Shipping lists were still used until 1965, when the card system was introduced for sea passengers. In 1958 the card was revised to allow visitors to be classified as 'in transit' or 'travelling for business, holiday, education or other'. The information collected included country of residence, age and sex, intended length of stay and country of last embarkation.

In 1975 the Australian Bureau of Statistics began regular collections of data on various kinds of accommodation. This was developed as a quarterly census which, by the end of 1997, covered nearly 10 000 establishments: 4900 hotels, motels and guest houses with facilities, 2700 caravan parks, 1600 holiday flats, units and houses (39 000 individual units) and 400 visitor hotels. From 1998 the survey was reduced because of budget cuts to cover only hotels, motels, guest houses and serviced apartments with 15 or more rooms, though data on all the types previously included was to be made available on an annual basis.

The ABS also produced a number of other statistical collections relevant to tourism, including surveys on specific industries such as hospitality, amusement and theme parks, motor vehicle hire and so on. It developed statistical standards, including a Framework for the Collection and Publication of Tourism Statistics, and worked on standards with the World Tourism Organization.

Various bodies carried out tourism research before the creation of the Australian Tourist Commission in 1967, but it was scattered and non-comprehensive. Piesse (1966) refers to a number of ANTA surveys—of overseas visitor spending, of attractions and tourism plant, and of potential markets abroad—but also notes that travel research was 'comparatively underdeveloped in Australia'.[1]

In 1965 the New South Wales Department of Tourist Activities appointed a research officer and conducted a pilot survey of the tourism industry at Port Macquarie. Results of surveys in 1964 showed that in that year 53 000 people took conducted tours of the Snowy Mountains Scheme, 28 500 visited the Northern Territory, nearly half a million spent approximately $21 million in South Australia and the value of the 'tourist trade' to the Gold Coast was nearly $72 million.[2]

The first studies that allowed Australia to put scale and value to its tourism with real assurance were produced in the 1970s. The ATC first produced an Overseas Visitor Survey in 1971 and did so annually until 1975 when the project was abandoned because of cost. It was reinstated in 1979 as the International Visitor Survey (IVS). The States and the ATC then decided to jointly finance a Domestic Tourism Monitor (DTM) to gather information on domestic travellers; the first was carried out in 1978–79.[3] The ATC conducted its first psychographic market research in 1977–78 in New Zealand, with Qantas, Air New Zealand and TAA. In 1979 the Bureau of Industry Economics produced its Research Report 4, *Economic Significance of Tourism in Australia*.

There was virtually no interest in tourism research at universities or other higher learning establishments at the time, although the first postgraduate thesis focusing on tourism had been completed in 1968.[4] Neil Leiper, a lecturer at Sydney Technical College in 1977, asked the editors of three overseas academic journals dealing with tourism research about their subscribers in Australia. Only one had any—and these totalled just four, of whom Leiper was one and the Sydney Technical College another. A check of universities in the late 1970s showed only three or four masters' or doctorate students whose research had any kind of link to tourism.[5] In the 20 years to 1988 there were 31 tourism-related theses—an average of only one-and-a-half a year. Only three of these were PhD dissertations.[6]

However, the Australian Standing Committee on Tourism (ASCOT), an intergovernmental committee, organised an annual Australian Tourism Research Workshop over a number of years starting in the late 1970s, the main objective being to foster the development of research techniques and skills.

308   The Bureau of Tourism Research was formed in 1987, funded by the Commonwealth, the States and the Territories, to undertake statistical collection and research in travel and tourism. It took responsibility for the IVS and the DTM and maintained a constant research program covering many aspects of tourism, economic as well as marketing.

> The creation of the BTR clearly represented a significant step forward in the development of tourism research in Australia. With the concentration of resources into a single research agency, a 'critical mass' of expertise was established and economies of scale in the deployment of resources could be achieved. Furthermore, it has provided a focus for the development of a more co-ordinated approach to tourism research between the Commonwealth and State/Territory tourism agencies, while some progress towards improved co-ordination at a broader level was achieved through the staging of research conferences ... and joint projects with some tourism industry bodies. (Hall, in Faulkner et al., 'Tourism research in Australia: Confronting the challenges of the 1990s and beyond', 1995)[7]

In association with the University of Queensland, the BTR organised the first national conference on tourism in 1988, which included a one-day Australian Travel Research Workshop. By the 1990s interest in research at universities had grown to the point where an annual National Research Conference was held each year by the Council for Australian University Tourism and Hospitality Education (CAUTHE). The first was held in 1993. By that time Australia had its own research journal, *The Journal for Tourism Studies*, which was produced twice a year by James Cook University. The first issue was dated May 1990. An analysis of the domiciles of authors of articles in leading overseas journals as well as in *The Journal for Tourism Studies* showed that the introduction of that journal had doubled the output of articles by Australian authors in its first few years of publication and had raised the overall percentage contribution by Australians in leading tourism journals from 3 per cent to 5.5 per cent.[8]

Also, in 1987 the Australian Tourism Industry Association and the Australian Federation of Travel Agents formed the Australian Tourism Research Institute (ATR*i*). This was intended as a kind of clearing house for tourism research from different sources: government, university and industry. It also provided the initial funding for the first chair in tourism at an Australian university—James Cook University. Professor Philip Pearce was appointed to the post.

In the early 1990s, Professor Pearce estimated that there were only about 100 tourism research personnel in Australia, spread throughout universities, government bodies like the ATC and State tourism organisations and Commonwealth departments dealing with tourism, transport and the environment. Many of these were poorly funded.[9]

But the second half of the 1990s saw considerable advances. First, the Commonwealth Scientific and Industrial Research Organisation (CSIRO) developed its own tourism research program following a national industry and CSIRO workshop in 1995. This led to projects in four areas: information technology; a planning and management framework for resorts; the integration of tourism into regional environment, society and economy; and the evaluation of future choices for the industry.

Then in 1997, after lengthy approaches by the ATRi and several universities, the Commonwealth Government approved the establishment of the Cooperative Research Centre for Sustainable Tourism (CRC Tourism). This was a huge step forward, and was expected to provide funding for research from Commonwealth, industry and university sources of $60 million in cash and kind over seven years. By early 1999 the number of universities involved had grown from the initial six to thirteen. Other organisations that participated included TCA, AFTA, Qantas Airways, American Express, Ernst and Young, Touraust Corporation, Conrad Jupiters, Gold Coast City Council, Warner Bros. Movie World, the Restaurant and Catering Association, Atlas Travel Technologies and Compaq.

Funds were distributed through a variety of mechanisms to specific projects. As a result of co-operation between CRC Tourism and TCA, the Centre for Regional Tourism Research was established at Southern Cross University and it listed thirteen projects for 1998–99. CRC Tourism was expected to help fund 40 PhD students.[10]

In 1997 changes were made to both the major international and domestic surveys. The IVS, conducted in airport lounges after visitors from overseas had completed their stay in Australia, was revised by increasing the sample size and decreasing the number of data items sought from visitors. The revisions were intended to increase the reliability of the core data. The DTM was replaced by the National Visitor Survey (NVS), which had a larger sample size and collected data on expenditure and outbound tourism.

Education and training

Education for the travel and tourism industry in Australia began with trade schools. Here people could be trained in skills such as butchering

310 and cooking, which suited them for the hospitality sector. The origins of this sort of training go back a long way in the history of technical education. For instance, Mrs A. Fawcett Story was appointed supervisor of cookery in the Victorian Education Department in 1899; by 1901 eleven 'cookery centres' had been established in Victoria.[11] Some trade schools were set up well before the Second World War and their work was expanded as the industry grew after the war. The emphasis was still on hospitality sector skills.

In 1962 a new concept was introduced into the Victorian system. Len Watts, director of technical education, combined elements of courses from three schools under his jurisdiction—William Angliss, a food trade school; Emily McPherson College, which tought domestic science; and Footscray Technical College, which offered business courses. The result was a Diploma of Catering and Hotel Management, which took four years to complete. Part of each year was spent working in the industry; the Australian Hotels Association training committee was closely associated with the education authorities at the time. The quality of the course was recognised by Michigan State University when it accepted a Victorian Diploma graduate as a student for a master's degree by giving him credit for his Australian studies.[12]

There were hotel and restaurant management courses in Sydney and Hobart as well as Melbourne when the American consultants Harris, Kerr, Forster and Stanton Robbins surveyed Australian travel and tourism in 1965.[13] However, the Victorian diploma course was the only one that was full-time.

The consultants reported that 'accommodations and catering industry training courses' were available at these institutions in 1964:

- Sydney—East Sydney Technical College
- Melbourne—Footscray Technical College, William Angliss Food Trade School, Emily McPherson College of Domestic Science
- Brisbane—Brisbane Technical College
- Adelaide—South Australian Institute of Technology
- Perth—Mt Lawley Technical School
- Hobart—Hobart Technical College.

However, they considered that:

> … much more needs to be done throughout Australia to overcome the drop-outs in the courses, to obtain greater recognition and support by employers as to the value of employees thus trained, and to instill in existing and prospective employees a

recognition that education is a key toward their progress to a successful and satisfying career.[14]

The consultants made no recommendations about training for people working in airlines and railways, because these had been 'successful in achieving a good quality of service through the training programmes and service standard procedures'.[15] However, they did suggest certified courses for guides and driver guides (including taxi and hire-car drivers) and a national training course for national parks and wildlife reserve rangers. They urged the Australian Federation of Travel Agents (AFTA) to proceed with its plan to establish training courses for travel agents. As for their main concern, the hospitality sector, they recommended the establishment of one or two central schools for hotel, motel and restaurant management which would draw on the experience of Michigan State University, Cornell University and the University of Hawaii.

This did not happen, but in 1971 Australia's first degree course in hospitality management started. This was the work of Dr Don Smith at the Gatton Agricultural College at Lawes, which is now part of the University of Queensland. The next year a course offering a degree in hospitality management became part of the curriculum at the Footscray Institute of Technology, previously Footscray Technical College and now part of the Victoria University of Technology.

The driving force behind Footscray's interest in the subject was a lecturer in advanced accounting, Brian Wise.[16] He had read extensively about the work being done at Cornell University and Michigan State University in the United States and at Surrey University in Britain. He went on to spend twelve months overseas studying tourism course development and wrote a master's thesis on the subject. In 1976 he introduced a tourism management degree course at Footscray. This was not only the first such course in Australia, but was also one of the first of its kind in the world.[17]

The Australian community became more aware of travel and tourism as a result of the rapid increase in inbound tourism from the mid-1980s. As a result, the need for a larger, better-educated workforce became apparent and the number of courses in both technical training and management education multiplied.

In 1989 tourism education was finally recognised by an Australian university; as previously noted, the first chair in the subject was instituted at James Cook University in Townsville. In late 1990, the first National Conference on Tourism Education in Australia was held at the University of Canberra and was attended by tourism educators in private,

312 technical and tertiary sectors. The main objectives of the conference were to identify trends in tourism education, to achieve a better understanding of industry requirements, to establish closer links between tourism educators and the industry, to review government policy and to develop broad strategies for the future. The conference, as reported by C. M. Hall, 'had mixed success in meeting these objectives'.[18] Nevertheless, a start had been made and there was impressive growth in the 1990s—not just in the number of courses and enrolments, but also in industry acceptance of the need for tourism education.[19] The Council for Australian University Tourism and Hospitality Education was formed in 1992 and in 1998 had 32 members, all universities and university colleges.

By 1996 about 80 000 students were undertaking travel and tourism courses at all levels in Australia.[20] Twenty-six Australian universities offered undergraduate programs in tourism and hospitality subjects. A much smaller number (less than half) had postgraduate programs, mostly in the form of course work. There was dissatisfaction among educators that more academic research was not being carried out. The reason given was that tourism was still not well understood as a coherent and identifiable area of teaching and research—either within universities or by funding bodies.[21]

Vocational training

By the mid-1990s the level of vocational training was not recognisable from that of earlier eras. This was due to the introduction of the Training and Further Education (TAFE) system throughout Australia at the beginning of the 1980s. TAFE colleges[22] not only modernised existing travel and tourism courses but also extended their range. They now offered courses in tourism and hospitality management as well as a variety of studies in such subjects as food preparation, housekeeping, bartending, waiting, travel consultancy, tour guiding and even crowd control.

This was further extended by initiatives launched in 1998. Three comprehensive training packages were introduced into the TAFE system—in hospitality, tourism and the caravan industry. These offered courses from certificate to advanced diploma level and a wide choice to suit specific areas of interest. For example, in hospitality it became possible for students to choose, with combinations, from 100 certificate courses. There were six specialisations in Asian cooking.

In tourism, where formerly most TAFE activity had been directed at the retail sector, courses became available in such areas as meetings and events management, attractions and theme parks, and Aboriginal and

Torres Strait Islander Tour Guiding. Caravan industry courses included caravan manufacture, caravan sales and caravan park management.

Of all Commonwealth government funding for vocational training in 1998, 7.7 per cent was devoted to travel and tourism subjects. Tourism training was by then becoming part of the curriculum in secondary schools. It was particularly strong in Queensland but was spreading throughout the country as part of the national training agenda.

A network of private providers had also developed offering accredited courses, mostly in hospitality (some with university connections offering degree courses), travel consulting and tour guiding, though some providers also taught tourism management subjects. Private providers were sometimes connected with large travel companies. For example, Jetset had its own school for travel consultants and ID Tours South Pacific offered training in tour guiding. The Radisson Training Centre was conducted for Radisson by the Australian School of Travel and Hospitality in Melbourne. AFTA had established its own schools in several States to prepare students for entry into travel agencies and also ran a distance learning system for people in agencies who wanted to extend their education.

Some private providers were particularly innovative. An example was The Hospitality Training Company, which started in Parramatta and spread to 14 sites throughout the country. At first it operated at entry levels for hotels, restaurants and clubs, and later at more advanced levels. It took training to regional areas that lacked conventional facilities, overcoming the problem by using commercial premises, such as those of RSL clubs, during slack times. It also established training restaurants under the Ghekko's brand on the Gold Coast and in Adelaide, Cairns, Townsville and Perth.[23]

Company courses

The idea of offering continuing education within a company system appealed to some of the larger organisations. Qantas developed the 'Qantas College', offering courses to its staff from TAFE Certificate 4 to postgraduate levels; Ansett Australia had a Diploma of Management course, supplied by Southern Cross University; the SPHC Group had a course equivalent to a Graduate Certificate (University of South Australia); ITT Sheraton had its own MBA (Bond University) as well as a diploma course; and AAT-King's had a trainee managership program.

Some associations, such as the Meetings Industry Association of Australia, had education or training programs for members and made involvement part of the requirement for accreditation. The Restaurant

314 and Catering Industry Association of Australia worked with Southern Cross University to develop a Diploma of Food Service Management, which was delivered by distance education.

In association with the Pacific Asia Travel Association (PATA), Southern Cross University conducted a yearly seven-day tourism executive development program, which was typically attended by students from five or six other countries as well as Australia.[24] The same university had combined with the Hotel Inter-Continental in Sydney to operate the Australasian Institute of Hotel Management.

Educational establishments broadly divided their courses between 'tourism' and 'hospitality'. This had some historical justification: hospitality education was instituted before the word 'tourism' was used in a business sense, let alone thought of as a subject for business education.

Some universities were becoming more specific, in whole courses as well as in electives, in preparing students for careers in different branches of the industry—for example, in the MICE sector or in club management. While some universities (such as the Victoria University of Technology) had progressive histories of tourism and hospitality education going back more than two decades, for others it was relatively new. But overall the growth of interest in tourism and hospitality education shown by Australian universities in the 1990s was remarkable, as was the recognition by a previously sceptical industry that it needed a better-educated workforce in the future.

ENDNOTES

1 Piesse, op.cit., p. 1182.

2 ibid.

3 Don Beresford was an influential force behind the introduction of both studies. As assistant general manager of the Australian Tourist Commission he insisted that the IVS be conducted yearly because he wanted a reliable indicator of visitor trends. He was director of the New South Wales Department of Tourism during the negotiations leading to the DTM.

4 Hall (1991), cited in Faulkner et al. (1995), 'Tourism research in Australia: Confronting the challenges of the 1990s and beyond', in *Tourism Research and Education in Australia, Proceedings from the Tourism and Educators Conference, Gold Coast, 1994*, BTR, Canberra, p. 5.

5 Associate Professor Neil Leiper (Southern Cross University), interview June 1998. Professor J. R. Brent Ritchie, of Calgary University, who was president of The Travel Research Association (TTRA), wrote to Dr Leiper in 1982 asking him to help establish a chapter in Australia. He sent out letters to 40 people seeking their interest, but had no response.

6 Hall, op.cit., p. 5.

[7] ibid., p. 5.

[8] Faulkner et al., op.cit.

[9] ibid.

[10] Peter O Clery, Consultant/Industry Program, CRC Tourism, interviews, and CRC Tourism Fact Sheet dated March 1999. In 1999 Sir Frank Moore was the chairman of CRC Tourism, ATRi and the Tourism Forecasting Council. CRC Tourism was established under the Commonwealth Government's Cooperative Research Centres Program, designed to strengthen collaborative links between industry, research organisations, educational institutions and relevant government agencies. The Commonwealth's contribution over seven years was set at $14.7 million.

[11] By 1922 there were 65 (Department of School Education, Victoria, 1992).

[12] Professor Brian Wise, interview, March 1991.

[13] HKF Report, op.cit. Training and education are covered on pp. 287–90. Accommodation and catering training courses are listed in Appendix XIII-A, p. 340.

[14] ibid., p. 288.

[15] ibid., p. 287.

[16] Professor Wise, the source of much of the information in this section, retired as Dean of Business in 1997.

[17] Tourism as a subject was offered in European universities as early as the 1930s and in the US from 1963 at Michigan State University (Faulkner et al., op.cit., p. 4). However, the first recorded use of the phrase 'tourism management' occurred only in the early 1970s in a document related to the development of London tourism. The first international use was in a textbook published in the mid-1970s (Seekings, J., 1989, 'Components of tourism' in *Tourism Marketing and Management Handbook*, ed. S. F. Witt & L. Moutinho, Prentice Hall International, Hemel Hempstead, pp. 57–62.

[18] Hall, C. M. (1992), 'Tourism education in Australia: research notes and reports, *Annals of Tourism Research*, vol. 17(1), p. 138.

[19] The author bases this comment on interviews he conducted with more than 100 industry leaders in Melbourne and Sydney on behalf of universities between 1993 and 1997. The difference in attitude over previous decades—in some cases from the same people—was notable. At one time it was not unusual for industry people to talk of the 'school of hard knocks' and scoff at formal education at higher levels. However, executives in all sectors of the industry now look to employing qualified people. The human resources director of a large hotel chain told the author in December 1997 that executives without formal tertiary education were feeling the pressure of younger, better-educated people coming up; people with degrees generally had better skills than those without, and it was noticeable.

[20] *The Australian Financial Review*, 20 September 1996, p. 52.

[21] Robyn Bushell, chair of the Council for Australian University Tourism and Hospitality Education, 'Emerging field's greener pastures', *The Australian*, 1 October 1996, p. 28.

[22] There were 86 TAFE colleges in Australia in 1998. Some universities have TAFE sectors.

[23] At the time of writing, all but the Perth restaurant were in recess while the company evaluated their operations.

[24] A number of people were interviewed in March 1998. They included Professor Brian Wise, Bill Galvin (Tourism Training Australia), Aaron Johnson and Leonie Shaw of the Australian National Training Authority (Brisbane), Peter Ring (Victorian Office of Training and Further Education) and Jeremy McNamara (Hospitality Training Company).

Postscript: the past as a guide to the future

The problems of prediction

Books of history must reach their end, but the many-threaded story of Australian travel and tourism goes on, of course—part of what D. Horne calls 'the greatest continuing mass movement of peoples in human history'.[1] Now it is pertinent to ask: what comes next for Australian travel and tourism?

> Predicting the future requires the perspective of history. The future is part of a seamless continuum and emerges from roots deep in the past. (G. T. T. Molitor, 'Trends and forecasts for the new millennium', *The Futurist*, 1998)[2]

That would seem to make forecasting the future relatively easy. It isn't so. The past is full of worthwhile lessons, but knowledge of what happened in earlier eras does not always make predicting the future easier.

Sometimes the continuum is clear and the next stage predictable. For example, international travel will get faster. The First Fleet took more than eight months to get to Australia from England. Some 150 years later the smart liners were making the trip in four weeks and flying boats were covering the distance in nine days.[3] Now planes are scheduled to fly between Australia and Britain in less than a day. With developing knowledge of new propulsion methods, we can see the day when it will be possible to fly between Australia and Europe in less than an hour.

We can also predict with certainty that more and more people will **317** travel. In chapter 8 we noted that there were 25 million international tourist arrivals in 1950 and that this figure had grown to 594 million by 1996 (pages 129, 135). The world's population is increasing, travel is becoming easier all the time and social and economic changes are making it possible for a greater proportion of people to take holidays. Growing middle classes in the most populous nations in the world, China and India, are but one indicator of the potential for the future. The WTO is expecting one billion international arrivals annually by 2010.[4] While that forecast may be out by a year or two, we can be reasonably sure that, barring a world catastrophe, it will hold good.

We cannot predict everything. Wars, natural catastrophes and economic crises can come unexpectedly, and they all affect travel and tourism. The forecasters made no allowance for the Asian economic crisis that began in 1997 and placed a check on travel within the East Asia and Pacific region. For some Australian operators, their businesses will never be the same again. In the past they had planned on the basis of uninterrupted growth of inbound visitors—some for as far ahead as 20 years or more—but in 1997 or 1998 the pattern was broken and the future became uncertain in a way it never had been before.

Not surprisingly, by late 1998 there were two views among experienced Australian travel and tourism operators of what would happen in the years to come. The optimistic view was that the rearrangement of world exchange rates had made Australia a more attractive destination for Europeans and North Americans and that the Asian markets would be rebuilding in two or three years. The pessimistic view was that a good part of the world was on the brink of recession and the tourism markets would become increasingly unstable.

Few predicted the most influential technological change of our times: the information revolution. It crept up on us. Its main components, the telephone, television and the networked computer, had been with us for a long time. The telephone was invented in 1876, the first television transmission was made in 1926 and the electronic computer was devised in the mid-1940s.[5] But even as recently as the late 1980s and early 1990s, when great strides were being made in key technologies,[6] few saw the full effects. Even though we were alerted to the possibilities, it was still difficult to know what was going to happen. In 1995 Robert Allen, chairman of AT&T, one of the world's great telephone companies, said:

> One could reasonably expect the chairman of AT&T to know what his corporation will be in ten years from now. He doesn't. One

318   could, within reason, expect the chairman of AT&T to be able to predict how technology will transform his business a decade hence. He can't. At the least, he should know who his major competitors will be in 2005. Stumped again. But here is what he does know: something startling, intriguing and profound is afoot.[7]

That 'something' will continue to affect everybody. Like Robert Allen, those in the Australian travel and tourism industry are wondering how it will transform their businesses in the years ahead. Regrettably, history is an uncertain guide. However, it does have valuable information that can help us achieve success in the future. And in broad terms the influences that shaped travel and tourism in the past—political, technological, economic, social and environmental—will be the same.

Technology: the Global Village

Besides cheaper and faster travel, it was the advances in telecommunications, made possible partly by computer technology and satellites, that ended Australia's isolation. The same processes also helped turn travel and tourism into the world's biggest business by making possible the integration of national industries.

The Australian industry now works in an environment in which even a small operator, catering for the domestic market, is not immune to some far-distant event that affects tourism. As for the big operators, they regard being international as a fact of life if they are to survive. To Qantas, the biggest Australian travel and tourism company, being a member of a top-quality world airline alliance was 'absolutely critical' to its long-term viability.[8]

The smallest companies, as well as the biggest, can use electronic networks like the Internet to appeal to customers all over the world. This means that many more products can be offered to potential travellers, allowing them to pick and choose what they will see and do when they are travelling.

> One may contact the 'entire world' and at the same time create specific products for very different segments. (WTO, *Tourism and Technology Bulletin*, 1997, p. 14)

The Internet

While the growth of the Internet may have been 'the most astonishing technological phenomenon of the late twentieth century',[9] perhaps even more astonishing is the fact that it is bringing about such change **319** in its infancy, with its real promise still to come. Literally speaking, nothing like the 'entire world' could be contacted in the 1990s. Some 57 million people were using it in 1997: about one-hundredth of the world's population. It was expanding rapidly, but no longer doubling every year as it once did. It was inefficient—a great amorphous mass of web sites that made searching for what you wanted difficult—and there were problems with security, which hindered the operation of business when payments were required.

As the *Economist* put it in 1997, just finding something to buy on the Internet was a triumph, let alone comparing prices and paying for the commodity: 'For most consumers today's Internet, far from being a perfect market, is the high street from hell.'[10]

Nevertheless, the Internet was offering people around the world services that were different, and better than any other means. It combined the computer's ability to process and store enormous amounts of information at a low cost with the telephone network's ability to reach millions of people around the world. It offered:

> … a glimpse of the communications future: a world where transmitting information costs almost nothing, where distance is irrelevant, and where any amount of content is instantly accessible.
>
> But it affords only a glimpse. The Internet is merely a prototype of something much more sophisticated. (F. Cairncross, *The Death of Distance*, 1997)[11]

Access to the Internet was becoming easier as the twenty-first century approached. The integration of telephone networks, television and computers resulted in devices such as set top boxes and screen telephones.[12] It was becoming increasingly a part of everyday life.

> Eventually, the Internet will be integrated into other products. It will be part of the telephone service, part of the way a television works, part of a games console. It will connect computers in an office and computers between offices. People will stop thinking of the Internet as a separate entity and will be aware only of the services it delivers rather than the technology itself. (Cairncross, op.cit., 1997)[13]

Those services will include tourism information and reservation services, which the Internet provides now—but with much greater efficiency and security.

320 The new vehicles

The modern tourism revolution began with steam-powered vehicles, and until the Information Age it was vehicle technology of one sort or another that brought about the major changes. The process is continuing. For instance, bigger and faster aircraft are on the drawing-boards in Europe and the United States. The Airbus A3XX, designed by the European Airbus Industrie consortium to seat 550 on two decks, is expected to be flying by 2004. In the United States McDonnell Douglas, now part of Boeing, has tested models of a giant flying wing capable of carrying 800 passengers. It could be in the air by 2010.

European, American and Japanese manufacturers have been working on possible replacements for the supersonic Concorde airliner. The Boeing company favours an aircraft carrying between 285 and 300 passengers at 2.4 times the speed of sound, with a range of 10 000 kilometres.[14]

Experiments are also being made with new forms of propulsion, which will be as revolutionary in reducing travel time as the steam engine was in the nineteenth century. One method in which scientists see great promise is the so-called 'air spike system'. American and Russian engineers have been experimenting with microwave energy, with the idea of creating shock waves ahead of a saucer-shaped vehicle and harnessing them to produce speeds of up to 24 000 kilometres per hour. Commercial craft propelled by this method could take passengers between Australian cities and New York in under an hour; part of the journey would be a glide through space.

Hypersonic shock tunnel tests of various aspects of this propulsion system have been conducted since 1995 by Dr Leik Myrabo, Associate Professor of Engineering Physics at Rensselaer Polytechnic Institute in Troy, New York. These proved that the theory worked for speeds up to Mach 10 (more than 11 250 kilometres per hour)—not yet full speed, but a promising start. The scene then moved to Edwards Air Force Base in California, where in 1998 Dr Myrabo used pulsed laser energy to propel tiny models of the 'lightcraft' 30 metres into the air.

The success of these experiments led the United States Air Force and the National Aeronautics and Space Administration (NASA) to jointly fund further development, with the aim of producing a twelve-person, 20-metre-diameter lightcraft by 2025.

The size of the lightcraft is dependent on the low-altitude power satellite necessary to beam the microwaves to the vehicle. The solar-powered satellite needed to produce the energy for a 20-metre lightcraft will be shaped like a bicycle wheel, ten thousandths of an inch

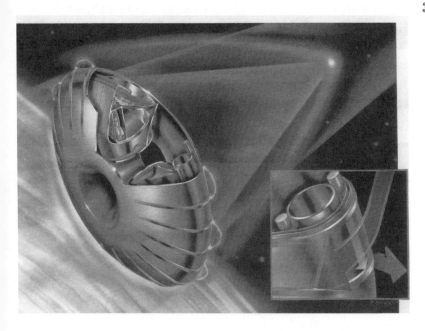

The shape of flight to come. Artist: P. DiMare. (Published by permission of NASA and the US Air Force Research Laboratory)

The saucer-shaped lightcraft in flight around 2025, travelling at speeds of up to 24 000 kilometres per hour. Electrodes can be seen in the drawing set around the rim of the craft and superconducting magnets are shown in the cutaway. The lightcraft uses electrodes, magnets and special antennae to create motive power. The fuel consists of microwaves converted from solar energy by low-altitude satellites and beamed to the craft, where they are picked up by antennae that refocus them at points just outside the rim. The microwaves heat the air, turning it into an ionised gas—plasma—that acts as a conductor for air between the electrodes. The interaction of flowing current and magnetic fields along the rim produces the thrust to propel the vehicle. Computers change the direction of the thrust for steering. An internal antenna focuses microwaves ahead of the craft to create an 'air spike' which acts as a nose cone, greatly reducing drag. The inset shows the flow of forces at the vehicle's edge. The upper circling arrow represents the accelerated airflow and the lower arrow the applied magnetic field. The intersecting arrow indicates the direction of the electric current. The magnetic coils can be seen on either side of the toroidal tube, which is part of the main structure of the craft.

322 (0.010 inch = 0.254 mm) thick and a kilometre in diameter. In 1998 NASA began studying the feasibility of building this extraordinary structure and putting it into space.

There is still a long way to go, but a picture of future long-range travel by lightcraft is emerging. It will be environmentally friendly—the lightcraft will not carry fossil fuel to produce noxious emissions, nor will it create a sonic boom. It will be relatively cheap, reducing the cost of space travel by a factor of 1000—it cost between $US5000 and $8000 to put a kilogram of cargo into space in the late 1990s; the lightcraft will reduce this to below $US10 per kilogram. It will not require airports: using solar power, the lightcraft will be able to 'motor' between passenger pick-up points at between 50 and 80 kilometres per hour before going to a microwave boost station to take off for another continent via space.[15]

In general, land travel in the future will be faster and safer and the vehicles far different from those of today. A new generation of superfast trains will not have wheels. A new technology, magnetic levitation ('maglev'), will result in the introduction of trains that will run up to 700 kilometres per hour within the first decade of the new century.

With maglev, magnetic power is used to lift the train and guide it forward millimetres above the track. Power is transferred into the carriage while the train is in motion to provide electricity for lights and other services. The linear motors have no moving parts, so the trains will travel without noise or vibration.

Experimental models have been built in Germany and Japan. One of the most advanced is at Emsland in the north of Germany, operating on a 31.5-kilometre test track. The consortium developing the system includes aircraft manufacturer Messerschmitt-Bolkow-Blohm (MBB), and the train has been designed to compete with aircraft. The Japanese maglev system is being developed by the Railway Technical Research Institute. A test vehicle achieved speeds of 517 kilometres per hour on a seven-kilometre test track in 1979 and a prototype maglev train made its first trial run on a 42.7-kilometre track near Tokyo in 1997.

The limiting factor for maglev is that an entirely new infrastructure is necessary; it is not possible to change existing track to suit it. Therefore it will be used mostly in heavily-travelled corridors where the potential revenue can justify the cost of building guideways. The first operational line in Germany is being built between Hamburg and Berlin, where the first train is due to run in 2004.[16]

The first Australian very fast train, to run between Sydney and Canberra, will have wheels, but the big corridor is Sydney–Melbourne and a maglev train could make the journey between city centres in about two hours. It is probably the only route in Australia on which, at present, the maglev train could make money.[17]

An immense amount of work is taking place around the world to make motor vehicles more efficient, less damaging to the environment and safer. The world's motor vehicle population was about 650 million in 1998 and is expected to reach one billion by 2025.[18] As motor vehicles already account for more than 20 per cent of the world's energy usage and are the cause of much of its pollution, it is essential to ensure that cars of the future use much less energy and produce much less pollution.

The ultimate aim is to do away with petrol-driven cars and their noxious fumes. But they are likely to continue to dominate roads in the next few decades, so making their engines more efficient and less damaging to the environment is of great importance. One research program in the United States is attempting to produce a car that will be able to travel 2000 kilometres on a single tank of petrol.

In the longer term we can expect environmentally-friendly vehicles that use one or more sources of energy other than petrol: electricity, methanol, natural gas or hydrogen. Some experimental cars have been built and tested which significantly reduce emissions compared with petrol-driven cars. Electric vehicles are the closest to providing pollution-free transport while, of the liquid or gas fuels, hydrogen is the cleanest because its only significant by-product is steam. Methanol and liquefied or compressed natural gas burn more cleanly than petrol; experimental engines that use them have reached efficiencies comparable to those of conventional internal combustion engines.

Research is also taking place into fuel cells, in which hydrogen and oxygen react to create water, generating an electrical flow, and hybrid systems in which a small liquid-fuel engine is used to extend the range of a battery-electric car.[19] Ford, Daimler Benz and Ballard Power Systems announced an alliance in 1998 to develop a fuel cell power train to support the commercialisation of fuel cells by 2004.[20]

The car of the future will monitor itself, its surroundings, its driver and the road. Vehicles will progress from being completely controlled by the driver to depending on the driver mainly for steering. In the more distant future cars may even drive themselves on roads in which sensors have been planted.

Navigational devices have been installed in the more expensive cars for some time. These use global positioning systems (GPSs), which rely on satellites to pinpoint the position of a car and provide directions to

324 a given destination. They will be improved and fitted to cheaper cars and make life easier for tourists driving in unfamiliar surroundings.

There is a prediction, too, of a 'Great Global Highway' connecting five continents and more than one hundred countries. Australia is not one of them because joining it by bridge or tunnel to other land masses is not yet contemplated, but no doubt Australians will be among the first who drive around the other continents.

> Imagine driving from Scandinavia down to Europe, across Germany, France, and Spain, then through a tunnel at Gibraltar to Africa. After circling the continent, you leave the eastern Mediterranean and drive across much of Asia and China before moving up along the Pacific Coast to Siberia. Using a tunnel beneath the Bering Strait, you join the Pan-American Highway across Canada, the United States, Mexico, and Central America. Driving from Panama over the elevated highway spanning the Darien Gap, you arrive in Colombia. Then you are free to visit the various nations of South America.
>
> Not too far into the twenty-first century, the news media will document the first such tour. (M. Conway, 'Super projects: rebuilding and improving our planet, *The Futurist*, 1996)[21]

Technology and the industry

It is sometimes easier to make predictions about the effect of technology on travel and tourism businesses in the more distant future than to contemplate the next few years. This is certainly true of information technology. For instance, we can say with confidence that the global distribution systems will disappear in their present form, but how will their services be integrated into a post-Internet system and when? That is too hard a question to answer.

The present travel agency system will disappear in time, but at least part of its function will remain: the need for interpretation and advice, for first-hand knowledge to support electronic information retrieval. Travel agents themselves expect a change, which is also being driven by airline cost-cutting. Despite dire predictions of its imminent demise over the previous five years, at the end of 1998 the travel agency system in Australia was bigger and stronger than ever. Change will come, but when?

Some believe that technology will revolutionise the hospitality industry. The International Hotel & Restaurant Association, at its 1997 conference, brought together a 'Think Tank' of 47 representatives from **325** leading technology companies and hotel organisations to discuss the future. They decided that the global hospitality industry could not continue in its present form. The major driver of change was the Internet.

It will redefine how guests discover and purchase hospitality products, and how hotels and restaurants interact with their suppliers. (WTO, *Tourism and Technology Bulletin*, 1997)[22]

Among the findings of the Think Tank were:

- The Internet was giving rise to a new sense of immediacy created by real-time transactions.
- Customers armed with instantly available information were more demanding.
- Hoteliers should develop the use of data warehousing and data mining techniques to make sense of the huge volume of guest information collected electronically.

The implication of this was that the hospitality industry could not continue as it had because the Internet was changing the customer. The 'segment of one' was becoming the norm.

Internet technology enables us to customize the hotel product and anticipate individual needs and expectations. This determines our edge in a competitive environment and provides the added value hotel guests are now seeking. (Rudi Scherb, a Think Tank participant, 1997)[23]

Technology and the customers

The electronic networks are supporting two marketing strategies concurrently: globalisation and segmentation. The number of products being offered is increasing enormously and so is the market reach; at the same time products are becoming more specific and take into consideration individual preferences.

Theories like 'the segment of one' and 'mass customisation' are appropriate for the hospitality industry's business market and are in harmony with the characteristics of the 'new tourist' of the 1980s (see pages 145–6), who can be seen turning away from escorted groups and the standardised offerings of tour operators in favour of more personalised travel experiences. Ken Chamberlain, a former executive of the

326   Pacific Asia Travel Association, had his own name for them: the 'curious travellers':

> They do not take to artificial waterfalls, crazy shaped swimming pools and potted plants. They prefer the real thing and want to get out of the built environment into the natural one. Many of them like hiking, diving, wildlife or following some other special interest. They want to mix with the local community and experience the local culture. They are looking for a unique experience not a rest ... (Chamberlain, in a paper delivered at Southern Cross University's Tourism Executive Development Program, 1997)[24]

We can find these tourists so interesting that we forget they are not the majority. To them 'small' may be beautiful, but it is 'big' that makes money. As examples, Chamberlain points to the huge cruise ships of more than 100 000 tons, the tallest hotel in the world on the Dubai shoreline and a 1000-room resort with three 18-hole golf courses on the small island of Antigua.

Many people just want to have fun when they travel; they do not want to risk 'the paradoxes and fiascos and spiritual perils of tourism'.[25] They are the 'indulgent tourists', those who fill the large cruise ships or stay in man-made surroundings, usually preferring the hotel pool to the ocean and a theme park to a local village. Often indulgent tourists will only leave a resort to go on the obligatory sightseeing tour with shopping.

> They look for as much luxury, glamour and name brand as they can get for the money they are prepared to pay...
>
> Whatever one's view, without this market segment, many aircraft, hotels and tour buses would lie unprofitably empty and many of us would be unemployed. (Chamberlain, op.cit., 1997)[26]

Which should Australian travel and tourism operators cater for in the future—the curious tourists or the indulgent tourists? Both, no doubt, but in what proportion? A mix of attractions is necessary to ensure growth in an environment of increasing complexity and competitiveness. But getting the mix right may not be easy in what E. L. Shafer and G. Moeller call 'a world of paradoxes in tourism and leisure ... where existing opposites operate simultaneously'.[27]

They point out that these days the same individuals shop at both down- and up-market shops and go to McDonald's for lunch and a four-star restaurant for dinner. Accountants sky-dive, campers drive 4air-conditioned vans to rough it in the country. Consumer tastes and preferences are changing rapidly and the multiple-profile consumer is **327** here to stay.

> ...the conventional ways of looking at tourism behavior are not only outdated but dangerous, and new approaches for analyzing the market need to consider the effects of oncoming [science and technology] on future demand and supply... Furthermore, in the tourism strategic planning game, many times it is the S&T *outside* the normal sphere of tourism research that can affect most dramatically tourism demand and supply patterns. (E. L. Shafer & G. Moeller, 'Science and technology in tourism', in Witt & Moutinho, eds, *Tourism Marketing and Management Handbook*, 1994)[28]

Managing future tourism

The management of tourism and its impacts will become critical as the number of overseas tourists in Australia doubles and triples and keeps on growing.[29] Scale matters: the more tourists there are the more important it is that we are alert to potential problems, and that our facilities, institutions and procedures are adequate to the task.

This is one area where we can learn from the mistakes of the past. There is no shortage of examples: failing to manage the tourism inflow from some Asian markets, which resulted in low yields and customer dissatisfaction; building hotels in the wrong places for the wrong reasons;[30] allowing planning controls to 'slip through bureaucratic cracks';[31] making tourist visas in some countries much easier to obtain through the introduction of the Electronic Travel Authority System (ETAS) and more costly in countries where it is difficult to get one, such as the emerging markets of China and India; and so on.

A considerable number of government agencies at all levels and industry associations are involved in the tourism management process. Some of the government agencies—departments or authorities—are not specifically concerned with tourism, but are involved with the physical, regulatory, fiscal and social framework in which tourism operates.

There is a clear need for improvement in some areas; for example in the administration of planning controls between the various levels of government—and perhaps in the controls themselves. A 1998 report spoke of 'a disjointed approach by bureaucracy [making] the already risky business of developing regional tourism harder'.[32] Part of the problem is a difference in cultures—private enterprise and public service—and basic lack of communication.

328   Town planners have generally not been exposed or achieved any
significant understanding of the market dynamics which drive the
tourism industry and as a result have often found it easier to
ignore tourism or deal with it in a peripheral way. (D. Dredge &
S. Moore, 'A methodology for the integration of tourism in town
planning', *Journal of Tourism Studies*, 1992)[33]

The environment will continue to be a matter of concern and dispute in
Australia well into the twenty-first century. The industry is already tack-
ling the issues of conserving resources and minimising the ecological
effects of tourism and sustainability, but good practice is by no means
universal and controls are not always sufficient. Projects still go ahead
without adequate environmental or social impact studies.

Within the industry, issues relating to sustainability are the responsibility not only of developers, but also of marketers. Sustainability
issues can affect decisions on the desired rate of growth of tourism, on
whether to promote to mass markets or the independent traveller and on
the provision of products that (a) cater for the growing interest in
nature tourism and (b) minimise social and environmental impacts.

Sustainable tourism is not cheap—it needs a responsible
approach, careful management and controlled planning, creative
and selective marketing, education and training. (A. Jefferson,
'Prospects for tourism—a practitioner's view', *Travel Management*,
1995)[34]

Government and industry co-operation

In the 1990s Australia, with its federal system, was not short of government organisations that had been created specifically to develop
and market tourism. The variety and number of organisations had
made co-ordination—and therefore coherent management—difficult
in the past. The production of the first national tourism plan by the
Commonwealth government in 1998 was a step in the right direction;
co-ordination in planning is the best hope for co-ordination in implementation. However, prospects would have been improved if the States,
Territories and regions had had more direct involvement in the planning process.

The most powerful organisation at the Commonwealth level was the
Department (or Office) of Tourism. It exercised influence over the
ATC,[35] the Tourism Forecasting Council and the Bureau of Tourism
Research. But its most important function was that of representing
tourism interests to Cabinet.[36] The Department also carried the respon-

sibility for development of the industry. In its relationship with the **329**
industry, it suffered from being a government department in Canberra
(or part of one) with a detachment from the realities of commercial
life and from the adoption of what was primarily an economist's view
of tourism.

The ATC, charged with the marketing of Australian tourism overseas,
had the confidence of the Australian travel and tourism industry and
was something of a public icon. The industry looked upon the budget
allocated to the ATC each year as a barometer of the Commonwealth
government's support of tourism.

The eight State and Territory tourism organisations had grown from
public service-style bureaus into sophisticated, professional bodies that
had no parallels in other fields of endeavour in Australia. They were
partly commercial, partly institutional 'half-way houses' between
industry and government (see pages 276–86). They did not split functions with others, as did the federal tourism organisations, and so they
could tackle a range of marketing, developmental and regulatory objectives in a co-ordinated way. They had relationships with the industry at
various levels, including the regions.[37]

Tourism Council Australia (TCA) was the main national association
for the Australian travel and tourism industry. It was generally uncritical
of government agencies; for example, it was more interested in seeing
that the ATC got what it considered an adequate budget than in worrying about how the money was spent. However, in 1998 it showed that
it was prepared to play a role co-ordinating some State governments'
activities in domestic tourism.

There was also a need for co-ordination of development plans
between different levels of government and an argument for giving
them a new focus. Most government plans had Australian social, economic and political needs as their basis. The logic for this was perfectly
reasonable from a government's point of view and few would quarrel
with programs such as those aimed at increasing the variety and viability of regional and rural tourism. However, from an industry point of
view messages from the marketplace were extremely important, and
these seemed to be ignored. For instance, there was no response to well-
publicised calls for new destination areas by Japanese tour operators in
the first half of the 1990s as high growth levels from Japan fell away.[38]

The difficulties of marketing co-operation between organisations
with different business cultures and different objectives had been com-
pounded by a policy of demarcation over the years. While the intention
had been admirable—avoiding duplication by agreement on what
organisations should do—in practice demarcation had not worked.

330   This was most noticeable overseas. With the formation of the ATC in 1967 it was thought that the States and Territories would confine themselves to domestic promotion. However, Western Australia took a promotional team to North America in 1974 and within a few years the States and the Northern Territory had begun to open overseas offices. In the 1990s there were more than 40 of them—most of them small, some of them of doubtful quality—with little status in the marketplace. From an overall Australian point of view this hardly made sense, though in a country as big as Australia at least some of the States and Territories had distinctively different attitudes to markets because of access, distance and varying attractions. Therefore, they viewed direct overseas representation as essential.

The problem of who should do what overseas between the States and Territories and the ATC arose first in the late 1970s, when the Tourism Ministers' Council agreed on what functions should be undertaken by the different organisations and what responsibilities should be shared. Demarcation discussions had been going on from time to time since and in 1990 became detached from reality, when the Tourism Ministers' Council agreed on guidelines summarised as follows:

- The ATC has prime responsibility for marketing the 'Australia' brand as an international destination to overseas consumers
- the States and Territories have prime responsibility for undertaking trade marketing activities for their respective areas
- the industry has a key role in product development and promotion.[39]

These guidelines could not work because they split the marketing effort between organisations that had different objectives. They might have had some merit if all the parties involved worked to the same marketing plan, but of course they did not. Co-ordinating a marketing plan containing a diversity of action plans can be difficult enough within a single organisation, as happened with the Hogan campaign in the United States in the early 1980s. Here a vital element of the marketing plan was not carried out and the whole plan failed. Allotting different organisations the 'prime responsibility' for different marketing functions when there was not a common planning mechanism was a prescription for failure.[40]

While experience showed that demarcation did not work, it also proved that co-operation did. The Partnership Australia program, an initiative of the ATC, was an example that showed how that organisation, State and Territory organisations and the industry could work together successfully—a microcosm perhaps of how the whole overseas marketing effort might have worked if it had been planned that way.

TCA adopted the formula with its Partnership Australia Domestic program in the late 1990s. Originally titled the Australian Domestic Tourism Initiative, it looked unpromising when the States refused to fund a generic advertising campaign. But in late 1998 TCA announced that it and the States had formed an advisory committee under the Partnership Australia Domestic (PAD) name. Among the initiatives proposed was a national online tourism network of all domestic product, which for the first time would give Australia a national product inventory. Other key points of agreement concerned a national events strategy and an enhanced research effort to provide a better understanding of the domestic tourism market. The ATC managing director, John Morse, was to be consultative member of PAD because of the ATC's experience with Partnership Australia.[41]

The directive taking away from the ATC the prime responsibility for work with the industry in overseas markets had the potential to do the most harm. If history has taught us anything about destination marketing, it is that the first responsibility of a national tourism organisation is to understand the industry in the market it is operating in—the structure, the links, the destination preferences and, in particular, the thinking of the influence leaders. Only when the industry is ready to play its part can the NTO properly plan its approach to the consumer (which may be direct or jointly with the trade).

In the 1990s support for tourism from all levels of government in Australia was stronger than ever, but overseas national governments had been showing increasing signs of disengagement from tourism.

> The trend partly reflects the increased efforts on the part of governments to curb public expenditure. But it is also due to the growing climate of liberalisation over the past decade—not to mention the political and economic shift to market driven economies—which have encouraged a re-examination of activities traditionally undertaken by the public sector. (WTO, *Towards New Forms of Public–Private Sector Partnership*, 1996)[42]

In some cases the structure of a country's national tourism organisation had been changed so that the industry and government planned and implemented overseas programs, and paid for them, jointly. In Australia the industry made substantial contributions to the ATC budget, but this was to pay for individual companies' involvement in promotional opportunities, which the ATC organised. Other countries produced programs that accommodated both national 'branding'

332 promotion and the promotion of specific interests of industry sectors or individual companies. The French Tourist Office, Maison de la France, even funded new overseas offices without any contribution from the French government.[43]

Whether or not Australia will follow suit is problematic, but some time in the future it is possible. Such a change would require willingness on the parts of both the Commonwealth government and the travel and tourism industry.

The Commonwealth government might welcome a combination private–public sector organisation if it placed less reliance on government funding than there is under the current arrangement. It might also be prepared to remove some of the administrative restraints that are imposed on the ATC; this would be a considerable advantage in overseas operations.[44]

From an industry viewpoint, the major deterrent to a joint venture is the old one: big budgets are needed for destination promotion and it is not possible to persuade industry members to contribute to generic promotions for which they cannot relate their expenditure to their own profit and loss statements. The industry has seen its role as being to persuade governments to spend as much money as they can on tourism, and as a consequence it has accepted government leadership.[45]

But times are changing. While small companies will still predominate, collectively the industry will grow in size, wealth and influence in the years to come. Universities are already helping to bring about changes in thinking. Those entering managerial ranks now have usually been given a broader education in tourism than their counterparts 20 years ago. As they reach senior positions, accustomed to working in a globalised industry and with a much wider array of research available to them, they can be expected to see the need for the industry to assert itself more than it has in the past. In the 1990s TCA initiatives in research, regional tourism and, in particular, domestic tourism indicated that the process had already begun.

We can only guess how far it will go, but from necessity there must be more fusion of interests, ideas and procedural mechanisms on both the demand and the supply sides in the future.

A final question: can our product stay Australian?

While technology and research help travel and tourism businesses find out more about their customers' preferences, it still takes people to deliver what they want. Interesting tales have been told about

Australian service, like the Len Evans story of the waitress shouting at breakfast guests 'Ands up oos for porridge' (page 114) or, going back to an earlier period, the response to a guest in a Brisbane inn inquiring about dinner: 'You'll have to take what ye can get.' (page 56).

Some Australians believe that as a nation we are still not service-oriented—that we find giving service demeaning. This is an illusion. Statistics quoted by King (1994) showed that 89 per cent of American tourists and 83 per cent of Japanese were satisfied with the service provided in Australian hotels and restaurants, with only 6 per cent dissatisfied in either case.[46]

A huge effort goes into service training; formal TAFE hospitality courses, in-house training and the AussieHost scheme are part of this. Then we have a nation-wide quality assurance program run by Tourism Council Australia, a widely-supported industry accreditation program in Victoria and other accreditation schemes administered by individual trade associations.

Has all this 'homogenised' us? In following internationally accepted standards, have we helped make Australia like every other place on the world tourism circuit? Today our waiters and waitresses dress as if they were from Europe, but in learning which side to serve from have they lost their Australian individuality?

We have a theme park that mimics Hollywood; the cuisines of the four corners of the world can be found in our restaurants; many of our hotels carry international brand-names; our products are listed in global distribution systems; our population is cosmopolitan. Can we say our tourism product is essentially Australian?

It can be argued that it is, because it is here. Australia is different from any other country; Australians on the whole are different from any other people. Just because some dress the way they do so that you know a waiter when you see one, or because a tourist can have a Batman ride on the Gold Coast, or eat a croissant in the Sydney Hilton hotel to a formula devised in Montreal, this does not mean that the setting and the overall ambience, style and customs that distinguish Australia from elsewhere are obliterated. As for service, well-trained Australians have proven that they can not only perform as well as anybody else, but that they often do so with an attractive, open attitude that visitors find distinctive and refreshing.

But other questions remain. Have we developed tourism product which cannot be sampled elsewhere, and which leaves those who have experienced it a sense of uniqueness? Is it authentic?

334   We have seen how a distinctive Australian cuisine was developed by applying experience with imported food styles to Australian foods. That makes Australian cuisine a hybrid. The same could be said of the Australian tourism product generally: some of it represents imported innovations and values; some of it is unmistakably Australian; the overall flavour is distinctive.

It was ever thus. Our early theme parks were based on those in London or Coney Island, just as today's Warner Bros. Movie World is directly derived from Hollywood. However, Australian individuality is represented in attractions built in recent decades—for example, Sovereign Hill, Old Sydney Town, the Tjapukai Aboriginal Cultural Park and our maritime museums.

While Australian cities may have some of the same features as cities anywhere, they also have those that belong to them alone—the Sydney Opera House and the Melbourne Cricket Ground, for example. The outback is unmistakably Australian and so is most of the tourism product associated with it. The great natural attractions—Ayers Rock (Uluru), the Flinders Ranges, Monkey Mia, the Great Barrier Reef and the whole island of Tasmania—could not be somewhere else.

> We are intrigued and fascinated by unusual and scenic natural environments and by the different lifestyles and characteristics of people outside our communities. It is these differences that motivate large numbers of people to travel. (L. E. Heber, cited in B. King, 1988)[47]

Since Australians first began promoting tourism they have been conscious of the need to define their products in terms that differentiated them from others. They have used unique natural features like the Great Barrier Reef and Ayers Rock and man-made structures like Sydney's Harbour Bridge and then its Opera House as symbols that would create an image recognisable as Australian. King has cited Ayers Rock as an example of tourism appropriating the icons of regional and national identity.[48] It could also be argued that it was the other way round: tourism helped define the elements of regional and national identity and made icons out of some of them. The history of Australian travel and tourism represents a significant contribution to the development of Australian nationhood.

ENDNOTES

1 Horne, D. (1992), *The Intelligent Tourist*, Margaret Gee Publishing, Sydney, p. ix.

2 'Trends and forecasts for the new millennium', *The Futurist*, Aug.–Sept.1998, p. 54.

3 But even then, the 'tyranny of distance' still applied. Only about 25 000 Australians travelled overseas in a year and the number of visitors to Australia was but a few thousand more. Immediately after the Second World War, airliners were flying between the two countries in just under two days. Nevertheless, it was 1962 before 100 000 overseas visitors came to Australia in a single year and 1963 before Australians made 100 000 trips abroad. It was jet aircraft, offering faster and cheaper travel, that finally made the difference. In the late 1990s Australians were making some three million trips abroad annually and people from overseas were making well over four million visits to this country. Australia was a considerable participant in the mass movement of peoples.

4 *WTO News*, issue 1, March 1997, p. 1.

5 Cairncross, F. (1997), *The Death of Distance*, Harvard Business School Press, Boston, Mass., p. 4.

6 Among them a vast increase in long-distance telephone capacity because of satellites and the extensive laying of fibre-optic cable; a big increase in the number of television channels because of digital compression and satellite broadcasts to small dishes attached to homes; the invention of the World Wide Web in 1989 and a multi-media browser in 1993, which opened up the Internet to non-academic users.

7 Cover, S. (1996), ed., *Beyond the Internet: Restructuring the Communications Market*, Analysys Publications, Cambridge, UK, p. ix, cited by Cairncross, op.cit., p. 2.

8 James Strong, Qantas managing director, *The Australian Financial Review*, 24–25 October 1998, p. 28.

9 Cairncross, op.cit., p. 87.

10 'A survey of electronic commerce', *The Economist*, 10 May 1977, p. 4.

11 Cairncross, op.cit., p. 89.

12 Of course, computers were always digital. Telephone and television networks are converting from analogue to digital format. Set top boxes allow people to use the television set as a simple PC, sending and receiving e-mail and exploring the World Wide Web. Screen telephones perform the normal functions of telephones and also provide access to the Internet and other networks, displaying text and graphics on a small screen. There was some small distribution of set top boxes in Australia in 1998, but a more extensive sales effort was expected to be made in 1999. In 1998 several screen telephones were under consideration for distribution in Australia the following year.

13 Cairncross, op.cit., pp. 117–18.

14 *Weekend Australian*, 11–12 July 1998, Cover IT, pp. 4–5; *Air Transport World*, September 1995, p. 61; *Herald Sun*, 9 September 1998.

15 Dr Leik Myrabo, interviews December 1998, January 1999. Although early lightcraft may be relatively small and able to move at car-like speeds at low altitudes over short distances, they should not be envisioned as family car replacements. The object is to replace B747-type jets with lightcraft. They will not be craft just for the elite, like the Concorde.

16 Eastham, T. R. (1995), 'High-speed rail: Another Golden Age', *Scientific American*, September, p. 74A; *Weekend Australian*, 1–2 March 1997; *SYTE*, pp. 1 & 7.

17 *Weekend Australian*, 1-2 March, 1997; *SYTE*, pp. 1 & 7. Professor John Black, of the University of New South Wales, said the maglev was 'the only medium that could seriously challenge air travel. The tilt train would only compete against existing rail services.'

He also said: 'A Sydney–Melbourne link might make money, but a Perth–Melbourne link—far too expensive' (p. 7).

[18] Molitor, op.cit., p. 58.

[19] Zetsche, D. (1995), 'The automobile: Clean and customized', *Scientific American*, September, p. 79. Also *The Futurist*, Nov.–Dec. 1995, pp. 8 & 11; *Tech Notes*, Spring 1996, bulletin from Pacific Northwest National Laboratory, which is involved in the New Generation Vehicle research program of the US Council for Automotive Research.

[20] *The Australian Financial Review*, 28 January 1998, p. 14. The report stated that Ballard was a pioneer in fuel cell development, while Ford had developed advanced electric power-train technology and Daimler-Benz had experimented with alternative drive systems and automotive fuels. The new technology would not see the end of the internal combustion engine in the short term, but Ford had made the point that products with a lower environmental impact would be a competitive factor in the next century.

[21] M. Conway, 'Super projects: Rebuilding and improving our planet', *The Futurist*, March–April 1996, p. 30.

[22] WTO (1997), *Tourism and Technology Bulletin*, August–September, 1997, p. 9.

[23] Rudi Scherb, general manager of the ANA Hotel Singapore, a Think Tank participant, in WTO (1997), op.cit., p. 9.

[24] Chamberlain (1997), p. 7.

[25] Horne, op.cit., p. x. He used these words in referring to writers of a certain kind of text-book, but they also fit the 'indulgent tourist'.

[26] Chamberlain, op.cit., p. 7.

[27] 'Science and technology in tourism' in *Tourism Marketing and Management Handbook*, eds S. F. Witt & L. Moutinho, 2nd edn, Prentice Hall International (UK) Inc., Hemel Hempstead, p. 381.

[28] ibid., p. 381.

[29] While the bulk of tourism in Australia is domestic, the main growth is from overseas and, given the type of facilities needed for overseas tourism, its influence is paramount in considering most management issues. The proportion of expenditure from overseas tourism will change. For Australia as a whole it was 25% in 1995–96, measured by expenditure. By the year 2010 New South Wales, Australia's biggest tourism State, expects that nearly 80% of its tourism revenue will be from international markets (Tourism New South Wales, *New South Wales Tourism Masterplan to 2010*, 1996, p. 29).

[30] In the mid to late 1980s developers and financiers 'were primarily motivated by rising property values and potential capital gains rather than by considerations of cash flow and operational revenues'. (King, B. & McVey, M., 1996, 'Accommodation: Hotels in Australia', *Travel & Tourism Analyst*, no. 2, p. 38).

[31] *The Weekend Australian*, Financial review, 14–15 March 1998, p. 8.

[32] ibid. The report was prepared by Arthur Andersen for the Tourism Task Force.

[33] 'A methodology for the integration of tourism in town planning', *The Journal of Tourism Studies*, vol. 3, no. 1, p. 9.

[34] 'Prospects for tourism—a practitioner's view', *Travel Management*, vol. 16, no. 2, p. 104. The establishment of a Co-operative Research Centre (CRC) for Sustainable Tourism by the Commonwealth government, with industry support, is an indication that the issue is being taken seriously in Australia.

[35] Besides having responsibility for administering the Australian Tourist Commission Act, the Department is represented on the ATC board and can directly influence the ATC marketing policy as the result of the Act, which in part reads like a primer in corporate and operational planning. It requires the ATC to submit to the Minister each year the corporate plan, and a revision of the corporate plan, which 'has no effect until it is

approved, in writing, by the Minister.' In 1995 the author asked an assistant secretary in **337** the Department how successive governments managed to find ministers who were experts in tourism planning. He said that of course it was not really the Minister who made the judgements—meaning it was the Department, which then advised the Minister.

[36] In the second Howard Government in late 1998 there was a Minister for Sport and Tourism outside the Cabinet. The Office of Tourism was part of the Department of Industry, Science and Resources and it was the Minister who carried that portfolio who represented tourism in Cabinet.

[37] All States and the Northern Territory have regional systems.

[38] Examples can be found in *The Australian*, 'Lack of top-class resorts threatens Japanese tourism', 19 October 1994, p. 3; *The Australian Financial Review*, 5 August 1993, 'Honeymoon is over for Japanese tourists', pp. 1 & 3.

[39] Commonwealth Department of Tourism (1992), *Tourism: Australia's Passport to Growth: A National Tourism Strategy* (1993), Implementation Progress Report no. 1, Canberra, p. 19. The full guidelines are given as Appendix D, p. 92.

[40] The directive taking away from the ATC the 'prime responsibility' for work with the industry in overseas markets had the potential to do the most harm. If history has taught us anything about destination marketing, it is that the first responsibility of a national tourism organisation is to understand the industry in the market it is operating in—the structure, the links, the destination preferences and, in particular, the thinking of the influence leaders. Only when the industry is ready to play its part can the NTO properly plan its approach to the consumer (which may be direct or jointly with the trade).

[41] TCA media release, 12 November 1998.

[42] WTO (1996), p. 1.

[43] ibid., p. 19. The Taiwan office, opened in February 1995, was being funded by selected members and partners of Maison de la France, including the Champagne-Ardennes provincial tourist office, the French Railways, the department store chain Galéries Lafayette, the inbound operator-cum-sightseeing company Paris Vision, and the Concord Hotels group.

[44] The reason for the current restraints has little to do with a power grab by tourism bureaucrats, but a lot to do with a desire to protect ministers from attack and an ingrained suspicion of statutory authorities in general, not just the ATC, in powerful departments like Treasury, Finance and Prime Minister and Cabinet.

[45] And government likes to control. 'He who pays the piper calls the tune' is an often-repeated proverb in Canberra. Another problem is that few in the industry understand the finer points of destination marketing, although this is changing due to better education.

[46] King, B. (1994). 'Bringing out the authentic in Australian hospitality products for the international tourist: A service management approach', *Australian Journal of Hospitality Management*, vol. 1, no. 1, pp. 1–7.

[47] ibid, p. 4.

[48] ibid.

References

Aboriginal and Torres Strait Islander Commission & National Office of Tourism (1997). *National Aboriginal and Torres Strait Islander Tourism Industry Strategy*, Canberra.

Allcock, J. B. (1994). 'Sociology of tourism' in *Tourism Marketing and Management Handbook*, eds S. F. Witt & L. Moutinho, 2nd edn, Prentice Hall International (UK) Ltd, Hemel Hempstead, pp. 73–81.

Allen, G. F. (1983). *Railways of the Twentieth Century*, Sidgwick & Jackson Ltd, London.

Anderson, K. (ed.) (1987). *Australia 200 Years and Beyond*, John Fairfax & Sons, Sydney.

Anderson, W. K. (1994). *Roads for the People: A History of Victoria's Roads*, Hyland House Publishing, Melbourne.

Andrews, G. (1994). *Ferries of Sydney*, 3rd edn, Sydney University Press in assoc. with Oxford University Press Australia, Sydney.

Archer, F. (1984). *Tell Me More: More of the Story of Menzies Hotel*, Fred Archer, Melbourne.

Atkinson, A. & Aveling, M. (1987). *Australians: 1838*, ed. A. Atkinson & M. Aveling, Australians: A Historical Library series, Fairfax, Syme & Weldon Associates, Sydney.

Atkinson, B. (1993). 'A pat on the back for ATC prophets', *Galah Gazette*, June. The *Galah Gazette* is a journal circulated to former Australian Tourist Commission staff members.

Australian Bureau of Statistics (1991). *Multicultural Australia*, Cat. no. 2505.0, ABS, Canberra.

Australian Government Inquiry into Tourism 1986 (1987). *Report*, vols 1 & 2, AGPS, Canberra.

Austroads (1997). *Roadfacts '96*, Sydney.

338

Bertie, C. H. (1927). *The Story of the Royal Hotel and the Theatre Royal,* **339** *Sydney,* Simmons Ltd, Sydney.

Blainey, G. (1975). *Triumph of the Nomads: A History of Ancient Australia,* Macmillan, Melbourne.

Bond, R. (ed.) (1997). *The Story of Aviation: A Concise History of Flight,* Greenhill Books, London.

Brendon, Piers (1991). *Thomas Cook: 150 Years of Popular Tourism,* Secker & Warburg, London.

Brett, R. (n.d.). Alan Greenway and the Travelodge story, unpublished manuscript. Brett supplied the author with a copy of the first part of the biography of Greenway he was writing.

Brimson, S. (1987). *Ansett: The Story of an Airline,* Dreamweaver Books, Sydney.

—— (1988). *The History of Australia's Airlines,* PR Books, Sydney, first published as *Flying the Royal Mail in 1984,* Dreamweaver Books, Sydney.

Brooke, S. (1984). *Railways of Australia,* Dreamweaver Books, Sydney.

Bureau of Industry Economics (1979). *Economic Significance of Tourism in Australia,* Research Report no. 4, AGPS, Canberra.

Bureau of Tourism Research, Domestic Tourism Monitor, published annually

Burke, D. (1991). *Road through the Wilderness,* NSW University Press, Sydney.

Cairncross, F. (1997). *The Death of Distance,* Harvard Business School Press, Boston, Mass.

Caldwell, J. C. (1987). 'Population' in *Australians: Historical Statistics,* ed. W. Vamplew, Australians: A Historical Library series, Fairfax, Syme & Weldon Associates, Sydney, pp. 23–41.

Cannon, M. (1993). *Melbourne after the Gold Rush,* Loch Haven Books, Melbourne.

Centre for South Australian Economic Studies (1993). *The Economic Significance of Alpine Resorts,* Adelaide.

Cervero, R. (1995). 'Why go anywhere? Millions of people could be liberated from their vehicles', *Scientific American,* September, pp. 92–3.

Chamberlain, K. (1997). International tourism: Trends, opportunities and threats, paper delivered at Southern Cross University's Tourism Executive Development Program, Ballina, NSW.

Clark, I. & Larrieu, L. (1998). Indigenous tourism in Victoria: Products, markets and futures, paper presented at 'Symbolic Souvenirs', a one-day conference on cultural tourism with the Centre for Cross-Cultural Research, ANU, Canberra.

340 Cole, R. K. (1950). 'Early Melbourne hotels', *The Victorian Historical Magazine*, vol. XXIII, no. 2, June, Royal Historical Society of Victoria, Melbourne.

Commonwealth Department of Industry, Science and Tourism (1998). *Tourism: A Ticket to the 21st Century: National Action Plan*, Canberra.

Commonwealth Department of Tourism (1992). *Tourism: Australia's Passport to Growth: A National Tourism Strategy* (1993), Implementation Progress Report no. 1, Canberra.

—— (1993). *A Talent for Tourism: Stories about Indigenous People in Tourism*, Canberra.

—— (1994). *National Ecotourism Strategy*, Canberra.

Commonwealth Department of Tourism and Recreation (1972). *Statement for the Royal Commission on Australian Government Administration*, Canberra.

Conway, M. (1996). 'Super projects: Rebuilding and improving our planet', *The Futurist*, March–April, pp. 29–33.

Correll, Ted (1986). *The History of South Australia's Department of Tourism*, South Australian Department of Tourism, Adelaide.

Corzé, J.-C. (1989). 'Theme and leisure parks' in *Tourism Marketing and Management Handbook*, eds S. F. Witt & L. Moutinho, Prentice Hall International (UK) Ltd, Hemel Hempstead, pp. 459–62.

Cottee, M. (ed.) (1995). *Beyond the Dawn: A Brief History of Qantas Airways*, Qantas Public Affairs, Sydney.

Cox, G. W. (1986). *Bass Strait Crossing*, Melanie Publications, Hobart.

Curr, E. M. (1883). *Recollections of Squatting in Victoria*, Australiana Facsimile Editions no. 130, reproduced by the Libraries Board of South Australia from a copy held in the State Library of South Australia, 1968, Adelaide.

Daniele, R. & Inbakaran, R. J. (1996). An overview of the evolution of electronic distribution of travel and tourism in Australia, working paper submitted for the Australian Tourism and Hospitality Research Conference, Southern Cross University.

Darby, G. E. (1991). 'An overview of information technology for travel agencies' in 'Telecommunications and the travel industry: Impacts on national and regional development', ed. L. S. Harms, *Proceedings of the Pacific Telecommunications Council's Mid-Year Seminar*, Bali, Indonesia.

Davis, V. C. (1959). *Let's Talk Motels: Motel Guide for Australia*, 2nd edn, The Australian Motel Magazine Company, Sydney.

Davison, G., McCarty, J. W. & McLeary, A. (eds) (1987). *Australians: 1888*, Australians: A Historical Library series, Fairfax, Syme & Weldon Associates, Sydney.

Deakin University (1986). *The Australian City. Unit A: Marvellous* **341** *Melbourne: A Study of Nineteenth Century Urban Growth*, Melbourne.

Dean, I. (1991). *Great Ocean Liners: The Heydey of Luxury Travel*, B. T. Batsford Ltd, London.

Department of School Education, Victoria (1992). *Timeline: A History of Technical Education in Victoria*, Melbourne.

Des Cars, J. & Caracalla, J. P. (1984). *The Orient-Express, A Century of Railway Adventures*, trans. George Behrend, Great Express Books, London.

Douglas, Ngaire & Douglas, Norman (1996). 'P&O's Pacific', *The Journal of Tourism Studies*, vol. 7, no. 2, pp. 2–13.

Dredge, D. & Moore, S. (1992). 'A methodology for the integration of tourism in town planning', *The Journal of Tourism Studies*, vol. 3, no. 1, pp. 8–21.

Dunbar, S. (1915). *A History of Travel in America*, The Bobbs-Merrill Company, NY. New edn, Tudor Publishing Company, NY, 1937.

Dunstan, K. (1991). *Flag: The First 30 Years*, Flag International Ltd, Melbourne.

Dutton, G. (1984). *City Life in Old Australia*, Currey O'Neil Ross Pty Ltd, Melbourne.

Eastham, T. R. (1995). 'High-speed rail: Another Golden Age', *Scientific American*, September, pp. 74–74B.

Echtner, C. & Jamal, T. (1997). 'The disciplinary dilemma of tourism studies', *Annals of Tourism Research*, vol. 21, no. 1, pp. 868–83.

Emmett, E. T. (1958–59). History of Tasmania's Tourist Bureau, unpublished manuscript.

Faulkner, W., Pearce, P., Shaw, R. & Weiler, B. (1995). 'Tourism research in Australia: Confronting the challenges of the 1990s and beyond', in *Tourism Research and Education in Australia, Proceedings from the Council for Australian Tourism and Education Conference, Gold Coast, 1994*, Bureau of Tourism Research, Canberra, pp. 3–24.

Feifer, M. (1985). *Going Places: The Ways of the Tourist from Imperial Rome to the Present Day*, Macmillan London Ltd, London.

Ferguson, W. C. (1987). 'Mokaré's domain' in *Australians to 1788*, ed. D. J. Mulvaney & J. P. White, Australians: A Historical Library series, Fairfax, Syme & Weldon Associates, Sydney, pp. 120–45.

Finn, E. ('Garryowen') (1888). *The Chronicles of Early Melbourne 1835–1852*, vol. 2, Fergusson & Mitchell, Melbourne.

Fitzgerald, R. (1984). *A History of Queensland: From 1915 to the 1980s*, Queensland University Press, St Lucia, Qld.

Franck, I. M. & Brownstone, D. M. (1986). *The Silk Road: A History*, Facts on File Publications, NY.

342 Freeland, J. M. (1977). *The Australian Pub*, Sun Books, Melbourne.

Gee, Chuck Y. & Lurie, M. (eds) (1993). *The Story of the Pacific Asia Travel Association*, Pacific Asia Travel Association, San Francisco.

Gee, Chuck Y., Makens, James C. & Choy, Dexter J. L. (1989). *The Travel Industry*, 2nd edn, Van Nostrand Reinhold, NY.

Gilltrap, Terry & Gilltrap, Maree (1981). *Romance of Australian Transport*, Rigby Publishers Ltd, Adelaide.

Glaser, W. (1988). 'A guide to casinos in Australia', *Tempo Australia*, vol. 6, no. 25.

Goding, A. (1990). *This Bold Venture: The Story of Lake Tyers House, Place and People*, Alison Goding, Melbourne.

Goldsack, R. (1995). *Captain Cook Cruises: A Silver Jubilee*, Fendwave, Sydney.

Gould, D. (ed.) (1995). *How was it done? The Story of Human Ingenuity through the Ages*, The Readers Digest Association Ltd, London.

Griggs, T. (ed.) (1997). *Superbrands: An Insight into 65 Australian Superbrands*, Superbrands Pty Ltd, Sydney.

Gunn, J. (1989). *Along Parallel Lines: A History of the Railways of New South Wales, 1850–1986*, Melbourne University Press, Melbourne.

Hall, C. M. (1992). 'Tourism Education in Australia: Research Notes and Reports', *Annals of Tourism Research*, vol. 17, no. 1, pp. 138–9.

Harris, Kerr, Forster & Company & Stanton Robbins & Co. Inc. (1965). *Australia's Travel and Tourist Industry*, Australian National Travel Association, Melbourne.

Harrison, L. J. (1963). *Victorian Railways to '62*, Victorian Railways Publications & Betterment Board, Melbourne.

Hawkes, N. (1992). *Man on the Move: Great Journeys by Land, Sea and Air*, RD Press, Sydney.

Hibbert, C. (1997). *Wellington: A Personal History*, HarperCollins Publishers, London.

Hicks, B. (1991). 'But I wouldn't want my wife to work there! A history of discrimination against women in the hotel industry', *Australian Feminist Studies*, no. 14, Summer.

Hirschhorn, C. (1981). *The Hollywood Musical*, Octopus Books Ltd, London.

Horne, D. (1992). *The Intelligent Tourist*, Margaret Gee Publishing, Sydney.

Howard, A. (1982). *Coaches, Riverboats and Railways*, Bay Books, Kensington, NSW.

Hutchinson, G. & Ross, J. (eds) (1997). *200 Seasons of Australian Cricket*, Pan Macmillan Australia Pty Ltd in assoc. with the Australian Cricket Board, Sydney.

Hutchison, J. (1997). Tourism: Getting it right for the millennium, a **343** report to the Hon. John Moore, MP, Minister for Industry, Science and Tourism, providing industry input to the development of a National Tourism Plan, Canberra.

Hvenegaard, G. T. (1994). 'Ecotourism: A status report and conceptual framework', *The Journal of Tourism Studies*, vol. 5, no. 2, December.

Inbound Tourism Organisation of Australia (1997), *ITOA: 25 Years Serving Inbound Tourism 1971–1996*, Sydney.

Industries Assistance Commission (1989). *Travel and Tourism*, Industries Assistance Commission Report no. 423, AGPS, Canberra.

Inglis, B. (1989) 'Transport' in *Technology in Australia 1788–1988*, Australian Academy of Technological Sciences & Engineering, Melbourne.

Inskeep, E. (1991). *Town Planning: An Integrated and Sustainable Development Approach*, Van Nostrand Reinhold, NY.

International Hotel Association (1996). *Into the New Millennium: A White Paper on the Global Hospitality Industry*, Paris.

Isaacs, K. (1988). 'Aviation' in *The Australian Encyclopaedia*, vol. 1, The Australian Geographic Society, Sydney, pp. 320–39.

Jefferson, A. (1995). 'Prospects for tourism—a practitioner's view', *Travel Management*, vol. 16, no. 2, pp. 101–5.

King, B. (1994). 'Bringing out the authentic in Australian hospitality products for the international tourist: A service management approach', *Australian Journal of Hospitality Management*, vol. 1, no. 1, pp. 1–7.

King, B. & McVey, M. (1996). 'Accommodation: Hotels in Australia', *Travel & Tourism Analyst*, no. 2, pp. 38–57.

Kludos, A. (1975). *Great Passenger Ships of the World*, vol. 1, *1858–1912*, trans. Charles Hodges, Patrick Stephens Ltd, Cambridge, UK.

Koskie, J. (1987). *Ships that Shaped Australia*, Angus & Robertson, Sydney.

Lafferty, P. & Rowe, J. (1996). *The Hutchinson Dictionary of Science*, Helicon Publishing Ltd, Oxford.

Larkins, J. (1973). *Australian Pubs*, Rigby Ltd, Adelaide.

Lattin, G. W. (1990a). 'Hotels', in *Collier's Encyclopaedia*, vol. 12, Macmillan Education Co., NY.

—— (1990b). 'Motel', in *Collier's Encyclopaedia*, vol. 16, Macmillan Education Co., NY.

Lawson, W. (1949). *Blue Gum Clippers and Whale Ships of Tasmania*, facsimile edn 1986, D. & L. Book Distributors, Launceston.

Lay, M. G. (1984). *History of Australian Roads*, Special Report no. 29, Australian Road Research Board, Vermont, Victoria.

344 —— (1993). *Ways of the World: A History of the World's Roads and of the Vehicles that Used Them*, Primavera Press, Sydney.

—— (1996). 'Roads and Roadmaking' in *The Australian Encyclopaedia*, 6th edn, Australian Geographic Pty Ltd, Terrey Hills, NSW, vol. 7, pp. 2592–4.

Leiper, N. (1980). An interdisciplinary study of Australian tourism: Its scope, characteristics and consequences, with particular reference to governmental policies since 1965, thesis for the degree of Master of General Studies, University of NSW.

—— (1995). *Tourism Management*, TAFE Publications, Melbourne.

Leisure and Recreation Concepts, Inc.(1978). *Economic Profile of Dreamworld: A Proposed Family Entertainment Center in Coomera, Queensland, Australia*, Dallas, Texas.

Lindberg, K. & Johnson, R. L. (1997). 'The economic values of tourism's social impacts', *Annals of Tourism Research*, vol. 24, no. 1, pp. 90–116.

Lloyd, J. M. (1986). *Skiing into History, 1924–1984*, Ski Club of Victoria, Melbourne.

Longmire, A. (1989). *The History of St Kilda*, vol. III, *St Kilda: The Show Goes On: 1930–38*, Hudson Publishing, Melbourne.

Maddock, J. (1992). *The People Movers: A History of Victoria's Private Bus Industry 1910–1912*, Kangaroo Press, Kenthurst, NSW.

McBryde, I. (1987). 'Goods from another country: Exchange networks and the people of the Lake Eyre basin' in *Australians to 1788*, ed. D. J. Mulvaney & J. P. White, Australians: A Historical Library series, Fairfax, Syme & Weldon Associates, Sydney, pp. 252–73.

McCallum, J. (ed.) (1995). *Australia: A Gourmet's Paradise*, Focus Publishing, Sydney.

McKercher, Bob (1996). 'Differences between tourism and recreation in parks', *Annals of Tourism Research*, vol. 23, no. 3, pp. 563–75.

McRobbie, A (1984). *The Fabulous Gold Coast*, Pan News Pty Ltd, Surfers Paradise, Qld.

Mistilis, N. & Leiper, N. (1998). The Australian Tourist Commission's early years reviewed by former senior managers, submitted for publication. Originally prepared as a working paper for the 1998 Australian Tourism & Hospitality Research Conference, February 1988, Gold Coast, titled 'Policy issues of the Australian Tourist Commission: Views of some early general managers'.

Molitor, G. T. T. (1998). 'Trends and forecasts for the new millennium', *The Futurist*, August–September, pp. 55–9.

Montgomery-Massingberd, H. & Watkin, D. (1989). *The London Ritz*, new edn, Aurum Press, London.

Morley, C. L. (1990). 'What is tourism? Definitions, concepts and char- **345** acteristics', *Journal of Tourism Studies*, vol. 1, no. 1, pp. 3–8.

Mulvaney, D. J. (1987). 'The end of the beginning: 6000 years ago to 1788' in *Australians to 1788*, ed. D. J. Mulvaney & J. P. White, Australians: A Historical Library series, Fairfax, Syme & Weldon Associates, Sydney, pp. 74–112.

Mundy, G. C. (1855). *Our Antipodes: Or Residence and Rambles in the Australasian Colonies etc.*, 3rd edn, Richard Bentley, London, pp. 16–18, in *Such was Life: Select Documents in Australian Social History*, ed. R. Ward & J. Robertson (1969), Ure Smith, Sydney.

Nahum, A. (1990). *Flying Machine*, Collins Angus & Robertson, Sydney.

National Association of Australian State Road Authorities (1987). *Bush Track to Highway: 200 Years of Australian Roads*, Sydney.

Noller, J. (1994). *Milestones*, Ansett Australia Public Affairs, Melbourne.

O'Dea, D. (1997). *Tourism's Direct Economic Contribution 1995–96*, BTR Research Paper no. 3, Bureau of Tourism Research, Canberra.

Opperman, M. & Cooper, M. (1996). 'Databased marketing in the hospitality industry' in *Tourism and Hospitality Research: Australian and International Perspectives, Proceedings from the Australian Tourism and Hospitality Research Conference*, ed. Gary Prosser, Bureau of Tourism Research, Canberra.

Pacific Asia Travel Association (1992). *Endemic Tourism: A Profitable Industry in a Sustainable Environment*, ed. Ian Oelrichs & Gary Prosser, Sydney.

Parnell, N. & Broughton, T. (1988). *Flypast: A Record of Aviation in Australia*, AGPS, Canberra.

Patterson, E. (1995). Brief historical notes on tourism in Tasmania, unpublished, Hobart.

Pearce, D. (1989). *Tourism Development*, 2nd edn, Longman Scientific & Technical, Harlow, UK.

Pearce, P. L. (1993). 'Issues in Australian tourism research', in *World Tourism Trends to the Year 2000: Research Catalyst Workshop, 14–15 May 1993*, UWS Hawkesbury, University of Western Sydney.

Pemberton, B. (1979). *Australian Coastal Shipping*, Melbourne University Press, Melbourne.

Petzinger, Thomas, Jr. (1996). *Hard Landing: The Epic Contest for Power and Profits that Plunged the Airlines into Chaos*, Times Business, NY.

Piesse, R. D. (1966). 'Travel and tourism' in *Year Book Australia 1966*, Canberra, pp. 1158–84.

Plowman, P. (1992). *The Wheels Still Turn: A History of Australian Paddlewheelers*, Kangaroo Press, Sydney.

346 Poon, A. (1994). 'The "new tourism" revolution', *Travel Management*, vol. 15, no. 2.

Price, C. (1987). 'Immigration and ethnic origin' in *Australians: Historical Statistics*, ed. W. Vamplew, Australians: A Historical Library series, Fairfax, Syme & Weldon Associates, Sydney, pp. 2–22.

Priestley, S. (1984). *The Victorians: Making their Mark*, Fairfax, Syme & Weldon Associates, Sydney.

Queensland Tourist Development Board (1947). *Report on the Tourist Resources of Queensland and the Requirements for their Development*, Brisbane.

Richardson, J. I. (1995). *Travel and Tourism in Australia: The Economic Perspective*, Hospitality Press, Melbourne.

—— (1996). *Marketing Australian Travel and Tourism: Principles and Practice*, Hospitality Press, Melbourne.

Rickard, J. (1987). 'For God's sake keep us entertained!', in *Australians: 1938*, ed. B. Gammage, P. Spearritt & L. Douglas, Australians: A Historical Library series, Fairfax, Syme & Weldon Associates, Sydney.

Rizika, M. (1995). *A Quick Look at . . . U.S. Travel & Tourism Market*, Center for Advertising Services, information facility of the Interpublic Group of Companies, Inc., New York.

Rühen, C. (1995). *Pub Splendid: The Australia Hotel 1891–1971*, John Burrell in assoc. with Murray Child & Co., Cullaroy, NSW.

Russell, H. S. (1888). *The Genesis of Queensland*, Turner & Henderson, Sydney, quoted in *Such was Life: Select Documents in Australian Social History*, ed. R. Ward & J. Robertson, 1989, Ure Smith, Sydney.

Russell, J. (1982). *The First 25 Years: A History of the Australian Federation of Travel Agents Ltd*, AFTA, Sydney.

Rutledge, J. L. & Hunter, J. F. (1996). 'Relation, by States, between population and number of travel agencies', *Journal of Travel Research*, Spring, pp. 73–6.

Schmidhauser, H. (1989). 'Tourist needs and motivations' in *Tourism Marketing and Management Handbook*, ed. S. F. Witt & L. Moutinho, Prentice Hall International, Hemel Hempstead (UK) Ltd, pp. 569–72.

Seekings, J. (1989). 'Components of tourism' in *Tourism Marketing and Management Handbook*, ed. S. F. Witt & L. Moutinho, Prentice Hall International, Hemel Hempstead (UK) Ltd, pp. 57–62.

Shafer, E. L. & Moeller, G. (1994). 'Science and technology in tourism' in *Tourism Marketing and Management Handbook*, eds S. F. Witt &

L. Moutinho, 2nd edn, Prentice Hall International (UK) Inc., **347** Hemel Hempstead, pp. 381–6.

Shin, H. (1995). Aboriginal tourism, internal memorandum, Lintas Melbourne.

Sigaux, G. (1966). *History of Tourism*, Edito-Service Ltd, Geneva, English trans. Leisure Arts Ltd, London.

Sillitoe, A. (1995). *Leading the Blind: A Century of Guide Book Travel, 1815–1914*, Macmillan, London.

Simpson, M. (1995). *Old Sydney Buildings: A Social History*, Kangaroo Press, Sydney.

Spearritt, P. (1978). *Sydney since the Twenties*, Hale & Iremonger, Sydney.

—— (1987a). 'Motor vehicles' in *Australians: A Historical Dictionary*, ed. G. Alpin, S. G. Foster, M. McKernan & I. Howie-Willis, Australians: A Historical Library series, Fairfax, Syme & Weldon Associates, Sydney, pp. 276–7.

—— (1987b). 'Railways' in *Australians: A Historical Dictionary*, ed. G. Alpin, S. G. Foster, M. McKernan & I. Howie-Willis, Australians: A Historical Library series, Fairfax, Syme & Weldon Associates, Sydney, pp. 344–5.

—— (1987c). 'Cars for the people' in *Australians: From 1939*, ed. A. Curthoys, A. W. Martin & T. Rowse, Australians: A Historical Library series, Fairfax, Syme & Weldon Associates, Sydney, pp. 119–29.

Spicer, C. J. (1993). *Duchess: The Story of the Windsor Hotel*, Loch Haven Books, Main Ridge, Vic.

Steins, R. (1995). *Transportation: Milestones and Breakthroughs*, Raintree Steck-Vaughn, Austin, Texas.

Stewart, S. (1986). *Air Disasters*, Ian Allan Ltd, London.

Taylor, C. (1986). *Great Rail Non-Journeys of Australia*, University of Qld Press, St Lucia, Qld.

Taylor, J. W. R. & Munson, K. (1972). *History of Aviation*, Crown Publishers, NY.

Theobald, W. (ed.) (1994). *Global Tourism: The Next Decade*, Butterworth-Heinemann, Oxford.

Thomas, I. G. (1996). *Environmental Impact Assessment in Australia: Theory and Practice*, The Federation Press, Annandale, NSW.

Time-Life Books (1988). *Computerized Society*, Amsterdam.

Timothy, D. J. & Butler, R. W. (1995). 'Cross-border shopping, A North American perspective', *Annals of Tourism Research*, vol. 22, no. 1, pp. 16–34.

Tourism New South Wales (1995). *Regional Tourism Strategy*, Sydney.

348 —— (1996). *History of New South Wales*, paper issued by Tourism New South Wales, Sydney.

Towner, J. (1988). 'Approaches to Tourism History', *Annals of Tourism Research*, vol. 15, pp. 47–62.

Trafalgar Tours (1997). *Fifty Years of Excellence 1947–1997*, London.

Vader, J. & Lang, F. (1980). *The Gold Coast Book*, Jacaranda Press, Brisbane.

Vamplew, W. (1987). Introduction, *Australians: Historical Statistics*, ed. W. Vamplew, Australians: A Historical Library series, Fairfax, Syme & Weldon Associates, Sydney, pp. xiv–xvi.

Vamplew, W. & McLean, I. (1987). 'Transport and communications', in *Australians: Historical Statistics*, ed. W. Vamplew, Australians: A Historical Library series, Fairfax, Syme & Weldon Associates, Sydney, pp. 166–82.

Van den Hoorn, R. (1991). *Dreams, Destinations, Directions: The Changing Face of Tourism in South Australia 1900–1992*, Tourism South Australia, Adelaide.

Van de Braak (1995). 'The road less traveled', *BYTE*, October, pp. 17–20.

Walker, F. (1921). 'Australian roadside inns', *The Royal Australian Historical Society Journal and Proceedings*, vol. VII, no. III, pp. 104–28.

Wapping History Group (1988). '*Down Wapping*': *Hobart's Vanished Wapping and Old Wharf Districts*, Blubber Head Press, Hobart.

Wheatcroft, S. (1994). *Aviation and Tourism Policies: Balancing the Benefits: A World Tourism Organization Publication*, Routledge, London & New York.

White, J. P. & Lampert, R. (1987). 'Creation and discovery' in *Australians to 1788*, ed. D. J. Mulvaney & J. P. White, Australians: A Historical Library series, Fairfax, Syme & Weldon Associates, Sydney, pp. 3–24.

White, R. (1987). 'Overseas', in *Australians: 1938*, ed. W. Gammage, P. Spearritt & L. Douglas, Australians: A Historical Library series, Fairfax, Syme & Weldon Associates, Sydney, pp. 435–45.

White, R. & Frow, L. (1987). 'Tourism', in *Australians: A Historical Dictionary*, ed. G. Alpin, S. G. Foster, M. McKernan & I. Howie-Willis, Australians: A Historical Library series, Fairfax, Syme & Weldon Associates, Sydney, p. 402.

Whitelock, D. (1977). *Adelaide 1836–1976*, University of Queensland Press, St Lucia, Qld.

Williams, M. (1988). *Australia: We Remember the Twenties and Thirties*, PR Books, Sydney.

World Tourism Organization (1993). *Global Tourism Forecasts to the Year 2000 and Beyond: World*, leaflet.

—— (1994). *Recommendations on Tourism Statistics*, Madrid.

—— (1995a). *Concepts, Definitions and Classifications for Tourism Statistics*, Technical Manual No. 1, Madrid.

—— (1995b). *Collection of Tourism Expenditure Statistics*, Technical Manual No. 2, Madrid.

—— (1996). *Towards New Forms of Public–Private Sector Partnership: The Changing Role, Structure and Activities of National Tourism Administrations*, Madrid.

—— (1997). *Tourism & Technology Bulletin*, a WTO Affiliate Member Publication, Issue no. 2, August–September.

—— (1998). *Tourism Highlights 1997*, Madrid.

Zetsche, D. (1995). 'The automobile: Clean and customized', *Scientific American*, September, pp. 76–80.

Index